Arsy Varsy
Reclaiming The Gospel
in First Corinthians

Phillip A. Ross

Pilgrim Platform
Marietta, Ohio

©2008 Phillip A. Ross
All rights reserved.

ISBN: 978-0-9820385-1-2
Edition: 25.9.17

Published by

Pilgrim Platform
149 E. Spring St.
Marietta, Ohio 45750
www.pilgrim-platform.org

Printed in the United States of America

All biblical quotations are from the *New English Bible*, the British and Foreign
Bible Society, 1970, unless otherwise noted.
MKJB refers to the *Modern King James Bible*, Sovereign Grace Publishers, 1993.
LITV refers to the *Literal Translation of the Holy Bible*, Sovereign Grace
Publishers, Third Edition, 1995.
KJV or AV refers to the *King James Version of the Holy Bible*, public domain in
the United States.
WCF refers to the *Westminster Confession of Faith*, 1646.
All verse references in this form, (v. xx), refer to the current chapter section of
    Scripture under consideration.

OCLC#: 3 1 0 9 6 2 1 8 2

For Barack Obama
in honor of his election as the
44th President of the
United States of America
and for the people who have called for
change they can believe in

BOOKS BY PHILLIP A. ROSS

The Work At Zion—A Reckoning, Two-volume set, 772 pages, 1996.

Practically Christian—Applying James Today, 135 pages, 2006.

The Wisdom of Jesus Christ in the Book of Proverbs, 414 pages, 2006.

Marking God's Word—Understanding Jesus, 324 pages, 2006.

Acts of Faith—Kingdom Advancement, 326 pages, 2007.

Informal Christianity—Refining Christ's Church, 136 pages, 2007.

Engagement—Establishing Relationship in Christ, 104 pages, 1996, 2008.

It's About Time! — The Time Is Now, 40 pages. 2008.

The Big Ten—A Study of the Ten Commandments, 105 pages, 2001, 2008.

Arsy Varsy—Reclaiming The Gospel in First Corinthians, 406 pages, 2008.

Varsy Arsy—Proclaiming The Gospel in Second Corinthians, 356 pages, 2009.

Colossians—Christos Singularis, 278 pages, 2010.

Rock Mountain Creed—The Sermon on the Mount, 310 pages, 2011.

The True Mystery of the Mystical Presence, 355 pages, 2011.

Peter's Vision of Christ's Purpose in First Peter, 340 pages, 2011.

Peter's Vision of The End in Second Peter, 184 pages, 2012.

The Religious History of Nineteenth Century Marietta, Thomas Jefferson Summers, 124 pages, 1903, 2012 (editor).

Conflict of Ages—The Great Debate of the Moral Relations of God and Man, Edward Beecher, 489 pages, 1853, 2012 (editor).

Concord Of Ages—The Individual And Organic Harmony Of God And Man, Edward Beecher, D. D., 524 pages, 1860, 2013 (editor).

Ephesians—Recovering the Vision of a Sustainable Church in Christ, 417 pages, 2013.

Galatians: Backstory/Christory, 315 pages, 2015.

Poet Tree—Root, Branch & Sap, 72 pages, 2013.

Inside Out Woman—Collected Poetry, Doris M. Ross, 195 pages, 2014 (editor).

God's Great Plan for the World, 305 pages, 2019.

John's Miracles—Seeing Beyond Our Expectations, 210 pages, 2019.

Essays on Church—Ordinary Christianity for the World, 385 pages, 2020.

Thessalonians—Thorn, Thistle, and Throne, 160 pages, 2021.

Institutes of The Christian Religion, Emanuel V. Gerhart, 9 volumes, 2023 (editor).

Goodnews—Evangel 2022, 187 pages, 2023

Goodnews—Evangel 2023, 318 pages, 2024

Goodnews—Evangel 2024, 322 pages, 2024

Goodnews—Reformation Reloaded, forthcoming, 2025

The Heritage of St. Paul's Evangelical Church, 108 pages, 2024

TABLE OF CONTENTS

INTRODUCTION

What kind of title is Arsy Varsy? It's an old Puritan word similar to vice versa. Where *visa versa* means conversely or a change in order, *arsy varsy* (pronounced *ahr-see-vahr-see*) means 1. (adj.) wrong end foremost, i.e., completely backward, an arsy varsy way of doing things; and 2. (adv.) in a backward or thoroughly mixed-up fashion, i.e., the papers are all filed arsy varsy. Today we might use the expression *ass backward*, which suggests that something is happening the wrong way, with the rear coming first. It indicates the complete reversal of the correct order.

Why would a book like this be dedicated to a President? There is a long tradition among Christian writers to provide theological insight where it is needed, where its application can get the most bang for the buck, so to speak. Senator Obama campaigned for President on the platform of bringing needed change to America, and that is exactly what this book is about.

I will put forth the audacity to hope that all Americans want what is best for America, and that the President—any President—is called to provide what he can toward that goal. Granted that my concern is theological and not political, though the two things are intimately related. The old adage is that so goes the (Christian) church, so goes the nation. This is true because politics are the outworking of beliefs and beliefs are the product of theology. Theology is simply the expression of our beliefs about God. And everyone has a theology, even atheists. They *believe* that God doesn't exist.

The theological position espoused herein is neither Left nor Right, neither Liberal nor Conservative because it is both Left and Right, Liberal and Conservative. The traditional Left/Right, Liberal/Conservative dichotomy is inadequate to the reality of life. It is a false dichotomy built upon a false and shallow understanding of reality. And it is our understanding of the reality in which we live that is the subject of this book.

i

Paul's intent in writing to the Corinthians was to correct a false understanding of success that had captured and perverted the gospel of Jesus Christ into its service. My intent is to reiterate Paul's message in a way that is orthodox and makes sense to me—and God-willing, to my contemporaries. This is no more than all Christians are called to do.

The thesis of this book is that Paul thought, wrote, and taught that some of the leaders of the Corinthian church had things *arsy varsy* or ass backwards. And the reason that First Corinthians has been valued over the centuries is that many Christians and churches have found Paul's insights and teachings to be valuable. It's a common problem that has plagued Christianity since the time of the Corinthian church, and before that back into the history of the Old Testament to the Fall of Adam. Being a sinner means getting things wrong. Paul was trying to help the Corinthians get things right, and their getting things right meant that they first come to understand that they had things wrong.

Expositional preaching provides the best exposure to a truly biblical perspective of Scripture. By simply preaching through a book of the Bible we cannot avoid those particular Scriptures or ideas that we don't like. And if we are honest, we will admit that there is much in God's Word that we don't like. If we were God, we'd do things quite differently. Thank God we aren't! God has given us His Word (Scripture) in the order, and with the terminology and the emphasis He wants it to have. Let us endeavor to receive it as He has given it to us, and to pass it forward as we have received it.

The contemporary American churches in the dawning of the twenty-first century are in a situation that is remarkably similar to that of the ancient Corinthian church. So, I decided to preach my way through Corinthians with the hope that Paul's work with the Corinthians will have some pertinent analysis of and application to our own contemporary situation. My approach has not been to read everything I could find about Corinthians in the hope of adding something new to the historic dialog. Rather, my intention is less grand. I hope to see and reveal the trouble the Corinthians had gotten into as a church as clearly as possible in order to understand what Paul was saying to them in the hope of shining some light on our own problem because their problem is our problem. It's a recurring problem because it is a problem of gospel reception and transmission.

"Corinth was a city of wealth and culture, seated at the crossroads of the Roman Empire, where all the trade and commerce of the empire passed through. It was a city of beauty, a resort city, located in a very beautiful area, but it was also a city of prostitution and of passion. It was devoted to trade and commerce, but also to the worship of the goddess of sex"[1]

Many of the people in the Corinthian church didn't understand why Paul was so troubled with them. After all, they were a large, successful church. They were growing by leaps and bounds. Membership and attendance statistics were solid. They thought they were doing great.

But Paul was troubled by what they were doing and he made every effort to tell them so. His trouble with the Corinthians is our trouble because his trouble with them would be his trouble with us. Unfortunately, the popular Evangelical approach to Christianity today has left too many people thinking that the pinnacle of Christianity comes at conversion, when we first give our hearts and lives to Jesus Christ. The initial change of heart and mind that captures new Christians is so stark a contrast to life before regeneration that it is described as going from death to life, from darkness to light. And it is exactly that!

But for far too many Christians the emotional high that accompanied their initial conversion and the wonderful feelings associated with the release from the burden of sin establishes a kind of emotional "high water mark" in their lives. It is a "mountain top experience" and tends to fade as people return to the daily drudgery of ordinary life. The release from sin releases a stream of endorphins into the blood stream. This, of course, is not a bad thing, but a good thing because it associates good feelings with God. However, being awash in an endorphin high is not the state of heart and mind that God wants His people to live in day in and day out. Nor does God want His people to get stuck in an emotional rut, forever pining for and pursuing the pleasures of emotional indulgence.

Too many Christians today are like converted hippies of a former time, whose motto could be. "I used to get high on drugs, but now I get high on Jesus!" Too much Christianity today is patterned after an endorphin rush. Please understand me. There is nothing wrong with feeling good, but our own good feelings are not the heart of Christianity.

Rather, God wants His people to grow—emotionally, intellectually, relationally, in every way. We are to grow "until we all attain to the unity of the faith and of the knowledge of the Son of God, to mature manhood, to the measure of the stature of the fullness of Christ, so that we may no

---

1   Steadman, Ray. *Expository Studies in 1 Corinthians, The Deep Things of God,* chapter: The Corinthian Crisis, http://www.raystedman.org/1corinthians/3571.html.

longer be children, tossed to and fro by the waves and carried about by every wind of doctrine, by human cunning, by craftiness in deceitful schemes. Rather, speaking the truth in love, we are to grow up in every way into him who is the head, into Christ, from whom the whole body, joined and held together by every joint with which it is equipped, when each part is working properly, makes the body grow so that it builds itself up in love" (Ephesians 4:13-16). And more often than not growth—real growth—is hard work.

It is amazing how much application Paul's words to the Corinthians have to the contemporary churches at the beginning of the Twenty-First Century. It is amazing how Paul's analysis of their problem fits the contemporary situation. And of course it is true that Paul was writing to them in their time about some very specific problems. So, understanding Paul's words from their perspective, from the perspective of that first century Corinthian church is very important to the study of Corinthians today. However, if we only understand Paul from a first century perspective, as applying only to the Corinthian church, we will only have a history lesson. As important as it is to understand what Paul was saying to those who first received his letter, to place our primary focus there will blunt the sharp edge of Paul's analysis and prescription, and quench the Spirit (1 Thessalonians 5:19) who is also speaking to us today.

Of course Paul was writing directly to those first century Christians. I'm not disputing that. And it is important to understand what he was saying to them. But we must understand that Paul was not writing *merely* to them. Paul was quite aware of his own position as an apostle of Jesus Christ, of the importance of his words, and of their place in history should God be willing to preserve them. And He did preserve Paul's words for us. God preserved Paul's words for us because they were not just for those first century Christians at Corinth, but they were intended by God and by Paul for us who would come later (1 Corinthians 10:11). Consequently, our task is to understand, not merely what Paul was saying to the Corinthians, but also what he is saying to us today.

It is in this sense that the Scriptures are living documents. They are alive, just as Christ Himself is alive, and they speak the words of Christ to us through Paul across two millennia. This is the sense in which I have approached this series on Corinthians. And I pray that the Lord will bless these meager efforts to help make Paul's words come alive in the minds and hearts of His people in our day. It is a difficult task because, like the Corinthians, many contemporary churches are caught up in their own apparent success. Their numbers are good, people are coming, they're growing. So, what's the problem? Well, that is the subject of this book.

I pray that you will see and hear Paul's words—God's Word—through my feeble and fallible efforts. Whatever success toward this end that may accrue to this work belongs to our Triune God who lives in the words of Paul, the words of Scripture, the Word of God. Where my words fail to communicate God's message accurately the fault is my own. I am a weak reed. But our God is truly great! And I pray that He will intercede between writer and reader to communicate and bless you as you engage these words, that He may show you His purpose in Paul's words and their application to your life and to His churches today.

THANKS

I want to thank several people who helped improve this book. Paul Williams, a neighbor and confidant, also proofread the text. While Paul and I have many theological disagreements along the classical divides of the sixteenth century, we are sufficiently committed to the unity of the church and interested in the deeper things that we have become good friends. I never satisfy all of Paul's concerns, and he keeps me sharp.

Other friends have provided me with a lot of meat to chew on regarding various features of this work. Many good questions have helped to clarify various arguments, though I have not satisfied some of their most basic concerns. Three things stand out as the source of the discomfort of some people regarding this treatment of First Corinthians. First, my presuppositional approach is different from an evidential approach to biblical study. Second, the integration of Trinitarian categories regarding human nature as a genuine reflection of God's nature result in additional subtleties and complexities found in the biblical text. And third, the application of the above presuppositionalism and Trinitarianism to Paul's treatment of spiritual gifts yields richer explanations, more diverse applications and a more foundational position for spiritual gifts regarding both the lives of individual Christians and the structure of the church. These interactions have given me a greater appreciation of the importance of epistemology and its impact on theology.

My wife, Stephanie, continues to be a blessing to me as I have grown over the years. No one knows the extent of my growth like she does. We have gone through many twists and turns together, and weathered many storms. My work would not be possible apart from her continuing love and support.

My children, Adam, Austin, and Justin, provide the teleological impetus for my efforts, and for them I am thankful. I have appreciated them
all of their lives—and increasingly so as they have become young men.
They are familiar with the material here and I expect—hope, really—that
they will take it and run with it in the years to come. I am not pressing
for their agreement, but for their serious engagement.

Underneath and above all of this runs my thankfulness to God for Jesus Christ, apart from whom nothing would matter, and in the light of
Whom everything matters so dearly.

Phillip A. Ross
Marietta, Ohio
November 2008

1. Lookin' Good!

Paul, a called apostle of Jesus Christ through the will of God, and Sosthenes our brother, to the church of God which is in Corinth, to those who are sanctified in Christ Jesus, called out with all those in every place who call on the name of Jesus Christ our Lord, both theirs and ours. Grace be to you, and peace from God our Father and the Lord Jesus Christ. I thank my God always on your behalf for the grace of God given you in Jesus Christ, that in everything you are enriched by Him, in all speech and in all knowledge; even as the testimony of Christ was confirmed in you; so that you come behind in no gift, waiting for the revelation of our Lord Jesus Christ. He shall also confirm you to the end, that you may be blameless in the day of our Lord Jesus Christ. God is faithful, by whom you were called to the fellowship of His Son, Jesus Christ our Lord. But I exhort you, brothers, by the name of our Lord Jesus Christ, that you all speak the same thing and that there be no divisions among you; but that you be perfectly joined together in the same mind and in the same judgment. For it has been declared to me concerning you, my brothers, by those of Chloe, that there are contentions among you. But I say this, that every one of you says, I am of Paul, and I of Apollos, and I of Cephas, and I of Christ. Is Christ divided? Was Paul crucified for you, or were you baptized in the name of Paul? I thank God that I baptized none of you except Crispus and Gaius, lest any should say that I had baptized in my own name. And I also baptized the household of Stephanas. Besides these, I do not know if I baptized any other. For Christ did not send me to baptize, but to preach the gospel; not in wisdom of words, lest the cross of Christ should be made of no effect.

— 1 Corinthians 1:1-17

Paul called attention to the fact that he was "called by the will of God" (1:1). He was called to be an apostle, to fulfill a specific role in the early church. We need to take care that we don't dismiss the nature and reality that all Christians are called into the church for particular reasons, and that every Christian has a particular role to play in the church. It is true that all Christians are not called to be apostles, all are not called to be deacons or elders, but all Christians are called to be something.

I am referring to the doctrine of vocation. Martin Luther is credited with reasserting the doctrine of vocation as a foundation stone in the Reformation of the church.

> "Therefore I advise no one to enter any religious order or the priesthood, indeed, I advise everyone against it—unless he is forearmed with this knowledge and understands that the works of monks and priests, however holy and arduous they may be, do not differ one whit in the sight of God from the works of the rustic laborer in the field or the woman going about her household tasks, but that all works are measured before God by faith alone" (Luther, Martin. *The Babylonian Captivity of the Church*, 1520).

All Christians are called by God Himself to play a particular role, fill a particular office, and/or accomplish a particular task, job, or function within the body of Christ. However, it also needs to be noted that the body of Christ is not coterminous with any particular denomination or 501(c)(3) manifestation of a local church organization. Rather, the body of Christ includes what has been traditionally known as the Church Militant and the Church Triumphant. The church of Jesus Christ is in time and beyond time at the same time.

Just as we are members of the church on Sundays when we gather for worship, we are still members of the church during the week when we are scattered for service. We gather for encouragement, instruction, fellowship, and worship. Then we scatter throughout society for service in the name of Jesus Christ. The church is not a static institution, but a living being, with a complex and dynamic identity—a Trinitarian identity because Christians are made in the image of God (Genesis 1:26).

What is commonly understood as the *church* in contemporary society is a mere husk when compared with the church in Scripture. The church of the New Testament was a vibrant fellowship of people from diverse backgrounds, traditions, and ethnicities who celebrated, not merely their human diversity, but their unity in Christ. They shared a common vision and purpose, communicated by Paul and the other apostles—not perfectly or without struggle, of course. But the power of their common vision and purpose overcame their differences.

We note several things of importance in this first verse. God calls all Christians to faithfulness where they are, in the midst of their current job, family, and neighborhood. And at the same time all Christians are called out of worldliness and into godliness. We are called to abandon the immorality of the world and to practice the morality of the Kingdom, and to do it right where we are—in our current job, family, and neighborhood. We are not called to create a Christian ghetto or to remove ourselves from our current obligations. Rather, we are called to be transformed people right where we are. We are not to run from the world, we are to be transformed in the midst of it.

Paul recognized the Christians in Corinth, those who were the immediate recipients of his letter, as people who were "sanctified in Christ Jesus, called to be saints" (v. 2). All Christians are called by the will of God to be saints. The Greek word translated as *saint* is *hagios*. The word means sacred, physically pure, morally blameless or religious.

Hagios is used throughout the New Testament to refer to God's holiness. Christ is the Holy One of God. Scripture refers to the Holy Spirit, the Holy Father, holy Scriptures, holy angels, holy brethren, and so on. The secular and pagan use of the word pictured a person separated and dedicated to the idolatrous pagan gods and carried no sense of moral or spiritual purity. The pagan Greek gods were as sinful, deranged, and immoral as the people who worshiped them. There was no sense of morality or righteousness associated with pagan worship. The worshiper of the pagan gods celebrated and mimicked the character of the pagan gods and the immoral religious ceremonies connected with its worship. We know that the Greek temple at Corinth housed and employed a large number of harlots who were connected with the worship of the Greek gods. Thus, the character of the Greek worshiper was licentious, depraved, and abandoned to the celebration of raw emotion.

Paul's use of the word hagios (saint) represented something filthy that had been washed and set apart for a completely new purpose, different from its original purpose. The traditional idea of a saint provides a picture of salvation. Those who were filthy with sin had been washed in the blood of Christ, and set apart from sin to serve God's purposes. The common understanding down the ages has been that saints practice a superior morality, that being a Christian or being called by God resulted in moral growth or refinement. That common understanding is not wrong, but more often than not it is misunderstood.

NOT PERFECT

Christians are not perfect and never will be, apart from the fullness of the Kingdom of God in glory. Yet, it is common that non-Christians accuse Christians of thinking that they (the Christians) are better than ev-

eryone else. And Christians are too often infected with the pride of thinking the same thing—sometimes blatantly, sometimes subtly.

There is a sense in which this idea of moral superiority is true, and a
sense in which it isn't. Christians do in fact grow and mature in morality,
so they do enjoy a kind of moral upgrade. Moral improvement is one of
the benefits of Christianity.

At the same time it is a supreme folly and sin for Christians to think
that they have been saved *because* they are morally superior to anyone else.
Too often the reverse is actually true. Many heathens are in fact morally
superior to many Christians. The point is not that Christians are morally
superior to heathens in general, because some are and some aren't. Rather,
the point is that Christians grow in moral purity. A Christian should always be more moral, more honest, more righteous than he or she used to
be. We are not to compare ourselves with others (2 Corinthians 10:12)—
Christian or heathen, but with Jesus Christ. Jesus Christ alone is our
model.[1]

Nor are Christians saved *by* their moral superiority to other people.
No one can practice moral improvement in order to become a Christian.
It doesn't work like that. No matter how hard we try, we cannot measure
up to the moral requirements established by God in the Bible. It cannot
be done, and the fact that it cannot be done is one of the central lessons
that the Bible teaches. Israel failed to be what God called her to be. The
faithful Jews in Israel were very righteous, very moral by any human
standard, including our own—but not by God's standard.

While moral improvement is a result of salvation, it is not in any
sense a cause or foundation of salvation. Rather, salvation is in Christ
alone. Augustus Toplady was correct when he wrote:

> Nothing in my hand I bring,
> Simply to the cross I cling;
> Naked, come to Thee for dress;
> Helpless look to Thee for grace;
> Foul, I to the fountain fly;
> Wash me, Savior, or I die.

At the same time, there is no salvation apart from moral improvement. Christians are "called to be saints" (v. 2, Romans 1:7) who are

---

1   Comparison to others is not the same as imitation. See the chapter on "Imitation," p.
     61.

"sanctified in Christ Jesus" (v. 2). Christians grow in grace, grow in obedience, grow in faithfulness, grow in righteousness, grow in moral improvement. Christians are not necessarily better than anyone else, but they are necessarily better than they used to be.

And Christians cannot claim any personal credit (or glory) for their moral improvement. We are what we are, not because we have worked hard to become good Christians, but solely because Jesus Christ died on the cross and dispatched His Holy Spirit to us while we were still awash in sin and disobedience. The Holy Spirit grabbed us by the scruff of the neck and hauled us aboard the life raft known as Jesus Christ. We had nothing to do with it until we found ourselves in Christ. Good thing, too! Because we, like Israel before us, are completely unable in our own strength and ability to be what God has called all people to be. Nor are we now—yet—what God has called us to be. But Christ has satisfied God's demands, deflected God's wrath, and provided a way for us to grow in godliness.

Paul proclaims, it is the "Lord Jesus Christ, who will sustain you to the end" (vs. 7-8). Here is a clear expression of the doctrine of assurance. Our salvation is assured, not because of anything that we can do, but solely because of what Christ has done. Christ's grip on us is much stronger than our grip on Him. Our assurance of faith rests in His grip on us, not in our grip on Him.

DIVISIONS

Paul goes on to address divisions in the church. Why does he talk about divisions in the church? Shouldn't he be talking about love and unity among the brethren? Paul was committed to the truth. He believed Jesus when He said that "the truth will set you free" (John 8:32). The truth was that there were divisions in the church. There are divisions in every church, always have been.

Paul not only acknowledged this truth, but went on to provide the cure for church divisions, "be united in the same mind and the same judgment" (v. 10). He was talking about doctrinal unity, about everyone being on the same page doctrinally. That's a pretty tall order. It was then and it still is today. Why? Partly because of the contemporary cultural emphasis on diversity, but also partly because we are all unique individuals with different perspectives, different thoughts, ideas, and analysis.

For instance, no longer is America considered to be a "melting pot" where immigrants shed their cultural background in order to become

Americans. Now Americans are taught to celebrate and maintain their cultural and ethnic perspectives and customs and to resist accommodation into American culture.

To keep us from getting confused about what Paul said, we need to note that there are two kinds of diversity—ethnic diversity and doctrinal (or philosophical/theological) diversity. We know as a fact that Jesus gave the church incredible ethnic diversity. Simeon prophesied that Jesus would be "a light for revelation to the Gentiles, and for glory to your people Israel" (Luke 2:32). Jesus commanded His people to go and "make disciples of all nations" (Matthew 28:19). Paul said that the gospel was "the power of God for salvation to everyone who believes, to the Jew first and also to the Greek" (Romans 1:16). Later he reminded the Galatians that "there is neither Jew nor Greek, there is neither slave nor free, there is neither male nor female, for you are all one in Christ Jesus" (Galatians 3:28). When the Holy Spirit poured out upon the saints gathered in the Upper Room there were "devout men from every nation under heaven" (Acts 2:5) dwelling in Jerusalem among the Jews.

> "And at this sound the multitude came together, and they were bewildered, because each one was hearing them speak in his own language" (Acts 2:6).

There can be no doubt that Christianity is for people of all ethnic backgrounds.

But the essence of Christianity is not doctrinal diversity, nor is it intended to be. Like a flower, Christianity is simple to behold, but complex to analyze. Flowers are composed of petals, pistils, stems, stalks, and roots —no two of which are exactly the same. Like God's Word, Christianity is a unified whole, a unified whole, that is simple to behold, but complex to analyze. In addition, people understand things differently, from different perspectives. That's to be expected. But those differences in understanding are a function of our sin. They are not to be normative. Doctrinal diversity is not the ideal or the goal. Doctrinal unity is the goal. Paul says, "be united in the same mind and the same judgment" (v. 10), the same mind, the same opinion, the same purpose. This is no fluke verse or idea. Jesus prayed,

> "I am no longer in the world, but they are in the world, and I am coming to you. Holy Father, keep them in your name, which you have given me, that they may be one, even as we are one" (John 17:11).

Paul wrote to the Philippians,

"Only let your manner of life be worthy of the gospel of Christ, so that whether I come and see you or am absent, I may hear of you that you are standing firm in one spirit, with one mind striving side by side for the faith of the gospel" (Philippians 1:27).

And later in that same letter,

"So if there is any encouragement in Christ, any comfort from love, any participation in the Spirit, any affection and sympathy, complete my joy by being of the same mind, having the same love, being in full accord and of one mind" (Philippians 2:1-2).

Ethnic diversity is the goal of the church, not ethnic unity or purity. On the other hand, doctrinal unity is the goal of the church, not doctrinal diversity or division. Jesus wants all kinds of different people to believe the same thing. He doesn't want all the people who are in the church to believe different things.

God created people as unique individuals and has allowed for some variation in perspectives and explanations regarding the complexity of Christian analysis. We should find overwhelming agreement in the simplicities even while we find striking differences in the complexities. Sometimes the differences are divisive, and therein lies the rub. Knowing when our differences contribute to Christian unity and when they result in division (as opposed to diversity) is the primary subject of Paul's letters to the Corinthians.

Peace And Purity

All Christians need to seek the peace and purity of the church. This is no small task because sin has set peace and purity at odds with one another. Those who seek doctrinal unity or purity, those for whom truth is the primary category of faithfulness, are often charged with disturbing the peace of the church because they meet with opposition when they teach or assert various unpopular doctrines. And those who seek peace, those for whom fellowship is the primary category of faithfulness, are often charged with disturbing the purity of the church because they want to maintain fellowship and camaraderie at the expense of truth. The one trumps fellowship with truth, and the other trumps truth with fellowship.

Scripture, however, insists on both peace (or fellowship among the saints) and purity (or doctrinal unity among the saints). Paul addresses this issue in its fullness in his letters to the Corinthians.

Note Paul's first defense of the gospel here in chapter one. His first attempt at telling the saints what they need in order to manifest both purity and peace in the church is very interesting. He spoke of baptism because that was the issue of presentation. People had been dividing themselves into groups based upon their baptisms. They separated themselves based upon who baptized them, upon whom they were baptized into. It makes a kind of sense. Baptism is a mark of entry into the church. It is a common belief that how a person got into the church suggests his or her position in the church.

The Reformed camp certainly understands this. They argue that people are brought into the church by the power of the Holy Spirit through regeneration, and not under their own power or by their own decisions to join or to be baptized. That's why they baptize infants as well as confessing adults. In other words, if you haven't been regenerated by the power of the Holy Spirit—which is a function of baptism broadly defined and not tied to the time of baptism, you are not really a church member, no matter what you or anyone else may think.

Yet, as much as people hold fast to this understanding of church membership, Paul brushes the issue of baptism aside, suggesting that the act of baptism is not in and of itself a sufficient indicator of church membership. Baptism is not a magic action that opens the doors of heaven. Rather, it is a symbolic ceremony. The symbolism is important, but not so important that it should disturb the peace and purity of the church.

"For Christ did not send me to baptize but to preach the gospel" (v. 17).

So, Paul's first defense of the gospel is not baptism. Paul will go on to say that the gospel is sufficient to defend itself, "for it is the power of God for salvation to everyone who believes" (Romans 1:16).

Paul tells us that worldly wisdom is not sufficient to make any judgments about the gospel of Jesus Christ. He is saying that those who are wise in the eyes of the world are not able to think correctly about the gospel. And who are the wise in the eyes of the world? Professors, intellectuals, scientists, think-tank scholars, university scholars, news anchors, etc. There's nothing wrong with being a professor or an intellectual or a scientists or a scholar or a news anchor, and there is great need for Christians to occupy these fields of endeavor. The problem is that the tools of these professions, inasmuch as they are committed to the wisdom of the world—that is to say wisdom without God, or wisdom apart from the light of Scripture—will always fail to understand even the most basic things about God or Jesus Christ. They will always and consistently get it wrong. Oh, they may stumble over a true thing now and then, but they will themselves fail to understand the fullness of any truth they come upon apart from Jesus Christ. Paul said it better,

> "For the word of the cross is folly to those who are perishing, but to us who are being saved it is the power of God" (v. 18).

He meant that Christianity will always look stupid to the world, to those who do not begin their thinking with the reality of God. How could it be otherwise? Those who acknowledge God and those who deny God have completely different understandings of the facts.

2. Smart Arse

For Christ did not send me to baptize, but to preach the gospel; not in wisdom of words, lest the cross of Christ should be made of no effect. For the preaching of the cross is foolishness to those being lost, but to us being saved, it is the power of God. For it is written, "I will destroy the wisdom of the wise, and I will set aside the understanding of the perceiving ones." Where is the wise? Where is the scribe? Where is the lawyer of this world? Has not God made foolish the wisdom of this world? For since, in the wisdom of God, the world by wisdom did not know God, it pleased God by the foolishness of preaching to save those who believe. For the Jews ask for a sign, and the Greeks seek after wisdom; but we preach Christ crucified, to the Jews a stumbling block, and to the Greeks foolishness. But to them, the called-out ones, both Jews and Greeks, Christ is the power of God and the wisdom of God. Because the foolish thing of God is wiser than men, and the weak thing of God is stronger than men. For you see your calling, brothers, that not many wise men according to the flesh are called, not many mighty, not many noble. But God has chosen the foolish things of the world to confound the wise; and God has chosen the weak things of the world to confound the things which are mighty; and God has chosen the base things of the world, and things which are despised, and things which are not, in order to bring to nothing things that are; so that no flesh should glory in His presence. But of Him you are in Christ Jesus, who of God is made to us wisdom and righteousness and sanctification and redemption; so that, according as it is written, "He who glories, let him glory in the Lord."

— 1 Corinthians 1:17-31

Paul wasn't interested in baptism or fancy talk. He was not out to impress anyone with his knowledge or his communication skills. He didn't give a hoot what the world thought of him or of his preaching. When Paul said that he aimed at "what is honorable not only in the Lord's sight but also in the sight of man" (2 Corinthians 8:21) he did not mean that he was appealing to the values of sin, but that people would eventually see that what honors God also honors man. And the way to keep this clear is to keep our eyes on the cross, not on the pew. This is a lesson that the church has yet to learn—particularly those who appreciate scholarship and social credibility.

American Christians lost this battle before the founding of the United States. Harvard University was founded in 1636 by the Great and General Court of the Massachusetts Bay Colony. To vote at that time required membership in a Congregational church. The Congregationalists of that day were consistent Calvinists, whose Puritan worldview was to be perpetuated in the institutions of higher learning in order to train future leaders of society in Christianity and Calvinism. They intended to build American society upon a Reformed Christian foundation.

An early brochure, published in 1643, justified the College's existence: "To advance Learning and perpetuate it to Posterity; dreading to leave an illiterate Ministry to the Churches."

With the dawn of the Enlightenment too many Christians in higher education began to believe that science and scholarship were leaving the church in the dust. Christians began scrambling to keep up with the latest scientific discoveries in order to apply them to the Bible. Many, like Charles Darwin who wrote in the 1800s, worked vigorously to adapt the Christian faith to newly discovered "truths" of science. Those efforts pushed the church down the slippery slope of compromise with the world in the name of scientific scholarship. The church endeavored to impress the world with its ability to adapt itself to the world of science in order to remain relevant.

Relevancy is a cry that we again hear in contemporary society and even in contemporary churches. More and more people are saying that the church must be relevant to the people it is trying to reach, that the Bible must be relevant to the world in which we live. Of course this is true, but the question is: Who are the people the churches are trying to reach? Here is where covenant theology plays a distinctive role. Obviously, the churches are trying to reach the "lost." But the lost come in two flavors—the unsavable lost and the not-yet-saved lost.

LOST FLAVORS

Paul noted this difference when he said that "the word of the cross is folly to those who are perishing, but to us who are being saved it is the power of God" (v. 18).

There are some people who will *not* respond to the grace of God, period. Others, of course, will respond. But *we* don't know exactly who will or who won't respond to the gospel. We don't know which individuals will respond and which won't. But we do know that some will and some won't, and that is very important information.

Knowing that some of the lost will respond to the gospel we must make our proclamation of the gospel appeal to those who will respond, to those who will eventually recognize the truth of Scripture and grow in grace and godliness. By way of contrast, it is futile to make our presentations of the gospel appeal to those who will not ever respond, to those who think that the gospel is foolish and who will never think differently.

Our presentation of the gospel and of ourselves as Christians must reflect the truth of the gospel. We must make our appeal by using the values and aesthetics of Scripture because it is precisely those values and aesthetics that will appeal to those who will ultimately respond to God's grace. Those who will eventually respond to God's grace will come to appreciate biblical values and aesthetics. Conversely, to use the values and aesthetics of the world in the presentation of the gospel is a waste of time and resources because those who see the values and aesthetics of Scripture as silly and irrelevant are exactly the people that Paul is talking about in this verse. They are or consider themselves to be "worldly wise," and they consider the gospel in and of itself—without embellishment—to be foolish and powerless. These are the people who will always reject the gospel (Luke 16:31).

Christians don't need to make an appeal on the basis of worldly values and aesthetics because those who will respond will respond to the power of the gospel alone. They will not be dissuaded by what the world sees as a foolish and irrelevant message. It is a waste of time and resources to try to make the gospel appear to be wise and/or relevant to the world. It is in and of itself already relevant to those who will be saved. What we win people *with* is what we will win them *to*. If we win people with worldly values and aesthetics, we will win them to a worldly church, a church that has already watered down the gospel to make it appeal to those who do not love the Lord.

Many very smart Christians get caught up in trying to impress the world with their learning, abilities, and/or stylishness—scientists, scholars, theologians, musicians, and artists. They are not trying to be unfaithful. Rather, they are trying to keep Christianity on the cutting edge, to keep it relevant in the face of astounding scientific discoveries, with advances in academic research, and with cutting edge anthropology, with new styles in music and art. We don't want to sell them short. They are trying to do what they think is right. Most of them are a lot smarter than we are. Nonetheless, the point to be made is that such Christians are chasing the culture, not leading it. They are following the world, not the Lord.

That is the point that Paul makes in the latter half of this first chapter of Corinthians. Paul said that the gospel of Jesus Christ is opposed to the wisdom (*sophia*) of the world. It is not opposed to intelligence per se, but wisdom that is based on the values and presuppositions of the world, apart from God. Paul did not say that Christians are not intelligent. Many are, and all should be growing in this regard. Paul suggested that the gospel needs to be preached "not with words of eloquent wisdom, lest the cross of Christ be emptied of its power" (v. 18).

The power of the gospel is lost through eloquence (*sophia*) and worldly wisdom. We can extrapolate and say that the gospel does not need to be couched in cutting edge musical forms or with the latest dramatic formulas, it does not need to fit into the latest anthropological theories about the origins of humanity, or in accord with the latest astronomical discoveries, in as much as those things are driven by godlessness. It does not need to be relevant to worldly godlessness. That is not what will attract the not-yet-saved.

But this is not what most people in the churches today believe. This perspective goes against modern evangelism techniques (techniques, I should add, which are not really working very well. The church in America has not grown in raw numbers for decades). Christians today want their preachers to be persuasive and powerful in their preaching. That's what it means to be eloquent. Aristotle defined the art of public speaking in the West. He called it rhetoric, and taught the skills of public speaking and argumentation (or persuasion). We might think of it as the art of story telling, both written and verbal.

RHETORICAL SUPPRESSION

Public speakers are taught to tell the audience what you are going to tell them, then tell them, and then tell them what you told them. Keep your messages simple and repetitive. It's a standard technique to make three points in any speech, and to repeat each point three times in different ways. You are probably familiar with this wisdom. But is it biblical? Did Paul do this? How about Jesus? No, the Bible doesn't engage this kind of worldly wisdom.

There are many rhetorical devises—alliteration, allusion, analogy, hyperbole, metaphor, simile, and a host of others. These are the tools of the public speaker and the story teller. Are they biblical? The Bible is in fact filled with such things. The Bible uses them liberally. The Bible intends to persuade through story telling, the telling of His-story. So, is Paul saying that preaching should not use the tools of rhetoric? The issue for Paul is not rhetoric per se, but godlessness. It is the godlessness of the world that accounts for its academic folly. It is the effort of the godless "who by their unrighteousness suppress the truth" (Romans 1:18) that is the problem.

The unrighteous suppress the truth. The church, in contrast, needs to proclaim the truth boldly, without equivocation or eloquence, to speak the truth plainly, directly, and without embellishment. And by presenting the gospel as Scripture presents it—simply, plainly, clearly, without dressing it up in the latest worldly fashions, it becomes clear that it works by the power of God and not by the power of dynamic communication skills, rhetoric, or marketing techniques.

Paul identifies two categories of people in verse 18: those who are perishing, and those who are being saved. For the one, the "word of the cross (Scripture) is folly." For the other, it is "the power of God" (v. 18). These are two very different perspectives. Paul doesn't say that those who don't understand Scripture are lost, rather he says that those who are lost don't understand Scripture. Nor does he say that those who understand it do so because they are saved. Rather, he says that those who are saved are able to understand it. The difference is critical. It is the difference between works-righteousness and salvation by grace. It is the difference between allowing the power of God to direct the not-yet-saved into salvation and directing the unsavable to go through the motions of religious affiliation for the appearance of success in evangelism and church growth.

Paul makes an astonishing statement, "in the wisdom of God, the world did not know God through wisdom" (v. 21). This essentially means that people cannot know God through their own efforts. God cannot be learned through study. God cannot be discerned through science. We cannot build a bridge to God. And that's exactly the way that God wants it! The only way that God can be known is by grace through faith (Ephesians 2:8). If God doesn't provide it of His own free will, it can't get got!

TWO GROUPS OF TWO

Paul went on to tell us that people make two kinds of foolish demands on the Lord (v. 22). He was talking about the two kinds of people

—those in the family of God (the Jews), and those outside the family of God (the Gentiles). We know that there are two kinds of people *in* the family of God—the saved and the lost (Romans 9:6), but there are also two kinds of people *not in* the family of God—the unsavable and the not-yet-saved (Luke 2:32).

The Jews required signs or miracles to confirm the mission of the Old Testament prophets who were sent to them. That's the traditional way that they certified their prophets. It was quite natural for them to insist on a sign to prove that Jesus was the true Messiah. Like the Jews of old, many people in the churches today are still waiting for a miracle to establish their faith. Yet, Jesus performed many miracles during His life on earth, and was resurrected from the dead and seated at the right hand of God as the ultimate miracle. Makes me wonder what people are waiting for today!

Paul also said that those outside the church, those who don't know the Lord seek wisdom—and not knowing the Lord, they seek worldly wisdom, godless wisdom. Many of them seek it as a substitute for God, as a way of salvation. Indeed, liberalism teaches salvation through knowledge or education. The civil government currently preaches salvation through education in their public schools. According to the state, education is the standard cure for everything—poverty, crime, drug abuse, domestic violence, etc. Again, it is not education per se, or wisdom or intelligence itself that is the problem. The problem is godlessness. Godless education or godless wisdom is futile because only God can change the heart. Only God can change the mind.

I'm not trying to undercut the importance of education. It is very important. But education does not save people from sin. Everyone needs education, both categories of the saved and both categories of the lost will benefit from biblical education. The saved need to be educated in godliness for their own sanctification. The lost who are not-yet-saved need to be educated in godliness in order to draw them into salvation and sanctification. The unsavable need to be educated in godliness in order to keep them from being as evil as they can be. Even the unsavable benefit from a biblical education. They aren't saved by it, but they learn about the role of law and the fact that the state has been instituted to punish those who break the law, and knowing that contributes to better behavior, which benefits everyone, including themselves. Conversely, there is no need for godless education. Ignorance of the Bible only serves to encourage god-lessness and sin.

God did not choose what was popular (v. 28). He didn't choose successful people, or beautiful people, or smart people. He chose what was despised—*exoutheneō*, that which is contemptible, least esteemed, most unpopular. Why would the Lord do that? Because Scripture teaches that people are sinners and that sin likes to be dressed in wisdom, intelligence, popularity, and beauty.

Sinners are caught up in their own thinking, their own values. They are caught up in themselves, and will not yield to a superior wisdom. Sinners will not heed Scripture. They refuse to learn from history. They are unteachable because they think that they know better. They cannot escape the limitations of their own desires. They are proud of themselves, even when they are soft-spoken.

Conversely, Paul tells us that God has arranged things "so that no human being might boast in the presence of God" (v. 29). God alone "is the source of your life in Christ Jesus" (v. 30). Everything in Scripture and history points to the fact that God is the author and finisher of human salvation, and that people are sinners and completely unable to save themselves. Salvation is by and through Jesus Christ, "whom God made our wisdom and our righteousness and sanctification and redemption" (v. 30). There is no salvation at all apart from biblical salvation in Jesus Christ alone (Acts 4:12). Therefore, as it is written, "Let the one who boasts, boast in the Lord" (v. 31).

All pride is forbidden, except pride in Jesus Christ. We are not to take pride in anything—not in our favorite sports team, not in our own accomplishments, not in our abilities, not in our generosity, not in our theology, not in our church, not in our nation. The only pride a Christian has should be pride in Jesus Christ, and the road to that kind of pride goes through the valley of humility.

This is not an argument against cheering on a home team, nor against the playing or watching of sports. But it does stand as an accusation against the contemporary sports industry that drives an unhealthy sports mania that promotes values that are opposed to the gospel.

3. Shifting Sands

And I, brothers, when I came to you, did not come with excellency of speech or of wisdom, declaring to you the testimony of God. For I determined not to know anything among you except Jesus Christ and Him crucified. And I was with you in weakness and in fear, and in much trembling. And my speech and my preaching was not with enticing words of man's wisdom, but in demonstration of the Spirit and of power, so that your faith should not stand in the wisdom of men, but in the power of God. But, we speak wisdom among those who are perfect; yet not the wisdom of this world, nor of the rulers of this world, that come to nothing. But we speak the wisdom of God in a mystery, which God has hidden, predetermining it before the world for our glory; which none of the rulers of this world knew (for if they had known, they would not have crucified the Lord of glory). But as it is written, "Eye has not seen, nor ear heard, nor has it entered into the heart of man, the things which God has prepared for those who love Him." But God has revealed them to us by His Spirit; for the Spirit searches all things, yea, the deep things of God. For who among men knows the things of a man except the spirit of man within him? So also no one knows the things of God except the Spirit of God. But we have not received the spirit of the world, but the Spirit from God, so that we might know the things that are freely given to us by God. These things we also speak, not in words which man's wisdom teaches, but which the Holy Spirit teaches, comparing spiritual things with spiritual. But the natural man does not receive the things of the Spirit of God, for they are foolishness to him; neither can he know them, because they are spiritually discerned. But he who is spiritual judges all things, yet he himself is judged by no one. For who has known the mind of the Lord, that he may instruct Him? But we have the mind of Christ.

— 1 Corinthians 2:1-16

Paul did not preach with lofty speech or persuasive words of wisdom. The focus of Paul's preaching and testimony was not on the words he used, but on the content of the message he proclaimed. He wasn't trying to craft a good speech or a compelling testimony. He wasn't engaged in classical rhetoric. He wasn't trying to win a debate, or to overpower the opposition. Nor was he trying to use a particular style of language in order to identify with his audience. He wasn't trying to move his hearers to an emotional or intellectual crisis that would result in new birth or conversion. The focus of his attention was not on his audience. Paul was not customer-centered or consumer-oriented.

Rather, Paul was God-centered and Christ-oriented. His focus was on the Lord, not on the Lord's people. His eyes were on the cross, not on the pew, nor on the pulpit. His intention was to communicate the gospel of Jesus Christ, crucified and risen.

He made a decision before he came to them to speak to them of nothing but Christ crucified. While he was a well-educated man, a pharisee of pharisees, a Rabbi of Rabbis, an intellectual of intellectuals, a teacher of teachers, he would speak of nothing but Christ crucified. He would build his case, or champion the cause of Christ on the basis of Scripture alone. He would not call upon the wisdom or literature of the world to bolster his testimony of grace alone through Christ alone on the basis of Scripture alone.

As Christians, and as a church, we need to take our cues from Paul, from Scripture, and not from the world. We need to understand terms like faithfulness and success from a biblical perspective, and not apply ideas and/or programs of worldly success to the church.

CHURCH GROWTH

Unfortunately, however, churches by and large have accepted and followed the ideas and values of the world for a very long time. For instance, the Church Growth Movement has had a serious impact on denominations and local churches. The Church Growth Movement is transforming the Christian landscape through the development of large, mega churches. This fact is well-documented in current literature and media—no church is exempt from its influence and impact.

Please understand that I am not against church growth. I do understand evangelism to be a central function of the church. Nor am I against the use of modern marketing and advertising technologies. But I am against using marketing and advertising technologies as the world uses them in the church. I am arguing for a more faithful and Christ-centered use of modern media. There is nothing wrong with modern media in and of itself. There is, however, a problem with using it to promote and encourage the values and aesthetics of sin in the name of Christianity.

Churches and denominations—Christians—need to heed and apply Paul's wisdom found here in Corinthians to the practice of evangelism, including the use of modern media (marketing and advertising). We must not allow the wisdom of the world to determine the methodologies of the church. Do we do this? I believe that we do, that virtually all churches have been affected by the "success" of modern marketing and advertising practices.

Such practices belong to what Paul called the "wisdom of men" (v. 5) and the "wisdom of the world" (Colossians 1:20). The current popular understanding of evangelism and the methodologies engaged to reach the lost that have been hijacked by what the business world calls "marketing creep." Market-think has crept into the church and dominates our outreach efforts.

John Gage, Chief Researcher at Sun Microsystems Inc., warned software developers at the Global Grid Forum in Seattle in June, 2003, "everything we do gets hijacked by marketing." His observation has application to more than software development. It applies to virtually every aspect of business. Allow me to explain.

BETTER MOUSETRAP

It was Ralph Waldo Emerson who said, "Build a better mousetrap and the world will beat a path to your door." That sound advice has inspired entrepreneurs across the globe to make better products as the primary method of business success. The drive to make better products as the most effective avenue of business success is responsible for the development of modern technology, which has forever changed the way people think and live the world over. American entrepreneurs have led the way for centuries.

At the same time, modern marketing methods have also changed the nature of this formula for business success. How so? By changing the definition of the word *better*. The original understanding of *better* meant that a better mousetrap would catch more mice, or catch them more efficiently, or more humanely, or whatever. *Better* indicated an improvement in product function. The emphasis was on the improvement of the mousetrap (or product) itself.

However, the new definition of *better* is not about the mousetrap, but about mousetrap sales. It's about mousetrap (or product) marketing. Business success no longer means building a better mousetrap. It means selling more mousetraps than your competitors, or increasing the profit margin on your mousetrap sales, which can be accomplished in several ways. Again, this shift is the result of "marketing creep."

Please be aware that there is nothing wrong with increased sales, nothing wrong with increased production efficiencies, nothing wrong with greater profits or increased revenues. But if there is nothing wrong with these things, then what am I talking about?

I'm talking about a shift in the purpose or goal of the business, which affects the purpose of the product produced. I'm talking about a change in the reason for building mousetraps (making particular products). The original purpose or goal of the business was to build and produce a better mousetrap. The purpose of the business was product oriented.

The new and improved purpose is to sell more mousetraps or to earn more money through the sale of mousetraps. The new purpose is not focused on the product, but on product sales. The new purpose is focused on sales and profits rather than on the function, design, or usage of the mousetrap. It is a shift from being product-driven to being financially-driven. And again, there is nothing wrong with concern and control of finances. Any business that is not concerned about finances will fail.

The older purpose of the business was other-directed. It was focused on providing a social service, on identifying a need and producing something to meet that need. The new purpose of the business is self-directed. It is focused on company profitability. The new purpose is to make money for the business owners. Again, there is nothing wrong with making money.

But there is a problem associated with the new marketing-driven purpose, and that problem relates to integrity and the decrease in the quality of mousetraps when they are produced for sales as opposed to product function. The new emphasis eventually involves cutting production costs to increase profits, which involves less or cheaper materials and/or less time in production. To compensate for these measures a subtle kind of marketing deceit comes into play.

MARKETING DECEIT

How does this happen? Rather than using stainless steel, for instance, producers will use iron that is chrome plated. And the marketing department will shift attention away from the disadvantages of such a change by conjuring up some new and improved element of the mousetrap. We are all familiar with this process.

The point to be made is the shift in purpose from function to finance, from performance to appearance, from essentials to periphery, from substance to style. Please understand that I am not arguing against profit or against marketing or against efficiency or against financial concern. All I am saying is that when a business shifts its purpose from production to marketing, the likelihood of an inferior product increases.

It doesn't have to, but it usually does. The concerns of marketing take precedence over the concerns of product quality and performance. There is a shift of concern from what is best for the customer to what is best for the business. It is a shift of priorities from other to self. This shift is evidenced in the wide-spread decrease in customer service that has happened across the board over the last twenty, thirty, or fifty years.

So, how does this play out in the church? Worldly wisdom tells us that gospel success means more people in the pews. The emphasis is on the pew rather than on the Lord. Whereas, biblical wisdom tells us that gospel success results from the glorification of God. The chief end or purpose of man is to glorify God and enjoy Him forever, according to the *Shorter Catechism*, Question 1. The purity of the church requires the right people in the pews, people who are covered by the righteousness of Christ. The biblical emphasis is on right belief or right values, on the righteousness of Jesus Christ, crucified and risen.

The traditional focus of the churches was Christ. The central focus of worship and evangelism was Jesus Christ. Churches and Christians were concerned about serving the needs and desires of Jesus Christ. Whereas the Church Growth Movement is concerned about serving the needs and desires of the people in the pews. Biblically, worship and evangelism are Christ-centered, and are understood to be byproducts of faithfulness. Biblical worship and evangelism are accomplished through faithfulness to Jesus Christ. They are not accomplished through the mechanics of marketing and advertising (human effort).

Again, marketing and advertising do have legitimate functions in the church. However, they are not to be self-centered, they are to be Christ-centered. Biblical marketing and advertising should not be about the church or about the people in the church. Rather, they should be about Jesus Christ—and Him crucified, as Paul said in 1 Corinthians 1:23.

Christians should understand that Christianity is not about us, it is about Jesus Christ. *We* don't bring salvation, *Christ* does. We don't produce sanctification, Christ does. Salvation is not about what we do or who we are, it's about Jesus Chris—what He has done and who He is!

The Church Growth Movement and virtually all contemporary Christian marketing and advertising, while it pays lip service to Jesus Christ, is actually focused on the people in the pews. It is primarily concerned with noses and nickels related to particular institutions. It understands the purpose of evangelism to be to get people in the pews—and that focus lobbies against preaching or sharing any biblical truth that has a hard edge, that will make people uncomfortable, or that may be difficult to understand. And, like it or not, biblical truth will make us all uncomfortable. Various aspects of biblical truth are hard to understand—faith is required. All growth is painful at times.

Growing, or stretching our limitations, is often uncomfortable. Christian growth—sanctification—requires thinking outside of the box of our spiritual immaturity. It's hard. It's painful. And it will take us where we don't want to go. The Spirit opposes the flesh.

> "Those who live according to the flesh set their minds on the things of the flesh, but those who live according to the Spirit set their minds on the things of the Spirit" (Romans 8:5).

> "For the desires of the flesh are against the Spirit, and the desires of the Spirit are against the flesh, for these are opposed to each other, to keep you from doing the things you want to do" (Galatians 5:17).

Go to the church page of any newspaper and you can see what I mean. The ads are church-centered rather than Christ-centered. The basic message is "come visit our church," rather than extolling the excellencies of Jesus Christ. By and large the messages preached are about what Christ can do for you, rather than biblical exposition or extolling the excellencies or message of Jesus Christ.

As we go through our exegesis of First Corinthians I want you to look for Paul's invitation to visit the church at Corinth. You won't find it, but it is important that you see that it is not there. Why? Because this is not an evangelism-centered book.[1] It is a sanctification-centered book. The focus is on the maturity of Christians. And then as now, the focus on maturity will not immediately increase local church membership, but will likely decrease it. Please understand that I am not suggesting that

---

1   For a discussion of Paul's evangelism method see Ross, Phillip A. *Acts of Faith— Kingdom Advancement*, Pilgrim Platform, Marietta, Ohio, 2007.

churches initiate programs in order to decrease their membership rolls. Rather, I am simply pointing to what Paul did, and his concern for Christian maturity and growth in grace.

ANTITHESIS

There is an antithesis between Christian maturity and worldly wisdom. That means that they are mutually exclusive. They are opposed to one another. What serves to increase Christian maturity undermines worldly wisdom, and what serves to increase worldly wisdom undermines Christian maturity. And it is this antithesis that Paul highlights in these chapters of First Corinthians. It is precisely because of this antithesis that Paul has "decided to know nothing among you (the Corinthians), except Jesus Christ, and him crucified" (v. 2).

Paul was not ignorant of Greek literature and philosophy. Rather, he didn't want them to undermine the gospel by bringing in non-biblical ideas, even when those ideas might seem to the Greeks to support the gospel. He knew that they would not, that they would dilute and undermine it. But he was not opposed to wisdom, "among the mature we do impart wisdom, although it is not a wisdom of this age or of the rulers of this age, who are doomed to pass away" (v. 6). Rather, Paul imparted the "secret and hidden wisdom of God, which God decreed before the ages for our glory" (v. 7).

Repeatedly, Paul says that God's wisdom is not available to the ungodly. The *Westminster Confession* teaches that

"the inward illumination of the Spirit of God (is) necessary for the saving understanding of such things as are revealed in the Word" (WCF 1:6).

Paul taught that

"no one comprehends the thoughts of God except the Spirit of God. Now we have received not the spirit of the world, but the Spirit who is from God, that we might understand the things freely given us by God. And we impart this in words not taught by human wisdom but taught by the Spirit, interpreting spiritual truths to those who are spiritual" (vs. 11-13).

There is a gulf between the godless and the godly that can only be bridged by Jesus Christ. It cannot be bridged by human wisdom or human effort. Christians can understand the godless because we were once godless ourselves, but the godless cannot understand Christianity unless and until they themselves are born again or become regenerate.

"The natural person does not accept the things of the Spirit of God, for they are folly to him, and he is not able to understand them because they are spiritually discerned" (v. 14).

There is an important application of this concept related to church marketing and advertising that virtually no contemporary church marketer uses. Most contemporary church marketing programs are aimed at the godless. What I mean is that they use the language and aesthetics of the godless in order to appeal to the values or aesthetics of the godless. They try to make Christianity appear to be hip or cool or "in" or popular. They try to make it appear to be worldly by copying the latest marketing fads and techniques in order to make Christianity more appealing to the worldly minded. But Paul clearly teaches that the truth of Christianity cannot be known to the godless. It can only be discerned by the godly.

In contrast, the biblical use of marketing and advertising will not clothe Christianity in worldly garb, hoping to make it appeal to the worldly mind, but will show the truth of Christianity from a purely biblical perspective. Biblical Christianity does not need to appeal to the godless or look like the world. It doesn't have to pretend to be cool or hip or "in" or popular. Such practice is not authentic Christianity. The purpose of evangelism is not to make Christianity look like the world. Rather, it is to make the world Christian. Godless people need to understand that they are not Christian, and that they cannot bring their godlessness into the church—not even in the name of Christianity.

There is a difference between the savable who are lost and the unsavable who are lost. We don't know exactly who is savable and who isn't, but God does. The Spirit of Christ in the church speaks to the Spirit of Christ in the savable lost. The values of Christ resonate with the savable lost and draw them into the fold. The beauty of Christ reaches out to His lost sheep to guide them home.

We obscure the values and the beauty of Christ when we use worldly (godless) aesthetics and values in our outreach. We shoot ourselves in the foot when we try to appeal to heathen forms of popularity to communicate the gospel. Such efforts obscure the truth of the gospel and disturb the purity and peace of the church. The whole world needs to see the antithesis between Christianity and the world in order to perceive the necessity of conversion. To blur the antithesis between the world and Christianity is to blur the necessity of the new birth and conversion.

The church will grow in faith and in numbers when it is seen as a viable option to the ways of the world. It will grow by differentiating itself from the world, not by trying to integrate itself into the world, or by trying to grow on a foundation of worldliness. This is an important application of Paul's central message of chapter two.

4. Divisions

And I, brothers, could not speak to you as to spiritual ones, but as to fleshly, as to babes in Christ. I have fed you with milk and not with solid food, for you were not yet able to bear it; nor are you able even now. For you are yet carnal. For in that there is among you envyings and strife and divisions, are you not carnal, and do you not walk according to men? For while one says, I am of Paul; and another, I am of Apollos; are you not carnal? Who then is Paul, and who is Apollos, but ministers by whom you believed, even as the Lord gave to each? I have planted, Apollos watered, but God gave the increase. So then neither is he who plants anything, nor he who waters, but God who gives the increase. So he planting, and he watering, are one, and each one shall receive his own reward according to his own labor. For of God we are fellow-workers, a field of God, and you are a building of God. According to the grace of God which is given to me, as a wise master builder, I have laid the foundation, and another builds on it. But let every man be careful how he builds on it. For any other foundation can no one lay than the one being laid, who is Jesus Christ.
— 1 Corinthians 3:1-11

Paul previously made the case that God's wisdom is not like human wisdom, that the best wisdom, intelligence, and scholarship that man has to offer is foolishness compared to God's wisdom, the wisdom of Scripture. Paul made the case for the necessity of regeneration and/or conversion from the mindset of the world to the mindset of Christ. To become a Christian is to undergo a complete change of heart and of mind that brings people into unity with other like-minded people.

That change has a definite beginning, and then grows in fits and starts. This change is always personal—it always affects personal values, beliefs and behavior. And a personal relationship with Jesus Christ necessarily means a covenantal relationship because God always relates to His people covenantally. So, the change that allows one to profess Jesus Christ as Lord and Savior comes about as a realization that God's saving grace applies to the professor personally, that the professor of Christianity has changed from being a covenant breaker to being a covenant keeper, albeit by the grace of God.

Christians understand that there are two aspects of covenant keeping. First and foremost, they understand that God alone has kept His covenant through the faithfulness and righteousness of Jesus Christ—and that Christ has applied His covenant faithfulness to His people. Christians, then, having received Christ's applied covenant faithfulness then apply themselves toward the manifestation of Christ's righteousness in their own lives, knowing that Christ will provide guidance and strength toward that end. All of this is to say that there is such a thing as Christian maturity, and that maturity is different from immaturity.

Addressing this issue, Paul said that he could not address the Corinthians as "spiritual people, but as people of the flesh, as infants in Christ" (v. 1). Think about that for a moment. These first century Christians were not paragons of faithfulness, as we like to consider them. Rather, they were babes in Christ. They were so immature in their faith that Paul had to alter his ordinary way of speaking about God because they failed to understand the most basic concerns of faithfulness.

Was he saying that they were not saved? Yes and no. Some were and some weren't. He was saying that the Corinthian church was a mixed bag, that it contained people who were saved and people who were not saved. Churches, according to the *Westminster Confession* are always "more or less pure," so that the "purest Churches under heaven are subject both to mixture and error" (WCF, 25:4-5). However, this does not mean that every church member who errs is unsaved. Rather, it means that sometimes those who are actually saved behave like the unsaved. It means that it is possible, even likely, that those who call themselves Christians but who do not work at spiritual maturity, who do not make an effort to grow in faithfulness, may find themselves excluded from the kingdom. Yes, we are saved by faith. Yes, Christ alone provides salvation and sanctification. And yet, all Christians are commanded to engage in works, to grow in faithfulness. We are not exempt from works, but are called to works, called to maturity and faithfulness.

MATURITY

Those who call themselves Christians but don't grow in the faith are dead, not alive in Christ. Such people will find themselves on "rocky ground, where they did not have much soil, and immediately they sprang up, since they had no depth of soil, but when the sun rose they were scorched. And since they had no root, they withered away" (Matthew 13:5-6).

These words are from Jesus, which were given for the encouragement of God's people, to encourage us forward in faithfulness, to give us the courage to persevere in faithfulness. We are encouraged to dig down deep into the soil of Christianity. And what is that soil? It is what provides nourishment for spiritual growth—Scripture, history, and fellowship. The soil in this parable is the backdrop, background, context, medium, milieu, setting, and/or surroundings in which Christianity will flourish.

The Christians at Corinth to whom Paul was writing had an excuse for their immaturity. There wasn't much Christian Scripture (New Testament), or Christian history (the church was young), or fellowship (Christians were few in number). We don't have such excuses today, and God will judge us all the more severely for our Christian immaturity.

> "They were so far from forming their maxims and measures upon the ground of divine revelation, and entering into the spirit of the gospel, that it was but too evident they were much under the command of carnal and corrupt affections. They were still mere babes in Christ. They had received some of the first principles of Christianity, but had not grown up to maturity of understanding in them, or of faith and holiness; and yet it is plain, from several passages in this epistle, that the Corinthians were very proud of their wisdom and knowledge. Note, It is but too common for persons of very moderate knowledge and understanding to have a great measure of self-conceit. The apostle assigns their little proficiency in the knowledge of Christianity as a reason why he had communicated no more of the deep things of it to them" (Matthew Henry).

This whole chapter is a call to Christian maturity, which must begin with the realization of our own immaturity. Paul was disappointed in the level of Christian maturity he found in Corinth. Would he be more or less pleased if he came to minister with us today? Not just with the people at this or that particular church, but how would Paul respond to the churches across the globe—and particularly the American church today? George Barna has documented that Christians today are not much different than non-Christians in any measure.[1] According to Barna, there is no

---

1   Barna, George. *The Barna Report: What Americans Believe : An Annual Survey of*

significant difference between the lifestyles of the saved and the unsaved in today's social landscape.

John Gill said of verse one,

> "... not that they were in a carnal state, as unregenerate men are; but had carnal conceptions of things, were in carnal frames of soul, and walked in a carnal conversation with each other; though they were not in the flesh, in a state of nature, yet the flesh was in them, and not only lusted against the Spirit, but was very predominant in them, and carried them captive, so that they are denominated from it."

It appears that the church at Corinth to which Paul was speaking was very much like the church today. Thus, we need to listen carefully to what Paul said to them because he would likely say similar things to us. Gill continued,

> "they too much walked as other men, who make no profession of religion; that they were led by the judgment of men, and were carried away with human passions and inflections; and in their conduct could scarcely be distinguished from the rest of the world."[2]

Paul found much of the same immaturity in the church at Galatia. There he delineated the works of the flesh, identified the things that bring trouble to the church.

> "Now the works of the flesh are evident: sexual immorality, impurity, sensuality, idolatry, sorcery, enmity, strife, jealousy, fits of anger, rivalries, dissensions, divisions, envy, drunkenness, orgies, and things like these. I warn you, as I warned you before, that those who do such things will not inherit the kingdom of God" (Galatians 5:19-21).

And those who will not inherit the kingdom of God are not Christians. However, this does not mean that all those who were guilty of these things were not Christians, but that those who did not grow out of these things would find themselves excluded from the kingdom. All sinners are not banned from the kingdom, only unrepentant sinners, only those who continue in their sin, who sin willfully.

Of course, it is not enough to say what is forbidden. Paul also tells us what is necessary—what we are to do, how we are to be in Christ.

Values and Religious Views in the United States, Regal Books, 1991.

2   Gill, John. *Exposition of the Entire Bible,* 1763, public domain.

"But the fruit of the Spirit is love, joy, peace, patience, kindness, goodness, faithfulness, gentleness, self-control; against such things there is no law. And those who belong to Christ Jesus have crucified the flesh with its passions and desires" (Galatians 5:22-24).

When Paul went to Corinth preaching nothing but Christ and Him crucified, he meant to teach them to crucify the flesh with its passions and desires.

MORTIFICATION

The Puritans called it *mortification*—the subjection and denial of bodily passions and appetites by abstinence or self-discipline. Mortification is not a hard thing or a harsh thing that causes suffering. Rather, it is the abandonment of those feelings and desires that are the true cause of suffering. Paul was talking about mortification when he said

"that our old self was crucified with him (Christ) in order that the body of sin might be brought to nothing, so that we would no longer be enslaved to sin" (Romans 6:6).

And again in Ephesians 4:17-24:

"Now this I say and testify in the Lord, that you must no longer walk as the Gentiles do, in the futility of their minds. They are darkened in their understanding, alienated from the life of God because of the ignorance that is in them, due to their hardness of heart. They have become callous and have given themselves up to sensuality, greedy to practice every kind of impurity. But that is not the way you learned Christ!—assuming that you have heard about him and were taught in him, as the truth is in Jesus, to put off your old self, which belongs to your former manner of life and is corrupt through deceitful desires, and to be renewed in the spirit of your minds, and to put on the new self, created after the likeness of God in true righteousness and holiness."

And in Colossians 3:5-11:

"Put to death therefore what is earthly in you: sexual immorality, impurity, passion, evil desire, and covetousness, which is idolatry. On account of these the wrath of God is coming. In these you too once walked, when you were living in them. But now you must put them all away: anger, wrath, malice, slander, and obscene talk from your mouth. Do not lie to one another, seeing that you have put off the old self with its practices and have put on the new self, which is being renewed in knowledge after the image of its creator. Here there is not Greek and

Jew, circumcised and uncircumcised, barbarian, Scythian, slave, free; but Christ is all, and in all."

You have heard it said that the church is the bride of Christ, which means that Christ is the husband of the church. Do you know what it means to be a husband? Do you know what *husbandry* is? It's a word that you don't hear much today. Nonetheless, God's primary function in the world is husbandry.

"For we are laborers together with God: ye are God's husbandry, ye are God's building" (v. 9—KJV). Webster defines *husbandry* as

> "The business of a farmer, comprehending agriculture or tillage of the ground, the raising, managing and fattening of cattle and other domestic animals, the management of the dairy and whatever the land produces. 1. Frugality; domestic economy; good management; thrift. 2. Care of domestic affairs" (*Webster's Dictionary*, 1828).

God is raising a crop of people for harvest. Are you one of them? What about your children? Who is husbanding your children?

Paul is telling us in chapter three that divisions and dissensions in the church are the result of sin not yet overcome or purged from the body of Christ. But he is not suggesting that anyone be run out of the church because of some latent or manifest sin. Rather, he calls all Christians to grow up in Christ, to get over their attachments to sin and evil. Christian discipline (or discipleship) is self-discipline or self-control through submission to the power of Jesus Christ. This is the critical element that was missing in Corinth, and is missing in too many Christians today.

Yes, we are saved by grace alone, yet we are called to righteousness. Yes, it is the righteousness of Christ alone. The righteousness that saves is not ours, but Christ's. It is a foreign righteousness that is applied to believers by the power of God—but it is righteousness, nonetheless. Justification by the blood of Christ is immediately credited to believers, and is sufficient for salvation. Yet, sanctification through the mortification of the flesh must be willingly engaged and regularly practiced by those who persevere to the end. Sanctification is not possible apart from the power of Jesus Christ. It can't be faked. But neither is it magic. It doesn't happen automatically. It doesn't happen all at once. It doesn't happen without hard work. It doesn't happen without willing submission to Jesus Christ, who is alone the author and power of it. It is not works-righteousness, but it is righteousness and it does require work.

Reward

How else can we explain Paul's emphasis on the personal reward for perseverance in faithfulness. Paul said that "each one shall receive his own reward according to his own labor" (v. 8—*Modern King James Bible*).

Part of what this means is that the Corinthians would not be rewarded according to Paul's labor, nor will you be rewarded according my labor, nor will Reformed Christians be rewarded according Calvin's labor. Rather, each will be rewarded according to his own labor (2 Corinthians 5:10). Note that the reward is real, and so is the labor. We are saved *by* grace, and we are saved *for* works. Works apart from grace cannot save, but neither does grace apart from works—works of righteousness.

John Gill said of this verse that we are not given reward for our success—"not according to the success of it," but according to our willing engagement of the work given to us by Jesus Christ—works of mercy, works of service, and growth in righteousness by the grace of God. The reward does not come as a result of our success, but serves to encourage us toward greater faithfulness. In other words, God withholds rewards from those who do not grow, who do not mature in faithfulness, not as punishment but simply because faith is the means by which the rewards are provided.

Of all the churches mentioned in the New Testament the Corinthian church that Paul addressed is most like the contemporary American church today. The church in Corinth and the church today suffer from spiritual immaturity. Paul wasn't saying that they were not saved, he was saying that they were unacceptably immature, and that the primary evidence of that immaturity was the divisions that plagued the church and interfered with evangelism.

Ray Stedman said that

"the two major forces that were active in this city, creating the atmosphere in which the Corinthian church had to live, were these: intellectualism and sensualism. This was a city devoted to the worship of the goddess sex."

John MacArthur said that

"they had managed to drag into their church life all of the features of their former pagan existence. They had not made a clear-cut separation —they had not come out from among the world to be separate."

Like those who heard Paul in Athens (Acts 17), the Christ that they accepted was a christ of Greek origin, not the Hebrew Christ of the Bible. They accepted Christ only to put Him into their pantheon fully clothed in the robes of Greek mysticism and philosophy—Greek (human) wisdom.

This is why Paul spoke so hard against human wisdom in the first two chapters. In chapter three he said that the failure to accept the Christ of Scripture by substituting a christ of Greek or human wisdom results in, among other things, divisions in the church. The divisions arise from the false understandings produced by filtering the gospel through the categories of human wisdom, by submitting the gospel to the categories of academia. Nowhere does Paul suggest merging human wisdom with God's wisdom. Rather, he insists that human wisdom is not adequate to the task of interpreting God's wisdom. Nowhere does he try to make the gospel appeal to human wisdom. In fact, he says that such an appeal is futile because "the natural person does not accept the things of the Spirit of God" (1 Corinthians 2:14).

By extrapolation, then, the effort to make the gospel appeal to popular tastes is no different than trying to make the gospel appeal to the natural person. The Greek word translated as *natural* is *psuchikos*, which literally means *sensual*. So the natural person is a sensual person, a person dominated by feelings (passions). The effort to bring natural people into the church by appealing to their natural sensitivities is an invitation to trouble. It is destructive to the peace and purity of the church.

Rather, says Paul, build on the foundation you already have. Build on the foundation of Jesus Christ. Church growth is not a matter of packing the pews with natural people. Work the good ground that you have been given by Christ. Plant and till and water the soil you have. You don't need different soil or different seed or different water. What you need is the discipline of perseverance in faithfulness. What we need is to do works of righteousness where we are planted. What we need is God's wisdom to show us who God has called us to be, and how to live lives of grace in Jesus Christ. What we need is the spirit of Jesus Christ to give us the courage to be Christian in the midst of a culture that is not Christian. Having been called by the grace of God through Jesus Christ, we need to rely upon the power and presence of the Holy Spirit to make a difference. But we are not to make just any old difference. The difference we are to

make is the difference between God's wisdom and worldly wisdom, between righteousness and lawlessness, light and dark, Christ and Belial.

Paul sums up this concern in his second letter to the Corinthians:

"...we appeal to you not to receive the grace of God in vain. For he
says, 'In a favorable time I listened to you, and in a day of salvation I
have helped you.' Behold, now is the favorable time; behold, now is the
day of salvation. We put no obstacle in anyone's way, so that no fault
may be found with our ministry, but as servants of God we commend
ourselves in every way: by great endurance, in afflictions, hardships,
calamities, beatings, imprisonments, riots, labors, sleepless nights,
hunger; by purity, knowledge, patience, kindness, the Holy Spirit, genuine love; by truthful speech, and the power of God; with the weapons
of righteousness for the right hand and for the left through honor and
dishonor, through slander and praise. We are treated as impostors, and
yet are true; as unknown, and yet well known; as dying, and behold, we
live; as punished, and yet not killed; as sorrowful, yet always rejoicing;
as poor, yet making many rich; as having nothing, yet possessing everything. We have spoken freely to you, Corinthians; our heart is wide
open. You are not restricted by us, but you are restricted in your own
affections. In return (I speak as to children) widen your hearts also. Do
not be unequally yoked with unbelievers. For what partnership has
righteousness with lawlessness? Or what fellowship has light with darkness? What accord has Christ with Belial? Or what portion does a believer share with an unbeliever? What agreement has the temple of God
with idols? For we are the temple of the living God; as God said, "I will
make my dwelling among them and walk among them, and I will be
their God, and they shall be my people. Therefore go out from their
midst, and be separate from them, says the Lord, and touch no unclean
thing; then I will welcome you, and I will be a father to you, and you
shall be sons and daughters to me, says the Lord Almighty" (2 Corinthians 6:1-18).

5. Two Spirits

And if anyone builds on this foundation gold, silver, precious stones, wood, hay, stubble, each one's work shall be revealed. For the Day shall declare it, because it shall be revealed by fire; and the fire shall try each one's work as to what kind it is. If anyone's work which he built remains, he shall receive a reward. If anyone's work shall be burned up, he shall suffer loss. But he shall be saved, yet so as by fire. Do you not know that you are a temple of God, and that the Spirit of God dwells in you? — 1 Corinthians 3:12-16

The natural man, that is, the wise man of the world (1 Corinthians 1:19, 20), the wise man after the flesh, or according to the flesh (v. 26), one who hath the wisdom of the world, man's wisdom (1 Corinthians 2:4-6), a man, as some of the ancients, that would learn all truth by his own ratiocinations, receives nothing by faith, nor own any need of supernatural assistance. This was very much the character of the pretenders to philosophy and the Grecian learning and wisdom in that day. — Matthew Henry

Paul tells us in verse 12 that there are two spirits active in the lives of people—the "spirit of the world" and the "spirit who is from God." The spirit of the world could also be called the natural spirit in that it does not recognize or honor God, while the spirit who is from God does. Understanding the difference between these two spirits hinges on our yielding to the reality of God and denying the temptations and deceptions of the world.

Webster defines *spirit* as 1) an animating or vital principle held to give life to physical organisms; 2) a supernatural being or essence; 3) temper or disposition of mind or outlook; 4) the immaterial intelligent or sentient part of a person; 5) the activating or essential principle influencing a person, an inclination, impulse, or tendency; 6) a special attitude or frame of mind. Paul uses the word to distinguish something supernatural from something merely natural. The difference suggests a disposition of mind that is God-given and God-driven versus a disposition that denies God. Paul's use of the word *spirit* intimates a disposition of mind or an attitude.

Paul places these two spirits or attitudes in radical opposition to one another, as he has done previously in his discussion of godly wisdom versus worldly folly. There are some areas that these two perspectives overlap, but that is not Paul's concern here. Here his purpose is to differentiate the two, to indicate that they are actually very different, in spite of the fact that they may at times look similar.

Paul was in the process of differentiating two kinds or groups of people. We know them as the lost and the saved, or the elect and the non-elect, the church as the body of Christ and everyone else. There is a difference between the world and the church, and that difference is critical or foundational to Paul's message. That difference not only determines whether one goes to heaven or to hell, but it determines how people live their daily lives. The difference it makes is a matter of attitude, temper, disposition, inclination, impulse, tendency, perspective, and habit. Paul is not talking about heaven here.

HABITUAL

Faithfulness is habitual. It is in part a matter of practice and repetition. It is, of course, more than a habit, but it is also, in fact, a habit. It is more than a habit because faithfulness is the result of the power and presence of the Holy Spirit operating in one's life. It is life lived on the basis of the reality of the Holy Spirit. It is a matter of discarding one's own personal preferences and desires, and submitting to the preferences and desires of God's Holy Spirit. It is a matter of not doing what you want for yourself, but of doing what God wants for you. It is a matter of abandoning worldly preferences and submitting to godly preferences.

And yet, faithfulness is more than a habit because mere practice cannot produce it. If faithfulness could be acquired by practice, it would be a matter of works-righteousness. But, as we know, it is not a consequence of works-righteousness and cannot be acquired by practice. And yet, it is a habit.

How can this be? While faith cannot be *acquired* through practice, it can be *increased* through practice. And conversely, it can be decreased through a lack of practice. This, of course, begs the question, if it can't be acquired through practice, how can it be acquired?

Paul tells us that it is not *acquired* at all, but rather *received* as a free gift from God. It needs be noted here that our willful reception of the gift of grace is not the trigger that activates it. We cannot say that it is our personal (willing) reception of God's gift that makes the gift real or even that it makes it effective. Whether or not we willingly receive or acknowledge God's gift of grace does not change the fact that God has given it prior to any reception or acknowledgment of it on our part. Our reception of God's grace is always a response to His gift. The reception or response follows the giving.

God wants us to understand or know the things that he has freely given to us. That knowledge is not mere head knowledge or historical knowledge, but is also heart knowledge, experiential knowledge. There are two ways to know a thing. We can know about it and we can know it directly, experientially.

For instance, I can know about China. I can read about it and see movies about it. And that is a legitimate form of knowledge. But it is always second hand knowledge. It is knowledge that comes through someone else—the author of the book or the director of the movie, etc. This kind of knowledge is general and multi-perspectival. It comes through the perspectives of other people.

I can also know China by going there myself. The experience of being there gives me a different kind of knowledge. It is a more direct kind of knowing because it is not mitigated through someone else. Visiting China provides personal experience, which is deeper and more focused than the other. Both kinds of knowledge have their limitations. One is general, but shallow. The other is deep, but narrow.

Knowledge about China gathered from reading or movie watching lacks the element of personal experience. On the other hand, knowledge gained through personal experience lacks the breadth of perspective that can be gained by reading and watching movies. Reading and movie watching provide insight into perspectives other than our own.

God wants us to engage both kinds of knowledge. This means that wisdom and understanding are integral parts of our salvation. Salvation is not just a matter of personal experience, it is also a matter of wisdom and knowledge—both the breadth of historical knowledge and the depth of personal experience.

Born Again

Yet, there is a third element that is essential for salvation to be genuine. The *Westminster Confession* calls it "the inward work of the Holy Spirit" (WCF 1:5). John said that "unless one is born again he cannot see the kingdom of God" (John 3:3). Peter said,

"Blessed be the God and Father of our Lord Jesus Christ! According to his great mercy, he has caused us to be born again to a living hope through the resurrection of Jesus Christ from the dead" (1 Peter 1:3).

Later in the same chapter Peter further clarifies,

"Having purified your souls by your obedience to the truth for a sincere brotherly love, love one another earnestly from a pure heart, since you have been born again, not of perishable seed but of imperishable, through the living and abiding word of God; for 'All flesh is like grass and all its glory like the flower of grass. The grass withers, and the flower falls, but the word of the Lord remains forever.' And this word is the good news that was preached to you" (1 Peter 1:23-25).

Peter tells us that being born again in Christ is a necessary part—even the foundation—of the gospel or good news of Jesus Christ. Regeneration is not optional. It is a fact. All Christians are born again, and if someone is not born again he is not a Christian. God has sent His Holy Spirit through the ministry of Jesus Christ—his birth, death and atonement for sin. And there is no salvation apart from the invasion of the Holy Spirit into the life of the believer. Just as God invaded human history through the birth of Jesus Christ, so the Holy Spirit invades our personal lives through the regeneration of individual believers.

Yet, regeneration is not merely individual. The sending of the Holy Spirit is the initial or essential gift of God's grace, for the Holy Spirit carries the message of salvation and redemption to God's people. The Holy Spirit brings the message of salvation to each person individually, but also to the whole people of God, corporately. Through the Holy Spirit the message of salvation is internalized—made real in a personal way—because the Holy Spirit resides within the hearts and minds of Christians. But God's message is also social and historical. Paul wanted to "impart this in words not taught by human wisdom but taught by the Spirit" (v. 13).

Most versions of the Bible use the word *speak* rather than *impart*. The Greek (*laleō*) literally means to utter speech. It is important to note that the gospel is shared through words transferred from one person to another, sometimes spoken, sometimes written. This impartation of the Holy Spirit is not magical, but is a function of ordinary speaking and writing. No candles in a darkened room, no special charismatic languages, no mumbo jumbo, no special touch from the master. Just words. Paul's letters provide the example of how its done.

Paul was converted (born again) on the road to Damascus. He was convicted by the Spirit, not by men (Galatians 1:1). Paul's conversion changed his heart and mind, and he spent the rest of his life talking about Jesus. His talk consisted of preaching, writing letters, and individual counseling or conversations.

Paul tells us that his recommended method of teaching is to compare spiritual things to spiritual things. Worldly things are inadequate to explain spiritual things. Another way to say it is that the truth of Scripture is self-evident to the born again. Or Scripture teaches Scripture. Or analogous things in the world always fall short of biblical truth. The illustration of biblical truths with non-biblical, worldly stories always falls short.

Would you go to a natural man to learn spiritual truth? Of course not. Would you go to a non-Christian to learn about Christianity? Of course not. And why not? As Paul said,

> "the natural man does not receive the things of the Spirit of God, for they are foolishness to him; neither can he know them, because they are spiritually discerned" (v. 14).

Show me someone who thinks that Christianity is foolish, and I'll show you a worldly person. The reason that they think Christianity is foolish is that they cannot perceive the reality of God.

DENIAL

Such people cannot perceive the reality of God because they "suppress the truth in unrighteousness" (Romans 1:18). God's truth is available to them, as it is available to every creature. They can't suppress it if they don't already have it. It is in their possession, but they hold it down. They keep it below their conscious awareness. They don't want to see it. They don't want to acknowledge it. And so they ignore it or deny it.

Avoidance is a well-known psychological phenomenon. When Paul says that they suppress the truth in unrighteousness, he means that their commitment to unrighteousness will not allow them to admit the possibility of righteousness. There are several ways they rationalize the denial of righteousness.

Sometimes the acknowledgment of the reality and extent of sin keeps people from righteousness by suggesting that human sinfulness excludes the possibility of human righteousness. They (correctly) acknowledge that sin is our natural condition, and that its extent is all-encompassing, but fail to acknowledge the reality and power of Jesus Christ to overcome it. These people deny the power of God to overcome sin, and believe that the best we can do is to learn to live with our sinfulness, to accept it as normal.

Sometimes people deny that we (people) have access to any objective knowledge, that all knowledge is necessarily subjective and completely determined by personal perspective and preferences. They think that all human knowledge and experience are necessarily subjective. And they are right, except for the fact that God's knowledge and experience are objective, or at least a lot more objective than any human knowledge and experience. In denying the reality of God, or the possibility of God communicating with or through people, they deny the possibility of ever having anything other than subjective human knowledge. These people deny the power of the Holy Spirit, and His ability to transform lives.

Sometimes people deny the authenticity and/or veracity of Scripture. They believe that all religious stories are essentially equal. And since some stories seem to contradict others at various points, they dismiss them as being no more than historical embellishments intended to explain the unexplainable, or to otherwise help people cope with life's difficulties. They consider all religious stories to be essentially fictitious. It is easy for us to misunderstand verse 15, "The spiritual person judges all things, but is himself to be judged by no one."

Judgmentalism is a hot topic in today's politically correct world, but that is not what Paul is talking about. The spiritual person is a born again person—a saved by the blood of Christ and into the fellowship of believers person, who has submitted to the power and presence of the Holy Spirit in his or her life. He is a person who does not live on the basis of his own desires or preferences. Rather, he lives on the basis of God's desires and preferences for him. This is exactly what Paul means: the spiritual person considers or evaluates everything on the basis of Scripture. The spirituality of such a person affects everything that they think, say, and do. Such a person applies the categories of Scripture to everything, and, first and foremost, the wisdom of Scripture is applied to his own life.

SUPERIOR

The second phrase of verse 15 is another way of saying the same thing, because the categories of Scripture (or the realm of the Spirit) subsume the categories of the world. This means that the things of the world can be explained by the Spirit, but the things of the Spirit cannot be explained by the things of the world. Spirituality cannot be explained or properly evaluated by worldliness. If you think this sounds like I'm saying that spirituality is somehow superior to worldliness, you're right. It is. But I'm not saying it. I'm just clarifying it. Paul is saying it. And he is saying it because Jesus teaches it.

However, we must remember that God's values are the inversion of human values. For instance,

> "Jesus called them to him and said, 'You know that the rulers of the Gentiles lord it over them, and their great ones exercise authority over them. It shall not be so among you. But whoever would be great among you must be your servant, and whoever would be first among you must be your slave, even as the Son of Man came not to be served but to serve, and to give his life as a ransom for many'" (Matthew 20:25-28).

In the kingdom of God the servant is in a superior position to the master. All Christians are servants to the one Master, who was Himself a servant to all.

Thus, Christians are called to rule the world through service. The spiritual person is to be judged by no one because he will be judged by Jesus Christ. And first and foremost, he will apply the judgment of Jesus Christ to himself by submitting to God's desires according to Scripture.

The final verse of this chapter includes a quote from Isaiah 40:13, "Who has measured the Spirit of the Lord, or what man shows him his counsel?" Paul translated it, "For who has understood the mind of the Lord so as to instruct him?" (1 Corinthians 2:16).

Though the language is different, the meaning is the same, and it applies to the subject of this section of First Corinthians. Paul is saying that the unsaved are not able to understand spiritual things. Nor do they understand spiritual people. So, they are not in any position to evaluate anything spiritual.

However, Paul concludes this thought by saying that "we (the born again) have the mind of Christ" (1 Corinthians 2:16) He is not saying that Christians are above judgment or above the law, but that because Christians have the mind of Christ they are able to judge themselves and one another. He is saying that Christians are subject to the mind of the body of Christ—the church, which is subject to the Word of God.

Paul will return to this concern in chapter five where he said, "For what have I to do with judging outsiders? Is it not those inside the church whom you are to judge?" (1 Corinthians 5:12).

The Bible does not teach Christians to suspend judgment. It teaches them to judge according to Scripture and not according to our own desires and preferences. Judging according to our own human desires and preferences is what Paul calls folly and worldly wisdom. But judging according to Scripture Paul calls spiritual wisdom.

6. Christ's Umbrella

Do you not know that you are a temple of God, and that the Spirit of God dwells in you? If anyone defiles the temple of God, God shall destroy him. For the temple of God is holy, which you are. Let no one deceive himself. If anyone among you seems to be wise in this world, let him become a fool so that he may be wise. For the wisdom of this world is foolishness with God; for it is written, "He takes the wise in their own craftiness." And again, "The Lord knows the thoughts of the wise, that they are vain." Therefore let no one glory in men. For all things are yours, whether it is Paul, or Apollos, or Cephas, or the world, or life, or death, or things present, or things to come; all are yours, and you are Christ's, and Christ is God's. — 1 Corinthians 3:16-23

Paul has established that the Spirit of God dwells with believers. He makes an analogy to the Old Testament Temple by saying that believers *are* the temple of God. It is important that we understand who Paul refers to here. The Greek word translated as *you* is a second person plural present indicative. That means that the best translation is *y'all*. It is a plural term and indicates that the people of God are the temple, not simply individual believers.

Peter built upon this theme when he said, "you yourselves like living stones are being built up as a spiritual house, to be a holy priesthood, to offer spiritual sacrifices acceptable to God through Jesus Christ" (1 Peter 2:5).

Yes, the Spirit of God inhabits believers as they are born again, and each believer must protect the purity (or health) of his or her own body as part of the discipline of faithfulness. But the analogy primarily applies to the corporate nature of the church as the body of Christ. The purity of the church must also be protected.

Paul speaks of this in 1 Corinthians 12:12-ff,

"For just as the body is one and has many members, and all the members of the body, though many, are one body, so it is with Christ. For in one Spirit we were all baptized into one body—Jews or Greeks, slaves or free —and all were made to drink of one Spirit."

Just as individual bodies are not divisible, which is the root meaning of *individual*, so, the church is also individual—not just specific churches, but the Church Universal is individual—whole, complete, without division. Christians are bound together in a bond of love and fellowship with one another across the face of the globe and throughout the centuries. Christian unity is not something to be achieved, rather it is something to be realized. It is already the fact of the matter in that Christian unity has been decreed and is in the process of realization.

Love and Fellowship

This bond of love and fellowship between believers is not based upon how we feel about one another, or on what we think about each other. How we feel about each other and what we think about each other are secondary concerns or less—minor concerns—because the love of Christ is stronger than whatever appreciation or disdain we may have for other believers. The bond of Christian fellowship is not based on our love or respect for one another, but on Christ's love for His people—all of His people. Our feelings for each other are not the bonding element of Christian fellowship.

Nor are Christians bound together by their understanding of biblical doctrine. Doctrine is not the bond of Christian fellowship, either. Christ is. Our bond is not doctrinal or denominational, but personal. Jesus Christ is the bond of Christian fellowship. Christians have Christ in common, and all Christians are growing into

> "the unity of the faith and of the knowledge of the Son of God, to mature manhood, to the measure of the stature of the fullness of Christ, so that we may no longer be children, tossed to and fro by the waves and carried about by every wind of doctrine, by human cunning, by craftiness in deceitful schemes" (Ephesians 4:13-14).

This is not a disparagement of the value of right doctrine, nor the importance of the love of the brethren—both of which are biblically mandated. Doctrine is important, and we are called to love and honor one another in Christ. We are stewards of the temple of God, which is no longer a building made of stones, but is now in Christ a church made of believers (1 Corinthians 3:16, 1 Peter 2:5).

"If anyone destroys God's temple, God will destroy him. For God's temple is holy, and you are that temple" (v. 17). The KJV translates it, "If any man *defile* the temple of God" (italics added). The Greek word translated *defile* means to pine or waste, to shrivel or wither, that is, to spoil or to ruin by moral influences, to deprave, corrupt, or destroy. I prefer *defile* to *destroy* because it better suggests the process that leads to destruction. It tells us that contamination of the purity of the church can be lethal. It tells us that moral contamination or moral synthesis produces death.

But is the Church of Jesus Christ morally or doctrinally pure? No, not yet. Rather, it is growing in purity over time as it grows in faithfulness through the sanctification of its members, individually and corporately, in spite of what it may seem. The growth of the church is like the growth of the stock market in that there are cyclic fluctuations but an overall increase over time. Because we are not pure, because we are still sinners wrestling with a boatload of sin in our personal and corporate lives, and yet are members of Christ's body nonetheless, the purity of the church is retarded by our spiritual immaturity. I am equating spiritual immaturity with moral depravity because we are all saved from sin into Christ's righteousness. We are growing in faithfulness and in understanding in as much as we trust and depend upon Jesus Christ and the Word of God and not on the foolishness of men.

At the same time, we cannot deny the moral demand that Paul lays at our feet in this verse. Inasmuch as we defile the church, God will defile us. It appears that God will give back to us what we give to Him. If we give Him love and honor and praise, He will give us love and honor and praise. But if we give Him hate and dishonor and spite, He will give those very things right back to us. Being made in the image of God means that there is a reflectivity in our relationship with our Creator. The positive side is that we reflect His character inasmuch as we are true to His Word. And the negative side is that our failure to reflect His character results in the defilement of the church, and leads to our own destruction.

If the church were just another autonomous gathering of people with common interests, that would be one thing. But because the church is the moral linchpin of the greater society the defilement of the church produces the moral decline and eventual destruction of the greater society. This is the issue that has faced humanity since Adam and Eve left the Garden. When God told Adam that he would "surely die" (Genesis 2:17) in the day that he ate of the fruit of the knowledge of good and evil, he had this death in mind. He didn't mean that Adam would die before the sun set that particular day. Rather, He meant that human society would inescapably collapse from the moral rot that would ensue from the disobedience and/or disregard of God's Word.

> "Let no one deceive himself. If anyone among you thinks that he is wise in this age, let him become a fool that he may become wise. For the wisdom of this world is folly with God. For it is written, 'He catches the wise in their craftiness,' and again, 'The Lord knows the thoughts of the wise, that they are futile'" (vs. 18-20).

Again the KJV is instructive. It translates *aiōn* as *world* rather than *age*. "If any man among you seemeth to be wise in this world…." This is the primary theme of First Corinthians so far: "Has not God made foolish the wisdom of the world" (1 Corinthians 1:20)?

FOOLISHNESS

What appears to us to be the wise thing to do is foolishness compared to the truth of Christ. This has a very wide application in our lives, but for the most part we ignore it. We have been trained by the world, by the values of secular humanism through our public education, through the secular values and practices of the media and the workplace. That training has taught us to ignore the inner testimony of the Holy Spirit when that testimony is not in conformity with the values and practices of secular humanism. And Christians are not immune from the pervasiveness of secular humanism in contemporary society. It is virtually everywhere in contemporary culture. Yet, not quite everywhere. For a few people in a few churches cling to the truth that worldly wisdom, secular ideas and ways of doing things, are utterly foolish in the light of Christ. It's not a popular position in any church.

Oh, Christians often agree with such an idea when they're at church. When we see it in Scripture we do not deny God's truth. Yet, when we walk out of the doors of the church, we are confronted by the common values and practices of secular humanism that categorically and comprehensively deny the validity and applicability of Scripture. Nowhere do we see the wisdom of Jesus Christ lived out in the world! Another way to say it is, everywhere we see the wisdom of the world and the implementation of science and technology without any reference to Christ. Everywhere we see the domination of nature and the apparent success of market forces through the application of the values and practices of secular humanism. The experience and history of the modern world teach that the world has made foolish the wisdom of Christ.

SCHIZOPHRENIA

The result is that Christians live out schizophrenic lives, believing one way in church and another way outside of church. No matter how faithful we are, no matter how much we believe Scripture and trust Christ, we are bombarded by the opposite teaching because of the pervasiveness of secular humanism in the contemporary world. We cannot escape it.

To seriously challenge the common wisdom and values of secular humanism makes life difficult because people react negatively when their most basic beliefs are contradicted or suggested (or demonstrated) to be false. Trust me, I know! The more you try to systematically and comprehensively apply the wisdom of Christ in the world, the more people will think that you are crazy, and the more successful you are in this effort, the more angry people will get.

I often hear people joke about themselves being thought of as a little odd or crazy in the sense that eccentricities are increasingly tolerated because of the recent emphasis on cultural diversity. You'd think that the diversity police would like people who don't conform to the current cultural standards. And they do, to an extent. They will tolerate every kind of social nonconformity, except conformity to Jesus Christ. And the more serious you are in that effort, the less people are willing to tolerate you, and the less funny (or cute) the joke becomes. Nonetheless, Paul said that "the foolishness of God is wiser than men, and the weakness of God is stronger than men" (1 Corinthians 1:20).

Paul has been contrasting wisdom and foolishness. Sometimes he uses the same word to mean both the real wisdom of Christ and the false wisdom of the world. The contrasts are laid out several different ways to ensure that we don't misunderstand what he is saying. In verse 18 he urges his listeners to become foolish in the eyes of the world by proclaiming and acting upon the wisdom of Christ. Earlier he admonished his listeners to abandon the foolishness of the world. But the point is clear—God's wisdom and the world's wisdom are not the same.

"For the wisdom of this world is folly with God. For it is written, 'He catches the wise in their craftiness'" (v. 19). Paul quoted from Job 5:12. Job 5:8-16 tells us exactly how God deals with foolish people:

"Truly, I would seek to God, and to God I would put my plea, Who is
doing great things, even beyond searching; marvelous things without
number, who gives rain on the earth and sends waters on the field, to
set on high those who are low, so that those who mourn may be lifted
up to safety; frustrating the plans of the crafty, nor did their hands do
wisely. He takes the wise in their own craftiness; and the counsel of the
wily is carried headlong. They meet with darkness in the day time, and
grope in the noonday as in the night. But He saves the poor from the
sword, from their mouth, and from the hand of the mighty. And there
is hope for the weak, and injustice shuts her mouth" (Job 5:8-16).

Notice that He doesn't just smite them from the face of the earth.
Rather, He "frustrates the devices of the crafty" and "catches them in their
own craftiness." The Hebrew words translated as *devices* are interesting.
The basic idea refers to the employment of the mind or the activity of
thinking. It does not refer so much to understanding, as it does to creating new ideas, to what we call creativity. It is used most frequently to
suggest planning or devising. Let me also suggest that it applies to the
fruit of such planning, the devices designed and developed by the exercise
of creative thinking and planning—technology. It refers to what we call
technological development.

I'm not suggesting that technology itself is a bad thing, only that—
like everything else—when it is used apart from God, apart from God's
wisdom—it has the potential for great evil and destruction. The issue is
not technology itself, as the fruit of creativity, but the faithful development and use of technology and creativity. We must be faithful as we develop it and faithful as we use it.

ROPE

Again, God doesn't stop people from creative thinking and planning.
He lets us do it. And when our creative thinking and planning are in harmony with His Word we are blessed by the fruit of His providence. But
when our creative thinking and planning are not in harmony with His
Word, or when we ignore God's Word and think and plan our own ideas
apart from God, he also lets us do it. In Romans 1:24-28 Paul said that
"God gave them up in the lusts of their hearts to impurity," and further,
that "God gave them up to a debased mind to do what ought not to be
done."

God's way is to let the sinner sin. But why? Shouldn't God stop sinners from sinning? Have you ever tried to tell a two-year-old child not to

touch a hot stove? You can do that. You can tell the child. You can threaten the child. You can create all the rules you want. But the child *will* touch the stove, and you cannot stop it from happening.

Is it a bad thing? No, because often we learn from painful experiences better than we learn from careful explanations. Is it painful? Yes. Is it bad? No. In the same way, God allows people to carry out their evil plans because he knows two things: 1) His justice will prevail, and they will get their comeuppance; and 2) many other people will learn to avoid evil from their experience and the consequences of their actions. And God will get glory from both—from the exercise of justice, and from those who learn to heed His Word and avoid evil. The same idea is found in Psalm 9:15, "The nations have sunk in the pit that they made; in the net that they hid their own foot has been caught."

It's sort of a reverse Golden Rule. Rather than "whatever you wish that others would do to you, do also to them" (Matthew 7:12), we see that we should not do unto others what we don't want done to ourselves. The operative principle here is that you get what you give.

"So let no one boast in men" (v. 21). I've talked about pride many times before. Pride is a sin. Pride is theft—it's stealing glory from God. Too many people discount the sinfulness of pride and boldly proclaim their pride in their children or grandchildren, or their pride in their boss or their employees, etc. But being a proud parent or grandparent is still pride, and is no less sinful than any other kind of pride. Can't people be "pleased" with someone, or "happy" about something they did without being "proud"? Of course they can. But our language betrays us. Too many people are even proud to be Christians!

The problem with pride is that it suggests that the source of a person's success is his own effort. A proud person takes credit (or glory) for the accomplishment of something. Whereas Christians know that the only source or cause of any success they might enjoy belongs entirely to God. Christians don't work in the flesh, they work in the Spirit. Those who work in the flesh are proud of themselves and their accomplishments. But those who work in the Spirit give all the glory to God. Let's not be proud of anything, remembering that pride is a sin.

> "For those who live according to the flesh set their minds on the things
> of the flesh, but those who live according to the Spirit set their minds
> on the things of the Spirit. To set the mind on the flesh is death, but to
> set the mind on the Spirit is life and peace" (Romans 8:5-6).

Unity

Finally, Paul called for a spirit of unity among Christians.

"For all things are yours, whether Paul or Apollos or Cephas or the world or life or death or the present or the future—all are yours, and you are Christ's, and Christ is God's" (vs. 21-23).

How can all things be ours? Paul prayed that Christians everywhere

"may know what is the hope to which he has called you, what are the riches of his glorious inheritance in the saints, and what is the immeasurable greatness of his power toward us who believe, according to the working of his great might that he worked in Christ when he raised him from the dead and seated him at his right hand in the heavenly places, far above all rule and authority and power and dominion, and above every name that is named, not only in this age but also in the one to come" (Ephesians 1:18-21).

Note the hierarchy. The fact that all things are ours seems to put us at the top of the hierarchy. But they are ours only inasmuch as we are Christ's, only inasmuch as we live in love and obedience to the law of Christ (Galatians 6:2). And all things belong to Christ only because Christ belongs to God. Now we see the real hierarchy. We are not at the top, God is! We are under the authority of Jesus Christ.

And this fact of Scripture is the very fact that the world denies. The repentant are glad to be under the authority of Jesus Christ because that is the fact of their salvation. But the Godless deny that they are under Christ's authority, and that denial is the foundation of their foolishness. In the fullness of time they will come to understand that they actually are under the authority of Christ, whether or not they believe it right now. For just as Jesus Christ will reward the repentant in heaven, He will also condemn the unrepentant to eternal hell and damnation without regard for what they themselves think or believe about it.

The issue is not whether the unrepentant can make sense of the world without God. The fact that they think they can make sense of the world without God only adds fuel to the fire of their foolishness because we are not judged on our ability to make sense of the world. We are judged on the basis of Christ's righteousness and the propitiation He made for His people at the cross. Christ's righteousness is like an umbrella under which His people live and move and have their being, protected from the wrath of God.

The issue is whether or not we are under the umbrella of Christ's righteousness. We cannot afford to fool ourselves about this matter. The issue is not whether we go to church, or where we go to church. The issue is not walking the "sawdust trail" or praying a prayer. Oh, all of these things are fine, but they do not make a person Christian. The issue is repentance, not sin. The issue is faithfulness, not church membership (Isaiah 1:11-16).

No one is kept from salvation by sin. Rather, people are kept from salvation by a lack of repentance. Jesus Himself said, "unless you repent, you will all likewise perish" (Luke 13:3). And to repent is to have your mind changed by God, to change the way you live. To repent is to actively seek to flourish in the shelter of the umbrella of Christ's righteousness.

7. Wisdom and Foolishness

This is how one should regard us, as servants of Christ and stewards of the mysteries of God. Moreover, it is required of stewards that they be found trustworthy. But with me it is a very small thing that I should be judged by you or by any human court. In fact, I do not even judge myself. I am not aware of anything against myself, but I am not thereby acquitted. It is the Lord who judges me. Therefore do not pronounce judgment before the time, before the Lord comes, who will bring to light the things now hidden in darkness and will disclose the purposes of the heart. Then each one will receive his commendation from God. I have applied all these things to myself and Apollos for your benefit, brothers, that you may learn by us not to go beyond what is written, that none of you may be puffed up in favor of one against another.

— *1 Corinthians 4:1-6*

The context of these verses is Paul's distinction between the wisdom of God and the foolishness of the world. Paul has set these two things in complete opposition, without any middle ground. This opposition is easy to describe and easy to understand. Understanding it doesn't require any academic degrees, special instruction or special intelligence. Of course, the understanding God's Word and the nature of this opposition between wisdom and foolishness requires two things: 1) regeneration, and 2) diligence. But, its full extent—the pervasiveness of its application—is seldom realized, understood, or spoken of because it is so different from what we have all been taught from our earliest childhood.

Cornelius Van Til, a Reformed scholar at Westminster Seminary until his death in 1987 spent a lifetime working out the philosophical and theological implications of the differences between the wisdom of God and the foolishness of the world. Van Til's work can be easily summed up in the phrase: there is no neutrality. It means that no one can be neutral or objective about anything, much less the gospel of Jesus Christ. Everyone has a particular perspective. Jesus said the same thing, "Whoever is not with me is against me, and whoever does not gather with me scatters" (Matthew 12:30).

Conversely, no one has a multiple perspective. To be an individual is to have a unique perspective. While we all need to be considerate of others, and attempt to "walk a mile in the shoes of another" no one walks in quite the same way. If you walk a mile in my shoes you will have a very different experience than I do when I walk a mile in them. The point is that every individual has a unique—and different—perspective.

What is more, the matter of God's existence provides a veritable watershed for human consciousness and understanding, dividing the human perspective into two separate categories. Those categories are 1) those who believe in God, and 2) those who don't. This divide that Paul has spent the previous three chapters discussing is so basic, so fundamental, so all-pervasive that it affects everything about every human being ever born. It essentially divides humanity into two categories or two cultures. These two cultures can be—and have been—variously labeled as believers and unbelievers, or the saved and the lost, or covenant keepers and covenant breakers. Thinking that the difference between them had to do with race and nationality, the ancient Israelites called them Israel and Gentiles. But the difference is not national or racial, it is cultural.

No Common Ground

Is there such a thing as common sense or a universal human perspective that all people share? Not according to Scripture. Of course, you and I share many things in common and the foundation of our shared perspective is our faith in Jesus Christ. But those who do not share that faith have a radically different perspective. So different, said Van Til, that virtually nothing is understood in the same way. Even when we do math or hoe the garden we do it very differently than those who do not believe in God. Believers do whatever they do in service to God, unbelievers do not. In other words, God is both the first and the final referent in all that believers think, say, and do. Apart from that foundation people think, say, and do very different things. Even when it appears that they are doing the same things, they are not because faith in God fundamentally changes everything.

Paul teaches that there is no significant common ground between these two groups of people. Paul will speak more fully of this division in his second letter to the Corinthians.

> "What accord has Christ with Belial? Or what portion does a believer
> share with an unbeliever? What agreement has the temple of God with
> idols? For we are the temple of the living God; as God said, 'I will make
> my dwelling among them and walk among them, and I will be their
> God, and they shall be my people. Therefore go out from their midst,
> and be separate from them, says the Lord, and touch no unclean thing;
> then I will welcome you, and I will be a father to you, and you shall be
> sons and daughters to me, says the Lord Almighty'" (2 Corinthians
> 6:15-18).

Such is the difference between the wisdom of God and the foolishness of
the world.

Of course, the sun shines on the good and the evil, and the rain falls
on the just and the unjust (Matthew 5:45). But the sun also shines and
rain falls on spiders and algae. All of God's creatures have many common
experiences—rain and sunshine, food and shelter, death and taxes. (Well,
spiders and algae don't pay taxes—yet!) But believers and unbelievers do
not have the same kind of experience of anything. The reason that we do
not have a common sense is that faith in Christ makes a real difference in
our lives. If the difference that Christ makes is insignificant or trivial, then
we might say that our experience or perspective is not much different
from that of unbelievers. But if Christ makes a significant difference, a
real difference, then Paul is telling the truth. Because we don't see things
in the same light, we don't know or experience things in the same way.
We don't do things for the same purposes.

Paul's ability to discern this important difference, which is a function
of the power and presence of the Holy Spirit in his life, gives him great
wisdom, real wisdom. Paul was a wise man of God, and as such we accord him honor and respect.

This fourth chapter of Corinthians provides a part of Paul's instructions about how to treat him, how to treat the apostles. This an issue because some people wanted to treat him and the other apostles as gods.
Remember how the apostles were treated at Lystra.

> "And when the crowds saw what Paul had done, they lifted up their
> voices, saying in Lycaonian, 'The gods have come down to us in the
> likeness of men!' Barnabas they called Zeus, and Paul, Hermes, because
> he was the chief speaker. And the priest of Zeus, whose temple was at
> the entrance to the city, brought oxen and garlands to the gates and
> wanted to offer sacrifice with the crowds. But when the apostles Barn-
> abas and Paul heard of it, they tore their garments and rushed out into

the crowd, crying out, 'Men, why are you doing these things? We also are men, of like nature with you, and we bring you good news, that you should turn from these vain things to a living God, who made the heaven and the earth and the sea and all that is in them" (Acts 14:11-15).

REGARD

And so Paul began chapter four by saying, "This is how one should regard us, as servants of Christ and stewards of the mysteries of God." He acknowledged that he and the apostles did indeed know the mysteries of God, that they did really know the wisdom of God. Part of that wisdom was knowing that they were not themselves God or gods. This knowledge is very important. It is very significant because it reveals that Paul and the apostles were not caught in the error that beguiled Eve in the Garden. There Satan told Adam and Eve that they could "be like God, knowing good and evil" (Genesis 3:5). And, of course, this is the most basic and most prevalent sin known to man. This sin is the foolishness of the world.

Paul tells us that "it is required of stewards that they be found trustworthy" (v. 2). Most versions read *faithful*. The Greek word is *pistos*, which is usually translated as *belief* or *faith*, but *trustworthy* is fine. A steward must be worthy of trust and full of faith. But how can we know if someone is trustworthy? Upon what should we base our trust of anybody? Let me ask it this way: Do we trust people because they have the ability to be just, truthful, honorable, or faithful? Do we trust that they are good enough or strong enough or smart enough to prove themselves faithful? What about sin? Is anyone above sin? No, which brings us to option two. The option is to trust Jesus Christ to both change a person for the better and to maintain that change over time. Do we trust that Jesus Christ is good enough and strong enough to accomplish what He said he would do? Do we trust that Jesus Christ is just, truthful, honorable, and faithful? Do we trust the power of regeneration in Christ?

If we put our trust in people we will ultimately be disappointed because no one is above sin. But to trust Jesus Christ is another matter. When Jesus Christ enters the picture everything changes. To trust a Christian is to trust the faithfulness of Jesus Christ. Our trust in fellow Christians is stronger because of the shared perspective or common experience that Christians have. Jesus teaches His people about faithfulness, so we all understand faithfulness in similar ways. And the Holy Spirit provides the power to be faithful to Jesus Christ. Trusting a Christian means trusting the Holy Spirit to accomplish His work of regeneration and sanctification.

In contrast, we cannot trust unbelievers (also known as covenant breakers) in the same way that we can trust Christians because we know that unbelievers are in rebellion against truth itself. So, when Paul tells us that stewards are to be trustworthy he means that they are to be Christian. Because Christ is the most trustworthy, those who believe in Christ are more trustworthy than those who don't.

What about dishonest, untrustworthy Christians? There are many people who claim to be Christian who are no more trustworthy than anyone else. How can we account for this? In Romans 9:6 Paul said that not all Israel is Israel. Similarly, not all those who claim to be Christian are actually Christian. There can be no other explanation. Jesus said the same thing in Matthew 7:21, "Not everyone who says to me, 'Lord, Lord,' will enter the kingdom of heaven, but the one who does the will of my Father who is in heaven."

LIGHT OF HUMANITY

The next few verses are difficult to understand. The key phrase comes in verse 4, and we turn to the *Modern King James Bible* (MKJB) to read it because it makes the point clear. Paul said, "for I know nothing by myself" (v. 4). Here is the context,

> "But to me it is a very small thing that I should be judged by you, or by a man's day; but I do not judge my own self, for I know nothing by myself. Yet I have not been justified by this, but He who judges me is the Lord" (v. 3-4).

Other translations of the Bible read "*of* myself" or "*against* myself." But there is no such Greek word in the text. The preposition has been added. There is an implied sense of the knowledge that Paul speaks of in the verse as being against or apart from himself. Nonetheless, the literal Greek reads, *For I know nothing myself.*

Back up for a moment and look at the phrase, "or by a man's day" (v. 3). The Greek word translated as *by* (*hupo*) can also be translated as *of*, but literally means *under*. "Man's day" is a literal translation, but it is an unusual phrase. So unusual that I want to suggest that it is an idiom that suggests the light of man or the light of humanity. The phrase we are looking at literally means *under the light of humanity*. Putting this all together we could read the verse, "But to me it is a very small thing that I should be judged by you, or judged under the light of humanity" (v. 3—my translation). Paul was saying that human reason or human experience or human discernment (the light of humanity) is not sufficient to evaluate God or the works of God. Human wisdom is inadequate to judge or understand Paul because his conversion and regeneration are a work of God.

There are many layers of meaning in these few verses. We know that Paul was defending himself against accusations made against him by others in the church. The nature of those accusations is unclear. But we can surmise that they stem in part from his opposition to the worldly wisdom (the Greek perspective) that was common among Corinthian believers. He put himself and the heart of Christianity in opposition to the common sense and practices—the common (Greco-Roman) culture—of the day. He said that the wisdom of Christ is contrary to human wisdom, that the culture of the church (believers) is contrary to the culture of the world (unbelievers). Those who supported the superiority of human wisdom accused Paul of foolishness among other things.

So, following the basic themes of First Corinthians to this point, we understand that Paul's comment in verse 4 was an expression of the crux of his argument against worldly wisdom. The story of the Serpent in the Garden and the temptation and Fall of Adam and Eve tells us that the Serpent provided a way to know the world apart from God. Satan convinced Eve that truth was not dependent upon God, that truth could stand alone, apart from any reference to God. From this perspective, God and man (humanity) could both use reason to understand and discern truth because truth was thought to exist independently of God and man. And furthermore, said the Serpent, God knows that if you employ reason as the primary tool for understanding the world, "your eyes shall be opened, and you shall be as God, knowing good and evil" (Genesis 3:5).

When Paul said "for I know nothing ... myself" (v. 4) he meant that genuine knowledge of the world required a reference or anchor point beyond himself, beyond his own ability to know and understand. He meant that human knowledge required a point of reference that was eternally fixed and stable through history in order to overcome the self-deceptions that are inherent in a self-contained, self-dependent, or human-dependent perspective. If human knowledge is limited to human experience, then all knowledge is relative. You have your experience and I have mine, and who's to say that one is better or more right than another? If there is no dependable reference point outside of human experience and knowledge, then all knowledge is relative.

But if all knowledge is relative, if all knowledge is simply a matter of perspective, then nothing is truly or objectively knowable. In such a case knowledge does not reveal truth, but only perspective—opinion. If all knowledge is relative then everything depends on how you look at it. In such a system truth has no place. In such a system truth cannot have a consistent meaning and, therefore, is meaningless.

RELATIVISM

And this is exactly where our contemporary world is at. Relativism is the reigning doctrine that is taught in public schools and universities. People are taught today in these institutions that knowledge that is devoid of any reference to God or Scripture is the only knowledge that is reliable. Religion is understood today to be a matter of opinion, which means that objective knowledge must be purged of religion because opinion distorts objective knowledge. Thus, public schools and universities today pride themselves on the fact that they teach knowledge of the world without reference to God or Scripture. They think that they are teaching objective truth, that truth itself stands apart from God or apart from any reference to God or to Scripture.

What they don't recognize is that they have elevated human knowledge, human reason, human perspective, and/or human experience to the status or function of a god. Reference to God in the pursuit of knowledge is like reference to the North Star for purposes of navigation, of knowing where you are. Once you know the position of the North Star, the positions of the other stars indicate your position on the earth. If there was no North Star in the sky, no star whose position is stable year round, navigation would not be possible.[1] In a similar way, God and His Word serve as the objective, stable perspective from which all other human knowledge has any significant meaning.

And we all know this at some level. Paul quoted popular Greek poetry to the Greeks at Mars Hill.[2] A popular poet was quoted as saying, "In

---

1   This analogy breaks down in the contemporary world because we now use satellite technology for navigation on the oceans. However, it should be noted that such navigation depends upon man-made devices. Thus, the navigational references (satellites) remain a function of human knowledge and experience. They can help us understand where we are on earth, but not where we are in the universe.

2   Ross, Phillip A. *Acts of Faith—Kingdom Advancement*, Pilgrim Platform, Marietta,

him we live and move and have our being" (Acts 17:28). Paul was pointing out that the Greek pagans understood the importance of an objective, stable point of reference regarding life and the pursuit of knowledge. This Pagan Greek poet was right to suggest that all human knowledge and experience are dependent upon God.

Paul goes on to say that it is "the Lord who judges" (v. 4) him. Again, he offers a contrast between the judgment of the world and the judgment of God. His point in part is that it is not his own limited knowledge that has reached out to know (discern or evaluate) the Lord, but rather that it is the unlimited knowledge of God that has reached down to know him. And only through being known by God can Paul know his place in the world. It is not through knowledge of the world that we come to know God's place in the world. But rather it is by being known by God that we come to know our place in the world. The difference involves a seismic shift in perspective. It is a matter of coming to see things from God's perspective, not our own. It is a matter of regeneration in Christ.

WATERSHED

The gist of these verses is that human beings must take care not to issue judgment or discern things apart from reference to God. The word *judgment* is to be understood in its widest meaning here. It means making decisions, evaluations. And it incorporates the ability to discern meaning. Van Til goes on to say that all meaning issues from God, and apart from God all meaning vanishes. The only way that unbelievers can make sense of the world is to borrow meaning from God, while at the same time deny His very existence. Paul explains in Romans 1:19-20,

> "For what can be known about God is plain to them, because God has shown it to them. For his invisible attributes, namely, his eternal power and divine nature, have been clearly perceived, ever since the creation of the world, in the things that have been made. So they are without excuse."

They suppress the truth in unrighteousness. They deny the truth and justify what is not right, not true, according to God's Word.

In verse 5 Paul tells us that we cannot properly pronounce judgment, we cannot correctly discern or understand anything under the light of humanity—from our limited human perspectives. So, we must wait for

Ohio 2007. For a discussion of Paul's Mars Hill evangelism method see the chapters on Acts 17.

the coming of the Lord, for the power of regeneration in Christ, which will "bring to light the things now hidden in darkness and will disclose the purposes of the heart" (v. 5).

In Christ, through regeneration everything changes. Nothing is the same. In the light of Christ, the North Star of human history, we come to know our place in the world. Conversely, those who are not regenerated in Christ, who do not see in the light of Christ, who do not have the North Star as a stable point of reference, do not and cannot know where they are at. They are lost.

Such is the difference between the wisdom of God and the foolishness of the world.

8. Imitation

I have applied all these things to myself and Apollos for your benefit, brothers, that you may learn by us not to go beyond what is written, that none of you may be puffed up in favor of one against another. For who sees anything different in you? What do you have that you did not receive? If then you received it, why do you boast as if you did not receive it? Already you have all you want! Already you have become rich! Without us you have become kings! And would that you did reign, so that we might share the rule with you! For I think that God has exhibited us apostles as last of all, like men sentenced to death, because we have become a spectacle to the world, to angels, and to men. We are fools for Christ's sake, but you are wise in Christ. We are weak, but you are strong. You are held in honor, but we in disrepute. To the present hour we hunger and thirst, we are poorly dressed and buffeted and homeless, and we labor, working with our own hands. When reviled, we bless; when persecuted, we endure; when slandered, we entreat. We have become, and are still, like the scum of the world, the refuse of all things. I do not write these things to make you ashamed, but to admonish you as my beloved children. For though you have countless guides in Christ, you do not have many fathers. For I became your father in Christ Jesus through the gospel. I urge you, then, be imitators of me.

— 1 Corinthians 4:6-16

In these verses Paul sums up the theme he has belabored in this letter to the Corinthians to this point. That theme is the difference between the wisdom of God and the foolishness of the world. He has applied this difference in perspective to himself and Apollos. Why Apollos?

Apollos had first misunderstood the gospel when he had been instructed by the followers of John the Baptist (Acts 18:24). But under the tutelage of Aquila and Priscilla he came to a fuller understanding. Scholars speculate that Apollos was with Paul as he wrote this letter to the Corinthian church because Paul was commending Apollos to Christian ministry among the Corinthians. Consequently, he suggests that Apollos and he were of the same mind in their beliefs and teaching.

The point that he was making was that Apollos had originally misunderstood the gospel, but now understood it correctly. Apollos had been able to go from misunderstanding to understanding, from the foolishness of the world to the wisdom of God. Apollos had been

> "competent in the Scriptures. He had been instructed in the way of the Lord. And being fervent in spirit, he spoke and taught accurately the things concerning Jesus, though he knew only the baptism of John" (Acts 18:24-5).

Apollos had all of the qualities that are exemplary for Christians. He was educated and articulate. He knew the Bible well. He had received Christian training. He had fervor—passion for the Lord. And everything he said about Jesus was accurate. For all intents and purposes, Apollos was an ideal Christian, except that he knew only the baptism of John.

What was the baptism of John? According to Mark 1:4,

> "John appeared, baptizing in the wilderness and proclaiming a baptism of repentance for the forgiveness of sins." According to Matthew 3:1-2, "John the Baptist came preaching in the wilderness of Judea, (saying) 'Repent, for the kingdom of heaven is at hand.'" And as we know, when John the Baptist was arrested Jesus picked up John's followers and his message. According to Matthew 4:17, "From that time Jesus began to preach, saying, 'Repent, for the kingdom of heaven is at hand.'"

The other thing that John is known for is water baptism because John water baptized Jesus. And remember that when Jesus was baptized John saw "the Spirit of God descending like a dove and coming to rest on him" (Matthew 3:16). So, we see that Apollos, prior to meeting with Aquila and Priscilla, appeared to have everything right. Yet, Paul faulted him for knowing only the baptism of John, implying that there was something significant that Apollos lacked—some sort of baptism, or something related to baptism.

If we fail to see what Apollos was missing, we will fail to see the point that Paul is making in 1 Corinthians 4. So, we need to discuss baptism. Unfortunately, baptism is widely misunderstood in the church and that misunderstanding has divided the church for centuries.

BAPTISM

Please be aware that these comments about baptism do not reflect the historic position of the *Westminster Confession of Faith*, but neither are they contrary to the Confession. Understand that the views that follow are my own views, and they simply reflect my best efforts to understand baptism.[1]

First, Scripture speaks of three baptisms: water baptism, spirit baptism, and fire baptism (Matthew 3:11). We know about water baptism because the church has universally adopted it as the entrance ceremony for church membership. We are not concerned here about the mode of baptism—sprinkling, pouring, or immersion, or the candidates for baptism—infants or adults.

John knew about the other baptisms, and said to the crowds that followed him,

> "I baptize you with water for repentance, but he who is coming after me is mightier than I, whose sandals I am not worthy to carry. He will baptize you with the Holy Spirit and with fire" (Matthew 3:11).

The candidates for these baptisms are not specified. The reason that this is important is that Apollos knew only the baptism of John—water baptism, and lacked the baptism of the Holy Spirit. Fire baptism is for unbelievers not believers, and further discussion of it will take us too far afield at this point.

Contrary to Pentecostal belief, the baptism of the Holy Spirit is not about speaking in tongues, but is about being radically changed by the Holy Spirit. The Greek word *baptizo* literally means to dip or dye, as in the dyeing or bleaching of cloth. Unfortunately, the passion to defend immersion as the only legitimate baptismal mode has shifted the attention of well-meaning scholars from the purpose of baptism—dyeing, to the process—dipping. People have latched onto the meaning of the process of *baptizo*—to dip, and ignored the purpose—to dye, to change the character (color) of a thing.

If there is only one word that means both dip and dye, and I tell you that I have dipped/dyed my shirt a different color, which meaning is the most natural? Obviously, dye. The process may involve dipping, but the purpose of dyeing the material is to permanently change the color or character of the cloth. The process is important, and there are many possible dyeing processes. However, the purpose of dyeing is essential to the process. Purpose is always primary to procedure for God. God is not bound by a particular procedure. Because the ceremony (procedure) of baptism does not itself cause the requisite change of character, we know

---

1   Ross, Phillip A. *Trinitarian Baptism*, Pilgrim Platform, unpublished.

that God is not limited to dipping, pouring, or sprinkling. God's greater
concern is the end product, His purpose for changing people in the first
place, which is a change of character, a change of heart.

God has always been out to change the character of His people, to
dye them, if you will, in various stages (covenant administrations) or baptisms, to bring them ultimately "to the measure of the stature of the fullness of Christ" (Ephesians 4:13). In history there have been many biblical
covenants or administrations, but God has always been working to produce only one change of heart, one baptism (Ephesians 4:5).

The fact that God's eternal covenant—Adam's covenant, Noah's
covenant, Abraham's covenant, Moses' covenant, David's covenant—has
now come to Christians through Jesus Christ is shown in Galatians 3:14,
"That the blessing of Abraham might come on the Gentiles through Jesus
Christ; that we might receive the promise of the Spirit through faith."
God's covenant, given to Adam, Noah, Abraham, Moses, David, and others has, through Jesus Christ, been given to the Gentiles—to us.

How has it been given? Always by the power of the Holy Spirit.
How has it been received? Always by faith in Christ, the Messiah. The
Holy Spirit falls upon His people, brings them to faith through a change
of heart, thus fulfilling God's covenant, so that they may fulfill God's
covenant through faith in Christ.

The real issue of baptism is not sprinkling, pouring, or immersion—
but being permanently changed (dyed) by the power of the Holy Spirit.
Surely, God is more concerned about purpose than process. And even
when the process plays a role, we know that God's power is not mediated
by the ceremony of baptism, however it is done! The power is not in the
ceremony, but in God's Word. Nor is the result some outward affect, but
a changed heart, a changed life, a changed perspective in the lives of individuals.

Surely, God can bring about the requisite change of heart, whether
people are sprinkled, poured, immersed, or none of the above. The real
concern of baptism is the dyeing, the bleaching, the purification, the
changing of one's character, the rebirth, the regeneration, the new life.
God is always after this one thing—a new heart through baptism in the
Holy Spirit!

And in Acts 18 Paul identified that Apollos had been missing this one
thing. In spite of the fact that Apollos had been nurtured by and educated
in the essentials of Christianity, and had been teaching and preaching

about Jesus in a correct and accurate way, he was for a time still missing the central element of faithfulness—a changed heart or baptism by the Holy Spirit. Then under the tutelage of Aquila and Priscilla he was born again in Christ. He underwent a radical change, though he had known about and had even taught about Jesus Christ for some time.

It is not that Aquila and Priscilla somehow caused the baptism of the Spirit to fall upon Apollos. We don't control or direct the Holy Spirit. Probably what happened was that Aquila and Priscilla were able to show Apollos that something was missing in his confession. Then through prayer and submission to Jesus Christ, Apollos was subsequently converted or regenerated. And Apollos, being teachable, came to understand that though he had known all about Christ, he had not been fundamentally changed by that knowledge prior to his regeneration.

Prior to his baptism in the Spirit he had been lost in the foolishness of the world, though he had been a teacher of Christianity. He had no doubt excelled in the Greek academy. No doubt he had been a fine scholar, had an exemplary character, and had tried to incorporate what he knew about Jesus Christ into his Greek worldview. He was even able to teach and preach about how Christ fit into his understanding of the world. But Paul saw through it. Paul saw that Apollos' application of worldly knowledge to Jesus Christ produced only foolishness that sounded Christian.

In verse 4 Paul said that he had applied all these things to himself and to Apollos for the benefit of the church, so that we "may learn not to go beyond what is written" (v. 4) in the Scriptures, that none of us may be "puffed up," to keep us from being in favor of one Christian's view of things over another's. Apollos had gone beyond Scripture by incorporating Greek philosophy (worldly wisdom) into his understanding of Christianity. Paul's minor point was that by doing so, Apollos had turned Christianity into worldly foolishness.

His major point was that Apollos had recovered from this error and was now in a position—precisely because of his recovery—to serve as a genuine teacher and preacher of real Christianity, not the worldly imitation. Paul knew that Apollos was the right man for Corinth *because* he had undergone this kind of conversion *after* he became a Christian.

Paul warns us not to be puffed up. The Greek word (*phusioō*) literally means proud. Intellectual Christianity is proud Christianity because it is built on the ability of the human intellect or human understanding, rather than upon the Word of God, which is beyond human understanding. It's

not that we cannot understand the Bible. We can, by the grace of the
baptism of the Holy Spirit. By grace, our understanding of the Bible is
correct, but it is not comprehensive. We do not have a comprehensive
understanding of God, nor of His Word. But by grace what we do understand is completely trustworthy because God's Word is reliable.

Paul's point in verse 7 is that all Christians have the understanding
they have because they have been baptized by the Holy Spirit, and not on
account of any abilities or skills they may possess in the flesh. All Christian understanding is *received* understanding, not *acquired* understanding.
Christian (biblical) truth is revealed truth, not attained truth. The truth of
Scripture is not learned through mere study. If it were, we would have a
works-righteous faith. Rather, the truth of Scripture is given by grace,
and in obedience to the Lord of life we study Scripture to grow in grace
and become more effective instruments for service to Christ.

Apollos was an example of a Christian who had not been baptized by
the Holy Spirit, and consequently had failed to understand and preach
Christianity correctly (or in the Spirit). But through submission to Christ
he received the baptism of the Holy Spirit Apollos went on to enjoy and
teach Christianity correctly. Apollos, like Paul, had been moved from the
foolishness of the world to the wisdom of God, and that was why Paul
applied "all these things to himself and Apollos" (v. 4).

In verses 8-13 we find Paul using irony and sarcasm to show the
Corinthians that their concerns about and charges against him amounted
to nothing more than foolishness. Paul noted that the Corinthian church
had grown large and fast, and prominent members had risen to take credit
for the growth and success of the church. But Paul saw in them the same
problem that he had seen in Apollos. They looked like Christians and
talked like Christians, but they boasted about their worldly success and
wisdom like pagan Greeks. Their pride in the growth of the church revealed that their essential human character had not been changed. They
were boasting in the flesh, proud of what they had accomplished, which
demonstrated to Paul that they were not in the Spirit.

Paul acknowledged the accomplishments of the Corinthian church in
verse 8. They had indeed become rich. They had a large budget. They
had become like kings. They had substantial political power. Paul even
wanted the church to have substantial political power because it would
aid the proclamation of the gospel. Yet, there is a tone of irony in Paul's
voice. The irony was that they thought that they were responsible for the

growth of the church, that their superior knowledge, administration, faithfulness, perspective—whatever—had produced the growth. They thought that their worldly wisdom was responsible for the success of the Corinthian church, and they were eager to teach that worldly wisdom as if it were an element of Christianity.

GOSPEL SUCCESS

In verse 9 Paul contrasts his success with the success of the Corinthian church. He suggested that men like himself and Apollos were treated as if they had been sentenced to death, like they had become a spectacle or embarrassment to the church and to the world. Why? Because they preached that the foolishness of Christ was greater, stronger, and smarter than the wisdom of the world. He preached that the wisdom of Christ was opposed to the wisdom of the world, opposed to the wisdom of worldly scholarship and philosophy.

It is important to note that Christianity is not opposed to scholarship and philosophy per se, but to scholarship and philosophy that tries to function apart from or independently of God and His Word. God is not opposed to intelligence. He created it. What He is opposed to is intelligence that suppresses the truth in unrighteousness, that tries to hide the fact that all people are responsible to God for their behavior and beliefs.

Verse 10 draws a stark contrast between worldly success and gospel faithfulness. "We are fools ... you are wise. We are weak ... you are strong. You are held in honor, but we in disrepute" (v. 10). The difference is not subtle, but stark. Paul and Apollos were poor, buffeted (beaten) and homeless. And they worked with their own hands, as did the lowest social strata in Greek society. They were everything that was despised by successful Greeks.

But in spite of all outward appearances they were not defeated. Their mission was to rebuild human culture from the ground up. They remained focused on their mission.

> "When reviled, we bless; when persecuted, we endure; when slandered,
> we entreat. We have become, and are still, like the scum of the world,
> the refuse of all things" (vs. 12-13).

The point is that God's ways are not our ways, that what God treasures is not what people treasure—and again the difference is not subtle but stark. Paul has offered this list of stark differences between himself and those who opposed him, those who had brought accusations against him.

He had been trying to show the difference between the perspective of God's wisdom and that of worldly wisdom (or foolishness).

In verse 14 he tells the church that he has not written these things to shame them, but to warn or admonish them. A synonym for admonish is *discourage*. Paul was *discouraging* the saints in the use of worldly wisdom, which he also called foolishness. It is important to see that Paul engaged in *discouragement* as a method of teaching the gospel. Faithfulness involves not believing and not doing the wrong things as much as it does believing and doing the right things.

Paul was able to admonish the Corinthian believers because he considered himself to be a father to them. "For though you have countless guides in Christ, you do not have many fathers. For I became your father in Christ Jesus through the gospel" (v. 15). Paul falls back upon the character of the family to describe his relationship with the church. He does not consider himself to be a CEO or an administrator or a captain or king or counselor or a guide, but a father.

A father loves his family. A father has an obligation to care for his family, to teach them what is right and to point out what is wrong, to encourage them, but also to discipline and discourage them (from the wrong things). A father has authority, responsibility, and accountability within the extended family structure. A father doesn't work for the benefit of his family in order to get paid. Being a father is not a job. A father works for his family without consideration for his own benefit. A father is there in good times and in bad times, to encourage and to discourage, to point out the truth and the lies.

Finally, said Paul, "be imitators of me" (v. 16). Don't forget the context of this verse. Paul has been telling them about the differences between those who live according to the wisdom of the world—which he also calls foolishness, and those who live according to the wisdom of God. He has essentially told the Corinthians that the success of their church has come from their commitment to worldly wisdom. He will continue to admonish the Corinthians throughout this letter, and the next, because of their worldliness and sin. They were engaged in worldly thinking and outright sin—all in the name of Christianity! He told them that they were proud of the success that their church enjoyed—it's wealth and political power—because they were worldly minded and unfaithful to Christ. Their pride in their church was an expression of their faithlessness and their misunderstanding of the gospel.

In contrast to what they were believing and doing, Paul said, "be imitators of me" (v. 16). He wanted them to imitate real faithfulness rather than to faithfully believe in imitation Christianity. Like Apollos before them, they were trying to incorporate what they knew about Jesus Christ into their Greek worldview. They succeeded in making Jesus fit comfortably into Greek society, and the church had grown drastically as a result.

May we hear the wisdom of God's Word and live our own lives accordingly. Amen.

9. Coming

That is why I sent you Timothy, my beloved and faithful child in the Lord, to remind you of my ways in Christ, as I teach them everywhere in every church. Some are arrogant, as though I were not coming to you. But I will come to you soon, if the Lord wills, and I will find out not the talk of these arrogant people but their power. For the kingdom of God does not consist in talk but in power. What do you wish? Shall I come to you with a rod, or with love in a spirit of gentleness? — 1 Corinthians 4:17-21

Paul began by saying, "That is why" (v. 17). In order to refresh our memories and to put this section in its proper context we need to remind ourselves of the conclusion from the preceding section that Paul was building upon here.

Paul had been harping on the differences between gospel wisdom and worldly foolishness. In particular, he had been trying to get the Corinthians to see this difference by contrasting the apparent success of the Corinthian church, which had grown large, wealthy, and influential, with the apparent poverty of faithfulness experienced by himself and the apostles. It's almost as if he was suggesting that his poverty and difficulties were directly related to the unpopularity of the gospel he preached.

However, he was not arguing that faithful Christians must necessarily be poor and unpopular. Remember that he said that he hoped that the Corinthian Christians would be numerous, wealthy, and influential for the sake of the gospel—not for their own benefit, but for the sake of the gospel. The point that he had previously made was that the Corinthian Christians should not imitate the wisdom of the world, the wisdom of academic scholarship or the apparent success of the prevailing Greek culture. Rather, Paul called faithful Christians to imitate him. He offered himself as a model Christian, and called all Christians to become model Christians like himself.

It is important to note that he did not want others to simply regurgitate what he had taught them, though his teachings were very important, and Christians should know and understand what Paul taught. Rather, by calling on others to imitate him, he meant that they should not only be able to talk the talk that he talked, but they should be able to walk the walk that he walked. Imitation is more than being able to parrot what someone has said. To imitate Paul means to live in the same way he lived—not in the sense that everyone should be unmarried, itinerant preachers, but in the sense of having the same goals, values, and purposes that Paul had. Paul didn't mean that history should be frozen into first century technology or culture. Nor was he mandating a cookie-cutter Christianity, where all Christians look alike and talk alike.

Rather, Christians are to imitate Paul's compassion and commitment to Christ. In essence, Paul was arguing for the necessity of Christian culture. Not a Christian subculture, where ghettoized Christians only associate with Christians or work to produce Christian kitsch, but a culture in which Christ is at the center and foundation of everything.

The word *kitsch* refers to things that appeal to popular or lowbrow taste and are of poor quality. Think of trinkets and knickknacks. But it's more than that. Kitsch is a German word meaning trash that is used to categorize cheap art imitation that mimics great original art. Kitsch is the product of mass production. Kitsch is produced for only one reason—profit. It may be difficult for us to understand kitsch because we live in a mass produced world. It may be difficult for us to think of any reason to produce anything other than profit. But genuine art thinks otherwise.

In fact, the difference between kitsch and art provides another example of the difference between foolishness and wisdom, between the values and practices of the world and the values and practices of the gospel. Paul calls Christians to imitate him, but not to be mass produced copies of the real McCoy. Rather, Paul has called Christians to become life artists, artists whose medium is life itself, who work in the same style or genre that he works in—his genre was culture. Paul was a human culture artist. He was shaping or working with culture. He was not interested in mass-produced imitation Christianity. He was interested in an abundant flowering of genuine Christianity. The two may look similar, but they are not at all the same.

To show them exactly what he meant, he sent Timothy to them because Timothy embodied everything that Paul was talking about. Timothy was a genuine Christian, not a mass-produced counterfeit. Paul described Timothy as "my beloved and faithful child in the Lord" (v. 17).

Timothy was not Paul's biological offspring, he was Paul's spiritual offspring.

That's exactly what the gospel of Jesus Christ is all about—becoming children of God, heirs of the Kingdom of God, heirs of the covenant of God through adoption by Jesus Christ.

Timothy would remind the Corinthians of Paul's "ways in Christ" (v. 17). Here we see the primary element that is to be imitated—not Paul's dress, nor his way of speaking, or anything about him as an individual. We are not to imitate Paul's person, but his way in Christ. The Greek word translated *way* (*hodos*) literally means road, and by implication it refers to the way a person progresses through life, the way a person makes progress in the world. We are to grow or make progress in Christ in the same way that Paul grew and made progress in Christ. This is the imitation that is to be central to Christian living.

AUDIENCE

In the final phrase of verse 17 Paul tells us that he didn't change his message depending upon who he was talking to. Rather, he was teaching the Corinthians just as he taught all Christians "everywhere in every church." Paul endeavored to make his preaching and teaching message always serve the same purpose—to encourage the growth of genuine Christianity through imitation. Paul's primary message was always the same—salvation by grace alone in Christ alone through faith alone according to Scripture alone. This was not just the message of Paul's teaching, it was the message or central core of his life.

How is this done? How are we to imitate Paul? First of all, we must understand that imitation is not accomplished through original thinking. Christians are not called to be original thinkers. This is important to understand because it goes completely against the grain of contemporary belief and training. We are taught in our schools, colleges, universities, and through the media that being human means being original, that we become most human when we are most original. Indeed, Humanism is the celebration of original thinkers as embodying the best that humanity has to offer. Artists will know what I'm talking about. At its root, we tend to think that to be human is to be original—authentic, and the more authentic we are, the more human we are. When we say that something is authentic we mean that it is a genuine original, not a copy, or that it has original authority. *Authentic* and *authority* come from the same root.

Here's the rub. The Bible teaches that only God is original and authentic. Please hear me. The Bible teaches that human beings were created in God's image. We are not originals, but copies of the Original. Nor do we have original authority. Rather, all human authority is derived authority, human being is derived being, and all are derived from God. That's what the Bible teaches.

We don't think about these things much, but over the centuries Christian theologians have understood the Bible to teach that Christians are called, not to think original thoughts, but to think God's thoughts after Him. We are not called to be original thinkers but to meditate upon God's thoughts, to study and ruminate on Scripture. Only God is original. Everything and everyone else is derived. This issues from the fact that God is not a created being, but is the Creator of all other beings. So, to try to think original thoughts is to try to become what only God is.

From a practical standpoint this means that God—God's thoughts (Scripture)—are to be at the center of all our thinking. We are not to try to think what no one has ever thought before. Rather, we are to think what God has thought and written in Scripture. The most faithful Christians are those who emulate God's thoughts most accurately and most consistently. The problem with trying to think original thoughts (other than the fact that it is impossible) is that being original means that we must make a conscious effort to *not* think God's thoughts—to avoid Scripture—because all thought about God's thought is imitative. Original thinkers cannot be followers because followers imitate their leaders (at least ideally they do). To be a follower of Christ or Paul or Calvin or Luther or Buddha means to follow them in their thinking, to imitate them, to think and live the way that they thought and lived.

Paul sent Timothy to Corinth (v. 17) so the Corinthians could see how Timothy imitated Paul, so they could learn from Timothy's example how to imitate Paul, who was himself imitating Christ. They would find in Timothy the same concerns and teaching that they found in Paul.

Paul was passionate about this, even angry that some Corinthian teachers were not imitating him. Verses 19-20 must be understood to convey a single thought;

> "But I will come to you soon, if the Lord wills, and I will find out not the talk of these arrogant people but their power. For the kingdom of God does not consist in talk but in power."

Here Paul threatened those Corinthian leaders who disagreed with him with public exposure of their pride, the very pride that was the source of their worldly mindedness.

Note that Paul was not interested in talking to his detractors. He wasn't coming to debate them. He was coming to demonstrate the power —the effectiveness—of the gospel. He used the Greek word *dunamis*, which in other places is sometimes translated as *miracle* when it describes the work of God. Jesus used this word when the Sadducees were arguing with him about the reality of resurrection. "Jesus answered them, 'You are wrong, because you know neither the Scriptures nor the *power* of God'" (Matthew 22:29).

Paul conditioned his plans to visit them upon his own submission to the will of God. Paul was saying that his plans would only manifest if the Lord decided to use those plans to accomplish His purposes, if his visit conformed to the will of God. And, of course, all Christian planning should submit to God's will, not just in words but in actuality. And that is the point that Paul underscores in verse 20; "For the kingdom of God does not consist in talk but in power." Talk is cheap. Talk is easy. But Paul wanted results that conformed to God's will.

COGNITIVE DISSONANCE

To understand Paul's point we must understand the difference between what he means by words and power. I don't know who first said that talk is cheap, but it is an often repeated platitude because it is so true and so common. Just because someone says something does not make it true. Neither does believing in what you say make it true. Surprise, surprise, people can be wrong! Now add to this fact the manifestation of what psychologists call cognitive dissonance, a condition that is all too pervasive in contemporary society, and you have the context to understand what Paul was trying to get at.

Cognitive dissonance is a condition that involves holding two contradictory beliefs or thoughts at the same time, while denying the fact of their contradiction. Jesus illustrates this phenomenon in Matthew 6:19-24, and concludes by saying,

> "No one can serve two masters, for either he will hate the one and love the other, or he will be devoted to the one and despise the other. You cannot serve God and mammon (or money) ... For where your treasure is, there will your heart be also" (Matthew 6:21).

Our commitments will always follow our values. We will be committed to the things that we value, not simply the things that we talk about. It is very easy and very common for people to talk about their commitment to one thing, but in reality to be committed to something very different. It is common for people to talk about their commitment to God and Christ, while sacrificing or ignoring that commitment in their pursuit of money. It's easy to talk the talk, but walking the walk is another thing. That is why Jesus talked about this issue, it was a common practice in his time, and it still is.

Cognitive dissonance is saying one thing but believing another. Have you ever heard or said to your children, "Don't do what I do, do what I say?" That's cognitive dissonance. People who talk the talk but don't walk the walk are practicing cognitive dissonance. That is what Paul was getting at when he said, "I will not know the speech of those who are puffed up, but the power" (v. 19).

Remember that he had accused some of the Corinthians leaders of being caught up in the foolishness of the world, of having forsaken the wisdom of Christ for the foolishness of the world. Here he says that the difference between the wisdom of Christ and the foolishness of the world was not simply a matter of words or thoughts, but a matter of power.

In Mark 9:39 the word *dunamis* is translated as *miracle* in the KJV. The ESV translates it as *mighty work*. Elsewhere John asked Jesus about His power.

> "John said to him, 'Teacher, we saw someone casting out demons in your name, and we tried to stop him, because he was not following us.' But Jesus said, 'Do not stop him, for no one who does a **mighty work** in my name will be able soon afterward to speak evil of me.'" (Mark 9:38-9).

The Greek *dunamis* is the root of the English words *dynamic* and *dynamo*.

Paul was saying that the kingdom of God does not consist in talk but in *dunamis*—power, dynamism, dynamics. Paul was saying that what is important are the social, intellectual, and moral forces that are directed and empowered by God through men that produce activity and change in a given sphere, that actually bring about the kingdom of God. Words can describe the kingdom of God, but it takes power, defined as spiritual, social, intellectual, and moral force, to bring it about.

That does not mean that the kingdom of God can be brought about through human activity alone. Yet, the actualization of the kingdom engages human activity or *means*, in as much as any government (kingdom) involves the human activity of the people of its realm. The King establishes the kingdom, and the people receive it. The inhabitants of the kingdom must act in it, live in it, and respond to it—and in receiving it they engage the social, intellectual, and moral processes that affect every aspect of their lives.

INFLATED

In verse 18 Paul described some of the people in the Corinthian church as "puffed up" (*phusioō*). The word means inflated, proud, even haughty. He repeated the charge in verse 19. He spoke as if a major aspect of the problem that he was addressing—God's wisdom versus the foolishness of the world—was related to pride, as if there is a relationship between pride and foolishness. And that is a point worth repeating because there is such a relationship. Pride and the foolishness of the world are intimately related. They are cut from the same cloth. They emanate from the same spirit.

Paul threatened to visit Corinth in order to expose the pride and foolishness of those leaders with whom he disagreed, those who were teaching other than he had taught, those who were filling the heads of the Corinthians with worldly foolishness. How would he do that? He would come and be an example of Christ-likeness in their midst. The example of his own faithfulness and humility would stand in stark contrast to the pride and foolishness that the Corinthians were used to. He believed that his own imitation of Christ (or Timothy's imitation of him) would reveal their pride and foolishness by contrast. The light of truth would reveal what the darkness concealed. The example of his humility would reveal the reality of their pride. Finally, Paul asked them, "What do you desire? Shall I come to you with a rod, or in love and the spirit of meekness?" (v. 21).

Interesting question. This verse is hard, not because it is hard to figure out what Paul was trying to say, but because what he said so confounds our expectations of Christian behavior. Again, Paul was talking to the leaders of the Corinthian church. He was asking the leaders how they thought he should deal with them.

Imagine that Paul is your boss, who has been away, and you are talking to him on the phone. He has a disagreement with how you are handling things in his absence, and tells you that he will return next week. Then he asks you how you would like him to approach you about this problem when he gets back. Should he bring a "rod?" In other words, should he come brandishing the authority and power of his position? Or should he come with love and meekness? He's really asking whether you will have complied with his instructions by the time he returns. If you haven't, he will bring the rod—discipline. If you have, he will come in love and humble appreciation.

But what was Paul's threat? What would he do to them if they failed to comply? What was the "rod" that he threatened to bring? We don't know. Scripture doesn't say. And it doesn't really matter. The point is that Paul exercised his authority against a group of Corinthian leaders who had abandoned the gospel by substituting the values of Greek culture for the values of the gospel. It is a very contemporary message, one that speaks to the churches today. The message is that the values of the world have no place in the church, regardless of their ability to make churches large, rich, or influential.

The church cannot be what God intends it to be unless it is fueled by the biblical gospel itself. As Paul said to the Romans (1:16): "I am not ashamed of the gospel, for it is the power of God for salvation to everyone who believes."

The gospel itself is the power of God. So, if we want to get the church right, if we want to get evangelism right, we must get the gospel right. Our concern is not the results, not the growth, but the cultivation. Paul had previously reminded them that he "planted, Apollos watered, but God gave the growth" (1 Corinthians 3:6). Planting and watering are the work of cultivation. We do not need to be worried about church growth, that's God's responsibility. We need to do the work of church cultivation.

> "Look at the birds of the air: they neither sow nor reap nor gather into barns, and yet your heavenly Father feeds them. Are you not of more value than they? And which of you by being anxious can add a single hour to his span of life? And why are you anxious about clothing? Consider the lilies of the field, how they grow: they neither toil nor spin, yet I tell you, even Solomon in all his glory was not arrayed like one of these. But if God so clothes the grass of the field, which today is alive and tomorrow is thrown into the oven, will he not much more clothe you, O you of little faith? Therefore do not be anxious, saying, 'What shall we eat?' or 'What shall we drink?' or 'What shall we wear?'"—or How shall we grow our church?—"For the Gentiles seek after all these things, and your heavenly Father knows that you need them all. But

seek first the kingdom of God and his righteousness, and all these things will be added to you" (Matthew 6:26-33).

The gospel is the wisdom of God and stands in opposition to the foolishness of the world.

10. Repentance

It is actually reported that there is sexual immorality among you, and of a kind that is not tolerated even among pagans, for a man has his father's wife. And you are arrogant! Ought you not rather to mourn? Let him who has done this be removed from among you. For though absent in body, I am present in spirit; and as if present, I have already pronounced judgment on the one who did such a thing. When you are assembled in the name of the Lord Jesus and my spirit is present, with the power of our Lord Jesus, you are to deliver this man to Satan for the destruction of the flesh, so that his spirit may be saved in the day of the Lord.[1] — 1 Corinthians 5:1-5

This chapter begins with a difficult text. It is not difficult to understand what it says. The meaning is quite clear. Again, the difficulty is found in ourselves because we do not want to accept what it says as being true. Nonetheless, it is the testimony of the historic churches that these verses are true and can be trusted.

The primary subject of the first four chapters of 1 Corinthians has been Paul's concern about the confusion of the foolishness of the world with the wisdom of God (1 Corinthians 3:19). The leaders of the Corinthian church had grown the church into a large, wealthy, influential organization in the community. However, Paul found that they had done so by substituting the foolishness of the world for the wisdom of God (1 Corinthians 4:8-16). The whole point of Paul's letter to the Corinthians was to accuse the leaders of the church of being confused and faithless, and to call them to repentance, forgiveness in Jesus Christ, and a change of belief and behavior.

Beginning with this fifth chapter Paul set an example of their faithlessness before them. "It is actually reported that there is sexual immorality among you, and of a kind that is not tolerated even among pagans, for a man has his father's wife" (v. 1).

There are two ways that the Greek word *porneia* is translated. The older versions translated it as *fornication*, and the newer versions translate it

---

1   Also see Jeremiah 5 and Luke 24:36-47.

as *sexual immorality*. The problem with using sexual immorality is that the English lacks definition. What does sexual immorality mean? The term can mean different things to different people. Would Paul say that all sexual activity was okay between consenting adults, and that only the lack of consent constitutes sexual immorality? Hardly! If there is any confusion about this issue it is ours. Paul was very specific about what he said and about what he meant.

PORNEIA

The *Greek Lexicon* (Thayer & Smith) defines *porneia* as "illicit sexual intercourse." The word *licit* is Latin and means permissible by law. So, *illicit* means not permissible by law. Paul said that it had been reported to him that people in the Corinthian church were involved in illegal sexual activity, what was not permissible by law. The point is that Paul was talking about more than some generalized idea of immorality. His point was that leaders of the Corinthian church were engaged in illicit behavior—illegal behavior between a son and his father's wife. We should also note that Paul's specificity does not annul the more general interpretation accorded to sexual immorality. It's just that Paul was being very specific by citing particular people involved in a specific relationship.

The Lexicon goes on to define *porneia* more generally to include adultery, fornication, homosexuality, lesbianism, intercourse with animals, sexual intercourse with close relatives (Leviticus 18), or sexual intercourse with a divorced man or woman (Mark. 10:11-12). And just to be clear the English dictionary defines *adultery* as "voluntary sexual intercourse between a married person and a partner other than the lawful spouse."

But what law had been broken? Greece, and particularly the seaport of Corinth, was rife with such practices. Greek culture is well known for its sexual permissiveness. The civil law of Greece and of Corinth were very tolerant of such behavior. So, Paul was not talking about Greek or Roman civil law. Rather, he was talking about God's law, biblical law, the Ten Commandments, the Bible.

So far, all I have done is to define a word that Paul used in his accusation against the leaders of the Corinthian church. And it is very interesting to simply define Paul's terms and understand them as he understood them. This kind of clarification speaks volumes about our own abandonment of God's law in twenty-first century America. By simply defining a word, we come face to face with our own immorality. But we are not talking about our situation, we are talking about Paul's accusation of the people of Corinth. So, I will leave the application of this verse in our contemporary context to the exercise of the Holy Spirit and your conscience. Lord, bring conviction upon your people.

Paul went on to say that the behavior of these church leaders was "not tolerated even among pagans" (v. 1). Matthew Henry calls it "incestuous fornication." Suffice it to say that whatever was going on was not common practice, even among the pagan Greeks. This is fascinating. We usually think of the church of the first century as being more holy or more perfect or more faithful than we are today. And in some ways they may have been. But here we see Paul calling the leaders of one of the more successful churches of the first century on the carpet for gross immorality and faithlessness.

ARROGANT

"And you are arrogant! Ought you not rather to mourn?" (v. 2). And if this particular sin weren't bad enough, Paul went on to accuse them of being arrogant. The Greek word is *phusioō*, which literally means to inflate or puff up, and is often translated as *proud*. The clear implication is that they were proud or arrogant with regard to their sin, when they should have been humiliated and in mourning about it—and that is the greater problem here. Pride is worse than fornication because it is more subtle, more difficult to identify as sin.

The sin itself was not the main problem. All of God's people are sinners, to a person. No one is condemned because of some particular sin. Sin is the natural condition of humanity since the Fall. We are all condemned by Adam's sin. Paul says in Romans 3:10, "None is righteous, no, not one." So, in the light of Jesus Christ people are condemned, not by their sin, but by their refusal to repent of their sin, by their refusal to turn away from sin, by their refusal to acknowledge it as sin and to turn to Jesus Christ for forgiveness and salvation from the eternal consequences of sin. No, sin is not the problem. God can forgive any sin through Jesus Christ. But God will not forgive any sin apart from Christ, and Christ demands repentance. "From that time Jesus began to preach, saying, 'Repent, for the kingdom of heaven is at hand'" (Matthew 4:17).

There is a difference between the ongoing struggle against sin by repentant Christians and the celebration of sin as a God-given right by the unfaithful. The faithful are humbled by their sin and moved to repentance, but the unfaithful are proud of their sin because they believe they have a right to it. In fact, all unrepentant sin thrives on pride. Pride is what keeps people from repentance. Pride is what keeps people from Jesus Christ, and from salvation.

John wrote,

> "Do not love the world, nor the things in the world. If anyone loves the world, the love of the Father is not in him, because all that is in the world, the lust of the flesh, and the lust of the eyes, and the pride of life, is not of the Father, but is of the world. And the world passes away, and the lust of it, but he who does the will of God abides forever" (1 John 2:15-17).

The lust of the flesh, and the lust of the eyes, and the pride of life, these are the enemies of the gospel, the enemies of truth, and the stumbling blocks to salvation. Where pride leads, sin follows.

"Let him who has done this be removed from among you" (v. 2). John Gill said of this verse that the guilty parties should be removed,

> "not by excommunication, for that they could and ought to have done themselves; but by the immediate hand of God, inflicting some visible punishment, and taking him away by an untimely death, which the Jews call כרית, 'cutting off,' by the hand of God; and such a punishment, they say, this crime deserved."[2]

Ouch! Gill provides the traditional interpretation of this verse, which was that it deserved excommunication by the church and judgment by God. The Apostle Paul called the wrath of God down upon down upon these unrepentant sinners, these leaders of the Corinthian church. Had they repented, he would have called the mercy of God down upon them. Jesus said, "'I desire mercy and not sacrifice.' For I did not come to call righteous ones, but sinners to repentance" (Matthew 9:13—LITV).

Jesus didn't just come to call sinners, He came to call sinners *to repentance*. Big difference! To the Pharisees Jesus said, "Bring forth therefore fruits worthy of repentance" (Matthew 3:8). Jesus is always after our repentance. "For though absent in body, I am present in spirit; and as if present, I have already pronounced judgment on the one who did such a thing" (v. 3).

Wait a minute! Doesn't the Bible teach that we should be nonjudgmental? Yes, we ought not judge a repentant person on the basis of their sin because God's mercy is grater than any sin. The grace of God through the propitiation of Jesus Christ trumps all sin. There is no sin so great that it

---

2   Gill, John. *Exposition of the Whole Bible*, 1763, 1 Cor. 5:2.

cannot be forgiven by the grace and mercy of God through Jesus Christ—
save one (Matthew 12:31).

UNREPENTANT

But, on the other hand, the churches are called to judge those who
are unrepentant. Jesus said, "Do not judge according to sight, but judge
righteous judgment" (John 7:24). We should not evaluate things on their
appearance, but on the basis of God's righteousness, on the basis of Scripture alone. We are not to judge according to our own values, our own
ideas, but according to God's standards of righteousness, according to
Scripture. It is not the standards of the community that are to prevail, not
the standards of the civil government, or the standards of the press, or TV,
or popular opinion, but the standards of Scripture by which Christians are
to judge (or evaluate) everything. So, Paul could say to the Romans,

> "We know that the judgment of God rightly falls on those who do such
> things. Do you suppose, O man—you who judge those who do such
> things and yet do them yourself (note the lack of repentance)—that you
> will escape the judgment of God? Or do you presume on the riches of
> his kindness and forbearance and patience, not knowing that God's
> kindness is meant to lead you to repentance?" (Romans 2:2-4).

God's kindness, His grace and mercy are linked to repentance. God is
kind and merciful in order to allow people the time and opportunity for
repentance. God does not rush to judgment, but provides ample time for
repentance. But at some point the opportunity for repentance comes to
an end, and judgment follows.

We confuse ourselves when we neglect the fact that Scripture treats
repentant sinners differently than it treats unrepentant sinners. Repentant
sinners have the protection of Jesus Christ the advocate, where unrepentant sinners face the full consequences of God's law on their own. Repentant sinners have been pardoned, unrepentant sinners have not. Judgment
for repentant sinners has been suspended by the propitiation of Jesus
Christ, but judgment for unrepentant sinners remains.

Paul went on to provide these instructions to the Corinthian church,

> "When you are assembled in the name of the Lord Jesus and my spirit is
> present, with the power of our Lord Jesus, you are to deliver this man to
> Satan for the destruction of the flesh, so that his spirit may be saved in
> the day of the Lord" (vs. 4-5).

Here is how the church is to respond to unrepentant sinners in their midst.

MEETING

First, the church is to assemble. Worship is not the context of this situation, yet the spirit of Paul and the power of Jesus Christ are to be part of the assemblage. There is to be a church meeting. Paul provides specific instruction, and the power of Jesus provides the ability to act or see it through. But how is the church to "deliver this man to Satan" (v. 5)? As you might imagine there is much disagreement about what this verse means. But the bottom line seems to be that the unrepentant person is to be censured in the presence of the gathered congregation. Such censure is an act of excommunication.

However, it must be stressed that the purpose of excommunication is always to provide an opportunity for repentance and reconciliation. Matthew Henry writes,

> "The great end of church-censures is the good of those who fall under
> them, their spiritual and eternal good. It is that their spirit may be saved
> in the day of the Lord Jesus."

Excommunication is never to be the end of church membership. Rather, it means to forbid participation in the comforts of the church, which are the Lord's Supper and fellowship.

The "destruction of the flesh" (v. 5) that Paul talks about pertains to what used to be called mortification, which

> "refers to the sinful actions that are done by the body arising from the
> temptations and injections of Satan or the corrupt dictates of our own
> sinful heart" (Christopher Love).

Mortification is the process of starving the life of sin in the body, or avoiding sin. How was that done? By replacing the temptation to sin with the love of Christ. "And if Christ is in you, indeed the body is dead because of sin, but the Spirit is life because of righteousness" (Romans 8:10).

So, when Paul called the Corinthian church to deliver this sinner to Satan for the destruction of the flesh, he meant that the church should withdraw the blessings and comforts of Holy Communion and fellowship in order to turn up the heat regarding the immediate consequences of sin in the hope that the abandoned sinner would repent and seek reconciliation with Christ and His people. God is always working to bring His people to repentance and reconciliation (which are the fruits of salvation). And God goes to great lengths to accomplish this purpose. Damnation, then, is the result of the willful refusal to repent, the refusal to turn away from sin, to turn away from Jesus Christ who provides forgiveness and new life.

Jesus Christ is the source of forgiveness and salvation through regeneration by the Holy Spirit. And regeneration always brings about repentance as a matter of sanctification or growth in grace. So, if there is no repentance of sin, there can be no growth in grace. When repentance is lacking, salvation must be doubted because salvation is not guaranteed, nor is it universally applied to all people.

Jesus said,

> "Come to me, all who labor and are heavy laden, and I will give you rest. Take my yoke upon you, and learn from me, for I am gentle and lowly in heart, and you will find rest for your souls. For my yoke is easy, and my burden is light" (Matthew 11:28-30).

Note that there is a yoke and there is learning from Christ. There is a burden, and the burden is humble repentance of sin. Christians do not celebrate sin, they turn away from it.

11. Infection

Your boasting is not good. Do you not know that a little leaven leavens the whole lump? Cleanse out the old leaven that you may be a new lump, as you really are unleavened. For Christ, our Passover lamb, has been sacrificed. Let us therefore celebrate the festival, not with the old leaven, the leaven of malice and evil, but with the unleavened bread of sincerity and truth. I wrote to you in my letter not to associate with sexually immoral people— not at all meaning the sexually immoral of this world, or the greedy and swindlers, or idolaters, since then you would need to go out of the world. But now I am writing to you not to associate with anyone who bears the name of brother if he is guilty of sexual immorality or greed, or is an idolater, reviler, drunkard, or swindler—not even to eat with such a one. For what have I to do with judging outsiders? Is it not those inside the church whom you are to judge? God judges those outside. "Purge the evil person from among you."   — 1 Corinthians 5:6-13

We have seen that the corrupt leaders of the Corinthian church boasted about the very thing that corrupted them. Paul called them "puffed up" in verse 2. He repeated the charge in verse 6 by telling them that their "boasting is not good." As we saw in the previous chapter, their main problem was not the outright sin, though it was a very heinous sin. Rather, their main problem was their pride that kept them from repentance. God can forgive every sin, except the pride that keeps a person from coming to God for forgiveness.

Medieval theologian Thomas Aquinas said that pride or "inordinate self-love is the cause of every sin ... the root of pride is found to consist in man not being, in some way, subject to God and His rule (1,77)."

Pride is one of the classic Seven Deadly Sins. Pride not only gives birth to other sins, but even more deadly, it keeps people from turning to God for forgiveness and repentance. Paul was suggesting that the Corinthian pride in their church, in its success and affluence, interfered with their exercise of humility. Proverbs 3:34 tells us that God is stern in dealing with the arrogant, but He shows kindness to the humble.

Pride is built on spiritual blindness. To encounter God is to encounter our own frailty and sinfulness in the same way that a well-lit bathroom mirror shows the flaws in our complexion. Like Oedipus, people are driven to gouge out their eyes at the sight of their own wretchedness and wander away from our heavenly home, ashamed but unwilling to admit our shame. But unlike Oedipus, we build up lots of illusions about who we are and what we are about. We have a false understanding of ourselves.

We busy ourselves with career, family—even church work, thinking we are being driven by a strong work ethic, high moral values, or the fire of the Holy Spirit. But too often, we are turning away from God by turning away from ourselves, by not seeing ourselves truthfully. Everyone else can see that we are putting on a show, but we can't see it. There's a log in our eye. We are blinded by the glare of our own pride. Coworkers may dislike us (we rationalize that they are just jealous), our children may self-destruct or leave us (we rationalize that they are ungrateful), and we may never truly pray, but only stand in the presence of a god we have created to make ourselves feel better. And in the midst of it all we adamantly refuse to see what is before our very eyes.

Because humility is the opposite of pride, it serves as a kind of antidote to keep pride in check, to keep the infection of pride from giving birth to more sin. Pride is a kind of spiritual virus. Paul refers to it as leaven. Leaven is what you put in bread to make it rise or puff up. Leaven causes fermentation, which produces gas, which causes the bread to expand. Fermentation causes organic things to break down. It is a kind of rot.

INFECTIOUS

"Do you not know that a little leaven leavens the whole lump" (v. 6)? Paul alluded to all of this in his single question. Leaven spreads through a loaf of bread like a virus. A little leaven will affect the whole loaf. Paul doesn't use the word *virus*, it was not available to him or to the Greek language. Virus is a discovery of modern science—not that science invented the virus. Rather, science invented the technology which allowed us to identify the reality and function of viruses. Viruses have always been around (at least since the Flood), but prior to the development of modern science we didn't have the tools to see them or analyze them. Earlier generations called them diseases or illnesses of various kinds. Nonetheless, the analogy remains: pride is a disease.

As with any disease there are two primary concerns: 1) containment, and 2) cure. A disease must be contained to keep it from spreading to other people, and most often disease is spread through contact or proximity. Once it is contained, it must be cured.

Not only will a disease affect one's whole body, but it will affect one's family and friends if we are not careful. Paul's point was that pride is contagious just like diseases are contagious. Just like leaven affects the whole loaf, so the contagious disease of pride can affect the whole body of Christ, the church. The disease of pride must be contained just as a contagious disease must be contained to keep it from spreading. The person who is ill must be isolated from other healthy people to eliminate or reduce the possibility of contaminating others. We'll come back to this analogy shortly.

But first, note Paul's use of the Passover here. Doesn't it seem odd that the subject of the Passover comes up in the middle of Paul's rant against sexual immorality? He speaks of keeping the Passover festival or feast (*heortazō*) in honor of Christ, who he describes as "our Passover lamb" (v. 7). Yes, Paul was alluding to the Christian sacrament of Communion, but there is more. Yes, Paul was suggesting that Communion replace Passover as a Christian holiday or festival, but there is more.

COMMUNION

Paul was alluding to the very essence or substance of Christian culture—Communion. But I don't just mean the ten minutes it takes on Sunday morning to eat bread and drink wine together. Communion is more than that. Part and parcel of the service of Communion is Christian fellowship and all of the relationships, traditions, authorities, and associations implied therein. We see this fact in the previous section where Paul spoke of removing the offending person from the fellowship of believers.

Paul was alluding to excommunication, as we have previously discussed. Excommunication accomplishes two things: 1) it forbids the excommunicant from receiving Communion, and 2) it forbids the body of Christ from fellowshipping with those who are under this discipline. Communion and Christian fellowship are linked together through the structure, authority, and discipline of church practice. Communion is an expression of Christian culture, Christian social organization.

They linked because Communion is a reflection of the whole organizational structure—the biblical understanding of Christ as Lord, the authority of the church and its officers, and the common bond of love that is the basis of Christian relationships. Communion is both the root and the flower of Christian culture. Don't think of Communion as an isolated, fragmented part of a worship service. Rather, think of it as an integral part of Christian life, both of the life of the individual Christian and the life of the Christian community. Think of it as the glue that holds Christianity together.

Communion is not an isolated, fragmented element of Christian worship. Rather, Communion is an expression of the wholeness, interrelatedness, and integrity of Christian society. No one can celebrate Communion alone. It requires the whole structure or apparatus of worship, authority, and fellowship of the Christian church, which in turn is composed of individuals, families, traditions, practices, formalities, habits, laws, customs, relationships, etc. If we eliminate any of these constitutive elements or reduce the church to a subset of any of these elements, we diminish the church and the Lord of the church.

Paul was saying that Communion is like the Old Testament Passover. The Passover was a week-long festival set in the context of the Hebrew calendar and Hebrew society. It was a major cultural event in the life of Israel. Paul was using it to refer to the holistic or all-encompassing nature of biblical culture. Paul was saying that just as Passover had been a central event in the life of Israel, so Communion is the central event in the life of the Church.

Paul was telling us what we need to do to encourage and protect Christian culture. He said that two things are required: 1) cure, and 2) containment. The cure is salvation by grace, the foundation of Christian life. No one can be a Christian apart from God's gift of salvation by grace, or regeneration. Once people are Christian, once they have been saved and baptized into the church, then the need for containment comes into play. Here we come back to the analogy of pride or, more generally, sin as a contagious disease.

There are two aspects of this containment. First, Christians need to fellowship with other Christians. There are a lot of reasons for this. Because our values and interests change once we have been converted, we find that we have less and less in common with people who are not Christian. Our circle of friends changes because we like being with Christians more than with non-Christians. The old adage is that birds of a feather flock together. Christian fellowship becomes a source of friendship and joy.

But there is another aspect of this containment. Just as it is good for us to spend time with other Christians, Paul tells us that it is not good for us to spend time with certain sinners. Paul does not mean that we should avoid all sinners, because if we do that we can be with no one—not even ourselves. Paul says this in verse 9,

> "I wrote to you in my letter not to associate with sexually immoral people—not at all meaning the sexually immoral of this world, or the greedy and swindlers, or idolaters, since then you would need to go out of the world."

The effort to avoid all sinners is futile. It can't be done. It's impossible.

HYPOCRITES

But Paul goes on to specify one special kind or group of sinners that are particularly harmful to the body of Christ, and whom we should avoid.

> "But now I am writing to you not to associate with anyone who bears the name of brother if he is guilty of sexual immorality or greed, or is an idolater, reviler, drunkard, or swindler—not even to eat with such a one" (v. 11).

The problem is not unconverted sinners, not those who are merely unsaved. It is not a problem to associate or fellowship with heathens. Rather, Paul tells us that the real danger is associating or fellowshipping with people who identify themselves as Christian, but who continue sinning—hypocrites. Those who say they believe one thing but live as if they believe another.

The real danger to Christianity is not sinners, but hypocrites, people who identify themselves as Christian but who disregard the practice or essence of Christianity, which is submission to Jesus Christ and the avoidance of sin as it is described in the Bible. Again, we must note that no one is ever completely free from sin in this life. The difference between a Christian and a hypocrite is that a Christian repents of his sin—daily, whereas the hypocrite does not repent. He wallows or stagnates in sin. He makes no effort to resist or avoid it.

Christians struggle against sin. Christians make a serious effort to avoid sin. They don't wallow in it. They don't excuse themselves from the difficulties of sanctification or spiritual growth, which necessarily involves ongoing moral improvement. They understand that Christ has called His people away from sin and into righteousness. Christians are engaged in the struggle to avoid or resist sin.

The Corinthian leaders were hypocrites. They were proud of themselves, proud that they had been able to lead such a large, dynamic, and powerful church—even while engaging in the sexual shenanigans that Paul had previously mentioned. What did it matter? they thought. The church grew anyway. The success of the church made them think that their own sin was irrelevant.

To the contrary, Paul suggested that if the Corinthians continued to fellowship with proud and sinful leaders, they would become increasingly infected with pride and sin themselves. This is an absolutely crucial verse for understanding how Christians are to relate to each other and to the wider culture, to any culture that is not Christian, not biblical. It means that we are to avoid sin, to avoid those elements of culture that promote or celebrate sin.

That does not mean avoiding all people who are sinners, but it means avoiding people who disregard the subtly and seriousness of sin. We are to avoid those who don't use sin as an opportunity to personally repent and turn to Christ for forgiveness, to avoid those who are not thrown to their knees when they find themselves (again or still) entangled in sin. Christians cannot be hypocritical with regard to sin because people cannot disregard or celebrate sin and be genuinely Christian. A hypocrite is someone who professes beliefs and opinions that he or she does not hold in order to conceal his or her real feelings or motives.

Think of cognitive dissonance. Cognitive dissonance involves believing two or more completely incompatible things to be true at the same time. Believing that one can freely engage in known sin and still be a Christian is an example of cognitive dissonance or hypocrisy. Hypocrisy is going to church, but not being faithful, not practicing the discipline of the faith, not doing all you can to avoid sin. Hypocrites wink at sin. They don't take it seriously. Paul said in verse 11 that we are not to fellowship—or even to eat—with such a person.

We cannot avoid all hypocrites because we cannot avoid ourselves. Yes, we are all hypocrites to some extent because no Christian can be fully Christian apart from living in a Christian culture, and there is no such thing at this time. The critical issue seems to revolve around pride. Are we haughty hypocrites who make light of our lapses into sin? Or are we humble hypocrites who repent and turn away from sin by turning to the gospel of grace and freely—even enthusiastically—embrace the burden of Christ's discipline? Do we turn away from sin wherever we encounter it? Do we actively expose it as sin in order to warn our brothers and sisters of the danger?

In verse 12 Paul went on to say that Christians are to judge one another, and that we are not to judge those outside of the church. "God judges those outside" (v. 13). Don't miss the caustic damnation that is in Paul's voice and in his meaning here. He means that those outside of the church are subject to the judgment and damnation of God apart from Christ. God's mercy is directed to those who are covered by the blood of Christ, those who are in the church—Christians. All others are subject to God's judgment without regard to the propitiation of Jesus Christ. He means that God's grace comes only through Jesus Christ and His church.

Those in the church have submitted themselves to Jesus Christ and to His representatives—to the judgments of the leaders of the church, of whom Paul is included. However, Christians understand submission to the authority of the church to be a good thing because Christians have the well-being of other people as a top priority. It is by submitting to Jesus Christ through the church that Christians are spared exposure to the judgment and damnation of God. In the effort to help one another avoid sin Christians enjoy the benefits of spiritual growth and sanctification. Subjection to Christ is the only alternative to subjection to the Old Testament judgment of God, the judgment that destroyed Israel in A.D. 70.

Paul concluded by citing the command given many times in Deuteronomy to "Purge the evil person from among you" (v. 13). Paul said here that the heart or intent of the Deuteronomic law still applies to the church. Jesus said,

> "Do not think that I have come to abolish the Law or the Prophets; I have not come to abolish them but to fulfill them. For truly, I say to you, until heaven and earth pass away, not an iota, not a dot, will pass from the Law until all is accomplished. Therefore whoever relaxes one of the least of these commandments and teaches others to do the same will be called least in the kingdom of heaven, but whoever does them and teaches them will be called great in the kingdom of heaven. For I tell you, unless your righteousness exceeds that of the scribes and Pharisees, you will never enter the kingdom of heaven" (Matthew 5:17-20).

This is the good news of the gospel of grace because it has already been accomplished, and yet is still to be fully accomplished by Jesus Christ in the future.

12. COURTS

When one of you has a grievance against another, does he dare go to law before the unrighteous instead of the saints? Or do you not know that the saints will judge the world? And if the world is to be judged by you, are you incompetent to try trivial cases? Do you not know that we are to judge angels? How much more, then, matters pertaining to this life! So if you have such cases, why do you lay them before those who have no standing in the church? I say this to your shame. Can it be that there is no one among you wise enough to settle a dispute between the brothers, but brother goes to law against brother, and that before unbelievers? To have lawsuits at all with one another is already a defeat for you. Why not rather suffer wrong? Why not rather be defrauded? But you yourselves wrong and defraud—even your own brothers!

— 1 Corinthians 6:1-8

This section of Corinthians calls attention to a long lost social function of the church—church courts. First, some history. Before Rome fell it was choked with a backlog of civil disputes in the Roman legal system. It could take years before a particular case came before a Roman judge. The Roman legal system was choking on the rampant immorality and illegality that contributes to the rot of empires by generating social conflict. Great nations are more usually destroyed from within by moral decay long before they fall victim to invading armies. And Rome had been rotting for hundreds of years before it was sacked by the Visigoths in 410 A.D.

At the same time, Christianity had inherited the elder rule system from the Old Testament, in which the local court overlapped the ecclesiastical court. We must remember that, while Rome had a great and powerful legal system, it pales in comparison to the modern Western legal system in terms of its effectiveness and bureaucratization. Yet, even on the Western Frontier in early American history, civil courts were often few and far between. And in that context necessity required another way to solve disputes between people.

The structure of the Christian church, until the modern era, had a system of courts to adjudicate matters between Christians, precisely because of Paul's admonition to avoid civil courts run by unbelievers. In the modern era these church courts have, for the most part, fallen into neglect. As unbelievers (or non church members) began to outnumber believers in a given area, the unbelievers were hesitant to use church courts to solve their problems. Unbelievers usually think that church courts are biased against them. And often it was true, but it should not be true on the basis of personalities. We should not be biased against unbelievers because we don't like them. It doesn't matter whether or not we like them. Justice is not a function of personal preferences.

JURISDICTION

All courts are subject to jurisdiction, the territory in which they are able to operate. We often understand jurisdictions as regional—city, county, state, and national. Church jurisdiction is completely separate, and includes only church members. Thus, the first issue is that church courts only have jurisdiction over Christians. And when a member is an unbeliever, someone who is backslidden or unregenerate, Christians are commonly biased against such a person in a variety of ways and for a variety of reasons, some of which may be biblical and some of which are most certainly not. We are cautioned in Scripture against holding a bias with regard to personalities.

Deuteronomy 1:17 reads,

> "You shall not respect persons in judgment. You shall hear the small as well as the great. You shall not be afraid of the face of man, for the judgment is God's. And the cause that is too hard for you, bring to me, and I will hear it."

This was Moses speaking to the recently freed Israelites. Does this apply to Christians?

> "Truly I see that God is no respecter of persons" (Acts 10:34).

> "...your Master also is in Heaven. There is no respect of persons with Him" (Ephesians 6:9).

> "whatever you do, do it heartily, as to the Lord and not to men; knowing that from the Lord you shall receive the reward of the inheritance. For you serve the Lord Christ. But he who does wrong shall receive

justice for the wrong which he did, and there is no respect of persons"
(Colossians 3:23-25).

"But if you have respect to persons, you commit sin and are convicted
by the Law as transgressors" (James 2:9).

What does it mean to have no respect to persons? It means that we
should not judge or evaluate people on the basis of their personalities or
circumstances, which is exactly what we are always tempted to do. We
make all sorts of judgments and evaluations about other people all the
time. It cannot be avoided. It is part and parcel of ordinary living.
Nowhere does Scripture advise people to suspend all judgment. Rather,
Scripture advises people to avoid judgments that are based on personalities
and circumstances, that are based on personal preferences or the circumstances of providence. Personal preferences are our likes and dislikes. Circumstances of providence are the social attributes of birth—money, social
position, health, geography, nationality. None of these things enter into
God's judgment, and neither should they enter into ours.

Church courts are charged with keeping the peace and purity of the
church. And, as I've said before, that is no easy job because the very
things that contribute to the purity of the church often disturb its peace,
and those things that contribute to the peace of the church often contribute to its impurity. An emphasis upon right doctrine disturbs many
Christians. And an emphasis on "going along to get along" often pollutes
right practice.

Most of the things that church courts deal with are matters of doctrine and morality (or life style). But moral concerns can easily degenerate
into civil matters rather quickly. The point is that morality and illegality
are related, but not always matters of the same jurisdiction. Some things
are immoral, but not illegal, and that is the way it should be. The con-
verse of this is that some things that are legal are immoral. The point is
that church courts are to adjudicate cases that pertain to doctrinal and
moral concerns of Christians, with the hope that dealing with them as
moral issues will keep them out of civil courts as legal issues.

But over the last hundred years or so church courts have fallen into
utter disregard, except for a few small (usually) Presbyterian denominations. At least this is the case in principle.

Civil courts make an effort to deal only with breaches of civil law—
criminal activity. However, current American jurisprudence has been
creeping into the area of what are called "hate crimes." Legislation has

been enacted that adds additional punishments for crimes that are motivated by hate. The problem with hate crime legislation is that it is encroaching into areas of morality rather than illegality. It is not illegal to hate because any law against hate in and of itself cannot be adequately defined or effectively enforced. Laws that cannot be defined or enforced are not laws at all, but only moral injunctions. And, indeed, hate is a moral issue. Nonetheless, such law requires the correct identification of personal motivation. And a person's real motivation is privy only to God. Let me say only that hate crime legislation has the potential to undermine the genius of the American legal system, in my opinion.

Paul's point in these verses is to encourage and legitimize church courts by recommending that church members abide by them, and avoid civil courts. Christians should make every effort to avoid civil courts, period. Paul even goes so far as to say that it is preferable to be wronged and defrauded by a church court than to appeal to a civil court. And that's a strong statement!

While it is true, in the litigious mania that has captured modern Western people, this sentiment has decimated all semblance of church courts, as those less concerned with biblical faithfulness took advantage of those who believed and acted upon Paul's admonition. Often those who are willing to be wronged and defrauded as a testimony of obedience to Jesus Christ, are taken advantage of in this fallen world. Like so many things biblical, Paul's admonition only works when those involved are faithful. In the wake of unfaithfulness biblical morality and the social structures it engenders tend to break down. Why would Paul make such a strong statement? He knew "that the saints will judge the world" (v. 2).

SAINTS WILL JUDGE

The Greek word translated *world* is *kosmos*, and includes the globe we call earth and everything that inhabits it. By this he means that the Gospel of Jesus Christ will ultimately reach the highest courts of the world, and those courts will render judgments in faithfulness to Jesus Christ. He doesn't mean that you and I (or that every Christian) will be thrust into positions of worldly power. Rather, he simply means that the gospel will eventually reach those in positions of worldly power and that they will exercise their faith faithfully. However, he asked, "if the world is to be judged by you, are you incompetent to try trivial cases" (v. 2)? Here, the Greek actually does suggest that Paul said *you*, as in a particular person to whom he was speaking. Does it, then, have any relevance to us today?

Paul did himself bring the Gospel to Rome and to the highest courts of the known world of his time. And some of his friends accompanied him on that journey. So, it is possible that he was speaking only to specific people as he anticipated his journey to Rome.

However, given the context in which he was writing these words, it seems likely that he meant to suggest that it is always the same Holy Spirit who animates all of God's people. And that the same Holy Spirit, who would judge the world in the fullness of time in the highest world courts through particular regenerate saints (Christians), is certainly able to judge the more trivial cases that would commonly come to church courts through the ordinary saints of the church. He was speaking about the Holy Spirit who would be manifest in all of God's people throughout history.

He can say this because he knew and he was teaching that Christians are not to judge or evaluate on the basis of personalities or the circumstances of providence, but are to render judgments and evaluations on the basis of Scripture alone. Thus, the same guide, the Holy Spirit through the regeneration of believers in every generation, will always be or should always be the basis for Christian judgments and evaluations.

"Do you not know that we are to judge angels? How much more, then, matters pertaining to this life!" (v. 3). The Greek word is *aggelos*, and means messengers, in this case messengers of God. Strong's concordance goes on to say of this word in this context that it suggests by implication pastors, who bring the message of the Gospel. And, indeed, ordinary saints do in fact judge pastors through church courts. Church courts license pastors, approve pastors for particular callings, and discipline pastors. We don't need to turn to spiritualized explanations when common explanations exist.

"I say this to your shame" (v. 5). Paul mentioned all of this in order to play upon the shame of the Corinthian church. Paul was using shame to admonish and teach the Corinthians. This is very interesting. Is shame an acceptable method of instruction? It may be disliked and considered to be impolite, but it appears to be biblical. The shame that Paul brought upon the Corinthians was that they settled disputes in civil courts rather than in church courts. And it was shameful because it neglected—even denied— the presence and power of the Holy Spirit who dwells with God's people, and who should have been called upon to adjudicate disputes among them. Paul suggested that their neglect of church courts was actually a neglect of the Holy Spirit and of Scripture.

And here's the rub. If the Corinthians were shamed by Paul for neglecting to use church courts to settle disputes among professing Christians, should we not also be shamed for the same thing? Is it not to the shame of Christianity that Christians regularly neglect church courts and turn to civil courts—or worse, political manipulation—to settle their disputes today? Is it not to the shame of Christianity that the churches have all but abandoned church courts?

And yet, there is a contemporary movement to reestablish church courts in our time. Peacemakers® is a Christian reconciliation organization that provides training and counselors for churches, and trains Christians to provide arbitration services that are acceptable alternatives to civil litigation. Peacemakers® begins with local church education and counselor training. If I understand it correctly, at some point in the process Peacemaker trained counselors can also provide counseling and arbitration services for hire as they receive training that is recognized by the state to qualify them as counselors and arbitrators.

This is a great thing, and could provide an effective ministry for any church and a substantial outreach tool for any community in the name of Jesus Christ.

Yet, the fact remains that true reformation and revival of the Christian church will also reform and revive church courts as the desire to avoid civil courts grows among Christians. Indeed, as the civil court system continues to collapse from the backlog of cases and the moral corruption of the legal system, the Christian church may well find itself faced with an opportunity to actually be what God has called it to be—a vehicle of forgiveness and reconciliation among all people.

"But you yourselves wrong and defraud—even your own brothers!" (v. 8). Paul here accused the Corinthians of lacking—not merely civil morality and Christian manners—but the most basic family considerations. From time immemorial families have had a code of honor and honesty that has been regularly observed by family members. Not always, not perfectly, but generally family members have been both trusted and trustworthy with regard to other family members. Without honesty and trust all social relationships break down. Chaos and poverty result. Families are the most basic building blocks of society. So, it is no mere wives' tale to say that as the family goes so goes the civilization. The family is the cradle of civilization.

Paul's accusation was very serious. He was suggesting that the behavior of the Corinthians, of taking one another to civil courts and neglecting the use of church courts, threatened the very fabric of civilization itself. You may think that I'm overstating the case. I don't think so because, as we've seen, Paul's accusation of the neglect of church courts or church reconciliation amounted to the neglect of Scripture and the neglect of the Holy Spirit. The neglect of church courts is an act of faithlessness.

The Bible is pretty clear that apart from Jesus Christ, which means apart from the Holy Spirit who is in union with the Trinitarian God of Scripture, humanity is bound for hell and society is bound for destruction. If Christians in the churches don't take God seriously, then no one will. It is only as Christians recover biblical practices in their own lives, and in their own churches, that Christianity will grow and become what God has called it to become—the only means of salvation by the only God who matters, the only God who actually exists.

13. RIGHTEOUSNESS

Do you not know that the unrighteous will not inherit the kingdom of God?
Do not be deceived: neither the sexually immoral, nor idolaters, nor adulterers,
nor men who practice homosexuality, nor thieves, nor the greedy, nor drunkards,
nor revilers, nor swindlers will inherit the kingdom of God. And such were
some of you. But you were washed, you were sanctified, you were justified in
the name of the Lord Jesus Christ and by the Spirit of our God.

— 1 Corinthians 6:9-11

Paul plainly said that, "the unrighteous will not inherit the kingdom of God" (v. 9). Righteousness is the foundation of the kingdom of God. Because God is perfect He cannot allow or tolerate any unrighteousness in heaven. To do so would be to pollute and destroy His kingdom. And exactly where is the kingdom of God? It is obviously in heaven, but remember that Jesus taught us to pray "Our Father ... Your kingdom come, your will be done, on earth as it is in heaven" (Matthew 6:10).

Paul was not calling the Corinthians to greater effort on their part in order to achieve personal righteousness through a commitment to not sin any more. Rather, Paul was calling them to Jesus Christ because he knew very well that they—we—have no personal righteousness. The only righteousness available to them—and to us or to anyone at any time—is the righteousness of Jesus Christ. Paul was painfully aware of the sins of the Corinthians. And he was painfully aware that too many of them had hold of the righteousness stick by the wrong end. He knew that they had been chasing worldly foolishness and forsaking godly wisdom.

That's the reason that he wrote the letter. He wrote to them in order to help solve some of the very serious church problems that they were having. The church is the leading edge of the kingdom of God on earth, and Paul was trying to help them get it right because he saw that they had it wrong. Paul's letter contains admonishment, instruction, and encouragement. Paul was not teaching them how to get to heaven. He was teaching them how to manifest heaven on earth through the proper functioning of the church.

But before we get into the content of this section, look again at who Paul wrote the letter to. Like any letter, if it's not written to you, you will have trouble understanding what it says or benefiting from its instruction.

"To the church of God that is in Corinth, to those sanctified in Christ Jesus, called to be saints together with all those who in every place call upon the name of our Lord Jesus Christ, both their Lord and ours" (1 Corinthians 1:2).

WRITTEN TO WHOM?

Paul's salutation began very broadly and then narrowed down the group of recipients with several additional phrases. He began, "To the church of God"—not to everyone in the world, but only to those who comprise the church. This means that he was writing to all of God's saints, and by extension it includes faithful saints of all churches and ages.

Then he began narrowing down the list. This process is both inclusive and exclusive. He was writing to the particular branch of God's church that was in Corinth. But he didn't stop there. He was not writing to every member of the Corinthian church, but only "to those sanctified in Christ Jesus." He meant to address those who were growing in the Lord, those who were in the process of being sanctified by the power and presence of the Holy Spirit in their lives, those who were regenerate, born again. And to make sure that he was speaking to the right people he added, "those who in every place call upon the name of our Lord Jesus Christ" (v. 2),

To call upon the name of Jesus is to be actively engaged in prayer. Thus, he was addressing those who prayed a lot, who prayed everywhere they went. And finally, just to make sure, he added that he was addressing those who actually believed in the same Lord as he did, "both their Lord and ours." He meant to insure that there was no misunderstanding about who would benefit from his letter—growing, praying, born again Christians who have a right understanding about God and Jesus. Interestingly, those who are not intended recipients find the letter to be of little interest or any real value. What was Paul trying to say to these Christians?

"Do you not know that the unrighteous will not inherit the kingdom of God? Do not be deceived: neither the sexually immoral, nor idolaters, nor adulterers, nor men who practice homosexuality, nor thieves, nor the greedy, nor drunkards, nor revilers, nor swindlers will inherit the kingdom of God" (vs. 9-10).

The Greek word translated *unrighteous* literally means unjust. He meant to say that the unjustified, those who are not justified by the righteousness of Jesus Christ, are not and cannot be part of the kingdom of God.

Paul was not saying that only those who work hard to satisfy the demands of God's righteousness would inherit the kingdom. Paul was not lobbying for works-righteousness here. Rather, Paul was speaking of being justified. He was speaking about the doctrine of justification, and that one's justification needed to be right, prior to entrance into the kingdom. And people justified by the unmitigated grace of God through the propitiation of Jesus Christ. He was not calling the Corinthians to increased godliness that would result in their inheritance of the kingdom. Rather, he was calling them to faith in Jesus Christ, who is alone righteous, and who provides the only means of entry into the kingdom.

Of course, the result of faith in Christ is an increase in personal righteousness over time, though never perfect nor sufficient. But in Christ the Holy Spirit supplies what we lack.

But it was not Paul who was making the determination that unrighteous, unjustified sinners would not enter the kingdom. Jesus said the same thing.

> "Truly, truly, I say to you, an hour is coming, and is now here, when the dead will hear the voice of the Son of God, and those who hear will live. For as the Father has life in himself, so he has granted the Son also to have life in himself. And he has given him authority to execute judgment, because he is the Son of Man. Do not marvel at this, for an hour is coming when all who are in the tombs will hear his voice and come out, those who have done good to the resurrection of life, and those who have done evil to the resurrection of judgment" (John 5:25-29).

There is a fork in the road at judgment. The goats and the sheep will be separated.

SEPARATION

Few people actually believe this. They don't now, nor did they then. So, Paul warned believers about being deceived, which means that believers can be deceived about what they believe. Not all believers believe correctly. Salvation does not make people instant winners of the orthodoxy contest. Of course, we are not saved by what we believe. Rather, we believe because we have been saved, which also means that our ultimate salvation does not come into doubt when our beliefs are wrong.[1] So, Paul does not mean that believers can lose their faith if they believe wrongly. Though wrong belief has many unfortunate and unpleasant consequences, from which believers are not spared. And at the same time, the Lord values right or correct belief.

Similarly, there are many fortunate and pleasant consequences of right belief, many of which are also enjoyed by unbelievers. When God's church believes and teaches the Gospel correctly, benefits accrue to both the saved and the lost. Conversely, when God's church believes and teaches the Gospel incorrectly, liabilities accrue to both the saved and the lost. God wants people to believe and understand His gospel message correctly. It is important to Him because He uses the correct proclamation of the gospel as a means of salvation.

> "But how are they to call on him in whom they have not believed? And
> how are they to believe in him of whom they have never heard? And
> how are they to hear without someone preaching?" (Romans 10:14).

We could think of the process of salvation as logging into the data base of the Holy Spirit. It is as if the Lord has installed a special password in the hearts of the elect. Proper preaching of the Gospel contains an automated login script that activates that password. But if that automated login script contains junk code, it interferes with the correct execution of the script. Orthodox preaching contains elements of that script that trigger the pre-installed login password of believers. So, to get the gospel wrong interferes with the hearing of the Gospel by the elect. It doesn't keep anyone from salvation, it just gums up the process.[2]

Paul was trying to fix the process that was in effect in Corinth as a result of those who had been teaching the foolishness of the world in the guise of the wisdom of God. "Do not be deceived" (v. 6), he said, because he believed that they were actively in the process of being deceived. Deceived about what? About, among other things, who would inherit the kingdom of God. He had previously identified the fact that one of their leaders had been involved in gross immorality, shameful even by pagan

---

1   See Anselm's comment in footnote 1, page 3.
2   This analogy is useful to a point, but it limps when we try to put too much weight on it. God's people will hear the gospel even if we communicate it incorrectly. They will hear it from someone else.

standards. It wasn't that this person had committed a sin so vile that it could not be forgiven. Not at all! God can forgive any sin, save one (Matthew 12:31-32).

It was not the sin that was the problem. Paul knew that all Christians are sinners. "And such were some of you." he said. "But you were washed, you were sanctified, you were justified in the name of the Lord Jesus Christ and by the Spirit of our God" (v. 11).

The problem was not that some of the members of the Corinthian church were living in sin. Who isn't? The problem was that some of the members of the Corinthian church had not repented of their sin. They were in the process of justifying it to themselves and to the church, trying to make it okay in the eyes of God by suggesting that God forgives everyone of everything, that in the light of the amazing grace of Jesus Christ repentance and turning from sin doesn't matter.

The rationalizations go like this: "Salvation is all of grace, it's all God's work and none of mine," which is true enough, of course. But the rationalizations go further: "Since God saved me from time immemorial, before I was born, and my salvation does not depend on anything I do or can do, then God doesn't care what I do. It doesn't make any difference to my salvation. So, I can do whatever I want." Wrong! God does care what we do. He cares about what believers do and he cares about what unbelievers do. If he didn't care, he wouldn't impose His law on everyone or bring judgment on anyone. But he does! God's law applies to all of humanity. And God will bring everyone into judgment before the bench of Jesus Christ.

The point is that apart from Jesus Christ there is no correct (objective, rational, or perfect) morality, which means that only Christians can teach morality correctly (objectively, rationally, perfectly) by teaching *biblical* morality correctly. However, this does not mean that Christians are perfect. Perfection is like calculus, one approaches a definitive answer, and makes some valid assumptions and conclusions about it.

And what is more, morality affects everyone. It's not that Christian morality only affects Christians or that pagan morality only affects pagans. Rather, we are all interdependent, saved and lost. So, the wrong morality brings God's curses upon everyone, just as the right morality brings God's blessings upon everyone. That doesn't mean that everyone will be saved, and it certainly does not mean that anyone is saved by moral behavior. It just means that life will be better for everyone when God's love, peace, justice, and mercy—defined and implemented according to Scripture—provide the best possible social morals for the greatest number of people, saved and lost.

Short List

Paul created a short list of those who will not inherit the kingdom of God:

> "neither the sexually immoral, nor idolaters, nor adulterers, nor men who practice homosexuality, nor thieves, nor the greedy, nor drunkards, nor revilers, nor swindlers will inherit the kingdom of God" (v. 0).

The list could be longer. If you aren't on that list, you might find yourself on Timothy's list.

> "We know that the law is good, if one uses it lawfully, understanding this, that the law is not laid down for the just but for the lawless and disobedient, for the ungodly and sinners, for the unholy and profane, for those who strike their fathers and mothers, for murderers, the sexually immoral, men who practice homosexuality, enslavers, liars, perjurers, and whatever else is contrary to sound doctrine, in accordance with the glorious gospel of the blessed God with which I have been entrusted" (1 Timothy 1:8-11).

Note that Paul tells us that God is so concerned about unbelievers that he has set the law out for them in particular. And that "whatever else is contrary to sound doctrine" (1 Timothy 1:10) is equivalent to lawlessness.

What is this difference between believers and unbelievers? Paul said that there was no difference regarding sin. Believers are no less sinners than unbelievers. It is not sin that makes the difference. Paul noted that the Corinthian believers were just as guilty of sin as the Corinthian unbelievers, "but," he went on to say, "you were washed, you were sanctified, you were justified in the name of the Lord Jesus Christ and by the Spirit of our God" (v. 11)—washed, sanctified, and justified. Matthew Henry says of this verse,

> "The wickedness of men before conversion is no bar to their regeneration and reconciliation to God. The blood of Christ, and the washing of regeneration, can purge away all guilt and defilement."

Paul mentioned three things: washed, sanctified, and justified.

The Greek word translated as *washed* is not an allusion to baptism. It is not the word *baptizo*. Paul was not talking about the sacrament or ceremony of baptism. He could have used that word if he wanted to, but he didn't. The word here literally means to wash off. It means to bathe in such a way as to remove something (dirt) that has attached itself to the body. The allusion here is to the cleansing of the body, the "cleaning up of one's act," if you will. It's not merely a spiritual thing, it is a bodily thing, a moral thing, a practical thing. He means that one's life, one's habits, one's actions and activities have been cleansed of filth—that which is offensive to God.

The Difference

Yet, Paul does not neglect the spiritual aspects of this difference between believers and unbelievers. He simply makes the point that the difference is not merely spiritual. It also manifests in the flesh.

The other two words deal with the spiritual aspects of this difference, one is centered in God and one is centered in the individual. The one centered in God pertains to justification, and means everything that the Protestant Reformers discuss under the title of *forensic justification*. It refers to God's act of justification, wherein God transfers the righteousness credit earned by Jesus Christ to the account of an individual sinner. It is an action of God in heaven that transfers Christ's righteousness to believers. It doesn't make sinners suddenly righteous. Rather, it acknowledges the promise and power of Jesus Christ to complete what God has begun. God has adjusted the heavenly balance sheet by transferring the credit earned by Christ on the cross to the debt of individual sinners. The debt of sin has been paid by Jesus Christ. That's what justification is.[3]

But that's not the end of the process. While the debt has been paid, and God no longer looks upon the sinner as a debtor, God is not stupid. He still knows the hearts of men, and while the hearts of believers have been changed, there is still much to do to bring believers into full possession of the righteousness that is now theirs. The seed of righteousness has been planted, but it has yet to grow to maturity.

And the process of that growth, powered by the presence of the Holy Spirit in the lives of individuals, is the process of sanctification. It is a process of growth and maturity in Christ,

---

3 Don't miss the point by putting too much stock in this analogy. God doesn't actually have a ledger sheet. The analogy simply points to God's sovereignty in salvation.

"until we all attain to the unity of the faith and of the knowledge of the Son of God, to mature manhood, to the measure of the stature of the fullness of Christ, so that we may no longer be children, tossed to and fro by the waves and carried about by every wind of doctrine, by human cunning, by craftiness in deceitful schemes" (Ephesians 4:13-14).

"You were washed, you were sanctified, you were justified in the name of the Lord Jesus Christ and by the Spirit of our God" (v. 11). That's the difference between believers and unbelievers. And to blur that difference is to lose sight of the purpose of God and the purpose of salvation. To ignore or confuse the difference between believers and unbelievers is to deny the power and purpose of God Himself.

14. MEMBERS

And such were some of you. But you were washed, you were sanctified, you were justified in the name of the Lord Jesus Christ and by the Spirit of our God. "All things are lawful for me," but not all things are helpful. "All things are lawful for me," but I will not be enslaved by anything. "Food is meant for the stomach and the stomach for food"—and God will destroy both one and the other. The body is not meant for sexual immorality, but for the Lord, and the Lord for the body. And God raised the Lord and will also raise us up by his power. Do you not know that your bodies are members of Christ? Shall I then take the members of Christ and make them members of a prostitute? Never! Or do you not know that he who is joined to a prostitute becomes one body with her? For, as it is written, "The two will become one flesh." But he who is joined to the Lord becomes one spirit with him. Flee from sexual immorality. Every other sin a person commits is outside the body, but the sexually immoral person sins against his own body. Or do you not know that your body is a temple of the Holy Spirit within you, whom you have from God? You are not your own, for you were bought with a price. So glorify God in your body.

— 1 Corinthians 6:11-20

Paul began this section by quoting some of the popular sayings of his day and contrasting them with God's Word. He was providing case studies to show them precisely how God's wisdom differs from the wisdom of the world. The Corinthians, and particularly their leaders, those whom Paul had been criticizing from the beginning of this letter, had been using various popular sayings to justify their belief and practice of worldly wisdom. Paul interacted with those popular sayings.

Paul, like a doctor examining a patient, put his finger on the sore spot —sexual immorality—in order to determine and demonstrate to the patient that there was indeed a problem that needed to be treated. He began with the age-old idea that people are free to do whatever they want, that their moral freedom was a God-given right. The popular saying of the day was, "All things are lawful for me" (v. 12).

This is an argument for the gospel of Jesus Christ that Paul himself made to the Galatians because the Galatians had slipped back into a faith of works-righteousness. Paul was adamant that Christians are to oppose every aspect of works-righteousness because works-righteousness opposes every aspect of the gospel of Jesus Christ. Paul's argument is that Christians are free from the religion(s) of work-righteousness in Christ. We are free *in* Christ, but not *apart from* Christ. But does that mean that we can do whatever we want as long as we acknowledge Jesus Christ? No, because the issue is not merely acknowledging Jesus Christ, as if He were some sort of talisman or charm. Rather, the issue is being *in Christ*, actually being in Christ.[1] Those who are actually in Christ are not free to do whatever they want. They are free to do what Christ wants them to do. This is Christian freedom.

Clearly, Paul does not mean that Christians are free to rape, murder, and pillage to their hearts' content as long as they "acknowledge" Christ. Not at all! Nor are Christians free to lie, gossip, and slander because they have received the forgiveness of Jesus Christ. It doesn't work like that.

CONSENTING ADULTS

The popular understanding of Paul's day, the understanding that Paul was arguing against, was that fornication (sex outside of marriage) was okay because of the Greek belief that there was a strict separation of body and spirit. This isn't something that people normally think much about. It is, rather, an assumption or presupposition that people have. A presupposition works in the background to approve certain kinds of decisions and disapprove others. It is a kind of prejudice, and most people are not aware of their own prejudices. But in fact, everyone has all kinds of prejudices, and not all of them are bad or wrong. For instance, Christians have a prejudice toward God. We call it *love*.

The Greeks had a prejudice about the human body. They believed that all of its activities and functions were evil and corrupt. And that the human spirit was above the fray and was, therefore, divine and perfect. Salvation for the Greeks (and those who believed and thought like the Greeks, as we do) was a matter of the spirit and did not involve the so-called corruptions of the body.

---

1   See Ross, Phillip A. *Colossians—Christos Singularis*, Pilgrim Platform, Marietta, Ohio, 2010.

The Greeks produced two schools of thought on this matter. The Gnostics sought to disengage themselves as much as possible from bodily functions and focused on the purity of the mind. They fasted, deprived themselves of sleep and became ascetics. They retreated from the body into the thoughts of the mind in the hope that they could dissociate themselves from the evil and corruption of the body. In Galatia, Paul was speaking against such Gnostics.

The other Greek school of thought was Libertine. The Libertines also thought that the body was evil and corrupt, but they thought that bodily activity had no connection with the purity of the spirit. So, it didn't matter what a person did in the body because the gulf between mind and body was unbridgeable. They believed that the activities of the body could not affect the spirit. Thus, they didn't fast, they partied. In Corinth, Paul was speaking to Libertines.

Christianity through the centuries has generated a great deal of confusion about this matter because, for the most part, Christian theologians have remained captive to Greek modes or categories of thought. Intelligence and intellectual endeavors in the West have always been defined by Greek categories. Even today our world is dominated by this kind of thinking. It's a kind of mentality that tends to compartmentalize various aspects of life, and is reflected in the fundamental dualism of mind and body. Most of our philosophical disagreements boil down to some version of Platonism verses some version of Aristotelianism. Modern thinking of this kind tends to analyze things by setting up opposing categories, like mind/body, conservative/liberal, right/left, Republican/Democratic, etc.

GREEK DICHOTOMY

Such thinking often creates a false dichotomy that overlooks the central issues. I'm not suggesting that all dichotomies are false. They are not. All I am saying is that the categories of analysis determine the acceptability of a solution. The way a question or issue is approached determines its resolution. You may have heard it this way. "To get the right answer, you have to ask the right questions." Most Christian theology suffers from the same problem. It sets up false dichotomies, asks the wrong questions, and fails to adequately reveal or "get at" the essential message of the gospel of Jesus Christ.

What do I mean? Rather, what does *Paul* mean? Paul teaches that Christianity is neither Gnostic nor Libertine because, according to Paul in this section, Christianity opposes the very categories of Greek analysis.

This is the issue that Paul was trying to get at in this letter to the Corinthians. And this is the issue that many people find confusing. Remember that Paul's letter to the Galatians preceded this letter to the Corinthians. And in all likelihood, the Corinthian leaders were aware of Paul's letter to the Galatians. However, the Corinthians tended to be Libertines rather than ascetic Gnostics. So, they took Paul's argument about freedom in Christ in a way that was never intended when he wrote to the Galatians.

Their argument, which really was Paul's argument to the Galatians, was that "All things are lawful for me" (v. 12). Yes, argued Paul, that is true enough, but it doesn't mean that "all things are helpful" (v. 12). The KJV translates the word as *expedient*. Not all things are expedient. Things that are expedient provide a means to an end, but not necessarily a principled or ethical means. Expediency usually suggests getting something done without regard for principle, morality, or ethics. It is the sentiment of the Nike® motto, "Just Do It!" Paul's opposition to this misunderstanding of his teaching to the Galatians reminds me of the children's song:

> Oh, be careful little eyes, what you see,
> Oh, be careful little ears, what you hear,
> Oh, be careful little hands, what you make,
> Oh, be careful little feet, where you go.
> There's a Father up above, looking down in tender love,
> So be careful little eyes, what you see.

Paul did not mean to say to the Galatians that it was okay for them to do whatever they wanted. They were not free to burn, murder, and pillage. Like everyone else in this God-created world they were still bound by the Ten Commandments. What Paul meant was that apart from Christ the Ten Commandments provided only a death sentence. But in Christ—and this is the crucial point, *only in Christ*—was the death sentence avoidable.

Obedience to Christ is possible, not because *we* can do it, but because Jesus Christ has already done it for Himself and will bring all of His people into willing compliance by the power and presence of His Holy Spirit. Paul was saying that sin does not keep God's people from salvation, but that God's grace is greater than sin. However, that does not mean that we are free to sin. Rather, like everyone else we will suffer the worldly consequences of sin, but not the eternal consequences. "'All things are lawful for me,' but not all things are helpful. 'All things are lawful for me,' but I will not be enslaved by anything" (v.12).

COMPARTMENTALIZATION

Verse 13 continues the same point,

"Food is meant for the stomach and the stomach for food"—and God will destroy both one and the other. The body is not meant for sexual immorality, but for the Lord, and the Lord for the body."

The worldly wisdom expressed in this popular saying was that bodily activities—eating, drinking, sexing, etc.—are intended for the body, and have no impact upon the mind or the spirit. It amounts to what can be called philosophical compartmentalization, which simply means that various elements of life and living can be sealed off from one another. For instance, they falsely believed that food has no effect upon the mind or spirit; that education has no effect on the body (it is for the mind or spirit), and that prayer or other spiritual practices do not impact the body.

We practice a similar kind of compartmentalization today. We think that we can cordon off our private lives from our public lives, or our home lives from our work lives, or our church lives from our work lives. Compartmentalization is simply the belief that some aspects of life and living have no effect or relationship to other aspects of life and living. Paul's example was that the Corinthians believed that extra-marital sexual relationships had no connection to their salvation or faithfulness. They argued that because their salvation did not depend upon what they did or didn't do or were able to do, that what they did or didn't do was in no way related to their salvation. Wrong!

Paul was saying that God trumps the body and everything related to it. "God will destroy both one and the other" (v. 13). God will destroy both the stomach (or body) and the food intended for it. He was trying to shake them out of their complacency by saying that arguments or postulates about God are categorically different than arguments or postulates about humanity. What is true for the human body is but a shadow of what is true for God.

And yet, God's truth is for the body. God's truth has taken the body and its various needs and activities into consideration. Here's the crucial verse: "The body is not meant for sexual immorality, but for the Lord, and the Lord for the body" (v. 13).

Our bodies are not free to express whatever they want, whatever they desire, whatever they think they need. Rather, we are to live in submission to God, to God's law, to God's desires in the light of Christ. Christians are not free to do whatever they want. They are free to do what God wants them to do *in Christ*. I pray that your ears will take care to hear this aright.

Just as it was necessary for Jesus Christ, the Son of God, to manifest in a human body, it is also necessary for God's Holy Spirit to manifest in the bodies of His people. Christianity is a religion of incarnation, of Christ's incarnation in the flesh, and the incarnation of His Holy Spirit in His people through regeneration. Paul ran with this argument by telling us that "God raised the Lord and will also raise us up by his power" (v. 14).

God raised what? By whose power? God raised the dead body of Jesus Christ who had been slain upon the cross. God raised His body, his human body, from death. But that's not all! God will also raise us. He will also raise Christians, those who willingly believe, those who have been born again, those who are blood-bought by Christ. Just as Christ's body was raised, so our bodies will be raised. Christians are resurrected people!

NOT JUST HEAVEN

Paul was saying here that Christianity is not so much about heaven. Please listen carefully. It is about heaven, of course. Heaven is real, and eternal life with Jesus Christ in heaven is real. But the greater concern for this world is the coming of the Kingdom of God (heaven) to earth. Christianity is about the manifestation of the Kingdom "on earth, as it is heaven" (Matthew 6:7). The point is not so much that Christians get to spend all eternity with Christ in heaven—though they most certainly do. The point is that Christians are the leading edge of the Kingdom of God on earth, which is in the process of manifesting on earth. Christians are the manifestation in Christ or through Christ of God's Kingdom on earth. The locus or theater of Christianity is not heaven, but earth, and the earth has been created for bodies.

"Do you not know that your bodies are members of Christ?" (v. 15). To be a member of something is to be part of a greater whole. The argument of membership in Christ is critical to overcoming the duality of Greek thinking. It is an argument that is uniquely Trinitarian. And like all discussion of the Trinity it is subtle, even difficult. But it is not difficult because it is hard to understand. It is difficult because our minds have been captured by Greek categories of thinking and analysis. All public education is saturated in Greek philosophy, so anyone who is a product of public education is a product of Greek philosophy—even today. The Trinity is a difficult concept because we have all been trained to think otherwise. The doctrine of the Trinity does not fit Greek categories.

Nonetheless, the reality of the Trinity is the linchpin of Christianity —its understanding and practice. The reality of the Trinity is difficult because it is below the surface of ordinary awareness. You can't tell if someone is a member of Christ by looking at him. We are not talking about membership in a 501(c)(3) organization or about attending a worship service in some particular place. We are talking about being a member of Christ. It's related to church membership, but it is not the same thing.

A *member* is an appendage, "a body part or organ: as a penis."[2] The Greek (*melos*—of uncertain affinity; a limb or part of the body: member) is no more helpful than the English here. Paul's argument is that our bodily parts—eyes, ears, hands, feet, etc.—are not just ours, they belong to God.

Paul uses an example of temple prostitution for two reasons. First, he has already identified that the Corinthians have misunderstood something significant related to God's teaching about sexuality, fornication in particular. And secondly, arguments related to prostitution have a long biblical history. The Old Testament prophets long described faithlessness as a kind of covenantal prostitution. Unfaithful people "live with" or "sleep with" other gods in violation of the covenantal relationship that God has established with all of humanity.

To be joined to a prostitute is to violate the covenant of the family, which is founded on the marriage covenant, which necessarily involves God. Contrary to popular opinion, marriage is not just between a man and a woman, but is between a man, a woman, *and God*. All family relationships and responsibilities are grounded and established on the biblical covenant of marriage, whether or not that covenant is acknowledged. Family membership is based upon the covenant of marriage which has given birth to the family. The family is a product of marriage, and marriage is a gift (or creation, or institution) of God. All sexual activity outside of marriage is, therefore, a violation of family membership. It is a

---

2   *Merriam-Webster Online Dictionary*—forgive me for getting graphic here, but it is important to understand this if we are to follow Paul's argument because Paul is alluding to a particular organ of the body, the organ of reproduction.

violation of one's personal identity as a human being, a part of the family
of man.

Paul acknowledged that sex is always a renewal—a remembrance and
consummation—of the marriage covenant given by God to all of humanity for our joy, health, and well-being. It is always that, and is never not
that regardless of the partners. Consequently, Paul argues that fornication
forges a union that is in conflict with God and family. But sex within
marriage reinforces one's individuality and, at the same time, one's
covenantal unity with one's spouse and family—and God.

The best way to deal with sexual immorality or sexual temptation, as
Paul notes, is to flee from it. Run! Get away before you are tempted, before you get near it because it will catch you in its web of sin. The fly
cannot defeat the spider. His only defense is distance. We need to run
from it because it will confuse and ultimately destroy both our individuality and covenantal unity.

Paul says it this way, "Every other sin a person commits is outside the
body, but the sexually immoral person sins against his own body" (v. 18).
All sin is primarily sin against God (Psalm 51:4, Luke 15:21) and secon-
darily against some other person—lying, slander, murder, etc. But the sin
of fornication is unique in that is constitutes a sin against one's self. Yes, it
violates God's covenant and involves another person, but in some way,
according to Paul, it is a violation against one's own body, and against
one's own soul. And because our bodies are members of Christ, it is a violation against membership in Christ. It is a violation against the character
of the Trinity and against the image of God in which we have been created.

UNITY & DIVERSITY

The nature of the Trinity is one in three, three in one—unity in diversity, diversity in unity. The doctrine of the Trinity teaches a unique
understanding of reality that allows for both particularity and unity. It is
the only perspective from which both particularity and unity can be
philosophically (or logically) justified.[3] But when a person is joined in one

3   I am employing the work of Cornelius Van Til, who has made a significant
     contribution to Christian theology. His work is a must read. Also see Rushdoony,
     R.J. *The One And The Many*, Ross House Books. Subtitled *Studies in the Philosophy of
     Order and Ultimacy*, this work, building on Van Til, discusses the problem of
     understanding unity vs. particularity, oneness vs. individuality. "Whether recognized
     or not, every argument and every theological, philosophical, political, or any other

flesh with someone apart from God's marriage covenant, the unique essence of the character of the Trinity is obscured. We are less able to understand or discern who God has created us to be because human sexuality is at the very core of human identity. And we are less able to understand or discern who God is because human beings are always related to God covenantally. To obscure the idea of covenant is to obscure God.

Yes, we have a personal relationship with Jesus Christ, but that personal relationship is always manifest through God's covenant. God's covenant is an essential element of reality. To perceive reality apart from God's covenant is to miss the Trinitarian character of reality. Truth cannot be seen apart from participation in God's covenant because the universe in which we live is necessarily Trinitarian. That is, it is the Trinitarian character of God Himself that allows for, or accounts for the existence of individual things and simultaneously, allows for participation in various classes of unity through covenantal relationships.

All things that belong to a group or class of any kind do so through a covenantal or legal relationship. It is God's law that holds everything together through unity and differentiation. God's law not only holds families together, but it holds the universe itself together. So, to obscure or confuse our understanding of covenantal relationship by violating the marriage covenant, for instance, we alter our understanding and our actual relationship with God because God always relates to humanity in terms of His covenant.

Thus, extramarital sex undermines God's unity or order in the universe by violating God's law, which is the only principle that allows for individuality within unity, or particularity in the midst of universality. A person is always more than an individual because all persons are necessarily related to various groups, like families, churches, nations, even humanity itself. And all groups are related covenantally, legally, according to God's law. And it cannot be otherwise. Thus, to dishonor the covenant of marriage, whether one is married or not, always amounts to the destruction of social coherence or unity. It is a form of social suicide.

exposition is based on a presupposition about man, God and society—about reality. This presupposition rules and determines the conclusion; the effect is the result of a cause. And one such basic presupposition is with reference to the one and the many." The author finds the answer in the biblical doctrine of the Trinity. Ralph Smith has also provided a helpful treatment of this issue in his book, *Paradox And Truth*, Canon Press, Moscow, ID, 2002.

Paul concludes this chapter with this thought, "do you not know that your body is a temple of the Holy Spirit within you, whom you have from God?" (v. 19). He refers to the bodies of believers as temples. The Old Testament understanding of temple—the temple at Jerusalem, in particular—as the place of God's presence. God was present in the temple. Of course, Jesus taught that God is present wherever two or three believers are gathered in His name (Matthew 18:20). And in the Old Testament, the temple was the place that God's people gathered. But the point is that the Spirit of God is present in the lives of believers, not in the temple itself, nor in some particular structure or geographical location.

It is the Trinitarian Spirit of God that provides for both the individuality and the unity of believers in Christ. And apart from that Trinitarian Spirit, there is no proper differentiation. The last phrase, "whom you have from God" (v. 19) simply repeats this truth. Some versions translate it *whom* and some translate it as *which*. It could be either in the Greek. The difference is whether it refers to the temple or to the Spirit. Either interpretation will do.

"You are not your own, for you were bought with a price. So glorify God in your body" (vs. 19-20). It could hardly be more clear that Christianity is about life in this world and in these bodies. Of course, it's about heaven, but that's later. Our bodies are now. Christianity is about the manifestation of God's Holy Spirit in the lives of believers in the midst of this fallen world for the sake of its redemption and our happiness.

15. Relations

Now concerning the matters about which you wrote: "It is good for a man not to have sexual relations with a woman." But because of the temptation to sexual immorality, each man should have his own wife and each woman her own husband. The husband should give to his wife her conjugal rights, and likewise the wife to her husband. For the wife does not have authority over her own body, but the husband does. Likewise the husband does not have authority over his own body, but the wife does. Do not deprive one another, except perhaps by agreement for a limited time, that you may devote yourselves to prayer; but then come together again, so that Satan may not tempt you because of your lack of self-control. Now as a concession, not a command, I say this. I wish that all were as I myself am. But each has his own gift from God, one of one kind and one of another. To the unmarried and the widows I say that it is good for them to remain single as I am. But if they cannot exercise self-control, they should marry. For it is better to marry than to be aflame with passion. To the married I give this charge (not I, but the Lord): the wife should not separate from her husband (but if she does, she should remain unmarried or else be reconciled to her husband), and the husband should not divorce his wife.

— 1 Corinthians 7:1-11

Having discussed the prohibitions of Christian morality regarding immoral sexual relations, Paul now provides counsel regarding proper Christian sexuality. Seven chapters into Paul's letter to the Corinthians Paul is still discussing the same subject, which suggests that it was a widespread and serious problem among church members. What subject? The confusion of worldly wisdom and biblical truth that was being expressed through sexual confusion, and in other ways.

All of their lives these Corinthians, who had only recently become Christians, had been under the influence of Greek culture. And, according to Scripture and history, Greek culture was saturated in sexual immorality and confusion. Because of the permissiveness or liberality of Greek culture, the proliferation of sexual perversions of every conceivable sort, Paul now turned his attention to some very basic and practical considerations regarding the exercise of sexual relations between husbands and wives. All sexual expression is reserved for biblical covenantal marriage. Scripture never speaks of sexuality between consenting adults as anything other than fornication and adultery.

The first thing to note is that the Corinthians had misunderstood something that Paul had said in a previous letter. That previous letter is lost, so we don't know exactly what he said, but we can piece together the misunderstanding from the issue raised in the first verse of chapter seven.

Immediately preceding this section Paul had been contrasting biblical beliefs with some of the popular beliefs of the time. And we noted that some of those popular beliefs were related to what Paul had taught to other Christians, namely to the Galatians. We noted previously that the Corinthians had taken what Paul had taught to the Galatians and applied it to their own Corinthian Libertine worldview, when Paul intended it to apply only to the Gnostic worldview of the Galatians. And the result was that the Corinthians misunderstood what Paul said to the Galatians when they applied it to themselves. I mention this only because verse 1 of chapter seven falls into the same literary pattern Paul used earlier, which suggests that it was part of that earlier thought.

Except in this case they have taken Paul's prohibition against sexual immorality (against fornication) and tried to correct their own error by jumping to the opposite view. The Corinthians reasoned that since Paul had spoken so harshly against the widespread sexual immorality that he found in Corinth, against the Libertine practices that they had been taught by their misinformed leaders, they thought that Paul intended to teach the Gnostic view of withdrawal from the world and the abandonment of bodily concerns. Thus, they surmised that Paul was teaching that "'It is good for a man not to have sexual relations with a woman'" (v. 1). But Paul was quoting a concern that they had brought to him in a previous letter, a quote that they had taken out of context.

They wrongly believed that because Paul taught against sexuality as it was understood and practiced in the permissive Greek culture of Corinth, that Paul intended to teach that all sexual activity should be avoided. Being Greek in their worldview, they jumped from one extreme (that of the Libertines) to the opposite extreme (that of the Gnostic Essenes). They jumped from the belief that everything sexual was okay to the position that nothing sexual was okay. Again, as we have seen before, their philosophical categories of analysis did not allow for the discernment of a Trinitarian position. Their Greek philosophical training (whether implicit or explicit) meant that they could only create a false dichotomy, the choice between two equally wrong positions.

Roman Catholic theologians have played havoc with this section of Scripture. Early Roman Catholicism in an attempt to be all things to all people interpreted biblical Christianity in Greek intellectual categories in an effort to appeal to the Greeks. They made the same error that these Corinthians had made. They failed to understand Paul's correction, and that failure still permeates the Roman Catholic Church.

Middle Position

Paul was *not* teaching that it is good *not* to have sexual relations. He was not teaching a Gnostic or Essene view of sexuality. He was correcting a misunderstanding. Greek thinking leads to the opposing positions that all sexual relations are okay or that no sexual relations are okay. The middle position that requires the discernment of a covenantal relationship (covenantal marriage) was completely foreign to them. They could not understand how or why biblical covenantal marriage could make any real difference. Biblical covenantal marriage was not even on their radar screens. Our world today is awash in the same false dichotomy, the same foolish thinking. So, it is important for us to understand what Paul was trying so hard to get at.

The first thing that Paul taught them was that all fornication is wrong, but that does not mean that all sex is wrong. It only means that all sex outside of marriage, outside of faithful adherence to God's covenant, is wrong. Greek dualism cannot conceive of the reality of the Christian Trinity. Within the categories of Greek philosophy, the Trinity makes no sense at all. It is foolishness to the Greeks. Greek analysis attempts to understand or define the Trinity in terms of its own duality, and necessarily confuses and obscures the role of God, the Holy Spirit, and His Word in the lives and practices of human beings. On the one hand, God's covenant with humanity is the linchpin of Trinitarian Christianity, and on the other it is invisible to Greek thinking. Inasmuch as we think that the Trinity is an unknowable mystery, we are stuck in Greek categories of thought. Again, this is the central focus of Paul's message in chapter seven.

He went on to say that part of the reason for the institution of marriage was to provide an outlet for sexual desire. God knew that abstinence was beyond most people. God created both sexuality and marriage to go together for the sake of the health and stability of the family. Each man should have his own wife, and each woman should have her own husband. Notice that the language that Paul uses implies ownership, ownership of the wife by the husband and ownership of the husband by the wife. And that is exactly what he meant—reciprocal ownership.

The next two verses (vs. 3-4) speak of the fact of that ownership. Not only does the wife *"not have authority over her own body,"* but *"the husband does not have authority over his own body."* Previously Paul said that we are not our own but that we "were bought with a price" (1 Corinthians 6:20). We are owned by Jesus Christ through His covenant with God, and we are owned by our spouse through our marriage covenant. Husband owns wife, wife owns husband, and God owns them both. Note that ownership is a legal relationship.

Knowing the weakness of the flesh, Paul told husbands and wives not to "deprive one another" (v. 5). Sexual drives and needs are real, and cannot simply be ignored without serious consequences. And marriage is the place to deal with those concerns. Note that he also suggested that prayer would at times take precedence over the marriage bed "for a limited time" (v .5). Paul suggesting that husbands and wives engage in prayer with the same enthusiasm and commitment as they have for the marriage bed. Prayer in that venue would also help provide protection from Satan, who often uses sexual temptation and perversion to lure his victims into his den of iniquity.

MARRIAGE COUNSELING

Paul continued to provide marriage counseling in the verses that follow, but the counsel that he provided is not a biblical command, but a personal recommendation based on his understanding of both Scripture and humanity. The recommendation was based upon his observations about the Corinthians and the problems they were having in the church. The recommendation comes from the person who wrote much of the New Testament, so it deserves our serious consideration.

He began by setting the context, "I wish that all were as I myself am. But each has his own gift from God, one of one kind and one of another" (v. 7). From very early in Christian history this verse was considered to refer to Paul's married life. But in spite of the fact that the Roman Catholic Church believes that he was not married, the evidence is not conclusive. He may have been married, or he may have been a widower when he wrote these words. There really isn't enough evidence to establish anything certain about his state of marriage.

Nonetheless, we note that the traditional understanding has been that Paul was not married, and that his celibacy is here spoken of as a "gift." But if we examine both the context and the implications of this idea, we will find that Paul was not speaking about celibacy at all. The idea that Paul was saying that celibacy is a gift is absurd for a couple of reasons.

First, he wished that "all" people were like he was with regard to whatever he was talking about. Do you think that Paul really wished that all people were celibate? Ridiculous! We know that Paul clearly understood that the gifts of the Spirit were many and diverse, and that their diversity was a strength. Paul celebrated the diversity of spiritual gifts (Romans 12:6; 1 Corinthians 12:1-12, 30). So, for him to want all Christians to have the same gift is ludicrous.

Secondly, Paul surely knew that if all Christians were celibate, they would die out. The Essenes believed that Paul wanted all Christians to be celibate, and they actually died out. Paul was not stupid. Celibacy is a strategy of death, not life. This all suggests that Paul was not speaking in this verse about celibacy as a gift of the Spirit. This misunderstanding has been read into the verse, not taken from it. Even more, it suggests that he was not talking about celibacy as a lifestyle at all.

We have already determined that Paul was trying to correct a Greek misunderstanding that lead to confusion about the nature of biblical sexuality, that the Bible taught neither that all sex was okay, nor that all sex was to be avoided. Rather, the Bible teaches covenant responsibility with regard to sex—covenant responsibility, or marriage. And celibacy is an avoidance of covenantal responsibility in as much as it is an avoidance of marriage. But don't jump to the false conclusion that this means that unmarried people are unfaithful. It does not mean that. The point is simply that the whole idea that Paul was talking about celibacy is a Greek misunderstanding about what the Bible teaches.

Paul's words are not perfectly clear. He assumed that his audience knew exactly what he meant, and it is likely that they did. The subject that Paul was talking about was assumed rather than stated. But it is nonsense to think that he wished that all Christians were celibate. It just doesn't fit with anything that Paul taught anywhere, and especially not here in First Corinthians.

Earlier Paul urged Christians to "be imitators of" him (1 Corinthians 4:16). In all likelihood, he was referring to this idea. It is more likely that Paul was referring to his commitment to Jesus Christ, to the fact that he had been waylaid by the Holy Spirit on the Road to Damascus, to the fact that he had been born again by the power and presence of the Holy Spirit, and to the fact that his regeneration had actually changed his life. This is what Paul wanted for every Christian. Paul was referring to the gift of regeneration, not celibacy. Paul wanted every Christian to be born again, to enter into a covenantal relationship with Jesus Christ and with the fellowship of saints.

NON-ISSUES

Paul went on to speak about the variety of gifts that are given by the Spirit, which means that he knew that all Christians could not be individually gifted as he was. Not every Christian was called to be an apostle. All he was saying was that he was so committed to Christ that the sins of fornication and adultery were simply non-issues for him. He understood and embraced his covenantal relationship with other believers. And that covenantal relationship protected believers from abuse of every sort from one another. He simply wished that fornication and adultery were non-issues for everyone, that everyone would come to a full understanding of the implications and responsibilities of the covenantal responsibilities they had with one another in Christ.

But he also realized that many—perhaps most—Christians were not as mature as he was in this regard. Paul was well aware that many people are tempted to sexual sin. So, he gave some practical advice.

"To the unmarried and the widows I say that it is good for them to remain single as I am" (v. 8). This verse puts Paul in the same category as the unmarried and the widows. This is the verse that Roman Catholic Priests cite to defend their celibacy because it suggests that Paul was unmarried.

But it equally suggests that Paul was a widower. It was far more common for Jewish Rabbis to be married than unmarried. The Jews have always had large families and strong family values. So, it is more likely that Paul was a widower than that he was simply unmarried.

In fact, Paul had such strong family values that he told those Christian wives who did not have Christian husbands that they should do everything they could to remain married; "the wife should not separate from her husband" (v. 10). Maintenance of the family structure was so important that Christian wives should do all they can to preserve their families. Don't divorce your unbelieving husbands, Paul said. Hang in there!

In addition, Paul said that, should a woman be single, she "should remain unmarried." And should a divorce ensue, the Christian wife should "be reconciled to her husband" (v. 11). Why does Paul not want the Christian divorcee to not remarry? Here Paul holds out the hope that the unbelieving husband will eventually be converted, and that the Christian wife should simply wait for and work for the conversion of and reconciliation to her estranged husband. Again, we see how important the family was to Paul. It is more important than the so-called happiness of the Christian wife—or of the husband, should the roles be reversed. Paul knew that the family is not an obstacle to happiness, but is a true engine of human happiness and fulfillment.

Clearly, for Paul marriage is not centered in sexual expression, but in family life. Paul understood God to have created marriage, not simply to contain the destructive power of illicit sexual relations, but rather, Paul understood God to have created marriage for the sake of healthy and happy families. For Paul the strength and health of the family is more important than sex and more important than the happiness or unhappiness of the individual. He knew that covenantal relationships are the foundation of cultural stability and joy in Christ, foundations that are much greater than mere self-satisfaction. Self expression and individual happiness are to take a backseat with regard to the covenantal relationships in Christ that bring joy, strength, and health to the families of believers.

In reality, Paul understood that family strength and health will serve the true happiness of individuals, sustainable happiness over a lifetime and beyond. Paul believed that when Christians put the desires of God and the needs of the family before their own personal desires, they will work toward a sustainable social structure that will deliver more peace and happiness to more people than could ever be imagined.

16. Called In Place

To the rest I say (I, not the Lord) that if any brother has a wife who is an unbeliever, and she consents to live with him, he should not divorce her. If any woman has a husband who is an unbeliever, and he consents to live with her, she should not divorce him. For the unbelieving husband is made holy because of his wife, and the unbelieving wife is made holy because of her husband. Otherwise your children would be unclean, but as it is, they are holy. But if the unbelieving partner separates, let it be so. In such cases the brother or sister is not enslaved. God has called you to peace. Wife, how do you know whether you will save your husband? Husband, how do you know whether you will save your wife? Only let each person lead the life that the Lord has assigned to him, and to which God has called him. This is my rule in all the churches. Was anyone at the time of his call already circumcised? Let him not seek to remove the marks of circumcision. Was anyone at the time of his call uncircumcised? Let him not seek circumcision. For neither circumcision counts for anything nor uncircumcision, but keeping the commandments of God. Each one should remain in the condition in which he was called. Were you a slave when called? Do not be concerned about it. But if you can gain your freedom, avail yourself of the opportunity. For he who was called in the Lord as a slave is a freedman of the Lord. Likewise he who was free when called is a slave of Christ. You were bought with a price; do not become slaves of men. So, brothers, in whatever condition each was called, there let him remain with God.

— 1 Corinthians 7:12-24

Paul now turns his attention from the marriages of believers to what we call mixed marriages, where one marriage partner is not a believer. This is a special circumstance and calls for special treatment.

When he says, "To the rest I say (I, not the Lord)," in verse 12, he suggests that what he is about to say has not been explicitly said anywhere else in Scripture. He is not demeaning his comment, as if to say that we are free to disregard it if we are so inclined. But rather, he is indicating that the Old Testament does not spell out how a believing spouse should treat an unbelieving spouse. Mixed marriages were simply not allowed in the Old Testa-

126

ment, but had grown in the New Testament era with the expansion of the Kingdom through the explosion of evangelism that gripped the Mediterranean area in the wake of Christ's crucifixion and resurrection—and particularly in the wake of the destruction of Jerusalem in A.D. 70. As the Gospel brought an increasing numbers of Gentiles into Christ's churches, and those Gentile Christians brought the problem of mixed marriages with them. Paul was simply addressing the problem, and noting that biblical scholars would not find reference to mixed marriages in the light of Christ anywhere else in Scripture.

Again, Paul was not saying that his instructions to Christians who found themselves in mixed marriages were optional. Rather, he was simply applying what he knew about Jesus Christ and the grace of the Gospel to this new situation. And by extension, he was showing us how to apply what we know about Scripture, the Gospel, and Jesus Christ to new situations. His application of the light of Christ provides a model for us as we encounter new situations that are not explicitly covered in Scripture. Here we see how the foundational element of God's covenant is to be applied in the light of the grace and mercy of Christ's work on the cross.

Paul went on to say, "if any brother has a wife who is an unbeliever, and she consents to live with him, he should not divorce her" (v. 12). Elsewhere Paul said "Do not be unequally yoked with unbelievers" (2 Corinthians 6:14). This includes the marriage yoke. The reference to a *yoke* suggests an agreement or covenant. In verse 12 Paul was directing his comments at unmarried people. So, if you are not yet married, Paul says not to marry an unbeliever. That is not the ideal situation because the unbeliever cannot recognize or honor their covenant with God, and it is the recognition of our prior covenant with God that provides the foundation for biblical marriage. Without that covenantal foundation, serious difficulties will ensue.

But if you are already married and become a believer and your spouse does not, what then? Paul turned his attention to this situation. And his advice was simple—remain married if your spouse is willing to remain married. The reasons for this are several. First, marriage provides a great picture of our covenantal relationship with God. It provides a building block and a model for covenantal relationships of various kinds. The picture that Scripture paints suggests that God will not divorce Himself from His people even if they willingly try to divorce themselves from Him. God's grace is extended to all, except those who willfully reject it, because

God knows that conversion will eventually come upon everyone who does not willfully reject Jesus Christ. This is not an argument against election, but is rather a goad to make one's calling and election sure. God will hang in there for the long run regardless of what the circumstances look like. And Christians should model God's love, patience, and persistence.

Conversely, sinners should also realize that God's commitment to His covenant means that their rejection of God is not the end of the matter. But rather, God will eternally pursue those who reject and break His covenant with curses and judgments. The rejection of God does not break or end God's covenant. It only confirms the individual as an unredeemed covenant breaker. Only God can break the covenant, but His promise is that He will not do so. God's covenant with humanity is eternal.

So, if the unbelieving spouse is willing to remain married, willing to honor the covenant of marriage with all its privileges and responsibilities—even apart from the realization of God's role in it, then that marriage should remain intact on three counts: 1) in the hope of the eventual conversion of the unbelieving spouse, 2) as a model for covenantal relationships more generally, and 3) as a pillar of strength and hope for the children of the marriage.

Verse 14 raises the issue of sanctification,

> "For the unbelieving husband is made holy (hagiazō—sanctified) because of his wife, and the unbelieving wife is made holy because of her husband. Otherwise your children would be unclean, but as it is, they are holy (hagios)."

Notice that he said that they *are* holy, not that they *will become* holy. Reflecting our baptistic and non-covenantal understanding of Christianity and marriage, we wonder how a believing spouse can be a means of sanctification for an unbelieving spouse—much less for the children of a marriage! This idea of covenantal sanctification is found elsewhere in Scripture. For instance: "For the promise is for you and for your children and for all who are far off, everyone whom the Lord our God calls to himself" (Acts 2:39).

This means that it is not the children of the flesh who are the children of God, but the children of the promise are counted as offspring (Romans 9:8).

"He will declare to you a message by which you will be saved, you and all your household" (Acts 11:14).

"And they said, 'Believe in the Lord Jesus, and you will be saved, you and your household'" (Acts 16:31).

The issue in these verses is about God's authority and the means of salvation. What makes the gospel effective unto salvation? How are people saved? Paul asked it this way to the Galatians,

"Let me ask you only this: Did you receive the Spirit by works of the law or by hearing with faith?" (Galatians 3:2).

"So faith comes from hearing, and hearing through the word of Christ" (Romans 10:17).

Putting them together we see that salvation comes by hearing God's Word.

HEARING

We know that God "chose us (the elect) in him before the foundation of the world" (Ephesians 1:4). We also know that the Holy Spirit is not awakened in God's people until they hear the Master's voice (John 5:25, 10:3, 10:27). So, salvation is a matter of hearing the voice of the Lord, of hearing the gospel correctly preached (read or spoken). If it is not correctly understood by the preacher, it is not likely to be correctly communicated. And if it is not preached in its fullness, in its totality, then it is not God's message and cannot be correctly heard by slumbering saints.

Paul is saying that if either spouse is a Christian, the whole family will at some point have the gospel spoken in their hearing (presented to them). Not all will hear it efficaciously, of course, but at some point in such a family the gospel will be spoken in their hearing. And the speaking of the Word of God is sufficient to awaken God's elect. Thus, a believing husband or wife is a sufficient means for the sanctification—or we could say *evangelization*—of his or her family.

And yet, there is another sense in which the believing spouse will sanctify his or her family. As we have talked about before, salvation is not merely a matter of entering into a personal relationship with Jesus, but is a matter of entering into a covenantal relationship with God, and with His people. Our covenantal relationships are a legal relationships by definition. A covenant is always a legal arrangement.

God's law was violated by Adam at the Fall and restitution was made by Jesus at the cross. Sin is not a matter of metaphysics or of being. It is not some physical, mental, or intellectual lack. Adam lacked nothing physical, mental, or intellectual that kept him from living in obedience to God's Word. Rather, sin is a moral issue. It is a matter of the will and of the spirit, which means that salvation does not impart anything physical, mental, or intellectual that turns an unbeliever into a believer.

Rather, salvation is a matter of the change of one's will, one's heart, one's spirit, from a spirit of willful rebellion against God's Word—God's law, to a spirit of willing obedience. Sin is a matter of being legally defined by God as a criminal because of Adam's sin and our willing complicity in the cause of sin. And salvation is a matter of being legally restored to full citizenship in God's Kingdom by the propitiation of Christ on the cross and our willing complicity in the cause of Christ, which is to bring honor and glory to God and to His Word.

The issue with regard to the legality of the covenant pertains to the legal status of ownership and the authority and comprehensiveness of God's covenant. God's covenant applies to all of life, every thought is to be held captive to Christ (2 Corinthians 10:5), every tongue is to confess and every knee is to bow to Jesus Christ (Romans 14:11).

We have already seen that the husband owns the wife and the wife owns the husband, and both are owned by God. The ownership of each spouse by the other implies that each is subsumed under the legal ownership of the other. God's covenant applies to everything a person owns. Thus, the ownership of the husband by the wife (as Paul notes in this verse) brings the husband under the authority structure of God's covenant. The same applies to the children of the marriage. The issue is not whether the spouse and children recognize that they are under God's covenant. The issue is the efficacy of the covenant, the power of God to apply His covenant to people whether they acknowledge or even recognize it. The issue is God's power and sovereignty.

UNBELIEVING SPOUSE

Paul goes on in verse 15, "But if the unbelieving partner separates, let it be so. In such cases the brother or sister is not enslaved. God has called you to peace." In essence Paul is saying that if the unbelieving partner walks away from a marriage because the other person has become a Christian, then the one who separates is not rejecting the believing spouse, but he or she is rejecting God. The rejecting spouse may argue that the believing spouse has changed since becoming a Christian, that the believing spouse is no longer the same person that he or she married—and we hope that that would be true! Nonetheless, it is a rejection of Christ and Christianity, not a personal rejection of the believing spouse.

Having rejected God, then, the unbelieving spouse who chooses to end the marriage should be allowed to do so. And the believing spouse should be at peace with the situation because it is God's will that unredeemable people not be yoked to believers. Let it be so. God has called believers to be at peace about it.

Verse 16 affirms that we cannot read the hearts of other people. We don't know whether our efforts will contribute to the salvation of a person or not. Salvation belongs to the Lord. So we must be at peace with providence, trusting in the sovereignty and wisdom of God in all things. Verses 17-24 conclude this thought with a general rule that Paul applied to all people in all churches. Because this applies to all Christians in all churches it is important.

> "Only let each person lead the life that the Lord has assigned to him, and to which God has called him. This is my rule in all the churches. Was anyone at the time of his call already circumcised? Let him not seek to remove the marks of circumcision. Was anyone at the time of his call uncircumcised? Let him not seek circumcision. For neither circumcision counts for anything nor uncircumcision, but keeping the commandments of God. Each one should remain in the condition in which he was called. Were you a slave when called? Do not be concerned about it. But if you can gain your freedom, avail yourself of the opportunity. For he who was called in the Lord as a slave is a freedman of the Lord. Likewise he who was free when called is a slave of Christ. You were bought with a price; do not become slaves of men. So, brothers, in whatever condition each was called, there let him remain with God" (1 Corinthians 7:17-24).

There is a contemporary saying that reflects the sense of this idea: *bloom where you are planted.* Becoming a Christian means being an agent and instrument of God in your current circumstance, whatever that circumstance may be. If you are married, be content to remain married unless the other person walks away. If you are not married, be content to remain unmarried unless the Lord leads you into marriage with a believer. If you work in a factory, be content to work in a factory. If you are the president of a bank, be content to be the president of a bank. Wherever you are, whatever you do, whatever your station in life, be content in it, and use your situation to forward the cause of Christ where you are. The first responsibility of believers is to be content to remain where they are and as they are.

Obviously, Christians should not be content to remain in sin. Obviously, we are not to be content to remain biblically ignorant or undisciplined. Rather, Paul is saying that we should remain in our social circumstance, and at the same time begin to avoid sin and to grow in biblical knowledge and discipline. What we are not to do is to use Christianity or other Christians as a means to get something that we want—power, position, wealth, happiness, etc. Christianity is not a matter of us using God to achieve our own purposes. It is a matter of God using us to achieve His purposes.

By remaining in our social position when converted our Christianity will be infused throughout the culture—and that is God's purpose. God doesn't want all faithful Christians to become accountants or politicians or pastors, or to all join the same church. Leaven does its work by spreading throughout the entire loaf. That's the model.

SLAVERY

Slavery provided a particular difficulty, and is defined as a function of debt in Scripture (Proverbs 22:7). So, Paul said that slaves who become Christian should similarly be content to remain as slaves. It is a heart concern. But at the same time, they are to work off (pay back) the debt that they owe, and through debt retirement regain their freedom. They should not run away from their lawful circumstance as slaves, not run away from their indebtedness, but should work diligently to repay their debts, and then live as free men and women, as people without debt.

By implication, Paul tells Christians to remain in whatever employment circumstance they find themselves. From an employment perspective, Paul does not believe that the ideal Christian life involves some church related job. You don't have to become a pastor to serve the Lord. Rather, the ideal is to bring Christian values and principles into whatever job or social position you already have. The ideal is not to concentrate Christian values and principles in the church, but to disburse them into society as leaven.

This is the rule that Paul has for all churches everywhere. Become a Christian, and then because your are a Christian be content to be in whatever circumstance you find yourself. It is out of that sense of contentment and peace that the Holy Spirit reaches out with the Word of

God spoken by you, by ordinary Christians in ordinary circumstances, to evangelize, convert, and reform the whole of society in the likeness of Jesus Christ. The Kingdom of God is not brought in by revolutionaries, but by people in ordinary circumstances who are content to remain in ordinary circumstances, and to speak the truth in love in the midst of their ordinary relationships. May the Lord so bless and empower all Christians in this regard.

17. Persecution Preparation

Now concerning the betrothed, I have no command from the Lord, but I give my judgment as one who by the Lord's mercy is trustworthy. I think that in view of the present distress it is good for a person to remain as he is. Are you bound to a wife? Do not seek to be free. Are you free from a wife? Do not seek a wife. But if you do marry, you have not sinned, and if a betrothed woman marries, she has not sinned. Yet those who marry will have worldly troubles, and I would spare you that. This is what I mean, brothers: the appointed time has grown very short. From now on, let those who have wives live as though they had none, and those who mourn as though they were not mourning, and those who rejoice as though they were not rejoicing, and those who buy as though they had no goods, and those who deal with the world as though they had no dealings with it. For the present form of this world is passing away. I want you to be free from anxieties. The unmarried man is anxious about the things of the Lord, how to please the Lord. But the married man is anxious about worldly things, how to please his wife, and his interests are divided. And the unmarried or betrothed woman is anxious about the things of the Lord, how to be holy in body and spirit. But the married woman is anxious about worldly things, how to please her husband. I say this for your own benefit, not to lay any restraint upon you, but to promote good order and to secure your undivided devotion to the Lord. If anyone thinks that he is not behaving properly toward his betrothed, if his passions are strong, and it has to be, let him do as he wishes: let them marry—it is no sin. But whoever is firmly established in his heart, being under no necessity but having his desire under control, and has determined this in his heart, to keep her as his betrothed, he will do well. So then he who marries his betrothed does well, and he who refrains from marriage will do even better. A wife is bound to her husband as long as he lives. But if her husband dies, she is free to be married to whom she wishes, only in the Lord. Yet in

my judgment she is happier if she remains as she is. And I think that I
too have the Spirit of God.   — 1 Corinthians 7:25-40

The sense of verse 25 is the same as that of verse 12, in that Paul
was not suggesting that people are free to disregard his advice,
but rather that he is speaking about things that have not been
covered in Scripture before. He was applying a principle to another new
circumstance.

The first concern here is to discover who Paul was talking *to* and
who he was talking *about*. The ESV translates the Greek word *parthenos* as
betrothed. The ESV varies from the well-established translation as *virgins*,
and I see no good reason to translate the word as anything other than *virgins*.

But we also need to remember that the word *virgins* in Paul's day
simply indicated unmarried females living in their father's home, women
living under their father's family covenant. Paul, no doubt writing a letter
to be read to a gathering of men, was simply turning his attention from
the special case of mixed marriages to the general case of potential marriages—young girls. It was as if Paul said, "Gentlemen, let us now consider your unmarried daughters." No doubt, some of these daughters
were engaged to be married, others may have been involved in the various stages of the marital partner selection process. In those days the mate
paring process was begun very early in the lives of children, in contrast to
common practices today. All young women and their families would
have been very interested in and concerned about their future roles as
wives, mothers, and homemakers.

Again, Paul reminded his audience that they would not find similar
instructions anywhere else in Scripture because he was in the process of
applying what he knew about Scripture, and about Christ's role as Messiah, to their present circumstances. Previously he had dealt with the new
circumstance of mixed marriages. Here Paul was addressing another unusual circumstance that first century Christians had been thrown into.
That circumstance was not only the gospel explosion that was growing in
the wake of persecution, but the fact of persecution itself.

Verse 26 mentions a "present necessity" (ESV) or "present distress"
(KJV). He was not talking about life as it normally unfolds, nor about ordinary circumstances involved in raising a family, but the extraordinary
or special circumstances that surrounded the impending destruction of
Jerusalem in A.D. 70. Consequently, what he had to say to and about un-

married girls during that time of struggle and increasing persecution of the church—of Christians—does not have the same application to Christians living during ordinary times, more peaceful times. He would go on to say that there would be great difficulty establishing a home and rearing a family during the period of great social upheaval and widespread persecution against Christians that was underway at the time.

He was also saying that the Christian faith is more important than family values. Ideally they work together, but when they don't, Christian faith trumps family values. Prior to A.D. 70 Christians needed to be light on their feet, ready at a moment's notice to run and to hide from those who threaten them with death. And having a family—babies and children in tow—would add to the stress and difficulties that would be involved. The same advice would apply to the Jews in Germany during the Nazi persecutions. It just wasn't a good time to try to establish a new Jewish family in Germany at that particular time in history.

Following his rule for all people in all churches (v. 17), he recommended that people—daughters—remain in whatever state they were in. They should not draw attention to themselves by engaging in the legalities and/or public celebrations of marriage. They should avoid garnering public attention to themselves.

At the same time, Paul was well-aware that the complete avoidance of marriage was neither possible nor necessary. "But if you do marry, you have not sinned, and if a betrothed woman marries, she has not sinned" (v. 28). He was not saying that it would be a sin to marry during such a time. Only that marriage would be difficult, more difficult than usual because of the growing persecution. Verse 28 goes on to say, "Yet those who marry will have worldly troubles, and I would spare you that."

WORLDLY TROUBLES

Exactly what kind of troubles did Paul mean? A more literal translation renders the phrase "trouble in the flesh" (LITV). The Greek word is *sarx* and refers to the meaty covering of the human skeleton.

There are two biblical purposes for marriage: 1) companionship, and 2) progeny—children. Paul was referring to children. He said that during the time of persecution, children would be an additional burden for Christian families. During times of persecution Christians would need to move quickly, run fast, and hide quietly—and children would add to the difficulties of doing these things. Paul was not speaking about sex, except that children are the natural product of sexual relations. He was not speaking about the experience of sex, but about the product—children.

Paul was aware that this recommendation would be both difficult to understand and difficult to accomplish. He went on, "This is what I mean, brothers: the appointed time has grown very short" (v. 29).

What appointed time? The Greek word is *kairos*, which literally means the "right or opportune moment." The ancient Greeks had two words for time, *chronos* and *kairos*. The former refers to chronological or sequential time—ordinary time, but the latter signifies "a time in between," a moment of undetermined duration in which something special happens. It refers to a period of time in which several dynamic events come to fruition to produce a particularly meaningful historical or personal event. The birth of Christ, for instance, was such a *kairos* moment in history.

In this case Paul was referring to the impending destruction of Jerusalem. He was aware of the winds of war—the political rhetoric, the growing persecution, and the movement of troops. It was in light of these things that Paul spoke to these new Christians, and to the fathers of young girls and their impending "prospects," to use a word from a former age. The winds of change were about to sweep the establishment of Judaism from the stage of history. War was immanent, Roman soldiers were gathering outside Jerusalem. Paul went on, "From now on, let those who have wives live as though they had none" (v. 29).

NON-ENGAGEMENT

What in the world does this mean? Were husbands to ignore their wives? To walk out of their marriages? Not at all, that's *not* what Paul meant. But there is a sense in which Paul was recommending that husbands sexually ignore their wives. Paul was trying to say as delicately as possible that the next few years or decades would not be a good time to have children. So, if you are married, if you have a wife, behave in this regard as if you do not. But that was not all. Paul continued,

> "and those who mourn as though they were not mourning, and those
> who rejoice as though they were not rejoicing, and those who buy as
> though they had no goods, and those who deal with the world as
> though they had no dealings with it" (vs. 30-31).

Here Paul went on to say that newly converted Christians needed to make a small public footprint. They needed to avoid public events wherein they would be identified as Christians—funerals (avoid mourning), parties (avoid rejoicing) and other public gatherings or meetings.

The MKJB better translates Paul's advice about buying, "And they who buy are as though they did not possess" (v. 30). Persecuted Christians should not try to preserve their possessions when it came time to run. They should not worry about the things they owned, because at a certain point they would be lucky to escape with their lives. And the same perspective must be applied to all of their dealings with the world; "and those who deal with the world as though they had no dealings with it" (v. 31).

Why was Paul so concerned? "For the present form of this world is passing away" (v. 31). What did he mean by "the present form of this world?" While the KJV translated the word as *fashion* (*schēma*), it would be a mistake to think that Paul was now talking about clothing styles or popular trends. He was talking about the scheme, the cultural order of the then current period of Jewish history, the temple administration. It was the same thing that Hebrews was talking about in—the closing of the Hebrew era and the opening of the Christian era. He was talking about the difference between the Old Testament and the New Testament. He was talking about the reason that the calendar would start over (at zero) at the birth of Jesus. Everything they knew would change in the light of Jesus Christ. The social and political system of temple sacrifices would soon be gone, swept from the stage of history by the hammer of the Roman army by the hand of God. That was the present form of the world that was passing away. And it was passing away in the midst of turmoil and persecution. He was telling young Jewish families that if they clung to the past, to their traditions, to their property, their stuff, they would be swept away too. He essentially said, "when the time comes, drop everything and leave Jerusalem."

And yet, in spite of the impending turmoil and persecution, Paul wanted them "to be free from anxieties" (v. 32). Jesus taught the same thing,

> "Therefore I tell you, do not be anxious about your life, what you will eat or what you will drink, nor about your body, what you will put on. Is not life more than food, and the body more than clothing?" (Matthew 6:25).

> "Peace I leave with you; my peace I give to you. Not as the world gives do I give to you. Let not your hearts be troubled, neither let them be afraid" (John 14:27).

AVOIDANCE

Paul went on to talk about how married people tend to be concerned about pleasing one another, and that unmarried people should be concerned about how to please the Lord, about holiness. Clearly, that particular period of history has passed away. His argument is a bit labored because he was trying to make a recommendation against worldly entanglements during the period of persecution prior to the fall of Jerusalem. But at the same time he wanted to make it clear that entering into such entanglements was not to be considered sinful. No one argued more clearly or vociferously than Paul that God would finish what he had begun with their callings and conversions to Christianity, and that God would provide for and protect His people in the midst of this fallen and sinful world.

His message in this section is actually pretty simple: avoid worldly entanglements regarding marriage, children, and business as much as you can. This will help to prepare you for the impending persecution. But don't go overboard by jumping into some hyper-survivalist way of life. Don't hoard weapons and food. Don't go off into the desert to live. Don't be afraid to marry and have children and do business. Just be aware that at some point in the near future, God may well separate you from everything you currently know and have. So, be ready to go with the flow, the Spirit.

In verse 35 Paul said that his purpose for having this little talk was not "to lay any restraint" upon them. He was not binding their freedom in Christ. Rather, his purpose was "to secure your undivided devotion to the Lord." He urged them all to be like unmarried couples in their devotion to God and to holiness, to purity of life and thought. They were not to abandon the ordinary practices of marriage and family life. But neither were they to abandon the practice of holiness,, and devotion. They were to bring the practice of holiness into their marriages, and not get distracted from God by their service to one another.

At the same time, Paul said in verse 36, if you get caught up in passion (sex) with your wife, don't worry. Don't be anxious about it. It's not a sin. Paul goes back and forth between these two perspectives in these verses.

In verse 37 he comes back to the theme of continence in marriage. The idea of being "firmly established in his heart" means to be steady and well-grounded, not to be dominated by one's feelings, but to demonstrate

equanimity in the face of temptation. He counseled them not to act under
"necessity," not to be driven by perceived needs, not to be emotionally
needy, but to have their "desire under control," not to be driven by desire.
To have "determined this in his heart" means to have made a commitment to do or not to do a particular thing, to have the matter settled in
one's own mind, and to be firm about it.

To have decided what? To be firm about what? "To keep her as his
betrothed" (v. 37). To behave as if they were not yet married. To abstain
from sexual contact. According to Paul, anyone who could do this, who
could make this commitment and stick with it would "do well." It was a
preferable course of action in the face of the impending persecution that
was about to be released upon the Christian community.

So, Paul concluded in verse 38, those who heed what I have said will
do well to marry. So, don't be afraid to marry. And don't worry if you
have children. God will look after you. But the better course of action is
not to give your daughters to be married at all. Paul was hearkening back
to Luke 21:20-24, where Jesus said,

> "But when you see Jerusalem surrounded by armies, then know that its
> desolation has come near. Then let those who are in Judea flee to the
> mountains, and let those who are inside the city depart, and let not
> those who are out in the country enter it, for these are days of
> vengeance, to fulfill all that is written. Alas for women who are preg-
> nant and for those who are nursing infants in those days! For there will
> be great distress upon the earth and wrath against this people. They will
> fall by the edge of the sword and be led captive among all nations, and
> Jerusalem will be trampled underfoot by the Gentiles, until the times of
> the Gentiles are fulfilled."

Paul was simply being faithful to the teaching of his Lord. So, if you
take anything away with you from this chapter, see the context of these
verses and understand that Paul was not arguing for perpetual Christian
celibacy. He was not arguing that the single lifestyle was preferable to
marriage—not at all. He was simply telling the gathered fathers that when
God's hammer fell on Jerusalem in the coming years, pregnant and nursing mothers would fare poorly. It was not a new teaching, but simply reflected the teaching of Jesus about the impending end of Jerusalem.

Paul wrapped up this talk to fathers of young women with two comments. First, he said that he believed that the young women would be
happier, that they would have a better life, if they remained single, at least

until the winds of change settled down. Second, he told them that he believed that this advice was given by the authority of the Spirit of God. That is, he believed himself to have been inspired.

There are two elements of his inspiration. One pertained to the instructions he gave to young families. The other pertained to the impending destruction of Jerusalem. Jesus had predicted it, and Paul said that it was imminent, that it would be upon them within that particular generation.

And it was. Paul wrote this letter to the Corinthians while he was in Ephesus during his third missionary journey, about 55 A.D. Jerusalem was destroyed in 70 A.D.

18. GILDING THE LILLY

Now concerning food offered to idols: we know that "all of us possess knowl-
edge." This "knowledge" puffs up, but love builds up. If anyone imagines that he
knows something, he does not yet know as he ought to know. But if anyone
loves God, he is known by God. Therefore, as to the eating of food offered to
idols, we know that "an idol has no real existence," and that "there is no God
but one." For although there may be so-called gods in heaven or on earth—as
indeed there are many "gods" and many "lords"— yet for us there is one God,
the Father, from whom are all things and for whom we exist, and one Lord, Je-
sus Christ, through whom are all things and through whom we exist.

— 1 Corinthians 8:1-6

Paul now turned his attention from the concerns of marriage and families to worship. "But concerning the sacrifices to idols, we know that we all have 'knowledge'" (v. 1). The context, "sacrifices to idols," involves holiday meals that were consecrated by false gods and celebrated by most everyone in the community. These religious and social events provided all the usual friendship, fellowship, and family time together that was then, and is still, enjoyed by people all over the world. Who can argue against the values and virtues of friendship, fellowship, and family?

Yet, new Christians in Corinth began to worry that the consecration of the food at such events, by what they now understood in the light of Christ to be false gods, might be offensive or counterproductive to their new faith in Christ. It's a real concern because all genuine converts gain a new sensitivity about offending Christ and a genuine concern for growing in grace and sanctification. Understandably, people don't want to put stumbling blocks in their own way.

They began asking if it was okay to join in such celebrations because they all had friends and family members who would host such events and invited them to attend. No doubt, they had been attending such events for years prior to their conversion, so their sudden absence would be a concern to those friends and family members who expected them to attend. That is the context of this chapter. They were concerned that such events constituted false worship or worship of false gods. In any case it is important to see that worship was the central concern.

The first thing that Paul addressed was knowledge (*gnōsis*). No doubt, all the various religious sects and their many philosophies taught some form of knowledge as the first step toward God. We know that the various Gnostics placed such importance upon special or secret knowledge. They taught that worshiping or understanding God required some special knowledge, and apart from that knowledge people were ignorant of things divine.

Note that Paul was still working on his very first consideration regarding the Corinthian:

> "For Christ did not send me to baptize but to preach the gospel, and not
> with words of eloquent wisdom, lest the cross of Christ be emptied of
> its power. For the word of the cross is folly to those who are perishing,
> but to us who are being saved it is the power of God" (1 Corinthians
> 1:17-18).

Though the words *knowledge* and *wisdom* are different, Paul was still talking about the same subject—the deceit of worldly wisdom, knowledge or Greek categories of thought.

OPPOSING KINDS

Paul has been trying to demonstrate that there are two distinct and opposing kinds of knowledge or wisdom. The ESV translates the verse well, "If anyone imagines that he knows something, he does not yet know as he ought to know" (v. 2). Other translations use the word *think* —"If anyone thinks that he knows something." Matthew Henry makes the point that Paul was arguing against those whose knowledge had been gained by experience. Those who had practiced divine *gnōsis* believed that they were in a superior position because they relied upon their own personal understanding. They were probably arguing that Paul didn't know what he was talking about because he was not a practitioner of *gnōsis*. So, how could he know about something with which he had no experience? It is a familiar argument.

Kent Hovind deals with it well when he considers a similar argument that is used to justify the use of drugs and alcohol. He says that it is not necessary to get run over by a truck in order to know that getting run over by a truck is not a good thing. It is a simple argument, and points to the false understanding that personal experience is required for knowledge to be true. Personal experience might enhance one's knowledge, and then again it just might skew genuine knowledge because personal experience is dependent upon one's own subjectivity. Again, subjectivity is not a problem unless it is confused with objectivity, which is a common problem.

A good example of this kind of confusion is found in the saying, "love is blind." The subjectivity, hope, and pleasure of romantic involvement changes the way we see things. Of course the saying refers to romantic attachment and not to godly love. For we know that God is love and that God is not blind. Nonetheless, those who find themselves romantically attached to a person (or thing) often justify their attachment in some amazingly creative ways. Dennis Peacocke says it this way, "the mind justifies what the heart chooses." People can justify anything because the mind naturally conforms itself to the desires of the heart.

Paul said that people who get imagination and knowledge confused don't know a thing as they ought. He suggested that there is a proper or better kind of knowledge than knowledge based on experience.

This preferred knowledge is based upon Christ, upon Scripture. And it is better because it is not based on or dependent on our own limited subjectivity. It is not based upon our own desires. Rather, biblical knowledge is based on the knowledge of God and interpreted or understood through the eyes of faithful Christians over thousands of years in many different cultural contexts. Biblical knowledge is as close as we human beings can come to absolute objectivity. This is the knowledge that all people ought to know. The word *ought* implies something that is morally superior. Paul was suggesting that biblical knowledge is superior knowledge, superior to personal experience and understanding.

ETHICS VS. MORALITY

The other night my brother, David, was talking about the difference between ethics and morality. He recently heard someone argue that the difference between them is that the ethical person knows what not to do, but the moral person simply refuses to do it. The implication is that there is a difference between knowledge in terms of abstract classification, and knowledge in terms of practical application. The ethical person, while knowing what he should or should not do, nonetheless often goes to great lengths to find ways to justify such action or to bend the rules legally. The moral person, on the other hand, will accept the fact that the action should or should not be done and will work to do it or to avoid doing it. He knows as he ought to know and avoids what he ought to avoid and does what he ought to do.

The ethical person has abstract knowledge about what is right and wrong, and has an intellectual understanding. His thinking is affected by his moral values. His morality determines the way in which he thinks about a thing. Whereas the moral person has concrete or visceral knowledge about what is right and wrong, and has a behavioral understanding. His behavior is affected by his morality. His morality determines the way in which he behaves toward a thing. One modifies thought, the other modifies behavior.

Paul said that knowledge puffs a person up. It inflates the ego. It makes people feel smart, even superior—which makes people want to tell others about what they know. For instance, if I can tell you something you don't know, something new, then I can feel superior to you. It strokes the ego to be a dispenser of knowledge. This is the dynamic that drives gossip. Gossip often masquerades as news. So, when we pass "news" about this or that person along, we often do so because it reinforces our sense of superiority. Those who pass the "news" on are in the superior position. News too often flies on the wings of pride.

In contrast to this, Paul tells us that love (*agapē*) builds up, love—charity—*edifies*. The Greek is *oikodomeō*, which literally means to be a house builder. Love is constructive. *Edify* does not mean what many Christians think it means. Many people think that Christian edification means spiritual or emotional encouragement, being nice, kind, supportive. The popular Christian radio station, K-love, understands itself to be involved in a ministry of edification. And, though I like some of the music they play, their format is sentimentalism in the name of Christian edification. It's goal is to make people feel good, not to impart biblical truth. They think that they are edifying by being positive, by making people feel good about themselves.

But biblical edification is not always positive, nor does the word mean to encourage. It can sometimes suggest encouragement, but the central meaning of the word is not encourage, but *instruct*. The word *edify* is from a Latin root that means to instruct or improve spiritually. One dictionary defines *edify* as to "make understand." So, edification is not merely encouragement. It is spiritual instruction—discipline—that perseveres in spiritual improvement and understanding. Edification is the effort to make people understand something correctly. Growth in grace and sanctification is not a magic pill. It requires discipline and effort.

Paul describes his own sanctification with racing language.

> "Do you not know that in a race all the runners compete, but only one receives the prize? So run that you may obtain it. Every athlete exercises self-control in all things. They do it to receive a perishable wreath, but we an imperishable. So I do not run aimlessly; I do not box as one beating the air. But I discipline my body and keep it under control, lest after preaching to others I myself should be disqualified" (1 Corinthians 9:24-27).

Paul turned our common understanding of love on its head in verse 8, "But if anyone loves God, he is known by God." It is not that we must understand God before we can love Him, but that our love for God is dependent upon His knowledge of us. John said it this way, "We love because he first loved us" (1 John 4:19). Our love of God is a response to God's love for us. It is dependent upon God's love for us. Our love of God is a reflected image of God's love for us. God's love for us is not sentimental. It is real. It is covenantal. It is not based upon God's feelings for us, but upon God's commitment to His own mercy, truth, and righteousness—His covenant.

Because God's love for His people is not based upon His feelings, but upon His covenant commitment, our love for God must not be based upon our feelings, but upon our covenant commitment, as well. And here is true love, true worship. True love of God—covenantal love—leads to worship, manifests in worship.

Of course, worship includes what happens when Christians gather on Sunday mornings, but it is much more than that. Genuine worship of God is the activity of covenant faithfulness every day. To worship God is to respond to God's covenant faithfulness, it is to reflect God's covenant faithfulness back to Him through covenant faithfulness of our own. To worship God is to grow in grace and sanctification, to grow in our knowledge of God, to grow in our faithful obedience to God, to grow in Christian responsibility and maturity.

HAPPY HOLIDAYS

"Therefore," Paul begins verse 4, concluding what has preceded. The first three verses of chapter eight establish the ground or basis of what follows. Because our love of God is based upon our mutual covenantal faithfulness, God's covenantal faithfulness toward us and our covenantal faithfulness toward God, a faithfulness that impacts everything that we say and do as Christians, then that covenantal faithfulness must also guide our approach and behavior with regard to the holiday festivities previously mentioned.

The Corinthians had been invited to attend certain holiday festivities where the food served had been blessed or consecrated to other gods. It had been "offered to idols" (v. 4). Should faithful Christians eat such food and participate in such events or not?

Paul responded by reminding the Corinthians that the idols in question were not real. They were not gods at all. They were false gods, illusions of the mind, imaginary. Thus, they had no real power or effect in the world. They were nothing. The God of Scripture is the only real God.

Verses 5 & 6 are understood to be parenthetical explanations of how it is that the world proclaims that there are many Gods, whereas Scripture proclaims that there is only one God who is Trinitarian. Verse 5 tells us two important things. First, that the many gods of the Greek and Roman pantheons are merely "so-called gods." They are gods only in name, but not in function or power. And secondly, that of these so-called gods "there are many ... and many 'lords.'" Many people are involved in the authority structures of these so-called gods. But in spite of all of this, Christians know that there is only one true God. Those who worship other gods are mistaken.

When Paul said,

> "yet for us there is one God, the Father, from whom are all things and for whom we exist, and one Lord, Jesus Christ, through whom are all things and through whom we exist" (v. 6),

he did not mean that there is one God for Christians and many gods for other people. He did not mean that it was true for Christians to believe in one God and that it was true for others to believe in many gods. He was not speaking relatively. He meant that for those who understand the truth —Christians—there is only one God, the God of Scripture.

NOT OUR OWN

The remainder of Paul's sentence tells us that we exist for God, for God's purposes and not our own. And that we exist through God, through Jesus Christ. He equates God and Jesus Christ and says that they are one. And that our own lives have been created by God and for God. We are not our own. In chapter six Paul said,

> "do you not know that your body is a temple of the Holy Spirit within you, whom you have from God? You are not your own, for you were bought with a price. So glorify God in your body" (1 Corinthians 6:19-20).

We belong to God, and God does with us whatever He desires (Romans 9:18).

Christians are not free in the sense that they can do whatever they want. Christians are free to want what God wants for them. We are free to be what God has created us to be. We are free to do what God wants us to do. We are not our own, but are owned by Another.

We cannot improve upon God's creation. At best we can be what God has called us to be in Christ. And through Christ we can work to overcome sin, but only as we participate in God's redemption plan. We cannot improve upon God's redemption.

All of this is to say that we must be who God has called us to be, do what God has called us to do, and worship as God has called us to worship. To do more or less is a function of faithlessness.

> "The Lord will open to you his good treasury, the heavens, to give the rain to your land in its season and to bless all the work of your hands. And you shall lend to many nations, but you shall not borrow. And the Lord will make you the head and not the tail, and you shall only go up and not down, if you obey the commandments of the Lord your God, which I command you today, being careful to do them, and if you do not turn aside from any of the words that I command you today, to the right hand or to the left, to go after other gods to serve them" (Deuteronomy 28:12-14).

19. More Guilding

However, not all possess this knowledge. But some, through former association with idols, eat food as really offered to an idol, and their conscience, being weak, is defiled. Food will not commend us to God. We are no worse off if we do not eat, and no better off if we do. But take care that this right of yours does not somehow become a stumbling block to the weak. For if anyone sees you who have knowledge eating in an idol's temple, will he not be encouraged, if his conscience is weak, to eat food offered to idols? And so by your knowledge this weak person is destroyed, the brother for whom Christ died. Thus, sinning against your brothers and wounding their conscience when it is weak, you sin against Christ. Therefore, if food makes my brother stumble, I will never eat meat, lest I make my brother stumble. — 1 Corinthians 8:7-13

The first six verses of chapter eight reminded the Corinthian Christians that the knowledge they had was a consequence of their regeneration. Our knowledge of God is a reflection of His knowledge of us. Remember that God's knowledge of us and God's love for us are not separate things. God loves us truly because He knows us truly, and God knows us truly because He loves us truly.

Yet, from the beginning Paul points out that, though we all have knowledge of some kind, we all do not know as we ought to know. We identified this concern as the continuation of the major theme of First Corinthians—the wisdom of the world versus the wisdom of Christ. We have further identified this theme as the difference between Greek thinking, which is dualistic, and biblical thinking, which is Trinitarian. Greek thinking is always necessarily humanistic because it cannot comprehend the true character of reality because it cannot see reality from God's perspective, the Trinitarian perspective. Greek thought exists in a kind of dualistic world that can only comprehend two dimensions, where reality is more three dimensional—Trinitarian. It is the reality of regeneration that brings the perspective of the Holy Spirit—of the Trinity—to the minds of believers and opens their eyes to God's reality and truth.

In verse 7 Paul said that "not all possess this knowledge," reminding the Corinthians that believers are fundamentally different than nonbelievers. Believers are different than nonbelievers because Christian faith is real. This reality, this difference is completely unbelievable and unacceptable to the unregenerate. The Trinitarian reality is only available to those who are inhabited by the Holy Spirit. "If anyone has ears to hear, let him hear" (Mark 4:23). "Truly, truly, I say to you," said Jesus, "unless one is born again he cannot see the kingdom of God" (John 3:3). This is true because it is not the flesh that sees or understands the things of God, it is the Holy Spirit.

> "He came to his own, and his own people did not receive him. But to all who did receive him, who believed in his name, he gave the right to become children of God, who were born, not of blood nor of the will of the flesh nor of the will of man, but of God" (John 1:11-13).

It is the Holy Spirit who inhabits born again believers, who sees the reality of the Trinitarian God of Scripture, not the eyes of the unredeemed flesh.

Thus, Paul wrote,

> "However, not all possess this knowledge. But some, through former association with idols, eat food as really offered to an idol, and their conscience, being weak, is defiled" (v. 7).

Some of the Corinthian Christians who had formerly been associated with false beliefs and false gods (idols) falsely believed that there was some reality associated with the sacrifices and worship activities related to their former religious beliefs, like the consecration of food and holiday (holy day) celebrations. Though they now associated themselves with Jesus Christ, they had not made a clean break with their former beliefs. They brought many of those former beliefs—false beliefs and the false worldview of Greek philosophy—into the Corinthian church.

Weak Conscience

Consequently, Paul described them as having weak consciences. It is not insignificant that those who had been captured by the categories of Greek thinking were described as having weak consciences, of being morally weak. It is common knowledge that both Greek and Roman societies had little regard for what we understand as biblical morality. The fact that biblical morality was a non-issue to the Romans and Greeks can be seen in Paul's lists of behaviors and character traits that would not be found in the kingdom of God.

> "Do you not know that the unrighteous will not inherit the kingdom of God? Do not be deceived: neither the sexually immoral, nor idolaters, nor adulterers, nor men who practice homosexuality, nor thieves, nor the greedy, nor drunkards, nor revilers, nor swindlers will inherit the kingdom of God. And such were some of you. But you were washed, you were sanctified, you were justified in the name of the Lord Jesus Christ and by the Spirit of our God" (1 Corinthians 6:9-11).

The Corinthians knew about the immorality of the Greeks and Romans because many of them were themselves Greeks and Romans. And it was precisely this mindset that was to be abandoned in Christ. This was the mindset that Paul described as morally weak and defiled. It was unrighteous, impure, immoral, degenerate, worldly, fleshly, limited, flawed, faulty, and wrong. And Paul told them so every chance he could get. "Not all possess this knowledge" (v. 7), he said. And he meant two things by it: 1) not all people possessed orthodox knowledge of God and Christ, and 2) not all Christians possessed it either. The whole problem in Corinth was that well-meaning Christians had brought their Greek thinking and Roman habits into the Corinthian church with them. This was the problem he was trying to correct.

"Food will not commend us to God. We are no worse off if we do not eat, and no better off if we do" (v. 8). In Acts 10-11 Peter had an encounter with the risen Christ that clarified and adjusted the ancient Jewish food laws that had established some foods as clean and some as unclean. In Acts, the Spirit instructed Peter that no foods were to be considered to be religiously unclean in Christ. Food is important, but it has no religious significance. So, Paul told the Corinthians that the consecration of food to a false god meant nothing. It was a non-issue or an imaginary issue that had nothing to do with reality.

MORAL ISSUE

However, there was an important moral issue related to the situation. But it wasn't about the food or the dedication of the food to false gods. It was about sanctification and growth in Christ. "But," said Paul, "take care that this right of yours does not somehow become a stumbling block to the weak." (v. 9).

Paul was talking about the right to ignore everything about idols and false worship. The right to participate in Christ's freedom, the right to participate in the holidays and festivals of false gods (the popular culture of the day) because those gods had no real power.

Paul would later tell the Corinthians, "But when one turns to the Lord, the veil is removed. Now the Lord is the Spirit, and where the Spirit of the Lord is, there is freedom" (2 Corinthians 3:16-17). One of the freedoms granted in Christ was freedom from the Old Testament food laws. The risen Christ instructed Peter, "What God has made clean, do not call common" (Acts 11:9). Later Paul would write to the Romans,

> "Do not, for the sake of food, destroy the work of God. Everything is
> indeed clean, but it is wrong for anyone to make another stumble by
> what he eats" (Romans 14:20).

In Christ we are free indeed. Yet, our freedom is not a license to confuse those who are not as mature in the faith as we are. Our individual freedom in Christ is bound by our love of and service to the body of Christ. We are free from our bondage to sin in order to become willing servants—slaves—to Christ, and through Christ, to His people, the church, the body of Christ. The mature in Christ are obligated and bound to assist in the sanctification of the immature in Christ, and at the very least, not to become stumbling blocks to them.

To the mature, Paul said,

> "Food will not commend us to God. We are no worse off if we do not
> eat, and no better off if we do. But take care that this right of yours does
> not somehow become a stumbling block to the weak." (v. 8).

There are no moral or spiritual consequences related to the consumption of food. The point is that the rights of some can lead others astray because the less mature do not discern their own weaknesses. Immature Christians often overestimate their own spiritual development. The ESV translates the Greek word, *exousia*, as *rights*, whereas the word also means authority, jurisdiction, liberty, power, and strength. *Exousia* is a freedom, an ability, an authority, a power. And it can be abused. The freedom of one person can become a means of sin and abuse to another.

The strong in Christ, the mature in Christ are not to live for themselves, not to overlook the special concerns of their weaker brothers and sisters. Rather, they are to protect and nurture them in Christ. The weaker brothers and sisters in Christ are just that—weak. The Greek is *astheneō*. "In all things," said Paul,

> "I have shown you that by working hard in this way we must help the weak and remember the words of the Lord Jesus, how he himself said, 'It is more blessed to give than to receive'" (Acts 20:35).

To the Romans Paul wrote,

> "Do not, for the sake of food, destroy the work of God. Everything is indeed clean, but it is wrong for anyone to make another stumble by what he eats. It is good not to eat meat or drink wine or do anything that causes your brother to stumble" (Romans 14:20).

> "The faith that you have, keep between yourself and God. Blessed is the one who has no reason to pass judgment on himself for what he approves. But whoever has doubts is condemned if he eats, because the eating is not from faith. For whatever does not proceed from faith is sin" (Romans 14:20-23).

It is not simply that insensitive and undiscerning freedom in Christ can offend those who are weak, those who are immature in Christ, but note that the prideful exercise of freedom in Christ can cause other Christians to become even weaker, even more immature, and fall into sin. We can better understand this through the analogy of alcoholism.

ALCOHOL

Alcohol is food. We consume it. And it is clean. It is not forbidden. It is even a blessing and a joy in Christ. However, it can be abused. We are free to consume it, but we must be cautious not to abuse it. In addition, we must take special care not to use it in such a way that it becomes a stumbling block to others.

Recovering alcoholics are not free to consume alcohol. They must avoid it because they have established habits of abuse. Their habit is to abuse it. So, to use it at all is to set the old habit into motion. Their weakness is their lack of control of that old habit.

Similarly recovering pagans had established patterns of beliefs and behaviors that were destructive to themselves and to the kingdom of God. Many, perhaps most of the Corinthian Christians were recovering pagans. Their weakness was the strength and tenacity of their old habits, their old patterns of belief and behavior. Like recovering alcoholics, recovering pagans found it difficult to engage their old habits without falling prey to them.

So, the problem was that if such a recovering pagan, a new Christian, saw some other respected Christian participating in pagan rituals and holiday celebrations, he might be tempted to participate as well, to engage in his old habits, his pagan worldview, before he has matured to the point that he could control those habits. He could easily get caught up in his old habits and ways of thinking, often without realizing it until it was too late. The truth is that we can all slip back into our own old habits of sin and immaturity all to easily. We are all creatures of habit and habits are hard to change.

While it is true that false gods have no power, idolatry and false belief are very strong human habits that have very deep roots in the human psyche. The false gods themselves have no real existence or power, but the habits of false belief and the behaviors they engender are very alluring and destructive. While alcohol consumption is not always a sin, a life of excessive drinking is deadly. It will interfere with and obstruct one's sanctification. So, even though it is not always a sin, said Paul, avoid it for the sake of your weaker brother. Don't let your knowledge of the truth, or your strength to not succumb to old habits become the undoing of others. "And so by your knowledge this weak person is destroyed, the brother for whom Christ died" (v. 11).

Paul makes this point later, "'All things are lawful,' but not all things are helpful. 'All things are lawful,' but not all things build up" (1 Corinthians 10:23). Just because we *can*, doesn't mean that we *should*. So, Paul counseled the Corinthians not to participate in the holiday celebrations or eat the food that had been dedicated to idols, not because it was a sin, nor because it would in any way harm them, but rather for the sake of the sanctification of those who were less mature, less stable in the faith, those who could still be drawn back into their old habits of false belief and destructive behavior.

CLEAN BREAK

The problem was that many Corinthian believers had not made a clean break with their former pagan beliefs and the destructive habits engendered by those false beliefs. So, Paul instructed the mature Corinthians to avoid participation in pagan holiday festivals in order to model the fact that genuine Christian faith was completely different than any former beliefs they may have had.

In his second letter to the Corinthians Paul defended himself and his teaching:

> "We have spoken freely to you, Corinthians; our heart is wide open. You are not restricted by us, but you are restricted in your own affections. In return (I speak as to children) widen your hearts also. Do not be unequally yoked with unbelievers. For what partnership has righteousness with lawlessness? Or what fellowship has light with darkness? What accord has Christ with Belial? Or what portion does a believer share with an unbeliever? What agreement has the temple of God with idols? For we are the temple of the living God; as God said, 'I will make my dwelling among them and walk among them, and I will be their God, and they shall be my people. Therefore go out from their midst, and be separate from them, says the Lord, and touch no unclean thing; then I will welcome you, and I will be a father to you, and you shall be sons and daughters to me, says the Lord Almighty.'" (2 Corinthians 6:11-18).

The Lord desires a clean and complete break with an unbelieving and pagan world, a clean and complete break with false beliefs that engender destructive behaviors. And such a clean break is the preeminent model of faithfulness. A model of faithfulness that does not provide a clean and complete break from false belief and immoral behavior, said Paul, would retard the growth and maturity of weaker Christians, all Christians really because the body of Christ is interdependent. Paul argued later, "if a trumpet gives an uncertain sound, who shall prepare himself for the battle?" (1 Corinthians 14:8).

It was the obligation of those who were mature in Christ to make their lives into Christian trumpets that sounded a clear and certain call to battle, a clear and certain separation from sin and from the temptations of old, godless habits—not the battle of a so-called holy jihad, but the battle call of faithfulness to Christ through obedience to His Word. Christians are not called to violence, death, or destruction, but to love, peace, life, knowledge, wisdom, and maturity.

Are you a Christian? asked Paul. Then act like a Christian!

Of course the Holy Spirit has the power to keep you from being personally affected by the silly cultural practices and beliefs associated with false beliefs and false gods. But God also uses sin to chastise and edify His people, to make them understand the importance of His ways. So, do not test God's power in this matter, or in any other matter. Rather, be who you were called to be. Be faithful. Be the church, the *ekklēsia*, the called out ones, those who really do dance to a different Drummer (Christ).

Don't get caught up in the false culture of false gods, even if you think you can dance that dance without tripping up. Avoid it because some other Christian who looks up to you may not be so light on his feet. Don't let your knowledge, strength, and freedom lead others into sin. In Christ we are free, yet in Christ we are bound by the love of God to the love and care of God's people.

20. QUESTIONS

Am I not an apostle? Am I not free? Have I not seen Jesus Christ our Lord? Are you not my work in the Lord? If I am not an apostle to others, yet doubtless I am to you, for you are the seal of my apostleship in the Lord. My answer to those who examine me is this: Do we not have authority to eat and to drink? Do we not have authority to lead about a sister, a wife, as well as other apostles, and as the brothers of the Lord do, and Cephas? Or is it only Barnabas and I who have no authority whether not to work? Who serves as a soldier at his own wages at any time? Who plants a vineyard and does not eat of its fruit? Or who feeds a flock and does not partake of the milk of the flock? Do I say these things according to man? Or does not the Law say the same also? For it is written in the Law of Moses, "You shall not muzzle an ox threshing grain." Does God take care for oxen? Or does He say it altogether for our sakes? It was written for us, so that he who plows should plow in hope, and so that he who threshes in hope should be partaker of his hope. If we have sown to you spiritual things, is it a great thing if we shall reap your carnal things? If others have a share of this authority over you, rather should not we? But we have not used this authority, but we endured all things lest we should hinder the gospel of Christ. Do you not know that those who minister about holy things live of the things of the temple? And those attending the altar are partakers with the altar. Even so, the Lord ordained those announcing the gospel to live from the gospel. But I have used none of these things, nor have I written these things that it should be done so to me; for it is good for me rather to die than that anyone nullify my glorying. For though I preach the gospel, no glory is to me. For necessity is laid on me; yea, woe is to me if I do not preach the gospel!

— 1 Corinthians 9:1-16

This chapter begins with a series of questions. The original letters in the New Testament were not divided into chapters. Rather, like any letter they just flowed from one thought to the next. By asking questions Paul was, in effect, making statements. The implied answer to each question is *yes.* Paul states: I am free. I am an apostle. I have seen the Lord Jesus. You (the Corinthian church members) are my workmanship in the Lord.[1] And finally, Paul tells them that they are the seal of his apostle-ship in the Lord. A seal is a mark of identity, or proof of authenticity and ownership. They themselves were the confirmation of Paul's authority, apostleship, and the effectiveness of his ministry.

Paul also told them that they themselves were the "defense to those who would examine" (v. 3) him. What examination was he talking about? What defense? What proof? Who was calling for an examination or a proof? Why was Paul on the defensive here? Who was calling his apostle-ship into question? And why?

It helps to keep the larger context of this chapter in mind. Paul was writing to the Corinthians in response to a controversy that had erupted in the church. That was the reason for this letter and his impending visit. A lot of issues were dealt with in this letter, and yet the context of the let-ter was laid out in the first chapter as being the wisdom of the gospel ver-sus the foolishness of the world (Greeks). That concern played itself out in several ways—sexual immorality, unity and diversity, food laws, spiritual gifts, etc.

Paul identified the underlying issue as a philosophical and/or theolog-ical dispute between two groups of people who had deep-rooted and op-posing views of things. He explained the issues by talking about how the wisdom of Christ was different than and opposed to the wisdom of the world. Today we call this kind of thing competing worldviews. One group interpreted everything through the eyes of the prevailing world-view of the day—various forms of Greek philosophy. The other group in-terpreted everything through the eyes of Christ.

Many new believers had been added to the roles of the Corinthian church, and in the midst of their growth pains one of the church leaders was found to be involved in an illicit romantic relationship with his "fa-ther's wife" (1 Corinthians 5:1). No doubt more was going on than what had been expressed in the letters to or from Paul.

The issue that had been presented to Paul concerned a church leader who had been teaching, implicitly or explicitly, that there was nothing wrong with such a relationship because in Christ Christians were free, in Christ Christians were no longer bound by the Old Testament or by their old moral habits. We tend to think that we in our day are different than

---

1   It is remarkable that a congregation is identified as God's workmanship. The Greek
     word *poiēma* signifies fabric, a weaving together of various life strands. The church as
     a work of art is a theme that needs to be further explored. See Ephesian 2:20.

the early Christians were, but here we see that things have not changed much regarding the fundamental concerns of the churches. Such concerns are still rife in the church today.

Paul was responding to a question (or a series of questions) that the Corinthians had written to him about. That original letter has been lost, but we know about it because Paul referred to it. In chapter seven Paul wrote, "Now concerning the matters about which you wrote: 'It is good for a man not to have sexual relations with a woman'" (1 Corinthians 7:1).

After answering that concern with the traditional biblical view of marriage in chapter seven, Paul clarified the issue of freedom in Christ using the concern of food sacrificed to idols in chapter eight. Yes, we are free in Christ, he said. But there are limits to our freedom that impact more than our own salvation and morality. There are social issues that involve us in the care and concern of our brothers and sisters in Christ. Though we may be technically free to do so, we must not model behaviors that can be misunderstood by others.

So, though we are free to eat food that has been dedicated to idols, though we are free to participate in pagan (popular) holiday festivals and celebrations, the better course of action, said Paul, the more mature and responsible thing to do is to avoid such activities, not because they are in and of themselves wrong or immoral, but because other Christians who are less discerning may misunderstand our actions and motivations and fall into temptation and sin as a result of misreading our actions.

Paul understood the tensions related to the issue of Christian freedom. Paul understood the ease with which the most sincere Christians can misunderstand the most basic things. On the one hand, freedom in Christ was the evangelistic cry of the Early Church in the face of political domination by the Romans and similarly in the face of religious repression by the Pharisees. The cry of freedom, then as now, was at the forefront of social and political change.

UNRESTRAINED FREEDOM

Against the tide of unrestrained freedom, Paul argued for caution and restraint. Here and elsewhere Paul argued that freedom in Christ did not mean that Christians were free to do whatever they wanted to do, even if there was nothing ultimately wrong with some particular action. But rather, Christians were free in Christ to live in obedience to Christ, free to care for and model behavior suited to the least discerning of Christ's people. Christians can err by improper evaluation of their freedom in Christ, and they can err by improper evaluation of their duties of obedience to Christ. But the danger dealt with here in First Corinthians lies in unrestrained freedom. Other dangers and concerns are dealt with elsewhere.

Paul's questions continue.

> "Do we not have the right to eat and drink? Do we not have the right
> to take along a believing wife, as do the other apostles and the brothers
> of the Lord and Cephas? Or is it only Barnabas and I who have no right
> to refrain from working for a living? Who serves as a soldier at his own
> expense? Who plants a vineyard without eating any of its fruit? Or who
> tends a flock without getting some of the milk? Do I say these things on
> human authority? Does not the Law say the same?" (vs. 4-8).

Paul's point here was that Christian freedom incurs a cost. Again, turning Paul's questions into statements, he said that Christians indeed have the right to eat and drink whatever they want. Apostles and pastors can marry just as anyone else can, and they can take their wives with them as they minister.

At this point Paul was struck with another thought. Speaking of wives, he implied that it is costly to care for a family and that those costs don't go away because a person is in the ministry. Ministers (pastors) have the freedom to marry and have families, but not everyone has the means to do so without actively working to support them. Those serving the Lord Jesus Christ in ministry should not have to pay all their own ministry expenses. It's just not realistic to try to engage in ministry and work another full-time job—and try to raise a family. Their just aren't enough hours in a day to do all that is required by all of these things.

The way that the question is phrased suggests that Paul was a little angry that he had to work a job *and* take the lead in the ministry of the church(es). Paul seems to be saying that it is unrealistic to expect pastors to work a secular job in order to pay for their own ministry expenses. The fact that Paul was not currently married was a blessing in this regard. It helped to keep Paul's expenses down. But many of Paul's experiences were not to be norms for ministry.

The synagogue model, upon which the Christian church was founded, required at least ten families to establish a local synagogue. Those ten families would then contribute ten percent of their incomes for the maintenance of the ministry, which would support a Rabbi and his family. As the synagogue grew, they could then engage in other ministry projects and mission efforts as more families and funds became available. The point is that the model for church growth was not only self-perpetuating, but would encourage young men to enter into ministry without sacrificing their natural passions and desires for their own family.

MINISTRY MODEL

Paul seemed to be suggesting that the model of church leadership that he had personally set was not the ideal. The ideal was not to roam the countryside as he had done, but to serve in an established or settled church. Paul's itinerant life as an apostle was not the norm for Christian leadership. We are to model Paul's faith, his commitment to Jesus Christ and his habits of study, prayer, etc., but not his itinerant lifestyle. That was particular to Paul's circumstance.

Paul's itinerant lifestyle was the result of his former position, his drastic conversion, and his change of political allegiance, and of course, the fact that the Jews perused him relentlessly because they wanted to kill him. In Paul's day, the church was under persecution by both the Romans and the Jews. During his entire life as a Christian, Paul had been running from powerful people who sought to stop his ministry and ultimately kill him. He knew that such a life was not normal. So, in these few questions he was lobbying for churches to provide for those who would take on Christian leadership. A settled ministry by a resident pastor was to be the norm.

Paul went on with his questions. You feed your oxen, don't you? Is God concerned about more than oxen than pastors? You feed the plowman and the thresher, don't you? All the workers of the fields share in the bounty of the harvest. Why should it be different in the churches? It shouldn't be. Paul was lobbying for a church model that collected tithes and administered local social welfare ministries, providing for the poor, widows without families, orphans, etc. These kinds of local welfare concerns were the providence of the local villages, synagogues and churches. This was the model for Christian churches that Paul taught. Obviously, local churches would help other local churches when the needs at hand were more than a local church could handle, as during the Jerusalem crisis (Romans 15:25).

In verse 11 Paul asks, "If we have sown spiritual things among you, is it too much if we reap material things from you?" Those who focus on the spiritual aspects of the gospel still have material needs. He continued,

"If others share this rightful claim on you, do not we even more? Nevertheless, we have not made use of this right, but we endure anything rather than put an obstacle in the way of the gospel of Christ" (v. 11).

The others who shared in the rightful claim upon the tithes of the church that Paul referred to were the local leaders, those who were opposed to Paul, those who were teaching false doctrine in the Corinthian church. Paul said that the Corinthians were rightly supporting their leaders, in spite of the fact that those same leaders were teaching falsehoods in their midst. And by extension, then, Paul, who came to correct the errors of the local leaders, was a legitimate recipient of the material care of the Corinthian church as well—even more so, because he was the spiritual father of the church.

And yet, in spite of that rightful claim upon the Corinthian purse, Paul did not request or receive any such care. He did not want to give the impression that his ministry was motivated by monetary concerns. He did not want to be perceived as a hired gun that had come in to clean up the Corinthian church. He did not want to put an obstacle in the way of the gospel of Christ. In order to ensure that he did not give the impression that he was in it for the money, he provided for himself. He worked another job and neither asked for nor received any compensation for his gospel work. But he wanted to make sure that they understood that his actions in this regard were not to be set up as a model for Christian ministry.

We can hear this concern in verses 13-15,

"Do you not know that those who are employed in the temple service get their food from the temple, and those who serve at the altar share in the sacrificial offerings? In the same way, the Lord commanded that those who proclaim the gospel should get their living by the gospel. But I have made no use of any of these rights, nor am I writing these things to secure any such provision. For I would rather die than have anyone deprive me of my ground for boasting."

This last phrase, "deprive me of my ground for boasting" is an unfortunate translation in that it is open to misunderstanding. Other translations render the phrase "make my glorifying void" (ASV), "make my reioycing vaine" (Geneva Bible), "nullify my glorying" (MKJB), "deprive me of this boast" (NIV). None of these translations do justice to this phrase, either. Paul was not boasting about the purity of his apostleship. As an apostle, he had a rightful claim upon some of the material wealth of the Corinthian church because he founded the church and because he was actively engaged in ministry in their midst. But he was not bragging or boasting about his claim upon them or about his position as an apostle. He was not boasting about himself at all, but about the gospel of Jesus Christ.

Verse 14 sums up this argument, "In the same way, the Lord commanded that those who proclaim the gospel should get their living by the gospel." He was merely stating the facts. He was saying that he would rather die than have anyone or anything undermine the truth of the message that he brought to them. Paul was not in it for the money, though he had a rightful claim on compensation for his expenses. Rather, Paul was in it for the glory of God, and he would do whatever was necessary to make that point clear. So, he neither asked for nor received any compensation for his efforts. But he insisted that this was not to be a model for Christian ministry.

Finally, in verse 16 Paul said, "For if I preach the gospel, that gives me no ground for boasting. For necessity is laid upon me. Woe to me if I do not preach the gospel!" There is no ground for personal boasting in the gospel because the gospel message is a message of both condemnation and salvation, in that order. If there is no condemnation from which to escape by the grace of God, then there is no need for salvation. The message of salvation contains within in, implicitly and explicitly, the understanding of a prior condemnation. Another way to say it is that the gospel message rightly preached convicts both the hearers and the preacher. The gospel truth applies to everyone. Paul was not an exception. He had nothing to boast about in and of himself. The gospel laid the necessity for salvation upon Paul just as much as it laid it on anyone else.

WOE

Paul's confession, "Woe to me if I do not preach the gospel" points to the fact that the gospel message is not a message of universal blessing upon all people. *Woe* is an expression of grief that issued from Paul's realization that God's curse was upon those who would not respond to the message of salvation in Christ Jesus, and it would apply to him if he acted apart from God's will. Yes, the gospel is a message of good news. But the news is good only if it is received and acted upon. To ignore the message of salvation in Christ means that God's prior covenant with humanity, the covenant that Adam had broken, the covenant that had brought all humanity into sin and damnation, was still in effect apart from Jesus Christ.

It is in the context of this prior covenant that the gospel of Jesus Christ is good news. Because all humanity and all children in perpetuity are party to Adam's covenant. Though not all people realize or accept it, it is already in effect for all humanity. Because all people are descendants of Adam, and later of Noah, all are involved in God's covenant. Another way to say the same thing is that all people are sinners. We are sinners because of Adam's broken covenant. All people are sinners, and all stand in the need of Christ's redemption. No one is exempt.

And what was the gospel that Paul preached? He summed it up for the Colossians:

> "And you, who once were alienated and hostile in mind, doing evil deeds, he has now reconciled in his body of flesh by his death, in order to present you holy and blameless and above reproach before him, if indeed you continue in the faith, stable and steadfast, not shifting from the hope of the gospel that you heard, which has been proclaimed in all creation under heaven, and of which I, Paul, became a minister" (Colossians 1:21-23).

Sinners have been reconciled through Christ's death on the cross in order that they may be sanctified and presented to God. Christians are Christ's gift to God, given to God for the glory of God—sanctified, holy and blameless before the judgment of God.

The Lord greatly blessed Paul's efforts. May He bless ours, as well. May the Lord bless you and preserve you from the only other option in the face of His judgment. Lord, have mercy.

21. Necessary Freedom

For if I preach the gospel, that gives me no ground for boasting. For necessity is laid upon me. Woe to me if I do not preach the gospel! For if I do this of my own will, I have a reward, but not of my own will, I am still entrusted with a stewardship. What then is my reward? That in my preaching I may present the gospel free of charge, so as not to make full use of my right in the gospel. For though I am free from all, I have made myself a servant to all, that I might win more of them. To the Jews I became as a Jew, in order to win Jews. To those under the law I became as one under the law (though not being myself under the law) that I might win those under the law. To those outside the law I became as one outside the law (not being outside the law of God but under the law of Christ) that I might win those outside the law. To the weak I became weak, that I might win the weak. I have become all things to all people, that by all means I might save some. I do it all for the sake of the gospel, that I may share with them in its blessings. Do you not know that in a race all the runners compete, but only one receives the prize? So run that you may obtain it. Every athlete exercises self-control in all things. They do it to receive a perishable wreath, but we an imperishable. So I do not run aimlessly; I do not box as one beating the air. But I discipline my body and keep it under control, lest after preaching to others I myself should be disqualified.   — 1 Corinthians 9:16-27

Paul said that "necessity" (v. 16) was laid upon him. He was talking about preaching the gospel, and the gist of his words suggest that he preached not out of desire, but out of necessity. It was necessary for him to preach the gospel. He could not do otherwise. What is necessary is required. What is necessary is not optional.

"Woe to me," he said, "if I do not preach the gospel!" (v. 16). To not preach would put him under God's woe, God's curse. For Paul not to preach would be an act of disobedience, and act of unfaithfulness, and would open him to God's chastisement.

To love God is to live in obedience to His Word.

"Whoever has my commandments and keeps them, he it is who loves me. And he who loves me will be loved by my Father, and I will love him and manifest myself to him" (John 14:21).

"And by this we know that we have come to know him, if we keep his commandments" (1 John 2:3).

"Whoever keeps his commandments abides in him, and he in them" (1 John 3:24).

"And this is love, that we walk according to his commandments" (2 John 1:6).

Verse 16 tells us that Paul understood that God had commanded him to preach, and he could not do otherwise. This raised the question that Paul answered in verse 17. Was he acting freely or out of necessity? Was he acting out of his own free will? Or was he being constrained by God's will? His answer was, "For if I do this of my own will, I have a reward, but not of my own will, I am still entrusted with a stewardship" (v. 17).

OF NECESSITY

He was talking about his call to preach the gospel. He was saying that if his preaching issued from his own will, he would receive a reward. The Greek word is *misthos*, and literally means *wages*. Jesus said, "the fields are white for harvest. Already the one who reaps is receiving wages (misthos) and gathering fruit for eternal life" (John 4:35-36).

Paul was saying that if he was preaching out of his own desire, out of his own willingness to obey God's call, then he would receive a just reward. And that is good. He would be rewarded for his obedience. However, if Paul did not preach out of his own will—but wait a minute! What does that mean? How can someone do something if they don't will to do it?

There are two possible meanings here. One, that Paul was preaching unwillingly, as in begrudgingly. We all know that obedience can be done begrudgingly. We can do something even if we really don't want to do it. We can do something when our hearts are not in it. It's an attitude thing. Is that what Paul meant? I don't think so because Paul doesn't have a begrudging attitude. That's not what we find in Paul's preaching any-where in his writings.

The second possible meaning is that Paul was preaching, not out of his own will, but out of God's will, or in response to God's will. Note that

Paul doesn't understand these two wills to be in opposition, but in harmony. And what is more, he seems to be saying that it is not his own will that is taking the lead in his cooperation with God, but that it is God's will that is in the lead and his will that is following. It was not that God was helping him to preach (though surely He was), but rather that he—Paul—was engaged in service to the will of God, in the cooperation of his will with God's will.

It wasn't so much that God was helping him, but that he was helping God. God's will was in the superior position. God was leading. God was dominant. Paul was subservient. He was following, but he wasn't following begrudgingly. He was following in willing obedience, gladly following. If you ask me to do something, and I do it willingly, whose will is accomplished? Yours. My will would be involved through my compliance, but doing the thing was not my idea. It was your idea. I would be doing your will. And I would not be doing it of my own accord, but in response to your request.

Paul understood himself to be a steward, a manager of someone's property. He had a stewardship entrusted to him. He had an obligation to properly care for and to properly invest the gospel, which was not his own but God's. He was preaching out of obligation, out of duty—yes! But that does not mean that he was doing it unwillingly or begrudgingly. Rather, it was for Paul a source of great joy, though it caused him much trouble, much difficulty and pain.

It was a labor of love. It was hard work, and he would be rewarded for his labor. But that was not why he did it. He didn't preach so that he would receive a personal reward. He preached because he was compelled to preach. He was obligated to preach, called to preach. He could do no other. It was his duty to invest his Master's talent, his Master's possessions, to increase his Master's holdings. Though he would be rewarded for his efforts, he was not motivated by his own reward, but by the obligation of his stewardship of the gospel. He put aside his former concerns and took the concerns of his Master to be his own. He put aside his own priorities and took up God's priorities.

EXPENSES

We mentioned previously that Paul's model of paying for his own ministry expenses was not the model for ordinary ministry, but that ministers should be paid a fair wage, even a double wage (1 Timothy 5:17) so that they could exercise and model greater personal generosity in their pastoral calling. "What then is my reward?" asked Paul (v. 18). He was not talking about his eternal reward, but about his wages and his job satisfaction, his salary as a minister and the satisfaction he received from doing his job well. Then he answered his question: "That in my preaching I may present the gospel free of charge, so as not to make full use of my right in the gospel" (v. 18).

In order to get the maximum return on his investment of the gospel in the hearts of the Corinthian believers, he understood that his presentation of the gospel needed to be unencumbered, that he must be able to present it free of charge, without cost, and without strings. He was not selling the gospel, nor was he providing gospel services for hire. He knew that maximum gospel growth would best occur if there were no obstacles to its presentation. So, even though he had a right to receive wages for his gospel work, he declined to "make full use of (that) right" (v. 18). Why? In order to maximize God's return.

Was it his own free will not to get paid for his work with them? No, he would argue that even an ox was fed from the threshing grain (v. 9), and by implication that the needs of pastors should also be provided for. He argued that pastors should be paid. Nonetheless, he accepted no wages from the Corinthians as a matter of God's will. So, he willingly—even gladly—accepted the honor to work for the Lord without pay. And because he worked without pay, he was free from their expectations, free from the strings that come with wages, free to preach the fullness of the gospel in their midst. God's will liberated Paul! Though he was free from them, free from the politics and pressures of a settled pastorate, he submitted himself to them.

"For though I am free from all, I have made myself a servant to all, that I might win more of them" (v. 19). Which *them* did he mean, exactly? Some of them? All of them? The rulers of the local church? He submitted himself to *them* that included Christ in their midst. He was a servant of Christ, not a servant to their personal desires. He was free, not to give them what they wanted, but to give them what Christ wanted them to have. That is the gospel freedom that is absent from too many pulpits. That is the freedom in Christ that wins souls.

PAUL'S STRATEGY

"To the Jews I became as a Jew, in order to win Jews. To those under the law I became as one under the law (though not being myself under

the law) that I might win those under the law. To those outside the law
I became as one outside the law (not being outside the law of God but
under the law of Christ) that I might win those outside the law" (vs. 21-
22).

These verses tell us Paul's strategy for soul winning. Paul was already
a Jew, so when he said that he "became as a Jew, in order to win Jews" (v.
21), he didn't mean that he had petitioned the local synagogue for membership. Paul was speaking culturally. He meant that when he was with
Jews he behaved as they did. He observed the laws and customs they observed because he didn't want anything to get in the way of his presentation of the gospel. He didn't want them to discount his testimony for any
reason. He wanted them to think well of him.

Next, to those "under the law"—he already mentioned the Jews, so
who was he talking about here? Paul clearly understood that there were
only two classes of human beings—the saved and the lost, covenant keepers and covenant breakers. Thus, he was extending the reach of the gospel
by defining and using the terms (words) he used. He could act like a Jew
because he was a Jew. He didn't say that to the Egyptians he would become as an Egyptian, nor to the Greeks that he would become as a Greek.

Rather, he was saying when he was with those who obeyed the law
and used obedience to the law as a fellowship shield, or a symbol of community identity, he would then also obey the law. What law? God's Old
Testament law. Even though he understood himself not to be under the
law, he obeyed it because obeying it in their presence would further the
gospel.

To those who were "outside the law," those who rejected strict obedience to God's law—not criminals, not rapists, thugs, and murders, but
people who didn't believe that complete conformity to Old Testament
law was a requirement for salvation—to these people Paul became as one
outside the law. He agreed with them that obedience to the law was not a
way of salvation. And yet he understood himself not to be "outside the
law of God but under the law of Christ" (v. 22).

He was not under the law, nor was he outside the law. Rather, he was
under the law of Christ or *in Christ*. It wasn't that Paul agreed with various people as they spouted the so-called cultural wisdom of whatever social or ethnic group they identified with, not at all. Paul was not being
culturally relative. He was not suggesting that all cultures are equally
valuable. Rather, he was saying that there are some elements of Jewish

practice and culture that are okay in Christ. The Jewish culture provided the context for these comments.

Jews did not have to give up everything Jewish to become Christians. Those who found life in obedience to God's commandments do not have to give up God's commandments to be Christians. And those who were burdened by the law, burdened by trying to live in obedience to every detail of the Old Testament law did not have to accomplish every jot and tiddle of the law to be Christians. Salvation was not a function of being Jewish, nor a function of obedience to the law, nor a function of the disregard of the law. Salvation was a function of Jesus Christ, period.

These verses reflect Paul's understanding of how Jesus Christ changed the relationship of God's people to Old Testament law. It is beyond our purposes here to discuss how Jesus Christ's fulfillment of the law affected the relationship of God's people to the law. But suffice it to say, as Paul says here, that Christians do not need to be Jewish, they do not need to be slaves to Old Testament law, but nor are they completely free of God's law because Christians are under the law of Christ. Christ changed the relationship of the Christian to God's law, but He did not negate it. "Bear one another's burdens, and so fulfill the law of Christ," (Galatians 6:2) Paul wrote to the Galatians. The relationship between God's people and God's law changed with the propitiation of Christ on the cross. That is what Paul was talking about in these verses. He went on.

"To the weak I became weak, that I might win the weak. I have become all things to all people, that by all means I might save some" (v. 22). Paul became feeble, impotent, sick, and without power or strength in order to win to Christ those who were feeble, impotent, sick, and without power or strength. Paul was a superstar, but he didn't act like a superstar. He always acted with humility. So, when he was with the downtrodden, he could relate to them because he was also downtrodden.

Yet, Paul was a superstar. He went on to talk about running a race, and that only one person would win the first place prize, only one person would wear the first place medallion or wreath. Comparing the walk of faithfulness with a foot race he encouraged believers to train hard, to exercise self-discipline in all things as both a method of training for faithfulness and as a lifestyle of faithfulness.

"So I do not run aimlessly; I do not box as one beating the air" (v. 26). The walk of faithfulness was not without purpose or aim. It was not a matter of working for a goal that was out of reach. Unlike a foot race where only one runner would win, in the race of faithfulness, all who ran in faithfulness and righteousness in Christ were winners already. Nonetheless, Paul encouraged believers to put all of their strength and energy into their exercise of faithfulness. Don't slack off because you know that in Christ you cannot lose, but rather pull out all the stops and run as if your very life depends on winning the race—because it does!

Christ expects His people to give themselves fully to the task of faithfulness. You may fool me. You may fool your parents or your boss that you are actually doing your very best, but you cannot fool God. He knows when you are holding back, when you could do better.

Finally, Paul said, "I discipline my body and keep it under control, lest after preaching to others I myself should be disqualified" (v. 27). He was not saying "do as I say not as I do." But rather, he made himself a model of Christian behavior. If you want to know what Christian faithfulness looks like, look at Paul. He knew that people would not listen to him if he failed to model in his own life what he preached to others.

Does this only apply to preachers, only to those called to peach? Not at all. Paul said that all Christians are called to the high calling of faithfulness. Mediocrity is not an option for Christians. Rather, Christians are called to be ordinary, not ordinary in the eyes of the world, not ordinary in the eyes of fellow Christians, but ordinary in the eyes of God. Living in faithfulness, running the race with all of our might, and winning the imperishable wreath of salvation in Christ is exactly what ordinary Christians are called to.

If you really want to go for the gusto, go for Christ. Christ calls us to do more than we think we can. He calls us all to exceed our own expectations because He has sent His Holy Spirit to dwell with His people to accomplish for them—for us—what we cannot of ourselves accomplish. The church and all of God's people are one of the means that God uses to accomplish His will, and God will not fail. Praise be to God!

22. Idle Worship

I want you to know, brothers, that our fathers were all under the cloud, and all passed through the sea, and all were baptized into Moses in the cloud and in the sea, and all ate the same spiritual food, and all drank the same spiritual drink. For they drank from the spiritual Rock that followed them, and the Rock was Christ. Nevertheless, with most of them God was not pleased, for they were overthrown in the wilderness. Now these things took place as examples for us, that we might not desire evil as they did. Do not be idolaters as some of them were; as it is written, "The people sat down to eat and drink and rose up to play." We must not indulge in sexual immorality as some of them did, and twenty-three thousand fell in a single day. We must not put Christ to the test, as some of them did and were destroyed by serpents, nor grumble, as some of them did and were destroyed by the Destroyer. Now these things happened to them as an example, but they were written down for our instruction, on whom the end of the ages has come. Therefore let anyone who thinks that he stands take heed lest he fall. No temptation has overtaken you that is not common to man. God is faithful, and he will not let you be tempted beyond your ability, but with the temptation he will also provide the way of escape, that you may be able to endure it. Therefore, my beloved, flee from idolatry. I speak as to sensible people; judge for yourselves what I say.   — 1 Corinthians 10:1-15

Chapter ten is difficult to get our minds around, but it will help to remember Paul's general theme of helping the Corinthians see the contrast between the wisdom of Christ and the wisdom of the world. To hear what Paul has to say about the baptism of ancient Israel we need to understand what he is contrasting it against. Paul continues to show the contrast between Christian thinking and worldly thinking.

To see the contrast more clearly, notice how often Paul uses the word *all* in these first four verses: "*all* (were) under the cloud, and *all* passed through the sea" (v. 1), "*all* were baptized into Moses" (v. 2), "*all* ate the same spiritual food" (v. 3), "*all* drank the same spiritual drink" (v. 4). Verse 5 then provides the contrast for the idea of *all*. He switches from *all* to *most*. "Nevertheless, with *most* of them God was not pleased, for they were overthrown in the wilderness" (v. 5)—*all, all, all, all,* but God was *not* pleased with *most.* Paul's emphasis on *all* changes to *most.* The contrast Paul was making in these verses is similar to what he was talking about in Romans 9:5-8:

> "They are Israelites, and to them belong the adoption, the glory, the covenants, the giving of the law, the worship, and the promises. To them belong the patriarchs, and from their race, according to the flesh, is the Christ who is God over all, blessed forever. Amen. But it is not as though the word of God has failed. For not all who are descended from Israel belong to Israel, and not all are children of Abraham because they are his offspring, but 'Through Isaac shall your offspring be named.' This means that it is not the children of the flesh who are the children of God, but the children of the promise are counted as offspring."

Paul's point in these first five verses of the tenth chapter of First Corinthians is not about the nature of baptism, but about the nature of regeneration. He cited baptism as a symbol of regeneration and as an example of the need for regeneration. Paul was saying that while all of the people of ancient Israel were involved in God's various baptisms, not all of those who had been baptized by God Himself were heirs to the kingdom of God. Paul was saying that, while they were baptized, their baptism did not save them. This has proven to be a hard lesson to get.

> "All ate the same spiritual food, and all drank the same spiritual drink. For they drank from the spiritual Rock that followed them, and the Rock was Christ" (vs. 3-4).

Paul said that they all drank from the well of Christ. Did that mean that they were all "saved?" Listen to Paul's answer: "Nevertheless, with most of them God was not pleased, for they were overthrown in the wilderness" (v. 5).

Though the ancient Israelites had all experienced and partaken of Jesus Christ (drank the water from the Rock) personally, some of them displeased God. And the result was that God allowed them to perish in the wilderness without entering the Promised Land. That is the lesson and the contrast that Paul was teaching here, and it's a hard lesson to swallow because it runs counter to what we want to believe about God and about ourselves.

EXAMPLES

Why would God bless His own people with genuine spiritual food, and then let them die in the desert? They were God's people, right? Why didn't God protect them? Why didn't God preserve or persevere with them? Why would God allow His precious baptized lambs to die in the wilderness? That is exactly what Paul was trying to get the Corinthians to see because that is exactly what God had done. So, Paul answered that very question. He said that "these things took place as examples for us, that we might not desire evil as they did" (v. 6).

Did you hear that? They died for our sake, to teach us a lesson about faithfulness, about not wanting the wrong things. Not all of them died, of course. Some lived and some died. That's the contrast Paul was making, and it begs the question—Why did some die? Why did some live? What was the difference between those who lived and those who died? Indeed, the contrast under consideration here is the same contrast that Paul has been teaching from the beginning of this letter. Paul continued to show them the difference between the wisdom (or foolishness) of Christ that is life itself and the wisdom (or foolishness) of the world that is death. The lesson that Paul was teaching is a matter of life and death. It is not trivial. It is not funny. It is serious. And it applies to us today.

Paul then clearly spelled out his central concern, so they wouldn't miss what he was talking about—idolatry.

"Do not be idolaters as some of them were; as it is written, 'The people sat down to eat and drink and rose up to play'" (v. 7). Paul quoted from Exodus 32:6. As Moses was up on the mountain receiving the Ten Commandments from God, the people demanded that Aaron make them a Golden Calf to facilitate their worship. Aaron did as he was requested, and the next day the people held a religious feast. About that particular feast Moses wrote, "The people sat down to eat and drink and rose up to play" (Exodus 32:6).

Paul's concern in these first few verses of chapter ten pertains to this story of Israel's idolatry. He was accusing some of the Corinthians of the same kind of idolatry.

How did God receive this idol worship that came from the minds and hearts of His people? "Twenty-three thousand fell in a single day" (v. 8), wrote Paul. God then commanded that the Levites take vengeance on the worshipers of the Golden Calf on behalf of the Lord.

"Moses stood in the gate of the camp and said, 'Who is on the Lord's side? Come to me.' And all the sons of Levi gathered around him. And he said to them, 'Thus says the Lord God of Israel, "Put your sword on your side each of you, and go to and fro from gate to gate throughout the camp, and each of you kill his brother and his companion and his neighbor."' And the sons of Levi did according to the word of Moses. And that day about three thousand men of the people fell" (Exodus 32:26-28).

Exodus 32 concludes with this verse, "Then the Lord sent a plague on the people, because they made the calf, the one that Aaron made" (Exodus 32:35).

Many more died from the plague. This is not a pretty picture, but it is the picture that Paul painted for the Corinthians to illustrate the severity of their error.

Paul summed up his lesson,

"We must not indulge in sexual immorality as some of them did.... We must not put Christ to the test, as some of them did and were destroyed by serpents, nor grumble, as some of them did and were destroyed by the Destroyer" (vs. 8-10).

Who had engaged in sexual immorality? Who put God to the test? Some of those ancient Israelites who had been baptized by God Himself in the cloud, in the sea, and in Moses. Notice Paul's contrast in these verses between *all* and *some*. *All* had been baptized, but *some* of God's own baptized people had been faithless, and God destroyed them. That's the point!

But why would God not protect and preserve all of His ancient people? Why did God not keep them from sin? Paul tells us. "Now these things happened to them as an example, but they were written down for our instruction, on whom the end of the ages has come" (v. 11). God killed them to teach a lesson to those to whom the end of the ages had come—Christians.

PRESUMPTION

This is a very important point. Don't miss it. *The Old Testament was written to teach Christians about faithfulness.* Another way to say it is that Christian faithfulness is aided by the lessons garnered from the Old Testament. Or this—Christianity cannot be understood apart from the teaching of the Old Testament, apart from learning the lessons of the Old Testament.

The point was that the Corinthians, like the Ancient Israelites, should not trust in their baptism alone. Paul said, "Therefore let anyone who thinks that he stands take heed lest he fall" (v. 12). Clearly, Paul meant that anyone who thought that he had a secure standing before the Lord because of his baptism needed to think again, and to repent of such presumption, lest he fall. He had in mind those Corinthian leaders who had opposed him by teaching the wisdom of the world as the wisdom of Christ. He had previously accused them of sexual immorality, here he accused them of idolatry and, ultimately, of faithlessness. This attack by Paul was directed at those who had broken covenant with God, and who had been leading the Corinthian church astray.

This doesn't mean that God doesn't protect and preserve His people. He does! It does not mean that baptism is not important, or that it is not an aid to faithfulness, because it is! Baptism is important and it is an aid to faithfulness. But that doesn't mean that God's people get to escape difficulties in this life. It doesn't mean that Christians escape testing and the need for the personal, ongoing discipline and practice in faithfulness. God accomplishes His purposes, not ours. God tests His people to prove them —and to improve them. God accomplishes His will, not ours. God does persevere with the saints, and part and parcel of God's preservation is His ongoing testing and our ongoing perseverance in faithfulness.

The old adage should be rewritten, "Once saved, always *being* saved." God's salvation is a process. This does not negate the fact that there is an historical moment of personal rebirth in the lives of saints. Rather, it puts that moment in a larger context. God's plan of salvation began before time itself and will culminate when the New Jerusalem comes down from heaven (Revelation 21:2). It has begun, but it has not finished. It's ongoing, moment by moment, twenty-four-seven. And it's not just that God is engaged moment by moment, but that God's people must be similarly engaged in the process. Once God begins a thing it will be completed, but Paul's point was that salvation is in the process of completion. It was both a done deal and yet still in process. Sometimes Paul spoke of salvation as a fact, and sometimes he spoke of it as a process not yet finished.

In verse 13 Paul turned his attention from the faithless to the faithful. Part of the confusion we find in this chapter (and elsewhere) is the result of the fact that Paul was speaking (writing) to two different groups of people, both of whom were members of the Corinthian church. That is what Paul was talking about in the first five verses—the difference between faithful Christians and faithless Christians. Some of Paul's words were aimed at the faithful Christians and some were aimed at the faithless Christians. Our task is to discern the difference.

As the Kingdom continues to unfold, some of the faithful will be revealed to actually be faithless, and some of the faithless will join the ranks of the faithful. There is some traffic between these two groups, and that is the issue that Paul is getting at.

> "No temptation has overtaken you that is not common to man. God is faithful, and he will not let you be tempted beyond your ability, but with the temptation he will also provide the way of escape, that you may be able to endure it" (v. 13).

The temptation is real and effects both groups—the faithful and the faithless. Note the abrupt change in tone. Paul has turned from addressing those with whom God was not pleased to those who had faithfully received the strength of Christ in order to provide for them what they could not provide for themselves.

God tests everyone, the faithful and the faithless. And the way in which people respond to those tests points to the difference between the faithful and the faithless. The faithful are encouraged and strengthened in the midst of trials and difficulties, the faithless are not. The faithful lean upon Jesus, who carries them to safety. The faithless do not, nor do they find safety. The trials of the faithful are productive, whereas the trials of the faithless are destructive.

God's faith in His Son, Jesus Christ, provides the model for faith. God's people are saved by God's faith in His Son, Jesus Christ, who will not—cannot—fail to bring all of His people into the Kingdom. The purpose of temptation, the trials and difficulties of the saints, is to drive them to greater dependence upon Jesus Christ, who provides the only safe passage through the troubles of this life. Those who will not rely upon Jesus Christ are driven away in anger and frustration—their own anger and frustration, I should add. God does not make them mad, rather they get mad at God and/or His people of their own accord.

RUN AWAY

Paul, then, singles out the faithful among the unfaithful and counsels them, "Therefore, my beloved, flee from idolatry" (v. 14). Flee from those who are tempting you to idolatry. Flee from idolatry into greater faithfulness by fleeing from those who preach and practice idolatry in your midst. Flee! The Greek word is *pheugo* and means run away.

"I speak as to sensible people; judge for yourselves what I say" (v. 15). Paul was not speaking to all of the members of the Corinthian church, only to those who were sensible, those who understood what he was talking about. The Greek word is *phronimos* and means thoughtful, sagacious, discreet. But it doesn't mean intelligent. The difference between the faithful and the unfaithful is not intelligence. It has nothing to do with intelligence. Rather, the difference is more like sensitivity or concern—better yet, a kind of common resonance, a common understanding. He was speaking to those who could resonate with what he was talking about, those who had been regenerated and were growing in grace through the Holy Spirit, those who were inhabited by the Holy Spirit. He was speaking to those who had been regenerated by the Holy Spirit, not to all who had been baptized.

There are two aspects to baptism. There is the outward ceremony of baptism, and there is the inward reality, what is sometimes referred to as the baptism *by*, *of* or *in* the Holy Spirit.

As I said, this is a hard lesson, not because it is difficult to understand, but because it is difficult to accept. Just as Jesus had criticized the Jewish leaders for their faithlessness, so Paul accused the Corinthian leaders for the same reasons. Is it surprising that a Christian church had apostatized so early in Christian history? Not really. Paul cited the example of those who fell into idolatry before Moses had returned from the mountain with the Ten Commandments. Human nature had not changed between the time of Moses and Christ, nor has it changed since.

The only thing that changes human nature is Jesus Christ, and He does so through regeneration by the Holy Spirit. Regeneration is symbolized by the ceremony of baptism, but the ceremony of baptism does not make regeneration real. It's the other way around (arsy varsy), regeneration makes baptism real.

What can we learn from all this? That our salvation is a done deal in the eyes of God only as we persevere in the trials of faithfulness. In other words, we can continue in our paltry efforts to be faithful because those efforts are guided by the God who cannot fail. But we must not presume on the success of our salvation, and think that it cannot be lost. We must persevere in the disciplines of faithfulness because that is what God's Holy

Spirit has empowered us to do. To fail such perseverance is an acknowledgment of the absence of God's Holy Spirit. Only in Christ are the means and the will—the desire and the ability—to actually live as a Christian.

23. PARTICIPATION

Therefore, my beloved, flee from idolatry. I speak as to sensible people; judge for yourselves what I say. The cup of blessing that we bless, is it not a participation in the blood of Christ? The bread that we break, is it not a participation in the body of Christ? Because there is one bread, we who are many are one body, for we all partake of the one bread. Consider the people of Israel: are not those who eat the sacrifices participants in the altar? What do I imply then? That food offered to idols is anything, or that an idol is anything? No, I imply that what pagans sacrifice they offer to demons and not to God. I do not want you to be participants with demons. You cannot drink the cup of the Lord and the cup of demons. You cannot partake of the table of the Lord and the table of demons. Shall we provoke the Lord to jealousy? Are we stronger than he?

— 1 Corinthians 10:14-22

Paul raised the ante of his accusations against the Corinthian leaders from sexual immorality to idolatry, as we saw in the previous verses of chapter ten. Note that Paul did not recommend that the faithful Corinthian Christians make the effort to save those who had been captured by idolatry. He did not recommend that they maintain fellowship and try to convince the idolaters about the truth of the gospel. Rather, he told them to "flee from idolatry" (v. 14) They were to separate themselves from the idolatry of the idolaters.

He knew that not all the Corinthians would hear him. Not all had "ears to hear" (Matthew 11:15). Some of those who had been baptized would not hear, would not heed his words, and would not be saved. He was speaking "as to sensible people" (v. 15)—"wise men" in other translations. But the wisdom of those to whom he spoke was not the wisdom of intelligence. He was not speaking of intellectual or academic wisdom. Rather, he had in mind the wisdom of Christ, which he had been preaching from the beginning of this letter. He was speaking to those who had ears to hear, to those who had the ears of the Holy Spirit, to those who had been regenerated by the Holy Spirit. He was not speaking to all who were listening, but only to those who were actively and actually in Christ, to those who could hear him.

But Paul did not know exactly who that was. He didn't know who was really born again and who wasn't. He didn't know who would be able to hear him. That knowledge belongs to God alone. We don't have access to the hearts and minds of others. Knowing this, Paul told them to "judge for (them)selves" (v. 15) what he had to say. Each person would have to judge (*krino*)—distinguish or decide—for himself whether Paul spoke the truth, and whether or not to heed the truth that Paul spoke. Understanding was not sufficient, Paul called them to action, to flee from idolatry.

Was Paul asking them to rely upon their own resources to make such a determination? Was he assuming that they had sufficient ability in-and-of-themselves to be able to hear him, to be able to correctly understand him, and to be able to make the right decision?

SELF-RELIANCE

No. Paul knew that they would not be able to do any such thing because he knew that he had not been able to do it on his own, and he knew that he was much smarter, much more committed, and better trained in religious disciplines than they were. He couldn't do it himself—and he didn't do it himself. Neither could they.

Paul had been saved against his own will, at least initially. He had been blinded and thrown in the dust while he still hated Christ. Once the Lord had his attention, Paul willingly conceded, of course. But the point was that Paul had not been called to rely upon himself or his own abilities in order to be saved—no Christian is. Rather, we are called to rely upon the ability and the reliability of God's Holy Spirit. We are called to rely upon Jesus Christ, not ourselves. We are called to regeneration, to rebirth. People do not cause their own birth, nor their rebirth. It is the power of God through the Holy Spirit who regenerates people, and it is upon that power that we must rely—before, during, and after, twenty-four-seven.

When Paul said, "judge for yourselves" (v. 15) he meant that he was teaching them how to make determinations about faithfulness and faithlessness—and that the principle application would always be to themselves. His purpose was to teach the Corinthians about the characteristics of faithfulness. He would lay out the characteristics of faithfulness and contrast them with the characteristics of faithlessness. We will watch for this pattern as his letters to the Corinthians unfold. By laying out the characteristics of faithfulness he would teach them how to judge them-selves, and how to grow in faithfulness. His intention was that Christians should judge themselves against the characteristics of faithfulness, and make necessary adjustments, by the presence and power of the Holy Spirit.

A better translation of this phrase is "you judge what I say" (MKJB). He was asking them to rely upon the Holy Spirit, who indwells believers. The Holy Spirit would evaluate the gospel that Paul taught and apply it to each believer's own life. With that in mind Paul immediately turned his attention to the sacrament of Communion. What has Communion to do with all of this? Everything.

Paul called upon the sacrament of Communion to illustrate what makes Christians Christian. At the heart of Communion and of Paul's il-lustration is the mystery of the Trinity. Paul's purpose in this letter to the Corinthians was to teach the difference between the wisdom of the world and the wisdom of Christ. That is the theme that he now illustrates with the sacrament of Communion—the mystery of the Trinitarian nature.

He mentioned earlier in this chapter about the role of baptism as a distinguishing mark of a Christian. Christians are baptized people, he said. But not all baptized people are faithful Christians. We discussed that in the previous chapter. Now Paul turned his attention to the other mark of a Christian—Communion. Christians are baptized people who participate in the Lord's Supper. By speaking about these two things—Baptism and Communion—Paul was identifying the central characteristics of Chris-tians, the building blocks of the church. A Christian is a person who has a new identity in Jesus Christ. And the Trinity is at the heart of our Chris-tian identity.

THREE IN ONE

Just as God is identified as Trinitarian, so are His people, and so is His world. We have been created in God's image, and God is Trinitarian. Christians are to understand the world through God's eyes, and God's eyes are Trinitarian. There is nothing outside of or apart from God. God is all encompassing, "infinite in being and perfection" (WCF 2:1). The point is that God is ultimately one and at the same time God is ultimately three. In God alone there is ultimate unity and ultimate diversity and/or individuality at the same time.

Let me illustrate and apply this idea. How can I be an individual, a unique whole, and at the same time be part of a distinct individual corporate entity (the body of Christ)? I am who I am in and of myself, yet my identity as a Christian is interwoven with all other Christians through the doctrine of Christian unity. While we use these distinctions all the time, it is quite difficult to provide an ultimate and rational explanation for such definitions and distinctions of personal and corporate identity.

While it is difficult to explain the Trinity, it is at the same time the most ordinary concept imaginable. Everyone intuitively understands that a thing can be both individual and corporate at the same time. Everyone intuitively knows what it means and uses such distinctions every day—everyone, not just Christians. And yet, a complete or comprehensive explanation of what the Trinity means or a survey of its implications is impossible. We use a lot of things that we don't understand—cars, computers, microwaves. We don't need to understand everything about a thing to use it. Yet, we can live more fully and more effectively when we understand more about how life works, about how reality is ordered. So, how does the Trinity affect our lives and our perceptions of things? Allow me to try to provide an explanation.

Being a Christian means being an individual Christian and at the same time being a member of a group of Christians, a member of a Church—the body of Christ. An individual person may be a Christian, but he cannot be a Christian by himself because being a Christian is always a matter of corporate identity as well as individual identity. Christians are called to love, so there must be an other—someone else to love. There's no such thing as a "Lone Ranger Christian." Christianity is always both an individual and a corporate affair.

Becoming a Christian means being born again, being regenerated by the Holy Spirit, who dwells in the hearts, minds, and lives of believers. Ask a young Christian under three feet tall how he knows he is a Christian and he will likely tell you "because Jesus lives in my heart." This is deep wisdom, and not mere childishness.

While "me" and Jesus live in the same body (sort of), it is not simply a matter of my individuality because Jesus, who lives in my heart, also unites me with a larger group of people, who also have the same Jesus living in their hearts, so to speak. Jesus also unites me with something beyond my own physical body, something eternal—God. Jesus is the bridge between me and God, and also the bridge between me and His people—the Church or body of Christ.

PARTICIPATION

"The cup of blessing that we bless, is it not a participation (a communion, a fellowship—*koinōnia*) in the blood of Christ? The bread that we
break, is it not a participation (a communion, a fellowship—*koinōnia*) in
the body of Christ?" (v. 16).

They are not real questions, they are rhetorical questions. Paul is stating facts about the Trinitarian God. To receive the cup is to participate in
or unite with Christ. To receive the bread is to participate in or unite
with Christ. Communion is for faithful Christians because it is a participation in and/or a union of sorts with Christ. It is an acknowledgment of
corporate membership in Christ. It is not a mere memorial or mere assent,
but involves all of the actual spiritual and legal rights and responsibilities
pertaining thereunto.[1]

It is not to be received casually or indiscriminately and especially not
unfaithfully. As we will see when we get to the eleventh chapter of First
Corinthians, people are to identify themselves as faithful Christians before
coming to the Lord's Table, lest they eat and drink judgment on themselves (1 Corinthians 11:29). Participation in the body of Christ requires
self identification as a Christian and faithfulness to that identity.

Most translations translate the Greek (*koinonia*) as *communion* rather
than *participation*, but either will do. Communion is not simple union, but
it is a kind of union. Where union is a kind of merging or loss of self in
something greater, communion is not a loss of self, but an expansion, a
clarification or extension of self. In communion both self and other remain clearly defined in the same way that God's Trinity—Father, Son,
and Holy Spirit—are clearly distinct, yet identical.

Christians have a unique individual identity, yet an overlap of common identity with Christ and with the community of Christ here on
earth and in eternity at the same time. There are common elements that
belong to the self, to other Christians, and to Christ. The Christian identifies with Jesus Christ, but He does not become Christ, nor does he lose
himself in Christ. Rather, his identification in Christ makes him—his self,
his individuality—more unique, not less. The sharing of Christian values
and Christian character gives his personality increased definition, increased clarity. He becomes more himself in Christ. People become more
in Christ than they could ever be apart from Christ.

---

1 Nevin, John Williamson & Ross, Phillip A. *The True Mystery of the Mystical Presence*,
  Pilgrim Platform, Marietta, 2011.

To participate in something is to take an active part in it. Participation and communion provide the foundation upon which social mores are built. Mores are strongly held social norms or customs, which derive from the established practices of a society or group. Taboos are a subset of mores that forbid a society's most unacceptable behaviors. Taboos are things like incest and murder. The word *morality* comes from the same root, as does the noun *moral*. Morality—behavior—is both individual and communal, personal and social. God's covenant is both personal and social. Being a Christian is both personal and social. God is both personal and social.

The point is that participation in the Lord's Supper provides the foundation for social mores and personal morals, which issue from the expression of Christian character through the imitation of Jesus. In other words, the Lord's Supper makes us who we are in Christ. It informs us as it forms us, both individually and corporately. It defines us as Christians and sets us apart from non-Christians. It is not magical, but it is mysterious. It is spiritual, but it is also real.

Paul goes on to say that our Christian identity is like the bread that we share. It is one loaf, but it is torn into many pieces. Yet, the tearing does not diminish the oneness of the loaf, but rather it enhances it because the loaf is not merely one loaf of bread, but it re-presents the one body of Christ. The division of the loaf into parts is an expression of the unity of Christ and actually increases the glory of Christ.

The same thing is true about the cup. It begins as one kind of grape, one flask or bottle of wine. Interestingly, the grapes from which it is made have only a resemblance to the wine itself. And again, the oneness of the bottle or skin in which the wine was carried is not diminished by those who drink from it. It remains one bottle (or skin), yet, it too is enlarged by the drinking because it re-presents the blood of Christ, the one sacrifice made for the people of Christ. It becomes part of the identity and the unity of the people of Christ. And the glory of Christ is increased with every individual who participates in it, whether they ultimately come to salvation or damnation.

In the Lord's Supper there is an intermingling of the elements, an intermingling of the unity and diversity of the elements, and of those who participate in the Supper, in such a way that the sum of the individual parts (or participants) is greater than the unity of the whole. Christ Himself is enhanced and expanded by the participation of His people in the

Supper (if we can think of God in terms of size, which of course we can't. Nonetheless, Christ grows with His people, as they grow more mature in the faith and as they grow in numbers.)

BOTH/AND

To clarify what Paul meant, he continued,

"Consider the people of Israel: are not those who eat the sacrifices participants in the altar? What do I imply then? That food offered to idols is anything, or that an idol is anything? No, I imply that what pagans sacrifice they offer to demons and not to God. I do not want you to be participants with demons. You cannot drink the cup of the Lord and the cup of demons. You cannot partake of the table of the Lord and the table of demons. Shall we provoke the Lord to jealousy? Are we stronger than he?" (vs. 18-22).

Pointing again to the distinction he made in Romans 9:6 he reiterates that the people of Israel are those who eat the sacrifices and participate in the "altar." All Israel participated in the sacraments of the Old Testament. That is what defined the people of Israel. And yet, his point was that in spite of the fact of their participation in the religious and cultural practices given to them, some of them were not genuine participants—"not all who are descended from Israel belong to Israel" (Romans 9:6). Many Israelites during many periods of history were not faithful. That's the story of the Old Testament. Idolatry continued to plague Israel throughout her existence until it culminated in the destruction of Jerusalem in A.D. 70.

In the same way the Corinthians were not immune from the temptations of idolatry. Paul clearly spelled out this implication when he said, that the Corinthians "cannot drink the cup of the Lord and the cup of demons" (v. 21) without falling into the same sin of idolatry that ancient Israel fell into. He said that Christianity is an exclusive religion because God is a jealous God. The effort to participate in pagan holidays and at the same time maintain Christian faithfulness is impossible. It can't be done. Christ is not part of a pantheon of Gods. His position and authority are not shared with other gods. All religions do not teach the same things. Christianity is unique because God is unique—Christ is unique. And any position that teaches otherwise is either pagan or apostate.

If you have heard what Paul has said, you will realize that we currently live in a time and in a culture that believes and teaches what is contrary to the truths of Scripture. Indeed, the effort toward religious tolerance that is taught everywhere today is a movement into paganism and apostasy—and it is justified by an appeal to reason, humility, and enlightened knowledge (or contemporary sensitivity).

These same things had been going on in Corinth, and Paul was trying to correct them. What some of the Corinthians leaders called reason, humility, and enlightened knowledge, Paul called worldly wisdom and contrasted such ideas to godly wisdom. His point was that what the non-Christian world thought was wisdom was revealed in Scripture to be foolishness in the light of Christ.

24. Not About "Me"

"All things are lawful," but not all things are helpful. "All things are lawful," but not all things build up. Let no one seek his own good, but the good of his neighbor. Eat whatever is sold in the meat market without raising any question on the ground of conscience. For "the earth is the Lord's, and the fullness thereof." If one of the unbelievers invites you to dinner and you are disposed to go, eat whatever is set before you without raising any question on the ground of conscience. But if someone says to you, "This has been offered in sacrifice," then do not eat it, for the sake of the one who informed you, and for the sake of conscience— I do not mean your conscience, but his. For why should my liberty be determined by someone else's conscience? If I partake with thankfulness, why am I denounced because of that for which I give thanks? So, whether you eat or drink, or whatever you do, do all to the glory of God. Give no offense to Jews or to Greeks or to the church of God, just as I try to please everyone in everything I do, not seeking my own advantage, but that of many, that they may be saved. — 1 Corinthians 10:23-33*

Paul had been talking about our freedom in Christ, that in Christ people are free from superstition and godless cultural practices. He began this section in chapter eight talking about various food prohibitions and practices as an example of Christian freedom. He had elsewhere discussed the fact that Christians are free from the Old Testament food laws. Here he showed that Christians are also free from pagan food practices.

What made the Old Testament food laws binding was the power of God. And what freed people from those Old Testament food laws was the power of Christ. Here he argued that only God has spiritual power, and God has given all spiritual authority and power to Jesus Christ (Matthew 28:18). Therefore, the pagan gods have no power. Their sacrifices and ceremonies have no consequences, and so whatever power was thought to be transmitted to food that had been sacrificed to idols was nonexistent because false gods have no power to begin with.

Therefore, Christians could eat food that had been sacrificed or dedicated to pagan idols because they knew that there was no spiritual power associated with such food. Pagan idols were dead and powerless to do anything. So, there was no danger or threat from such idols or from anything associated with them.

And yet Paul did make a case against eating food that had been sacrificed or dedicated to idols that was based, not on the power of pagan idols, but on the weakness of Christian brothers. Paul had argued that practicing radical Christian freedom in the presence of weaker Christians, Christians who did not fully or correctly take their own weaknesses into consideration, could result in the overestimation of their own strength, their own ability to resist the pull of their old pagan habits, and lead them back into sin. Therefore it was incumbent upon the more mature Christians to model faithfulness in such a way as not to lead other Christians astray. It was an argument, not based on Christian freedom, but based on Christian responsibility to one's weaker, less mature brothers and sisters. Of course Christians are free, but we are also responsible to God and for one another.

AVOIDED

"'All things are lawful,' but not all things are helpful. 'All things are lawful,' but not all things build up'" (v. 23). *Lawful* is a correct translation of the Greek, but in this context it means *permissible*. Paul was saying that while all things are permitted, not all permitted things are helpful, not all permitted things contribute to Christian growth and maturity. Sometimes some things that are permitted should be avoided, if not for our own sake then for the sake of others. Paul went on,

> "if someone says to you, 'This has been offered in sacrifice,' then do not eat it, for the sake of the one who informed you, and for the sake of conscience—I do not mean your conscience, but his. For why should my liberty be determined by someone else's conscience?" (vs. 28-29).

We may ask why we should not be free to express our freedom in Christ any way we please. God is sovereign, Christ is Lord, and Christians are free in Christ. All of these things are true. However, said Paul, "Let no one seek his own good, but the good of his neighbor" (v. 24).

This hearkens back to Jesus admonition in Matthew 20:25-28:

> "You know that the rulers of the Gentiles lord it over them, and their great ones exercise authority over them. It shall not be so among you.

But whoever would be great among you must be your servant, and
whoever would be first among you must be your slave, even as the Son
of Man came not to be served but to serve."

Having children provides this same lesson. Before they have children,
parents are free to do all sorts of things for their own benefit and pleasure.
But when children are in the home, some things must be curtailed—not
because they are wrong, not because they are forbidden or unlawful, but
because children are prone to mimic behaviors they see without discernment. "Monkey see, monkey do," as the old adage goes. Children learn
by imitation, so adults need to do only those things that will not be
abused or misused by those who are less discerning.

Christians are free to eat whatever is available at the market without
concerns about propriety, morality, or conscience. Because pagan rituals
have no spiritual power there is no spiritual danger from pagan ritual
foods. But if someone makes a point about the fact that the food is associated with pagan rituals, if someone brings it up, if someone points it out
to you, then there is another concern.

This new concern is not about the food, or your freedom to eat
whatever you want, but about the person who brought up the concern. If
it was not an issue for that person, he would not have brought it up. So, if
the concern is raised, it is a real concern. And it is incumbent upon the
more mature Christian to set an example that will not be misinterpreted
by the less mature Christian, or by the person who has yet to confess
Christ as Lord. At this point, the issue is not the food or the power of pagan gods, but service to a fellow or potential Christian. Our obligation to
be of service to others trumps our freedom in Christ to do what pleases us.

Paul has delineated an important principle here, that the controlling
conscience among Christians is the weaker conscience, or we could say
the more sensitive conscience. We should think of it as setting a good example. But let's not forget that while we want to set a good example, we
must not forget or neglect the greater responsibility to teach our children
how to discern good and evil for themselves.

That's what it's really all about—knowing the difference between
good and evil so that we can follow the good and avoid the evil. For children these things are pretty black and white. As we experience more of
the world, we find that what was once black and white shifts into various
shades of gray. With worldly experience comes accommodation and tolerance. The more we experience a thing, the more tolerant we become of

it and the more we accommodate ourselves to it, regardless of what we think of it. Over time it becomes more of a commonplace element in our experience. We take less notice of it and just accept it as part of our environment.

ACCOMMODATION

This psychological process of accommodation is the basis of the long strategy to make homosexuality (sin) acceptable. The first time a Christian encounters it he is repulsed. It is dismissed without consideration because of the biblical prejudice against it.

Make no mistake that the Bible is prejudiced against homosexuality—and against sin, as it should be. Prejudice is not a bad thing. I am prejudiced against getting run over by a truck, and against drinking poison, against theft, and against extortion, and a host of other things. I don't have to experience such things to know about them.

The Bible is not a balanced and objective philosophical treatise, it is simply true. Truth is not balanced and objective, where *balanced* means taking into consideration many perspectives and *objective* means not having a particular point of view. God does not have many perspectives, though we must not neglect the diversity of the Trinity. God has a particular point of view, and what is more, He wants us to share that particular point of view because it provides the only means of having a sustainable relationship with Him. God is not interested in examining the various points of view about a thing. He already knows what is right and what is wrong. God does not want us considering or thinking about things that are wrong (evil) in order to make some objective evaluation of them. God has already evaluated everything, and we are to follow God's determinations provided in Scripture.

Paul raised two questions that must be kept together.

> "For why should my liberty be determined by someone else's conscience? If I partake with thankfulness, why am I denounced because of that for which I give thanks?" (vs. 29-30).

They are actually the same question phrased differently in order to make a particular point. Again, Paul was not just asking questions as if he expected an answer. He was raising questions to make a point.

The point is that the relationship that Christians have with one another is more important than the exercise of our right to do whatever we want. If I give thanks to God for some food that has been dedicated to

idols, knowing that I am free in Christ to eat it without fear of the contamination of idolatry, then why does that freedom lead to my condemnation by others who are equally free in Christ, but who are still fearful of
being contaminated by sin. Clearly, these weaker Christians are at fault
for not believing or trusting in the power and authority of Jesus Christ to
protect them from the false power of false gods.

FOREGOING FREEDOM

And yet, while all of this is true, Paul makes the point that we must
forgo our personal freedom in order to maintain a relationship of trust
and unity with those whose faith is not as strong as ours. Paul's point is
that the bond of fellowship in the church is more important than our individual freedoms in Christ. The freedom to eat a particular meal or to
exercise a momentary pleasure pales in comparison with our responsibility
to maintain the bond of fellowship with others who are not as far along as
we are. Our greater responsibility is to help teach them the fullness of
God's truth. But we cannot do that if people do not trust us. Our freedom
in Christ cannot be used to disrupt the solidarity or unity of the church.

The point is that Christian freedom is not simply the freedom to do
whatever you want, but is the freedom to do what Christ wants you to
do. The point is not that Christians are free from God to follow their own
hearts or the cultural expectations of their society, but (arsy varsy) that
Christians are free from the cultural expectations of their society to follow
the dictates of God.

Why would Christians want to be free from God or free from doing
what pleases God? Why would *you* not want to do what pleases God? We
love God. We honor the Lord. We are followers of Jesus Christ, obedient
to the will of Jesus Christ, whose ministry enabled and enforced the will
of God in Scripture without changing a jot or tittle of God's law
(Matthew 5:18). In Christ Christians want to live in obedience to Scripture. If you don't want to live in such obedience, you need to reevaluate
your love for Jesus Christ and your understanding of the gospel. If you
are not willing to forsake a meal for the sake of your brothers and sisters
in Christ, how could you possibly be willing to take up your cross and
follow Jesus into persecution?

> "These things I command you, so that you will love one another. If the
> world hates you, know that it has hated me before it hated you. If you
> were of the world, the world would love you as its own; but because

you are not of the world, but I chose you out of the world, therefore the
world hates you. Remember the word that I said to you: 'A servant is
not greater than his master.' If they persecuted me, they will also persecute you. If they kept my word, they will also keep yours. But all these
things they will do to you on account of my name, because they do not
know him who sent me" (John 15:17-21).

Paul was saying that Christians who are hell-bent on exercising their
own freedom in Christ without regard for its effect upon others—even if
they are ultimately theologically correct, even if those effected are wrong
in their understanding of Christian freedom—should not be viewed as
leaders because their leadership is self-centered rather than other-cen-
tered. Christian leadership is not self-centered. Freedom without regard
for others is divisive and is not in harmony with God's call for Christian
unity and service. Again, service trumps freedom.

In summary of this section on Christian freedom that began in chapter eight, Paul said,

"So, whether you eat or drink, or whatever you do, do all to the glory
of God. Give no offense to Jews or to Greeks or to the church of God,
just as I try to please everyone in everything I do, not seeking my own
advantage, but that of many, that they may be saved" (vs. 31-33).

We are to give God glory in everything that we say and do. God is
the first priority of a Christian. Pleasing God and serving God are our first
priorities. Jesus said,

"do not be anxious, saying, 'What shall we eat?' or 'What shall we
drink?' or 'What shall we wear?' For the Gentiles seek after all these
things, and your heavenly Father knows that you need them all. But
seek first the kingdom of God and his righteousness, and all these things
will be added to you." (Matthew 6:31-34).

Whatever you do, do all to the glory of God.

Keep this in mind because the next thing that Paul said can come
into conflict with the idea of pleasing and serving God. What did he say?
"Give no offense to Jews or to Greeks or to the church of God" (v. 32).

But the Jews were terribly offended by Jesus and by Paul. Paul offended the Greeks on Mars Hill, and just about everywhere he went. And
now Paul was in the midst of offending the church at Corinth as he called
them from apostasy to faithfulness. So how are we to understand this?
How can we put God first without offending the world?

PLEASE EVERYONE?

Paul set himself up as an example to follow in this regard. He said that he tried to please everyone in everything that he did. Really? Well, that's what he said, and yet Paul is perhaps the most offensive of the biblical writers. The Jews hated Paul, the Greeks couldn't stomach him, and the church.... Again, there were those who loved Paul and there were those who hated him. And the difference had to do with Paul's instruction to "do all to the glory of God" (v. 31).

Those who loved God loved Paul. Those who loved God understood Paul. Those who loved God protected Paul (Acts 9:25). So, did Paul really try "to please everyone in everything" (v. 33)? Yes. But we need to keep these two injunctions together: 1) to do all to the glory of God, and 2) to work to please everyone in everything. The order is significant. The glory of God outranks pleasing people. We are not to please people at the expense of the glory of God, but are to refrain from offending people unnecessarily apart from doing things to the glory of God. We are not to go out of our way to offend people, but are to do everything possible to keep from offending them without demeaning the glory of God.

The only reason that anyone should have for being offended with us is that they don't like the fact that we always put God first. If someone is to be offended, they should not be offended by us. Our manners, consideration and comportment must be of the highest order. We must always operate above board, in the open with honesty and integrity—all the while putting God first in all things. Paul clarified himself by adding, "not seeking my own advantage" (v. 33). Paul was a servant of the Lord Jesus Christ, he was not his own servant. He did not put his own interests first, nor did he put them second. First was God, then he put the interests and concerns of others before his own. He put the good of the many—the people of God—before his own personal good.

But neither did he simply give people what they want. Rather, his concern was "that they may be saved" (v. 33). His first priority was God's glory, his second priority was to serve the cause or plan of salvation among the people of God. His concern was not their well-being, nor their happiness, nor their comfort or desires. Rather, his concern was their salvation. Paul simply reflected Jesus' command to "seek first the kingdom of God and his righteousness" (Matthew 6:33).

The kingdom of God is the realm of His people. God's people live in the kingdom of God. We seek to live in God's kingdom, to live as if God was king—because He is! And we are to seek His righteousness, not our own. We don't have any righteousness. The only righteousness that the people of God have is Christ's righteousness that has been imputed to us. It is real righteousness, but it is not ours. Yet, we are to strive for it by giving ourselves to Christ in everything. Thus, we are to give God the glory in all we do and help one another to give God the glory in all that they do.

No one is able to accomplish this by him- or herself. We must rely upon Christ first, and we must rely upon His people—the church—in mutual accountability and responsibility. We are to hold one another accountable and responsible to serve God and to give God the glory in all that we say and do. May it be so among us.

25. Covering

*Be imitators of me, as I am of Christ. Now I commend you because you re-
member me in everything and maintain the traditions even as I delivered them
to you. But I want you to understand that the head of every man is Christ, the
head of a wife is her husband, and the head of Christ is God. Every man who
prays or prophesies with his head covered dishonors his head, but every wife
who prays or prophesies with her head uncovered dishonors her head—it is the
same as if her head were shaven. For if a wife will not cover her head, then she
should cut her hair short. But since it is disgraceful for a wife to cut off her hair
or shave her head, let her cover her head. For a man ought not to cover his head,
since he is the image and glory of God, but woman is the glory of man.*
— 1 Corinthians 11:1-7

Monkey see, monkey do. That was Paul's advice to this church
whose leaders were engaged in apostasy and immorality. "Be
imitators of me, as I am of Christ" (v. 1). The KJV translates the
word (*mimētēs*) as *followers*, suggesting that followers imitate or mimic the
one they follow. Follower's are to reproduce the leader's thoughts and behavior, and sometimes even his looks. Paul was not so concerned with how
the Corinthians looked—though he had some concerns about clothing
styles that will come up shortly. Rather, his concern here was behavior. At
the same time, Paul was not unconcerned about how they looked because
dress, style, and mannerisms are all part of behavior, and all are a reflection
of values, beliefs, and morality.

Paul was engaged in the ministry of modeling. He was a model Christian. He set himself up as the one to emulate. Paul saw himself as a trend
setter in the Christian church. He understood himself to be a foundation
stone for a social movement that would utterly change the world—and it
did!

What does it mean to imitate Paul? How do we do that today? Can we
do that? Is it important? Paul answers these questions in the next verse:

"Now I commend you because you remember me in everything and maintain the traditions even as I delivered them to you" (v. 2).

Paul commended the Corinthians. He has trust and confidence in them in spite of the fact of the apostasy and immorality of some of their leaders. He had confidence that the body of believers would be corrected and strengthened by the Spirit of Christ—saving some and casting some out. His confidence was not simply in them as individuals, but in Christ and in Christ's power to save and sanctify all of His people. Christ is not stopped by apostasy and immorality. His truth marches on, healing and correcting the sin that He encounters. Sin does not stop Jesus Christ—not at all! He came to conquer sin and death, and is eager to confront it.

Normally, when something dirty touches something clean the dirt is transmitted and pollutes what was previously clean—sometimes a lot, and sometimes a little. However, when Christ touches a thing His cleansing and purity are transmitted. The dirt and pollution do not accrue to Christ, rather His purity and righteousness accrue to the thing touched. The point is that in Christ the normal transfers of purity and pollution are reversed. When Christ interacts with apostasy and immorality their unrighteousness does not flow to Him. Rather, His righteousness flows to them. The touch of the Lord purifies what He touches.

Paul commended the Corinthians because they remembered him. They remembered Paul's faithfulness, Paul's model. And they didn't just remember him now and then. It was not an occasional thoughtfulness of Paul, but they remembered him "in everything" (*pas*). Clearly, Paul was speaking to those who do in fact remember him in everything, but he was also speaking to the whole church and calling them all to remember him in everything, and to imitate him in all things. Paul was speaking to the whole Corinthian church, some of whom were faithful and some of whom were not. The point is that the moral imperative of obedience applied to them all.

PRECEPTS

Note also that there are three English words used to translate the Greek (*paradosis*)—traditions, doctrines, and ordinances. *Paradosis* means objectively, that which is delivered, the substance or content of a teaching. Secondly, it refers to the body of precepts, and ritual(s) associated with various precepts. It refers to doctrine, but not *merely* doctrine. Rather, it includes the social practices associated with doctrine. The Old Testament often prescribed various social rituals with various doctrines as a way to give life to the doctrines, and to help people keep various teachings in re-membrance. Paul used the word *paradosis* to suggest a passing on of something important by word of mouth, and it included both knowledge and the practice of cultural norms.

Paul tells the Corinthians to "maintain the traditions" (v. 2) of faith-fulness. He was not talking about the "traditions of men" (Mark 7:8, Colossians 2:8), but the religious practices and habits of faithfulness that are biblical, those which have been instituted by Jesus Christ regarding worship and ordinary life. He was speaking in particular about the tradi-tions that he—Paul—had given to them, and which he now went on to clarify.

The first thing that he did is to ground his clarification in a discussion of headship or authority—the power or right to give orders and make de-cisions. In a court of law the very first issue that is raised is the issue of ju-risdiction. Jurisdiction determines whether this or that particular court has the right and authority to adjudicate in a particular matter. Before a court does anything, it must determine whether it has proper jurisdiction. That is what Paul was doing in his discussion of headship.

"I want you to understand that the head of every man is Christ, the head of a wife is her husband, and the head of Christ is God" (v. 3). Paul was describing a kind of chain of command or jurisdictional order. It is important to note that Paul's language is universal, Christ is the head of *every* man. Not *some* men, but *every* man. We might be tempted to limit the context to the Corinthian church, and say that Paul meant that Christ was the head of every male *church member*. But we can only make such a determination by speculation that doesn't agree with Paul's actual words. We limit Paul's meaning because Jesus said that "all authority in heaven and on earth has been given to" Him (Matthew 28:18). If all authority was given to Jesus Christ, then He would indeed be the head of all, not just church members.

The fact that Jesus is Lord does not mean that His Lordship just ap-plies to people who agree with Him. Jesus is Lord *of* all, or He is not Lord *at* all. Paul penned one of the earliest Christian creeds in Romans 10:9, "if you confess with your mouth that Jesus is Lord and believe in your heart that God raised him from the dead, you will be saved."

The earliest and most consistent understanding of this creed was that it is universal. It applies to everyone, and at the same time it is conditional. *If* you confess—not everyone will, in spite of the universal imperative.

Paul continued, "the head of a wife is her husband" (v. 3). Just as Jesus is in submission to God the Father, so the husband must be in submission to Jesus the Son. Remember that Jesus did not do what He wanted to do, He did what God wanted Him to do.

"Father, if you are willing, remove this cup from me. Nevertheless, not my will, but yours, be done" (Luke 22:42).

"So Jesus said to them, 'When you have lifted up the Son of Man, then you will know that I am he, and that I do nothing on my own authority, but speak just as the Father taught me'" (John 8:28).

All authority is authority in submission, with God the Father at the top of the heap. Thus, the husband has limited authority over his wife because he must live in submission to Christ. His primary authority is the authority to follow Christ in obedience.

CHAIN OF COMMAND

So, the chain of command is: God, Christ, husband, wife. But we must understand that authority is not the same as status, and furthermore that Christian authority is not the same as worldly authority.

"Jesus called them to him and said, 'You know that the rulers of the Gentiles lord it over them, and their great ones exercise authority over them. It shall not be so among you. But whoever would be great among you must be your servant, and whoever would be first among you must be your slave, even as the Son of Man came not to be served but to serve, and to give his life as a ransom for many'" (Matthew 20-25-28).

Christian authority—headship—is, then, service and responsibility, not domineering power.

God is the head of Christ, who is the head of every man. And the husband is the head of his wife. Christian headship is, then, a biblical family office to which men are called and elected by God (and voted into office by the wife who votes *yes* to his proposal of marriage). In addition the office of headship provides a double bind. Husbands are under Christ and in service to their wives. Husbands are bound by the authority of Christ and by loving service to their wives, who by virtue of their marriage concur with God's calling and election of their husbands. Husbands are responsible *to* Jesus Christ for themselves, for their wives, and for their children. Wives are responsible *to* their husbands for themselves and for their children. And children are in the process of learning Christian service and responsibility. That's the model.

Paul now begins a discussion about the tradition of Christian worship, as he understood it. Differentiating between husbands and wives, Paul said that "Every man who prays or prophesies" (v. 4) does one thing, or does it one way, "but every wife who prays or prophesies" (v. 5) does it another way. Before we get into the different ways that husbands and wives attend to their various responsibilities in worship, notice that both husbands and wives are described as praying and prophesying. This has nothing to do with worship leadership, but everything to do with worship participation. Paul is not discussing worship leadership responsibilities, but common responsibilities in worship. From the earliest times Christians prayed and sang together. That's what Paul was talking about.

To see the ordinary way that this played out requires us to understand what Paul meant by *prophesies (prophēteuō)*. The Greek word can mean to foretell events and to divine, as in using divine powers to know things not knowable through the ordinary senses. Of course, Christians know God through the power and presence of the Holy Spirit through regeneration. And though Jesus spoke things that are difficult to understand, He did not teach mystical prognostication as practiced in pagan religions. Though there are mysterious things about Christianity, Christianity is not a mystery religion. Rather, in the context that Paul used this word, it is better understood to mean "speaking under inspiration." Again, we are not talking about some magical or mysterious thing, though the process remains mysterious because we don't know how it happens, other than attributing it to the power and presence of the Holy Spirit.

I want to suggest that Paul was talking about the ordinary things of worship—praying, singing, reading scripture, etc. All of these things occur under the influence and inspiration of the Holy Spirit, and both men and women do them. Both men and women are to live and worship under the influence of the Holy Spirit, and both will at times speak under the influence of the Holy Spirit in prayer and song.

At the same time, we must not limit our understanding of worship to mean an hour on Sunday mornings. True Christian worship is a way of living in thankfulness and faithfulness to God in all things—all things, not some things, all the time, not just some of the time. Thus, worship must be at the very center and heart of everything that we do. Worship affects the way we live our lives, not just what we do on Sunday mornings, though it has a particular focus on Sunday mornings.

CULTURAL NORMS

All that having been said, it seems most likely that Paul was discussing some of the cultural norms—Christian cultural norms—of worship participation, which affect Sunday mornings and often spill over into our everyday living. Paul called attention to the social norm that men who participated in Sunday morning worship with their heads covered dishonored their head—Christ. And the opposite was true for women. Paul's comments testify that such a norm was in existence at that time. That may seem odd at this point in history. But the traditional practice up until the 1960s was for men to take their hats off when they came into church, and for women to wear hats to church—and not just in America, but universally, virtually everywhere there was Christian worship.

What has happened since the 1960s is interesting. Women today seldom, if ever, wear hats to church, regardless of their denomination. Things have changed for women in response to the Women's Liberation Movement. Nonetheless, many men still remove their hats in church, if they wear them to church.

I doubt that God ultimately cares whether people wear hats. That is not the issue. Rather, the issue is honoring the principle of headship, and doing so in various cultural ways as a testimony to the wider society. Paul simply cited a particular cultural practice of the day that was in use to symbolize the idea of honoring authority. And that cultural practice continued from the first century to the twentieth. Styles of hats (head coverings) changed with national and historical trends, but the basic rules of hat wearing in church did not change for twenty centuries, until Women's Liberation became popular.

I had jury duty a couple of weeks ago, and before the judge (a woman) came into the room the bailiff instructed all who were present to remove their hats. Something of this biblical cultural practice regarding hats and authority still survives. There is real power in cultural norms.

Paul's point was that it was important to honor authority, and that because men and women had different kinds of authority they showed that honor in different ways. Men, husbands, who were in direct authority to Christ came to church "hat in hand" so to speak, in visible submission to Christ. And women, who were in authority to Christ through the authority of their husbands, kept their heads covered in honor of the authority of Christ through Christ's representatives—their husbands. Head covering symbolized authority and power, service and responsibility. There is some good symbolism in all of this, and I think that Paul's point was to honor God through various cultural practices or norms.

The issue is not women's rights or male domination, both of which are manifestations of pride and self-concern, and are—or should be—foreign to Christianity. This misunderstanding is not new. The issue is God's honor and authority. The disciples themselves had misunderstood Jesus' authority, and asked to "sit, one at your right hand and one at your left, in your glory" (Mark 10:37). The story continues:

> "Jesus said to them, 'You do not know what you are asking. Are you able to drink the cup that I drink, or to be baptized with the baptism with which I am baptized?' And they said to him, 'We are able.' And Jesus said to them, 'The cup that I drink you will drink, and with the baptism with which I am baptized, you will be baptized, but to sit at my right hand or at my left is not mine to grant, but it is for those for whom it has been prepared.' And when the ten heard it, they began to be indignant at James and John. And Jesus called them to him and said to them, 'You know that those who are considered rulers of the Gentiles lord it over them, and their great ones exercise authority over them. But it shall not be so among you. But whoever would be great among you must be your servant, and whoever would be first among you must be slave of all. For even the Son of Man came not to be served but to serve, and to give his life as a ransom for many'" (Mark 10:38-45).

The point is that the disciples misunderstood what Jesus was doing. They thought that He was conferring status and they wanted to be at the head of the line. But Jesus was not conferring status, at least not as they understood it. He was conferring obligation and responsibility—servanthood. They had been interested in getting the honor and status of association with Jesus Christ. But Christ was interested in serving the Lord Himself and enlisting others to serve the Lord in His stead. They wanted to *get*, He wanted them to *give*. It is a classic problem in the life of the church. People come to Christ and to His church with the wrong hopes and dreams. People have it arsy varsy. They want what is best for themselves. Christ wants what is best for God.

26. HEAD DRESSING

For man was not made from woman, but woman from man. Neither was man created for woman, but woman for man. That is why a wife ought to have a symbol of authority on her head, because of the angels. Nevertheless, in the Lord woman is not independent of man nor man of woman; for as woman was made from man, so man is now born of woman. And all things are from God. Judge for yourselves: is it proper for a wife to pray to God with her head uncovered? Does not nature itself teach you that if a man wears long hair it is a disgrace for him, but if a woman has long hair, it is her glory? For her hair is given to her for a covering. If anyone is inclined to be contentious, we have no such practice, nor do the churches of God. — 1 Corinthians 11:8-16

And the Lord will make you the head and not the tail, and you shall only go up and not down, if you obey the commandments of the Lord your God, which I command you today, being careful to do them. — Deuteronomy 28:13

Today, children—male and female—come from the bodies of women at birth. That's what motherhood means. But in the biblical story of Creation, the first woman came from or was made from the rib of the body of the man. Woman was a derivative creation of man.

The cultural practice regarding head coverings reflected and symbolized the biblical Creation story, the original order and authority structure in the world. The symbol is not about the subjugation of women or the superiority of men, but the universal submission to God's authority and the human responsibility that is necessary in order to live under God's authority. Both men and women were assigned various roles and responsibilities as a cultural reminder of God's authority, and of our responsibility.

Hats (head coverings) have been practically universal throughout history as people lived outside in the elements, unlike today when few Western people wear hats, and people live inside. Hats are a form of protection from the elements, warmth in the cold, shade in the sun, protection from the rain. Hats, then, symbolize care, protection, and shielding.

Men were to uncover their heads during worship, symbolizing their direct or unprotected and unshielded relationship with and responsibility to Jesus Christ. In contrast, Women were to cover their heads during worship, symbolizing their protection, their shielding from the harsh elements of reality by the power and authority of their husbands. Their head covering symbolized the fact that wives honored their husband's (or father's) protective authority and the fact that their husbands (or fathers) honored their own responsibility to Jesus Christ. Paul's head covering instructions were not just for women, but were for both men and women.

The couple was treated as a unit. It was a kind of double symbolism, reflecting the double bind of the husband's authority under Christ and his service to his wife and family, his commitment to their care and protection, and his commitment of faithfulness to God. It was also a symbol of the covenant union between husband and wife, and also symbolically reflected the covenantal relationship between God and His people.

REPRESENTATIVE GOVERNMENT

All biblical government is representative government, and it always exists and operates through various hierarchies of authority and responsibility. Thus, the wearing of a head covering was for the wife a cultural expression of the representative authority of her husband who was a recognized member of Christ's kingdom (and who was also under authority). He had authority over her, but his primary responsibility was her well-being because of Christ's authority over him.

When all authority is hierarchical, then every person has some other person to whom he or she is personally responsible. In the Christian scheme of things husbands are responsible to Jesus Christ through the various authorities He has established through the structures of church and state. Christian husbands are personally responsible to the elders of the churches to which they belong. And wives are directly responsible to their husbands. The personal relationship that wives have to Jesus Christ is a derivative relationship through their husbands, which means that the authority of Christ is real, and the derivative authorities He has established are equally real. In addition, the biblical structures of responsibility and authority reflect and symbolize the authority relationships within the Trinity. There is a hierarchy of authority in the Trinity, yet there is equality of being.

We must also remember that the positions of biblical leadership are positions of servanthood. Husbands were charged with acquiring and maintaining family provisions—food and shelter, protection from the elements (Ephesians 5:25-30). The husband's responsibility was to provide for the sustenance and protection for his wife and family, and her wearing of head coverings was a symbol of his protection and authority. It was also a symbol of devotion (Colossians 3:18), of the wife's love and devotion to her husband and the husband's love and devotion to Jesus Christ and to his (the husband's) wife.

"Nevertheless, in the Lord woman is not independent of man nor man of woman" (v. 11). Man and woman, husband and wife are not independent entities. The Greek word translated as *independent* (*chōris*) means without. The woman (*gunē*—literally female) is not without the man (*anēr*—literally male). Man (the species) is composed of male and female. "So God created man in his own image, in the image of God he created him; male and female he created them" (Genesis 1:27). Individuals are not independent units of humanity. Rather, one unit of humanity is male and female (Genesis 2:24). The unit is required for reproduction, for the sustainment of human life.

While there is nothing wrong with being unmarried, the Bible teaches that it is better to marry (1 Timothy 3:2). Paul does teach that there are times when it is better not to marry (Matthew 19:10), but the context of that advice was the destruction of Jerusalem in A.D. 70. This was not generic advice, but was intended for a specific time and circumstance. Paul also taught that it is "better to marry than to be aflame with passion" (1 Corinthians 7:9).

ECONOMIC UNIT

Until very recently in history, families, that is to say husband and wife, were considered to be a single economic unit. This is still part of the U.S. Tax Code. The word *economic* comes from the Greek word *oikos*, which means *household*. It did not mean that men "worked" and women didn't. It did not mean that men worked outside the home and women worked inside the home. Rather, it meant that the family household was the central focus and location of work. The household was an economic unit. With industrialization, work moved from the household to the factory and/or office. The point is that over time the focus of work has moved out of the household.

It is also a well-established fact that the industrialization that has occurred over the past 200 years has not only completely changed the most fundamental structures of human society, but has had a particularly detri-

mental effect on the family, on the bonds of family life, and on family responsibilities. It has also distanced contemporary culture from the values
and norms of the Bible. So, it is no surprise that we have difficulty understanding and/or adapting to biblical culture. At best biblical culture in
contemporary society operates in fits and starts. This is only to say that
the Kingdom of God is not yet manifest in its fullness.

Note that the Bible plays a key role in God's long range plan to move
biblical culture from the periphery to the center of human society. Christian culture today is a counter culture in that the dominant contemporary
culture is not Christian. And it is unlikely that it ever was completely
Christian. Nonetheless we must understand that God intends to change
human culture and the structures of human societies to conform to the
values and practices taught in Scripture. Thus, Christians cannot avoid
culture by retreating into various Christian ghettos (sub-cultures), nor by
being assimilated into the popular culture—not even in the name of Jesus.

Many Christians and their contemporary churches are just as worldly
as the surrounding culture, except that they practice their worldliness in
the name of Jesus—thinking and saying one thing while doing another.
This is not how things should be! Christians are to be actively involved in
the centers of human culture, influencing those centers with biblical values and practices. Christians are to influence the centers of culture, not be
influenced by them. The difference is critical and has proven to be difficult to accomplish.

The classic formulation is for Christians to be *in* the culture but not
of the culture, to live in its midst without being caught up in it, without
being defined by it, without finding their identity in it. Unfortunately,
too many people today are *in* the church and *of* the world. That is, they
are caught up in popular culture through a baptized version of it without
realizing that there is not much difference between those who covet sin a
little and those who covet sin a lot.

This is the primary mechanism that drains Christianity of its strength
in our day. People think that they are Christian because they "walked the
aisle," or because they go to church, or because they grew up in the
church. The world and the church are awash in a kind of logical discon-
nect, where people say they believe in something but act as if they don't—
except possibly sometimes at church. At church they dress their secular
beliefs in Christian clothes. They believe those who teach that church and
God and religion are fine, but must not mix with government, politics, or

the work place, that it is wrong to practice Christianity if someone objects to it.

CREATION ORDER

In God's culture Adam was created before Eve, and she was created differently, by a different process, a derivative process, and to function in a different role. Adam, the man, had greater responsibility because he was created first. So, his greater responsibility required greater authority. Women have envied Adam's position of authority over the years, thinking him to have been more important or of a higher status in God's eyes. That's not the way that God sees it, but it is the way that sinful people see it. Women have striven for equality without understanding that their claim to equality is based on the presumption that they know more than God, who created them, or that they are more moral than God, who did not institute the kind of equality that sinners want.

Paul wrote to the Philippians about this issue of social equality,

> "Have this mind among yourselves, which is yours in Christ Jesus, who, though he was in the form of God, did not count equality with God a thing to be grasped, but made himself nothing, taking the form of a servant, being born in the likeness of men. And being found in human form, he humbled himself by becoming obedient to the point of death, even death on a cross" (Philippians 2:5-8).

Jesus was not concerned about equality. He was concerned about God's justice and He appealed to God's grace. God knew that Jacob and Esau were not equal (Romans 9:13), nor are any other two people. Equality of being is a mirage.

The very heart of Christianity is about justice and grace, truth and mercy. And God's justice is representational justice, and His grace is representational grace because justice and grace are expressions of authority, and God's authority is always representational authority. Our union with Christ through regeneration is not a union of equality of any sort. It is, rather, a representational union. Christ is our head, our representative on the cross, and through His resurrection, in God's judgment court. He represents us before God, sort of like your senator represents you in the senate, or your defense lawyer represents you in court.

Adam was created and given a job—naming and classifying the animals. Only then he was given a wife. Why was Adam given a wife? Genesis 2:20 says it best, "there was not found a suitable helper for Adam." She

was not created to be an equal, but a helper. The Hebrew that is translated as *suitable helper* (עזר נגד) in this verse literally means exactly that.
Sinful people have assumed that being a helper is less valuable than being
the one helped. But Scripture does not suggest any such thing.

Is there anyone who does not work as a helper to someone else? I
doubt it. All jobs, all work is a form of some kind of help for someone
else. Everyone helps someone else and everyone has a boss. There is nothing demeaning about being an assistant, or in biblical terms, a servant.
Christians are called to be servants, and the "higher" people rise in Christian authority, the more service is expected of them.

Paul went on to show two things based upon verse 12, "for as
woman was made from man, so man is now born of woman. And all
things are from God."

First, he indicated that the way things are now is not is not the way
they were in the Garden. God's creation was categorically different in
form and structure from the natural processes we see in operation today.
At Creation, God made Eve from Adam's rib. But today men are born
from the wombs of women. God's ways and methods are not our ways
and methods. God established several cultural practices to remind us of
that fact, and Paul's injunction regarding head coverings serves in that ca-
pacity, as a reminder of the order of Creation and of God's authority.

Secondly, Paul tells us that God's authority is absolute, that "all things
are from God" (v. 12). Lest we begin to think that our ways are on a par
with God's, Paul reminds us that even the fact that women now give
birth to men is not a function of the power and authority of humanity,
but is simply another derivative authority that also belongs to God. So, if
you don't like the way that things are, the way that Paul has laid them
out, you need to take it up with God, not with Paul, and by extension,
not with the church, nor with the husband, but with God Himself—at
least as long as the husband and the church are functioning according to
God's Word. Where they are not in line with God's Word (Scripture)
they are liable to correction, but where they are in line with God's Word
they are due honor and respect. Obedience to a faithful husband—faithful
to Jesus Christ—is faithfulness to God.

CONSCIENCE

Having, then, established that Paul's understanding about head coverings is grounded and established in the Word of God, Paul appealed to

conscience, "Judge for yourselves: is it proper for a wife to pray to God with her head uncovered?" (v. 13).

Paul was saying that if you doubt his interpretation or his authority to make such determinations, then use your own judgment. Paul was not forcing his authority down their throats. Rather, Paul allowed—better yet, encouraged—people to rely upon their own conscience to determine what to do about head coverings. It is not a salvation issue. It's a cultural practice issue. It's a family issue, and it is an issue of conscience.

The KJV says that it is *comely* (*prepō*) for women to pray uncovered—proper, becoming, suitable, winsome, graceful, fitting, right. Webster said, "Applied to person or form, it (*comely*) denotes symmetry or due proportion, but it expresses less than beautiful or elegant."

Paul's teaching about head coverings appeals to a sense of propriety, of acceptable behavior or morality. Interestingly, for most of history in most cultures "uncovered" women were considered to be whores or prostitutes, to be without husbands, to be without the authority or protection of a father or husband—unprotected and vulnerable. Only in the modern and postmodern West has this changed. Or has it?

Verses 14 & 15 comprise one sentence or idea,

> "Does not nature itself teach you that if a man wears long hair it is a disgrace for him, but if a woman has long hair, it is her glory? For her hair is given to her for a covering."

Paul previously appealed to God's Word—and the various structures of authority given therein—and to human conscience. Here he appeals to nature (*phusis*) to make his point. Paul is appealing to something that is inwardly innate or self-evident. It is an appeal to character, specifically to Christian character.

Paul was appealing to the cultural maintenance of the social distinction between the sexes. In every human culture there are important social and cultural differences between men and women, differences that are manifest in dress, mannerisms, roles, and character. Some of these differences are apparent to an observer, and some are difficult for an untrained eye to see. At root Paul was appealing to the innate differences between masculinity and femininity. And Paul was saying that it is important to preserve such differences both personally and culturally. Men and women should look different and act different because they are different.

Defining or describing masculinity and femininity is quite difficult, if not impossible. Definitions and descriptions—words—struggle to capture the differences. And yet the differences are quite real. People tend to know the difference when they see it, to know it when they experience it. But putting it into words turns it into an abstraction. Words alone don't do it justice. And that is Paul's point here.

Paul was suggesting that God has distributed authority and responsibility differently to men and women, that God does not treat the sexes the same, so neither should we. And part and parcel of that difference will manifest—must manifest—itself in various cultural practices. It may not make any difference what those particular cultural practices are, as long as they are different. But if it doesn't really matter what they are, then there is no good argument for disagreeing with Paul's injunctions regarding head coverings.

Paul related the differences between men and women to their heads because Scripture provides a difference in authority and responsibility between husbands and wives. And the symbolism of head coverings points to the head, to authority. Men are not better than women, or visa versa. They are simply different, and the differences are a matter of character and culture as well as biology. The differences are also real and are to be respected personally and culturally.

Quit Carping

In conclusion Paul said, "If anyone is inclined to be contentious, we have no such practice, nor do the churches of God" (v. 16). John Gill sums up this thought well:

> if anyone will not be satisfied with reasons given, for men's praying and prophesying with their heads uncovered, and women's praying and prophesying with their heads covered; but will go on to raise objections, and continue carping and caviling, showing that they contend not for truth, but victory, can they but obtain it any way; for my part, as if the apostle should say, I shall not think it worth my while to continue the dispute any longer; enough has been said to satisfy any wise and good man, anyone that is serious, thoughtful, and modest; and shall only add, "we have no such custom, nor the churches of God;" meaning, either that men should appear covered, and women uncovered in public service, and which should have some weight with all those that have any regard to churches and their examples; or that men should be indulged in a captious and contentious spirit; a man that is always contending for contention sake, and is continually caviling and carping at everything that is said and done in churches, and is always quarreling

with one person or another, or on account of one thing or another, and is constantly giving uneasiness, is not fit to be a church member; nor ought he to be suffered to continue in the communion of the church, to the disturbance of the peace of it (Gill, John. *Exposition of the Bible*).

Strong words, but worthy of consideration.

So, should contemporary women wear head coverings? The first question to ask is, Who has jurisdiction to countermand Paul's teaching? Is it simply a women's issue? Or is it a family matter? Or should your local pastor weigh in? It seems to me that the pastor's job is to make the teaching of the Bible plain, and allow the freedom of conscience to dictate personal behavior, particularly in a case like this.

Christ abrogated several Old Testament practices as He fulfilled the Law's demands and brought the fullness of God's grace to bear upon the world. As far as I can tell, this is not one of them, but you may see it differently.

27. HERESIES

But in the following instructions I do not commend you, because when you come together it is not for the better but for the worse. For, in the first place, when you come together as a church, I hear that there are divisions among you. And I believe it in part, for there must be factions among you in order that those who are genuine among you may be recognized. When you come together, it is not the Lord's supper that you eat. For in eating, each one goes ahead with his own meal. One goes hungry, another gets drunk. What! Do you not have houses to eat and drink in? Or do you despise the church of God and humiliate those who have nothing? What shall I say to you? Shall I commend you in this? No, I will not. — 1 Corinthians 11:17-22

K-LOVE, a Contemporary Christian radio station whose motto is "Positive and Encouraging" will never express the content of verse 17, nor will K-LOVE ever consider those aspects of the biblical message that disturb or offend anyone. They know that people want encouragement and do not want chastisement, so they pander to the former and ignore the latter. The problem with such "positive thinking" is that its criteria for evaluation is not the content of a particular thought or idea, but one's own feelings about it. It is based upon a purely subjective criteria and tends to eliminate any thought or idea with which one is uncomfortable. In short, positive thinking is not based upon objective reality, but purely upon one's own subjective desires and feelings.

In contrast, Paul tells the Corinthians that he will not praise them with regard to certain aspects of their coming together for worship. Inasmuch as they imitate Paul, he does praise them. However, in certain aspects of worship they have not imitated him but have indulged their own selfish concerns. Calvin hit the nail on the head when he said of this verse, "that they were not of one accord as becomes Christians, but every one was so much taken up with his own interests, that he was not prepared to accommodate himself to others."[1]

Paul went on to say that they did not gather "for the better but for the worse" (v. 17). The gathering together of selfishness magnifies selfishness, just as the gathering together of selflessness magnifies selflessness. In other words, their attitude—that complex union of beliefs, feelings and values that each of us bring to all that we do—was not in proper alignment with Christ. Something was wrong with their worship. An unchristian attitude was undermining their worship.

ATTITUDE

An instructive definition of the word *attitude* pertains to flying aircraft. The attitude of the plane is its position in three dimensional space relative to a frame of reference, usually the horizon. The point is that the attitude of the craft indicates its position regarding a frame of reference. Applied to people, a person's attitude is that complex union of beliefs, feelings, and values that are derived from the person's frame of reference, from God who is our ultimate frame of reference. Thus, attitude is always an expression of one's faith, one's faithfulness or one's faithlessness, where faith is understood to be an expression of one's position with regard to Jesus Christ. Our attitude is a reflection of our beliefs, feelings, values, and disposition to act in certain ways. The way that we act is the fruit of our attitude. All of this is to say that attitude is a spiritual matter.

Paul notes that when the Corinthians gathered together as the church there were divisions among them, or so Paul was told. Someone noted divisions among the Corinthians and reported that observation to Paul. Was it true? Paul thought that it was, at least in part. I would even speculate that Paul hoped that it was true because Paul knew that the Corinthians were guilty of immorality and apostasy—at least some of them were. So, if there were divisions among them, then perhaps all of them were not guilty. Some of the leaders had fallen from grace, but a group of believers continued in faithfulness. Thus, the divisions in the church were for Paul a mark of hopefulness.

This insight comes from reading verse 19 back in to verse 18. Verse 19 reads, "there must be factions among you in order that those who are genuine among you may be recognized." This is a very interesting verse

---

1 Calvin, John. *Calvin's Commentaries*, XX, Baker Book House, 1993, p. 365.

because it suggests that, while Christians are to seek unity among believers, the churches will always have various kinds of divisions, schisms, and heresies because God uses those divisions to grow and sanctify His people, to help them grow in faithfulness and understanding. This suggests that, while identifying schism and heresy are important matters, the process of such identification cannot—should not—be shut down by banning the discussion of various perspectives within the churches.

No one enters into Christian faith as an orthodox believer. We are all guilty of sin and are inadequate to the task that Christ has called us to. We cannot be Christians in and of ourselves, but must rely upon the presence and power of the Holy Spirit through regeneration and lean upon the witnesses of history. In addition, no one reaches perfect sanctification in this life, which means that we continue to grow as Christians all our lives. And Christian growth is a double edged process. We grow

> "until we all attain to the unity of the faith and of the knowledge of the Son of God, to mature manhood, to the measure of the stature of the fullness of Christ, so that we may no longer be children, tossed to and fro by the waves and carried about by every wind of doctrine, by human cunning, by craftiness in deceitful schemes" (Ephesians 4:13-14).

We grow in faith and obedience that leads to ever increasing maturity. Because life in Christ is eternal, growth in Christ is also eternal.

DISILLUSIONMENT

The other edge of Christian growth and maturity involves the process of disillusionment. In Christ we are increasingly disillusioned of our sins, errors and false ideas. J.C. Ryle said,

> "The man whose soul is 'growing,' feels his own sinfulness and unworthiness more every year. He is ready to say with Job, 'I am vile,' and with Abraham, I am 'dust and ashes,' and with Jacob, 'I am not worthy of the least of all Thy mercies,' and with David, 'I am a worm,' and with Isaiah, 'I am a man of unclean lips,' and with Peter, 'I am a sinful man, O Lord' (Job xl. 4; Gen. xviii. 27; xxxii. 10; Ps. xxii. 6; Isa. vi. 5; Luke v. 8.)."[2]

Growth in grace produces an increased sensitivity and repulsion to sin, particularly one's own sin. The more people grow in grace, in faithfulness and obedience to Christ, the more they are aware of and disgusted

---

2   Ryle, J.C. *Holiness: Its Nature, Hindrances, Difficulties, and Roots,* 1879.

by sin. I suspect that this is part of the generation gap that seems to exist perennially between the young and the old. The process of Christian growth is the process of stripping us of our illusions and false ideas until we come to full agreement with God's perfect knowledge.

Consequently, it is not enough to ban thinking, reading, or discussion of aberrant theological views in the church. Everyone comes to Christ with all sorts of spiritual illusions and false ideas. It is not true that people are instantly stripped of all their false ideas upon regeneration. Rather the disillusionment process begins with regeneration as we see that we have been wrong in various ways and willingly acknowledge our errors and repent of our sin. However, that is not the end of the process. It is the beginning.

The job of church elders, then, is to engage people in theological discussion in a way and manner that convinces people of God's truth, not merely tagging various arguments as schismatic or heretical, but by providing convincing arguments that eliminate lingering false ideas in the minds of believers. Those who cling to their false ideas and beliefs in the face of God's truth will leave the congregation either from a lack of support or from the suggestion or request of the elders. God's Word always draws the faithful and repels the unfaithful through theological clarification.

The process of sanctification through discussion and clarification plays an important role in the life of the church. A lively, healthy church will not refuse to discuss aberrant ideas and/or theologies among its members, but will eagerly engage and defeat such ideas—not by bullying those who believe wrongly, nor by the use of power politics to shut them down, but by the superior arguments of God's truth, and with patience, perseverance, discipline, wisdom, discernment, and instruction (Psalm 86:11). The goal of reaching perfect sanctification in Christ cannot be reached apart from the process of growth that leads to it. To short-circuit the process for fear of where it may lead evidences a failure of faith in the power of Christ to persevere with His people and to bring them into all truth. Growth means being willing to learn and change our minds about what we believe in order to be better aligned with Scripture.

DIVISIONS

Thus, Paul said that various divisions in the church were normal because sin was both universal ("for all have sinned and come short of the glory of God"—Romans 3:23) and lingering ("If we say we have no sin, we deceive ourselves, and the truth is not in us"—1 John 1:8). There will be no perfect church this side of heaven, "for there must be factions among you in order that those who are genuine among you may be recognized" (v. 19). The factions (*heresies* in the KJV, *schisma* in the Greek) are used as a foil to prove, sharpen, and recognize genuine believers.

False beliefs "must be" in the churches, according to Paul, because

> "God from all eternity, did, by the most wise and holy counsel of His own will, freely, and unchangeably ordain whatsoever comes to pass" (*Westminster Confession of Faith* 3.1).

God's purpose is unalterable, and since there were false prophets during Old Testament times, it must be expected that false teachers would arise in the Christian churches. Satan is always busy sowing the seeds and tares of false doctrine. And human nature, being both weak and wicked, is gullible to the lies of Satan, and is easily deceived. John Gill wrote that "it cannot be thought that it should be otherwise."[3] Why would God allow falsehood to exist in His churches? For the teaching and training of the saints, for their sanctification and growth in grace, knowledge and understanding. Though God is not the author of evil, He uses evil as a backdrop from which to set apart holiness and to bring about its own destruction to the glory of His justice.

Verse 20 provides an example of how this process works. The example comes from the worship experience of the Corinthian church.

"When you come together, it is not the Lord's supper that you eat" (v. 20). Interesting. They probably thought that they were eating the Lord's Supper, but Paul told them otherwise. Here we learn that we are not always doing what we think we are doing, that we—human beings, and even Christians—are susceptible to self-delusion. Here we learn that it is possible to go through the motions of worship—eating the Lord's Supper—and still miss the point, purpose, and experience of genuine worship. This same principle is found in Matthew 7:21-23,

> "Not everyone who says to me, 'Lord, Lord,' will enter the kingdom of heaven, but the one who does the will of my Father who is in heaven. On that day many will say to me, 'Lord, Lord, did we not prophesy in your name, and cast out demons in your name, and do many mighty works in your name?' And then will I declare to them, 'I never knew you; depart from me, you workers of lawlessness.'"

3   Gill, John. *Exposition of the Whole Bible*, 1763.

"For in eating, each one goes ahead with his own meal. One goes hungry, another gets drunk" (v. 21).

Notice that not only did Paul tell them that they were not eating the Lord's Supper, but here he told them that they were eating their own supper. Verse 21 repeats the same point, that they were substituting God's thoughts and desires with their own thoughts and desires. They were not worshiping God, they were projecting themselves, substituting their own likeness for the likeness of God.

The human mind is able to both perceive and to project. It can both perceive patterns of information that exist objectively in its environment, and it can project organizational patterns onto its environment that exist subjectively in itself. We can read meaning *from* data, and we can read meaning *into* data. And it's not that the one is right and the other is wrong. Both are important. People do both all the time. Discerning order helps us understand. Projecting order helps us create. What is important is to know when to do the one and when to do the other, to know when we are engaged in the one and when we are engaged in the other.

The worship of the Corinthians, including their use of the Lord's Supper, failed to engage the objectivity of God's Word (God's thoughts and desires) in worship because they were projecting the subjectivity of their own words (thoughts and desires) in worship. Worship is one place we want to discern God's order and not project our own.

Young's Literal Version helps, "For each one takes his own supper first in the eating; and one is hungry, and another drunken" (v. 21). It is a difficult verse, but at root Paul alludes to three problems with what they were doing in their celebration of the Lord's Supper.

First, there was a kind of selfishness where each worshiper focused on *taking* rather than *receiving*. By *taking* the Lord's Supper the central actor was the taker. By *receiving* the Lord's Supper the central actor is the Giver —God. Do we *take* what is ours? Or do we *receive* what is given? It's an attitude thing.

Secondly, they were neglecting those who were hungry in their midst. It's another example of the wrong attitude, an example of self-concern and the neglect of others.

And thirdly, some were drunk. All three problems were the result of their focus in worship being on themselves and not on God. The focus was subjective, not objective. They were self-concerned and self-focused when they should have been God-concerned and God-focused. They were more interested in getting than in giving.

CHURCH ORDINANCE

Paul exploded in anger and frustration,

"What! Do you not have houses to eat and drink in? Or do you despise the church of God and humiliate those who have nothing? What shall I say to you? Shall I commend you in this? No, I will not" (v. 22).

Paul was not against eating and drinking. He was not opposed to feasting or wine. Rather, he was interested in the sanctification of the Lord's Supper—separating the Lord's Supper from common eating. The Lord's Supper had a special purpose and was to be differentiated from other eating and drinking. And secondly, it was a church ordinance not a household ordinance. It was officiated by the elders of the church, not simply the head of the household. It was a communal meal that was centered around the church community, not merely the household community.

To miss the church-centered aspects of the Lord's Supper was equivalent to despising the church of God because it failed to provide proper honor to the structures of authority established by Jesus Christ. Part of true worship involved caring for God's people, and when the needs of poor and hungry worshipers were ignored the poor and hungry were shamed by their lack in the face of the abundance of God's provision in the midst of the community. Poor people often feel out of place in a wealthy congregation, and the Corinthian church was wealthy.

God is not against wealth, but insists that wealth be used according to His dictates. God cares for His people. He provides for them by insisting that His people provide for their own, for God's people. God's church is not a place for the wealthy to hobnob. Rather, it is a place for service, for everyone's service, including—and perhaps even, especially—the wealthy.

Jesus' instructions to the rich young ruler are pertinent:

"When the young man heard this he went away sorrowful, for he had great possessions. And Jesus said to his disciples, 'Truly, I say to you, only with difficulty will a rich person enter the kingdom of heaven. Again I tell you, it is easier for a camel to go through the eye of a needle than for a rich person to enter the kingdom of God.' When the disciples heard this, they were greatly astonished, saying, 'Who then can be saved?' But Jesus looked at them and said, 'With man this is impossible, but with God all things are possible'" (Matthew 19:22-26).

What have we learned in this section of First Corinthians? First, Paul was not always encouraging, but would chastise people when they needed it.

Second, God uses people who think differently to sharpen each other; "Iron sharpens iron, and one man sharpens another" (Proverbs 27:17). Thus, theological discussion is not about winning arguments, but about learning God's truth. And when we are committed to God's truth, we are free to learn in every circumstance. The wisest Christian is never so wise that he cannot learn something from the dullest Christian. Paul's teaching about factions in the churches is about the distance between wise Christians and dull Christians, and growing in corporate unity through personal sanctification.

Thirdly, true worship is not about the worshipers who gather together, but about the God who gathers them.

And fourthly, we are all in continual need of God's grace and mercy because we continually get things wrong on our way towards perfect sanctification—and more so because we do not reach perfect sanctification in this life.

"Be merciful to me, O God, be merciful to me, for in you my soul takes refuge; in the shadow of your wings I will take refuge" (Psalm 57:1).

28. Body & Blood

For I received from the Lord what I also delivered to you, that the Lord Jesus on the night when he was betrayed took bread, and when he had given thanks, he broke it, and said, "This is my body which is for you. Do this in remembrance of me." In the same way also he took the cup, after supper, saying, "This cup is the new covenant in my blood. Do this, as often as you drink it, in remembrance of me." For as often as you eat this bread and drink the cup, you proclaim the Lord's death until he comes. Whoever, therefore, eats the bread or drinks the cup of the Lord in an unworthy manner will be guilty of profaning the body and blood of the Lord. Let a person examine himself, then, and so eat of the bread and drink of the cup. For anyone who eats and drinks without discerning the body eats and drinks judgment on himself.

— 1 Corinthians 11:23-29

W hat exactly did Paul receive from the Lord? What did he deliver to the Corinthians? Paul has been addressing this concern throughout this letter, and in particular here in the eleventh chapter. Paul received from the Lord and delivered unto the saints the "way" of Christ. He says so in 1 Corinthians 12:31, where he speaks of the greatest gift that Christ has given to His people: "But earnestly desire the higher gifts. I will show you a still more excellent way."

The spiritual gifts listed in chapter twelve are secondary to the way described in chapter thirteen. The gifts listed in chapter twelve serve to introduce what has become known as the Great Love Chapter, 1 Corinthians 13. We will speak more about this when we come to it. But note that Paul was setting up that discussion here. And it is significant that part and parcel of that set up is the institution of the Lord's Supper.

Paul received from the Lord the "way" (*hodos*) of Christ. Isaiah prophesied about this. John the Baptist, hearkening back to Isaiah, when he cried "in the wilderness: 'Prepare the way of the Lord; make his paths straight.'" (Matthew 3:3). Paul spoke of the Way when he witnessed to Felix in Rome:

"Neither can they prove to you what they now bring up against me. But this I confess to you, that according to the Way, which they call a sect, I worship the God of our fathers, believing everything laid down by the Law and written in the Prophets, having a hope in God, which these men themselves accept, that there will be a resurrection of both the just and the unjust" (Acts 24:13-15).

THE WAY

What Paul calls the *Way*, they called a *sect*. The Way of Christ refers to the entire cultural structure of Christianity in its wholeness, its totality. The Way of Christ is a way of life, a lifestyle. Paul received from Christ a vision of Christian society or culture and it was that vision, that cultural practice, that way of life, that Paul was passing on to the Corinthians. It was more than a mere vision. It was an institution, a cultural apparatus, a way of being human in the light of Christ.

The capstone of that Way is Communion or the Lord's Supper. The Lord's Supper represents and communicates the entire cultural structure of Christianity in its wholeness. At the center of that cultural apparatus is a story, the story of Jesus Christ, the story of His betrayal, death, and resurrection. But that story must be seen in its context, the context of Christ's birth as the long-awaited Messiah prophesied in the Old Testament. Thus, the entire edifice of Scripture—all of its various stories and histories—are implicated as Paul referred to the night when Jesus was betrayed. Understanding Christ's betrayal and death requires understanding the Bible, God's story—His-story—from Creation to Redemption.

And at the center of God's redemption is the body and blood of Jesus Christ. On that night Jesus

"took bread, and when he had given thanks, he broke it, and said, 'This is my body which is for you. Do this in remembrance of me'" (vs. 24-25).

Luke also recorded the story,

"And he took bread, and when he had given thanks, he broke it and gave it to them, saying, 'This is my body, which is given for you. Do this in remembrance of me'" (Luke 22:19).

The Lord's Supper is a mnemonic device to aid the memory. It helps us remember the Way of Christ. And yet the Lord's Supper is more than simply words, more than a mnemonic device. It also elicits action—eating and drinking, taking in sustenance to sustain life. So, the Supper calls us to action and not merely the remembering of old stories. It calls us to *our* place in God's Story of redemption, and to our various duties and responsibilities, joys and freedoms in Christ.

The bread is broken and given to us to remind us that Christ was given and broken for us, for our sins, not His own. People sometimes mistakenly say that they "take" communion, but such language is not biblical and conveys the wrong perspective regarding the Lord's Supper. To *take* something implies that we are the central actors, that the initiative and impetus are ours to take. Thus, it gives the wrong understanding of communion. We do not *take* it. Rather, it is *given* to us. It is a gift. Just as we do not *take* salvation from Christ, we do not take Communion. We *receive* them as gifts from God.

FINGERPRINTED

Let me also suggest that when you receive the bread of Communion and are holding it in anticipation of receiving it together in the fellowship of the church, press your thumb print into the bread. Notice that as you hold the bread, your thumb print, an expression of your unique and particular identity, is recorded in the bread. Your personal identification is pressed into the body of Christ. You are identified and fingerprinted in the bread of Christ. In the celebration of the Lord's Supper you are identified as part of the body of Christ. Your identity is impressed into the bread—the body of Christ.

"Do this in remembrance of me." The purpose of the Lord's Supper is to re-member, to reconnect with the body of Christ. This remembering is not simply a matter of memory, but a matter of membership. It is a matter of re-membership-ing, of reinforcing the bonds of membership.

> "In the same way also he took the cup, after supper, saying, 'This cup is the new covenant in my blood. Do this, as often as you drink it, in remembrance of me.'" (v. 25).

Where the bread represents the body of Christ, the wine represents the life of the Spirit of Christ. Where the bread suggests body life (action), the cup suggests covenant life (promise). As a cup holds liquid together, so the covenant holds life together. The New Covenant is none other than the final covenant of the God of Scripture through the resurrection of Jesus Christ to the glory of God the Father.

There are two elements in the Lord's Supper—bread and wine, body and spirit. And these two elements are Trinitarian in character.

"There is one body and one Spirit—just as you were called to the one hope that belongs to your call—one Lord, one faith, one baptism, one God and Father of all, who is over all and through all and in all" (Ephesians 4:4-6);

one God who is Father, Son and Holy Spirit. The bread represents the body, and the wine represents Christ's blood, Christ's Spirit, Christ's covenant. As the blood is the life of the individual body (Leviticus 17:11), so the covenant is the life of the corporate body, the church.

We equate spirit and covenant because the Spirit is the glue of God's promises that holds all things together. God's promise (His Word enfleshed in Jesus Christ and through regeneration in the lives of His people) "is the assurance of things hoped for, the conviction of things not seen" (Hebrews 11:1). Christian faith is faith in God's promises, in the veracity and reliability of God's Word.

Paul goes on to say that "as often as you eat this bread and drink the cup, you proclaim the Lord's death until he comes" (v. 26). Participating in the Lord's Supper, receiving Holy Communion is a kind of proclamation. It is an announcement that Jesus Christ is Lord and that you are His servant. It is a ceremony of covenant renewal, a reaffirmation of our commitment to God, to His truth and to His people. And it is a public proclamation in that it is made publicly in the light of day before a watching world. It is an intensely personal matter, but it is not private.

Paul said that it is a proclamation of the "Lord's death until he comes" (v. 26). Why did Paul call it a proclamation of Christ's *death*? Why not a proclamation of Christ's *resurrection*? In truth it is both, but Christ's death was the necessary condition for His resurrection. Paul's phrasing tells us that we currently live between the time of Christ's death and His return in glory. The phrase is descriptive of the most important element of the time in which we live, the time of "travail until Christ should be formed in you," as Paul said in Galatians 4:19.

"We know that the whole creation groans and travails in pain together until now. And not only so, but ourselves also, who have the firstfruit of the Spirit, even we ourselves groan within ourselves, awaiting adoption, the redemption of our body" (Romans 8:23).

The guiding paradigm of the history of this world began with Christ's death and will culminate in His return in glory.

UNWORTHILY

Having set the markers for all history—Christ's death and return, Paul set forth a caution. "Whoever, therefore, eats the bread or drinks the cup of the Lord in an unworthy manner will be guilty of profaning the body and blood of the Lord" (v. 27). The caution applies to whoever, suggesting that it doesn't matter who you are or who you think you are, the caution belongs to *you*.

To suggest that the Lord's Supper can be engaged improperly means that there is a proper way to participate in it, a correct way (*hodos*) to celebrate it. The issue is worthiness, and Paul has set the caution in the negative—unworthily (*anaxiōs*), irreverently, without respect. It is significant that Paul has told us how *not* to do it, rather than telling us how to do it. The negative caution provides maximum freedom of expression. If he had told us how to do it, there would only be one way to do it. But by telling us how not to do it, we are free to do it however we choose, as long as we don't do it that one certain way—unworthily. The Ten Commandments are set negatively in the same way for the same reason—to provide maximum human freedom.

In order to follow Paul's admonition, we must know the difference between being worthy and being unworthy to receive the sacrament. At first glance it would appear that we must find or provide our own worthiness, that we must do something or accomplish something that will provide our own worthiness, that we must be worthy of the sacrament in ourselves. But nothing could be farther from the truth. Rather, Paul was pointing to our unworthiness. Paul knows that we are unworthy, that we cannot provide any personal worthiness in and of ourselves. As long as we look to ourselves for worthiness we will be unworthy. Paul has set the bar of communion participation out of human reach, and he has done so intentionally.

If we could reach the bar ourselves, we could *take* communion. But we cannot take it ourselves. Rather, we must receive it. It must be given. We have no worthiness in and of ourselves, so any worthiness that may accrue to us must come from without. It must come from Christ alone who is alone worthy. It is only the power and presence of the Holy Spirit in us through regeneration that provides our worthiness for participation in the Lord's Supper. To participate in the Supper apart from personal regeneration is to participate unworthily, and to invite—to call down—the consequences of "profaning the body and blood of the Lord" (v. 27). To profane the name of the Lord is a violation of the Third Commandment, and constitutes serious sin with serious consequences.

The simple act of participating in the Lord's Supper brings about the separation of the saved and the lost by distinguishing the difference between them, that difference being regeneration or Christ-given worthiness. Participating in the Lord's Supper is not neutral. It is not irrelevant. Rather, it is efficacious. It has the power to bring about an effect.

EFFICACIOUS

It is not simply helpful for the saved, those who have been regenerated by the Holy Spirit. It is also harmful for the lost, those who have not been regenerated. Receiving the Lord's Supper helps the faithful grow in faithfulness by reaffirming their covenantal faithfulness. But it also harms the unfaithful by contributing to their covenantal unfaithfulness. When the unfaithful disregard Paul's caution and assume their own personal worthiness apart from the regeneration of Christ they profane God's name. By taking the sacrament apart from the worthiness that only Christ provides through regeneration, they falsely claim the name of Jesus Christ for themselves, and add to their violation of God's Word by engaging the sin of presumption (Romans 2:4, Deuteronomy 18:20).

This fact reinforces the truth that God's covenant through Jesus Christ carries both blessings and curses. It is a blessing to the faithful and a curse to the unfaithful. The salvation provided by Jesus Christ offers the last and only hope for redemption from the damnation that has been accruing to this world since the time of Adam's Fall. To ignore Christ, or to pretend or presume salvation apart from regeneration, is to continue on the road to damnation. And to disavow or disobey Christ is to get into the fast lane on the highway to damnation. The curse was set in motion by Adam. The blessing was set in motion by Christ. There are no other alternatives.

How can a person know if he or she is regenerate? Paul counsels us, "Let a person examine himself, then, and so eat of the bread and drink of the cup" (v. 28). Paul calls people to self-examination. And what is this examination looking for? It is looking for the worthiness to receive the sacrament. Because Christ alone provides that worthiness and because that worthiness must be present in those who receive the sacrament, it can only be concluded that Christ's worthiness must be present in the recipient through the power and presence of Christ alone through regeneration. The Spirit of Jesus Christ, the Holy Spirit, must actually be present in the recipient.

EXAMINATION

Paul calls for self examination because no other examination can reveal Christ's presence through regeneration. Church elders examine prospective members and the children of believers prior to their participation in the Lord's Supper, but the elders' evaluation of the assurance of salvation is not perfect. It is fallible. The elders do not have insight into the secret things of God. Only the individual believer can know for sure whether or not he or she is regenerate. But neither are there any infallible methods that can guarantee such assurance. Rather, the assurance of salvation is a function of faith, and "faith is the assurance of things hoped for, the conviction of things not seen" (Hebrews 11:1). For those who are regenerate, no proof is necessary, and for those who are not, none is possible. Thus, Paul calls for self-examination. It is a matter between the individual and God, though it should be concurred by the elders.

But please do not think that the charismatic understanding of regeneration that is so popular in contemporary culture is the biblical teaching regarding regeneration. I'm not suggesting that charismatics are not regenerate—some are, and some aren't (Matthew 7:21-ff). I'm only suggesting that God's regeneration is not programmable. It doesn't always happen in the same way. It is not always an Acts 2 Pentecostal tongues of fire experience. Sometimes it is a "fan(ing) into flame the gift of God" that has been given through baptism, as was the regeneration of Timothy (2 Timothy 1:6). Sometimes it is the simple response to God's call that is completely ordinary and unremarkable, as the regeneration of Simon and Andrew.

> "And walking along beside the sea of Galilee, He (Christ) saw Simon and Andrew his brother casting a net into the sea; for they were fishermen. And Jesus said to them, 'Come after Me and I will make you fishers of men.' And immediately they left their nets and followed Him" (Mark 1:16-18).

No bells, no whistles, no tongues of fire, just simple obedience. And we know that obedience to Christ is not possible apart from the power and presence of God's Holy Spirit in the lives of believers.

Paul then expressed another thought about the unworthy taking of the sacrament. "For he who eats and drinks unworthily eats and drinks condemnation to himself, not discerning the Lord's body" (v. 29). Again, note that the sacrament affects not only believers, but unbelievers as well. It provides, not only assurance of salvation for the faithful, but condemnation for the unfaithful. And Paul appends as an explanation for the condemnation the failure to correctly discern the Lord's body. Personal regeneration provides a particular insight and understanding—a discernment—of the Lord's body, the body of Christ.

The simple explanation is that the faithful (the regenerate) correctly understand themselves, their own bodies, to be included in the body of Christ. Whereas the unfaithful (the unregenerate) either completely ignore God or mistakenly presume themselves to be included in the body of Christ.

BODY

There are two important elements regarding this discernment of the Lord's body. One involves a correct understanding of the nature and extent of the body of Christ, and the other involves the individual's personal incorporation into the body of Christ. Regeneration is the central element of the second concern.

The first concern has proven to be more difficult to explain because it rests upon the Trinitarian character of God. The better understanding of the "Lord's body" requires a correct (or at least an adequate) understanding of the Trinity, an understanding given through regeneration. We can get at the issue by asking, "What is the Lord's body that Paul refers to?" Does Paul mean the physical body of Jesus, the man? Or the spiritual body of the resurrected Lord? Or the church as the body of Christ?

He means all of them. There is more to the body of Jesus than meets the eye. The body of Jesus walked on the sea (Matthew 14:25). The body of Jesus performed miracles (Matthew 8:3, 8:15, 9:20, 9:29, 14:36, 20:34, etc.). The body of Jesus rose from the dead (Acts 10:41, Romans 14:9). The body of Jesus will come in the clouds (Mark 13:26, 14:62, 1 Thessalonians 4:13, Revelation 1:7). The body of Jesus is the "bread of life" (John 6:48).

Clearly, the Lord's body that Paul spoke of is more than the mere body of a man. Yes, the body of the Lord is the body of the man Jesus Christ, but it is more than what we usually think of as a person's body, more than an individual, physical, body of flesh. Paul said in chapter ten, "The bread which we break, is it not the communion of the body of Christ?" (v. 16). Paul said in chapter twelve, speaking to the Corinthians, "you are the body of Christ, and members in part" (1 Corinthians 12:27); and in Ephesians 5:30, "we are members of His body, of His flesh, and of His bones." Clearly, Paul's understanding of the Lord's body was not limited to the physical manifestation of mere flesh and blood of the person of Jesus, the carpenter of Nazareth.

Paul understood the word *body* to also mean a group of persons associated by some common tie or occupation and regarded as an entity. A body includes all of the parts, the entire structure of an organism or entity. And the church—the body of Christ, the people of God—is not merely an organization, it is an organism, an entity.

When thinking of a body we are tempted to think in terms of the Greek word *sarx* when Scripture uses *sōma* here. Both words refer to body, but *sarx* is more akin to flesh while *sōma*, like the English word *body* can be used to describe people closely united into a society, or family; i.e., a social, political, ethical, or mystical body. Paul's use of the "Lord's body" employs the wider, more inclusive term (*sōma*). Paul used it to suggest Christian unity, as if Christianity is a unity, a whole, a body, an organism, or culture.

The discernment of the Lord's body has serious implications for the lives of believers and their understanding of Scripture. Our understanding of the Lord's body will impact our understanding regarding the biblical teachings of resurrection, the so-called rapture (meeting the Lord "in the air," 1 Thessalonians 4:17), and the second coming (Matthew 24:27).

From a Trinitarian perspective the Lord's body is the body of Jesus of Nazareth, but it is also the body of God Himself (whatever that is), and it is the body of the church, the fellowship of disciples. The body of Christ has both unity and particularity at the same time. It is mysterious and cannot be fully known, but it can be adequately known. And that is what Paul was talking about when he cautioned people to correctly discern the Lord's body prior to receiving the sacrament of the Lord's supper.

> "Likewise, my brothers, you also have died to the law through the body
> of Christ, so that you may belong to another, to him who has been
> raised from the dead, in order that we may bear fruit for God" (Romans
> 7:4).

And, said Paul,

> "the fruit of the Spirit is love, joy, peace, patience, kindness, goodness,
> faithfulness, gentleness, self-control; against such things there is no law.
> And those who belong to Christ Jesus have crucified the flesh with its

passions and desires. If we live by the Spirit, let us also walk by the Spirit" (Galatians 5:22-25).

29. Judged

That is why many of you are weak and ill, and some have died. But if we judged ourselves truly, we would not be judged. But when we are judged by the Lord, we are disciplined so that we may not be condemned along with the world. So then, my brothers, when you come together to eat, wait for one another— if anyone is hungry, let him eat at home—so that when you come together it will not be for judgment. About the other things I will give directions when I come.   — 1 Corinthians 11:30-34

Paul went on to say that many of the Corinthians had wrongly discerned the Lord's body and that their faulty discernment caused many among them to be weak and ill, and many to die (some translations use *sleep*). To die or to sleep (*koimaō*)? The Greek word can be translated either way, depending on the context. In this case, it doesn't really matter because the issue is that the lack of discernment results in a lack of responsiveness.

Paul has been speaking of the theological and philosophical differences between the wisdom of the world and the wisdom of Christ, but here he pointed to some of the very real and experiential consequences that accrue to a false belief that result in the false practice of the Lord's Supper, and ultimately lulls people into a kind of sleep or death. Here Paul pointed out proof that the sacrament is effectual even regarding those who participate in it wrongly, apart from regeneration and submission to the Holy Spirit.

It cannot be ignored that Paul links the malpractice of the Lord's Supper with illness and death. This is serious stuff! It should also be noted that the evils that come to those who take communion without regard for Paul's caution, take God's judgment upon themselves. And they do so of their own natural free will.

There is a remedy, a way to avoid the illnesses and deaths that result from the wrong participation in the Lord's Supper. Paul provided the remedy in verse 31, "But if we judged ourselves truly, we would not be judged."

This is a very important and little understood verse. It is divided into two clauses and appears to contrast the same idea or word in both clauses. The common word is *judged*. Most English translations use the same root word in both clauses, but they are different words in the Greek—and the difference is significant.

JUDGMENT

To better see the difference and the nature of the contrast we need to engage in a brief word study. The words are related, but different—*diakrinō* and *krinō*.

"But if we judged (diakrinō) ourselves truly, we would not be judged" (*krinō*—v. 31). The first instance is a modification of the second. Paul was saying that some sort of modified human judgment will help keep people from God's ultimate judgment.

Diakrinō is translated in many different ways:

"So when Peter went up to Jerusalem, the circumcision party criticized (*diakrinō*) him…" (Acts 11:2).

"And in the morning, 'It will be stormy today, for the sky is red and threatening.' You know how to interpret (*diakrinō*) the appearance of the sky, but you cannot interpret (*diakrinō*) the signs of the times" (Matthew 16:3).

"And Jesus answered them, 'Truly, I say to you, if you have faith and do not doubt (*diakrinō*)….' " (Matthew 21:21).

"Rise and go down and accompany them without hesitation (*diakrinō*), for I have sent them" (Acts 10:20).

"And the Spirit told me to go with them, making no distinction…" (*diakrinō*) (Acts 11:12).

"He did not stagger (*diakrinō*) at the promise of God through unbelief, but was strong in faith, giving glory to God" (Romans 4:20).

"For who makes you to differ (*diakrinō*) from another?" (1 Corinthians 4:7).

"I say this to your shame. Can it be that there is no one among you wise enough to settle a dispute (*diakrinō*) between the brothers" (1 Corinthians 6:5).

"But let him ask in faith, with no doubting (*diakrinō*), for the one who doubts (*diakrinō*, wavereth—*Authorized Version*) is like a wave of the sea that is driven and tossed by the wind" (James 1:6).

Of course context is important, but notice the many ways that the word is translated: *interpret, doubt, hesitation, distinction, stagger, differ, dispute,* and *waver.* Strong's defines the word first and foremost as "to separate thoroughly, that is, (literally and reflexively) to withdraw from, or (by implication) oppose." If we use this meaning for the word in the verse under consideration we have: "But if we judged (oppose, separate or withdraw from) ourselves truly, we would not be judged" (*krinō*—v. 31). To *separate from ourselves* can only mean that one subgroup of the Corinthian church separate from another subgroup—and the context is the church. Paul was talking about a separation within the church.

Is this the correct use of the word *diakrinō?* It is, because all of the various translations of the word suggest some element or consequence of differing opinions within the body of Christ that would lead to some sort of separation. It is the differing opinions between those who claim the wisdom of the world and those who claim the wisdom of Christ, and the conflicts and disagreements associated with such differences that result in division, separation, and withdrawal from common fellowship.

But surely Paul taught the unity of the church, the unity of Christianity! Of course he did. And yet it appears here and elsewhere (2 Corinthians 6:17) that Paul taught that some separation is consistent with Christian unity. Indeed it seems that Christianity can multiply through cell division as well as cell growth, much like biological cells.

Paul was saying in verse 31 that if the church would clean its own house, it would not fall under the judgment of God. This is very difficult to hear, and even more difficult to actually engage. Nonetheless, it appears to be what Paul said to the Corinthians. We—people in the churches—can avoid being disciplined by God by disciplining ourselves. We can avoid God's judgment through the exercise of church courts for the sake of the health of the church and the sanctification (growth in grace) of God's people. Paul taught here and elsewhere that faithless people should not be allowed to fellowship with the churches, and that if the churches become dominated by faithless people, then the faithful saints should separate themselves from the part of the body of fellowship that is dominated by faithlessness.

"Therefore go out from their midst, and be separate from them, says the Lord, and touch no unclean thing" (2 Corinthians 6:17). Paul went on to say that such separation was not a bad thing, but was a good thing.

"But when we are judged by the Lord, we are disciplined so that we may not be condemned along with the world" (v. 32).

When the churches fail to discipline themselves, they will come under the discipline and judgment of Jesus Christ, who brings trials and tribulations in order to test and sanctify the saints, to strengthen them through perseverance, and grow them in holiness, in order to keep His people from the final condemnation that will come to the world. This is indeed good news though it is not easy news, perhaps not even pleasant news—but it is good!

TABLE FELLOWSHIP

"So then, my brothers, when you come together to eat" (v. 33). Let's pause mid-sentence to note the common practice of the early churches known as table fellowship. Was Paul talking about the Lord's supper here? Of course he was in a sense. But there are two distinct aspects of the Lord's Supper that he alludes to. There is a formal aspect and an informal aspect, and if we fail to note which aspect he is now talking about we will misconstrue what is being said.

The whole sentence reads,

> "So then, my brothers, when you come together to eat, wait for one another—if anyone is hungry, let him eat at home—so that when you come together it will not be for judgment" (vs. 33-34).

Notice several things: 1) that the subject of this chapter, its context, is the Lord's Supper or Communion, 2) that Paul has been discussing the consequences of taking communion wrongly, and 3) that Paul now introduces the idea of eating at home. The third observation shows that Paul distinguishes between the Lord's Supper (as a formal celebration of Communion in a worship context) and the Lord's supper or table fellowship (as the informal practice of dining together in one another's homes apart from formal worship). Paul here introduced the idea of eating at home, and distinguished it from Communion in a worship context.

Let's also look more closely at the phrase "wait for one another." The Greek is composed of two words: *ekdechomai*, translated as *wait*, and *allēlōn*, translated as *one another*. The word *for* has been added to the English for clarity. However, it appears that the addition does not provide clarity, but glosses over what may be a more important meaning. The addition of the word *for* assumes that the phrase means that everyone should begin to eat at the same time, at the same moment. We envision people gathered around the table, and no one can begin eating until a signal is given. But there is no contextual reason for such a suggestion. And there is a better way to translate this phrase that provides greater consistency to the Christian calling in the given context.

The word *wait* has several senses in Greek, just as it does in English. It can mean "remaining inactive in one place while expecting something," or it can mean "to serve as a waiter or waitress as in a restaurant." The context determines which meaning should be invoked. But here the context is eating, so there is no good reason to assume the first and deny the second. Therefore, I want to suggest a better translation for this phrase, "wait *upon* one another." This sense captures the emphasis that Christianity places upon service, and upon the call to service that is related to Paul's discussions of the duties of deacon, recalling that the word *deacon* literally means *table waiter*.

As with all things Christian, there are both formal and informal realities and practices.[1] There are various things that the church is to do when she gathers together and there are various things that Christians do when they leave formal worship and scatter into the community. But Paul makes the case that, whether gathered together on the Lord's Day or scattered from one another during the week, Christians must be Christian all the time, twenty-four-seven.

The Trinitarian character of the Lord's Supper provides both vertical and horizontal relationships, to use a traditional description of Communion. The vertical element alludes to the individual, personal relationship that believers have with the Lord Himself. And the horizontal element alludes to the social or common relationships that people have with one another. Remember that social relationships are always mixed. Believers and nonbelievers always fellowship together in the world and in the church.

FORMAL & INFORMAL

There are both formal and informal aspects of both vertical and horizontal relationships, but here Paul pointed to the informal aspect of the horizontal relationships among believers. He said that one of the manifestations of that common horizontal relationship manifests in table fellowship or sharing a meal. It should also be noted that family meals—common meals shared in homes—are never reserved for believers only but

---

1   For a discussion of the informal realities of Christianity see Ross, Phillip A. *Informal Christianity—Refining Christ's Church*, Pilgrim Platform, 2007.

are always mixed gatherings. Jesus knew that biological families were mixed, that some believed and some didn't (Luke 12:53), and that gatherings of family and friends would also be mixed gatherings.

Another problem is that verse 34 has been translated as if it is singular, but it could just as well be plural. The Greek allows for either. But here it should be translated in the plural because Paul mentioned in verse 33 that he was speaking to "my brethren," to a group of people. He does not turn aside to address any one particular person, so it should be assumed that the whole thought is addressed to the group. Consequently, a better translation would be "if *some* are hungry, let *them* eat at home" (my translation). The plural translation is supported by the fact that we know that the early Christians ate together and fellowshipped often in each others' homes (Acts 2:46).

So, a better translation of this whole sentence would be

> "So then, my brothers, when you come together to eat, wait upon one another—if some are hungry, let them eat at home—so that when you come together it will not be for judgment."

Paul made a distinction between eating informally at home and formally receiving the Lord's Supper while gathered for worship. And that is the main point that Paul made here—the difference between home fellowship and church fellowship. Both are part of Christian fellowship, but they are different. They perform different functions and have different dynamics.

He closes by saying, "About the other things I will give directions when I come" (v. 34). There were other things to be spelled out. Exactly what those other things were is lost to antiquity. People speculate, but no one really knows. At best, it might be a reference to material covered in Paul's Second Letter to the Corinthians. We will simply note that Paul had more to say to the Corinthians than what we have recorded in his letters.

Paul said a lot in these four verses. He provided a diagnosis and a cure. His diagnosis was that many people in the church were weak and ill. And that, untreated, that weakness or illness leads to the sleep of death. His cure is to discipline the body of Christ, to discern between the wisdom of the world and the wisdom of Christ, and to gather around the wisdom of Christ and to forsake the wisdom of the world.

The wisdom of the world is out to *get* and the wisdom of Christ is out to *give*, so this is done through *service*, by waiting upon one another around a common table. Paul taught the Corinthians to practice waiting upon one another at home, so that it would be easier to do at church. That's Paul's advice here. While we wait for Christ to return in judgment, we can help reduce the negative consequences of that judgment by performing the duties of deacons—not by seeking the formal office of deacon, but by performing the informal function of table waiting—engaging in Christian service.

It's pretty simple, really. It may be too simple for those who are wise in the ways of the world, but not for Christians. Christians are called to service, ordinary service in the midst of ordinary living.

30. Gifts

Now concerning spiritual gifts, brothers, I do not want you to be uninformed. You know that when you were pagans you were led astray to mute idols, however you were led. Therefore I want you to understand that no one speaking in the Spirit of God ever says "Jesus is accursed!" and no one can say "Jesus is Lord" except in the Holy Spirit. Now there are varieties of gifts, but the same Spirit; and there are varieties of service, but the same Lord; and there are varieties of activities, but it is the same God who empowers them all in everyone. To each is given the manifestation of the Spirit for the common good.
—1 Corinthians 12:1-7

The word *gifts* in the first verse is not in the Greek, but is supplied by the translators for clarity. While it is true that this entire chapter is about spiritual gifts, this addition in the first verse is not necessary, and serves to limit Paul's broader spiritual concern to the subject of gifts. I understand Paul to have meant that he did not want his Christian brothers to be uninformed about anything spiritual, including spiritual gifts of course, but not limited to spiritual gifts. Having then referred to the general case (anything spiritual), he now turns in chapter twelve to the specific example of spiritual gifts.

Verse 2 provides the context for Paul's discussion. Prior to their regeneration they were not Christian, and did not have any Christian experience or understanding, nor did they have access to the Holy Spirit. They were thoroughly pagan (Gentile). The Greek word translated as *pagans (ethnos)* simply means that they were not Jewish. However, Paul used the word to mean that they were not of Israel in the sense of Romans 9:6. Of course some of the Corinthians were genetic Jews, but Paul's point was that they had not been raised in a culture that honored the God of Scripture. They had turned their backs on their true heritage as the people of God. They had no experience or training in biblical truth, nor had they been regenerated by the Spirit of Jesus Christ. Thus, they were pagan in all their beliefs and practices.

All of their cultural teaching and social practices prior to becoming Christians had been directed toward idols that were nothing. Those idols were deaf and dumb. They had no life whatsoever—spiritual or otherwise. They could not hear, nor could they speak.

The last clause of verse 2 tells us that any and all the arguments that may have been used to describe or analyze their idols had been entirely Godless. It didn't matter what those arguments were, they were without the illumination of the Holy Spirit and as such were spiritually futile. In whatever ways they had been led to appreciate Pagan idolatry, they had been led to false gods with false logic that led to false conclusions.

Human wisdom could not and would not lead to the Christ of God. Add to this the fact that all speculation about things divine will always fall short of God's revelation in Scripture. The only way that information about the only real God—the God of Scripture—could be made available to humanity was through the personal revelation of God. God would have to provide it Himself, and He had done exactly that through the Old Testament, and now through Jesus Christ. God had fulfilled that Old Testament prophecy.

Christ is the key to all knowledge and wisdom, both knowledge about God Himself and all true knowledge about the world in which we live. There is nothing that does not reflect, refer, originate, or conclude apart from Jesus Christ because all authority has been given to Him (Matthew 28:18).

JESUS IS LORD

Paul went on to say that "no one speaking in the Spirit of God ever says 'Jesus is accursed!' and no one can say 'Jesus is Lord' except in the Holy Spirit" (v. 3). Of course Paul knew that people can lie, that people can believe and say all sorts of foolish nonsense, and that people are often inconsistent and liable to various logical disconnections. So, Paul was not talking about merely saying a thing, but about actually believing it. No one can believe that Jesus is accursed if s/he is "in the Spirit of God." And conversely, belief that Jesus is Lord necessarily arises from regeneration, from the Holy Spirit Himself who abides in His people. Verse 3 simply reiterates the necessity of regeneration by the presence and power of the Holy Spirit in the lives of believers. There is no such thing as orthodox belief apart from regeneration, regardless of the intellectual content of such belief.

The fact that the Jews, represented by the Pharisees and others, hated Jesus and accused Him of all sorts of vile and evil things is well attested in history. And the Jews were very influential. Add to this the accusations of the foolishness of the gospel by the Greeks and those who had been captured by Greek philosophy, and you had a lot of people in Corinth who badmouthed Jesus. No doubt many of the Corinthian converts had been previously counted in that number. The faithful Christians in Corinth were besieged from without and from within. How could they know who was with them (with Christ, actually) and who was against them?

Paul answered this question in verse 3 by providing the first Christian creed or statement of faith: *Jesus is Lord!* To accept Jesus Christ as Lord and Savior requires that faithful Christians accept the gift and grace of salvation, or face the necessary default of their own damnation. People's response to Jesus Christ provides evidence of their belief or disbelief.

The idea of "speaking in the Spirit" (v. 3) is another allusion to regeneration. The idea is that one's speech is directed and guided by the Holy Spirit, or that the Holy Spirit Himself, who overshadows those whom He regenerates, speaks through the regenerate. This idea, however, does not suggest or lead to the infallibility of the Christian. It does not mean that everything a faithful Christian says is "of the Spirit" because the process of sanctification or growth in grace is long, arduous, and incomplete in this fallen world. Nonetheless, the Holy Spirit is real and has a real effect in the lives of believers.

VARIETIES

In addition, the activity or influence of the Holy Spirit is not the same in all believers. The Spirit works differently in different people. As Paul said, "there are varieties of gifts" (v. 4). Again, the topic of this chapter is spiritual gifts. In verse 1 Paul used the Greek word *pneumatikos*, and there the English word *gifts* has been added for clarity, as I said earlier. *Pneumatikos* refers more generally to spiritual things, more than to gifts specifically, but it includes gifts. So, the translation is okay. Just note that all the rest of the time Paul used the word *charisma*, which is translated as *gift(s)*. It is interesting to note that Paul did not use the two words together (i.e., spiritual gifts) in this chapter (or the next).

The Greek word, *charisma*, like the English (which is a simple transliteration rather than a translation) suggests a God-given gratuity, or a deliverance from danger or passion, or a spiritual endowment, or a supernatural faculty. To be charismatic is to be influential, generally speaking. A person who has charisma is a person who is attractive and influential among others. Paul's usage of the word in this chapter (and the next) suggests that spiritual gifts are used by God for the purpose of evangelism, attracting people through the means of Christian service. In other words, evangelism is an outgrowth or overflowing of Christian service. Christians engage in service and others experience it as evangelism.

One of the overarching themes in this section is the idea that there is only one real God. Paul emphasized a variety of things, but stressed that in spite of the variety, the unity of God holds the various things together; "… there are varieties of gifts, but the same Spirit" (v. 1).

He listed three things in verses 4, 5, and 6 in the same literary pattern: there are a variety of gifts, services, and activities, but in spite of the variety it is the same Spirit, Lord, and God "who empowers them all in everyone" (v. 6). Paul has set out a poetic threesome—gifts, service, and activities that are held together by the same Spirit, Lord, and God. We don't want to make too much of this literary device, but we don't want to miss its importance either, because Paul has used it to lay out some important tools of evangelism.

EVANGELISM

We can see that the evangelistic process involves both human elements and divine elements. The human elements are gifts, service, and activities; and the divine elements are Spirit, Lord, and God. The three-ness is not accidental.

Let's examine these elements. We already talked about gifts (*charisma*). The second term has been translated as *service*. The Greek is *diakonia*, which is related to *diakonos*, which is usually translated as *deacons*. The difference between the two words is the difference between the office of Deacon and the action of deaconing or performing service. Some translations read *administrations*, which suggests that an orderly service plan may be in view. Note also that the spiritual element related to *diakonia* is the Lord—*kurios* in the Greek. *Kurios* suggests a supreme authority or master. Where *charisma* is superintended by the Spirit and is subject to the influence of the Spirit, *diakonia* is superintended by the Lord and is subject to the authority of the Lord, of Christ, and His church.

The last pairing is *activities* (*energēma*) and *God* (*theos*), "there are varieties of activities, but it is the same God who empowers them all in everyone" (v. 6). Unlike the English word *energy*, which can be abstracted as a potential force, the Greek word *energēma* indicates the actual and active force that produces something. It is not a measure of potential, but the process and/or result of something actual. Think of it as the energy of Isaiah 55:11,

> "so shall My Word be, which goes out of My mouth; it shall not return to Me void, but it shall accomplish what I please, and it shall certainly do what I sent it to do."

This energy is superintended by and subject to God Himself. God accomplishes what He intends to accomplish.

As we think of these three things as elements of evangelism, we see that evangelism entails a Spirit-led charisma in the midst of a comprehensive plan of service opportunities that result in the actual accomplishment of God's Word. There are a variety of thoughts, ideas, feelings, plans, and activities, but in spite of the variety, all of these things pull together or are superintended by the unity of God. The unity that is in the midst of the diversity is the intentional focus upon Jesus, the Christ of God; and apart from this focus, there can be no unity.

Diversity in-and-of-itself, apart from the unity of the Trinitarian God of Christianity, is divisive. The unity of Christianity is a matter of God's superintendence while doing a variety of things, diverse things—gifts, service, and activities, but doing them all for the same purpose, in the service of the glory of God in Christ.

According to verse 7 there are two elements of this unity, one focuses on God and one focuses on humanity. The godly element is emphasized through the giving of various gifts to various people. The gifts are God's to give, and much like the economics of Adam Smith, the multiform, diverse, individual exercise of these gifts contributes to the uniform, social benefit and good of all. The key to the process is the manifesting or showing forth of the Spirit. And it needs to be noted that this manifestation is given to the saints. It is not something that we work up in our own energy. Rather, it is given, and part of the gift is the desire and ability to engage it.

It is important to note that the source of energy for the use of the gift comes from outside of us, from Christ, from the Holy Spirit through regeneration. And at the same time, this given energy is real energy that manifests itself in the lives of individuals. It is real, actual, and visible—it is a personal charisma that permanently changes one's life and perspective.

Unity In Diversity

Paul emphasized and repeated the idea of unity in diversity, and it needs to be noted in this day and age that the thing that provides the unity is God—Jesus Christ. To suggest that there can be unity in diversity apart from Jesus Christ is false. Apart from Jesus Christ, and the Trinitarian character of the Godhead, there can be no real unity nor any real diversity. Apart from Christ the emphasis on unity moves toward totalitarianism. Apart from Christ the emphasis on diversity becomes anarchy. Only in Christ is there genuine social unity; only in Christ is there genuine social diversity (or particularity).

Also note that these gifts are given to each Christian, not to some Christians. The Greek clearly means *each and every*, and the implication necessarily affects each and every Christian. All Christians are gifted in some way to contribute to the life of Christ's church and to evangelize within his or her circle of influence. This does not mean that all of these gifts are to be used at church, in the service of the building or the organization on Sunday mornings or throughout the week. All Christians are not called to hold church offices, serve on committees, or sweep church floors.

Rather, Paul has in mind a much larger vision of Christ's church. Paul has the whole of human society in mind. He intends that God's people serve Jesus Christ in everything that they think, say, and do. God's gifts to His people are to be used at home, at work, on the road, on vacation—everywhere and always. Jesus Christ has been given all authority, *all* not *some*. Being a Christian is a twenty-four-seven endeavor.

It is not a difficult thing to do, though it has its moments. There are times of stress, times of testing and chastisement. And yet the growth in grace that comes out of such times provides a kind of joy in the face of difficulties because we know that Christ will overcome all difficulties as His kingdom grows. He will subdue all of His enemies, and He will do it through the common service of His people who engage God's gifts in the midst of their ordinary lives.

Real evangelism is not arm twisting people into the kingdom. It is the exercise of faithful service in the midst of ordinary living.

31. God's Endowment

To one is given through the Spirit the utterance of wisdom, and to another the utterance of knowledge according to the same Spirit, to another faith by the same Spirit, to another gifts of healing by the one Spirit, to another the working of miracles, to another prophecy, to another the ability to distinguish between spirits, to another various kinds of tongues, to another the interpretation of tongues. All these are empowered by the same Spirit, who apportions to each one individually as he wills. For just as the body is one and has many members, and all the members of the body, though many, are one body, so it is with Christ. —1 Corinthians 12:8-12

Paul previously said that God works in His church, His people, through a variety of means. And that in spite of the variety of ways that God makes Himself manifest there is always a unity that binds the different manifestations of His work together. He now enumerates several of the more common gifts as examples of how this unity in diversity works. His list is not complete, but it is significant. There are other gifts that God gives to His people. In fact, all of what we call talents and abilities are gifts of God. While we don't want to limit God's gifts to these few that Paul mentions here, neither do we want to discount the importance of those listed.

Verse 8 distinguishes two important gifts: the ability to speak words of wisdom and words of knowledge. It is important to notice the difference between wisdom and knowledge. They are related, yet distinct.[1] *Wisdom* is the Greek word *sophia*. However, Paul did not have the Gnostic goddess Sophia in mind. Paul was not teaching Gnosticism, though that is what Gnostics think he was doing. Rather, Paul used the word in its generic meaning. According to Webster the word (*wisdom*) means the right use or exercise of knowledge; the choice of laudable ends, and the choice of the best means to accomplish those ends.

---

1   For a discussion of this difference, see Ross, Phillip A. *The Wisdom of Jesus Christ in the Book of Proverbs*, Pilgrim Platform, Marietta, Ohio, 2007.

Knowledge (*gnōsis*), on the other hand, is more akin to science and the gathering of information and facts in order to understand how things work. As Paul used these two words here, knowledge has to do with understanding how the world works, and wisdom has to do with using that knowledge in the service of God, according to Scripture.

We know that Paul is talking about the use of wisdom and knowledge in relation to God and not in a more generic sense because he said that they are "given through the Spirit" (v. 8). The Spirit is the vehicle of their delivery to the hearts and minds of Christians. Wisdom and knowledge are gifts of the Spirit that are manifest in the words (*logos*) of His people.

Of course *logos* means more than mere words. It also means the structure and energy that shapes and gives meaning to words. John wrote,

> "In the beginning was the Word (logos), and the Word was with God, and the Word was God. He was in the beginning with God. All things were made through him, and without him was not any thing made that was made" (John 1:1-3).

Logos is the root of the English word *logic*. From all this we see that the gifts of wisdom and knowledge make sense of the world and of God's Word—Scripture. We know that the correct understanding of Scripture requires personal regeneration because it requires the presence and power of the Holy Spirit to directly lead and guide the spirit of each Christian. And the same thing is true with regard to knowledge of the world. Regeneration is necessary in order to understand the world correctly, from God's perspective, from a biblical perspective—the only true perspective. And again, the only true perspective always comes "according to the same Spirit" (v. 8).

There is unity and corroboration between everything that comes from God. There is unity in the Scriptures, unity of doctrine (teaching), unity of purpose. But this unity is not a "cookie-cutter" type of unity. Rather, there is a great diversity of gifts, many different manifestations of the Spirit, a diversity of thoughts and ideas, different ways of doing things. But the diversity, the differences, are always trumped by the unity. And our best understanding of that unity is shaped by our understanding of the Trinity—one, yet three; three, yet one; all pulling in the same direction, all working toward or with the same purpose.

In verses 9 and 10 Paul listed other gifts that are subsumed under the unity of the Spirit: faith, healing (note the comma—not faith healing), miracles, prophecy, discernment, tongues, and interpretation of tongues. Let's consider each one in turn.

Faith

First is faith (*pistis*). According to Strong's *pistis* is defined as persuasion, credence, and/or moral conviction (of religious truth, or the truthfulness of God or a religious teacher), and especially reliance upon Christ for salvation. We might better understand this gift as faithfulness, being loyal and steadfast. But it is not generic loyalty, it is loyalty to Jesus Christ. Nor is it generic steadfastness, it is steadfastness to God's truth in Scripture.

Faith is related to our perseverance in Christ and God's preservation of His people. Being faithful is not simply a matter of believing and trusting in Christ, but believing rightly, correctly—that is to say, not believing falsely. It is both a commitment to being truthful and loyalty to God's truth. Paul wrote to the Ephesians, "For by grace you have been saved through faith. And this is not your own doing; it is the gift of God" (Ephesians 2:8). This gift is by grace and through faith, as are all God's gifts. And that means that all the other gifts stand on or issue from the gift of faith or faithfulness to Jesus Christ as the foundation and/or source.

Healing

Second on Paul's list is healing. The Greek literally means cure. There are two Greek words that are translated as healing in the New Testament. The most common is *therapeuō*, the root of the English word *therapy* and literally means to wait upon. We can think of it as a kind of nursing.

The other word (*iama*) is used only here and in Acts 4:22, "For the man on whom this sign of healing was performed was more than forty years old." It refers to the healing of the lame beggar in Acts 3.2 This healing provides a fascinating story of a social outcast who was reintegrated into the community as a result of his healing by Peter. Note several things about this healing: 1) Peter did it, 2) upon being healed the beggar, "stood and began to walk, and entered the temple with them, walking and leaping and praising God" (Acts 3:8), 3) his presence in the Temple amazed and upset the congregation, 4) Peter used the disturbance as an opportunity to preach, and 5) "as they (Peter and John) were speaking to the people, the priests and the captain of the temple and the Sadducees came upon them, greatly annoyed because they were teaching the people and proclaiming in Jesus the resurrection from the dead. And they arrested them" (Acts 4:1-3).

Clearly, the healing indicated by this particular word had an effect or an impact on more than the individual man who was healed. It affected the whole community. It revealed the bankruptcy of the Old Testament Temple culture, revealed Jesus Christ as the source of the miracle that healed the lame beggar, and resulted in the beggar's reintegration into society—the new culture of the New Testament church. All of this is to say that the gift of healing that Paul identified here has a holistic character that includes much more than the physical restoration of one person's health. The healing Paul had in mind was a cultural healing or restoration.

MIRACLES

Next in Paul's list of gifts is miracles (*dunamis*). *Dunamis* is often translated as *power* and means ability. Power is the ability to get things done. It requires the authority and competence to make things happen. *Dunamis* is not a personal ability of the flesh, but is the power of Jesus Christ to accomplish His purposes through the Holy Spirit. It is an alien power that belongs to God and is given to God's people through regeneration. Yet, it highlights particular individuals who find themselves in unique and important historical roles that provide an opportunity to testify to and promote the cause of Christ. The purpose of miracles is always to reveal God's work in history.

Paul's emphasis on miracles helps us understand how God works in the world. God always works through means, both ordinary and extraordinary. God's ordinary means are traditionally understood by Protestants to be Word and Sacrament. God acts through His Word—through Scripture—and through the Sacraments—through Baptism and the Lord's Supper.

God also acts through extraordinary means—through miracles. God's miracles always serve to accomplish God's purposes and magnify God's glory. Usually we see His glory manifested through His power to contravene what we perceive as the laws of nature. But God's primary purpose for miracles is to establish His authority and to identify His people. God works various miracles through particular representatives (prophets) to establish the veracity (truthfulness) of His Word in the service of His glory.

While all of life is miraculous, and God's grace is certainly miraculous, and God can contravene the laws of nature whenever He wants, God usually works through His ordinary means, through the preaching of God's Word and the administration of the Sacraments. God's ordinary means are the ordinary functions of His church. And because Jesus Christ came to establish and build His church on earth, God's emphasis since Christ's resurrection and the establishment of the Canon (New Testament Scripture) is upon His ordinary means, upon the purpose and function of His church. That is where God's people are to focus their energies, on the purpose and function of Christ's church. But not simply on the church as a particular social institution, but on the church in its wholeness as an expression of Christian culture. However, God reserves the right to exercise His extraordinary means as He pleases, whenever He pleases. But that is His business, not ours.

Paul's attention to miracles preceded the establishment of the New Testament as part of God's Word and justified the extension of the Bible to include the fulfillment of Scripture by Jesus Christ and the establishment of the Canon. With the closing of the Canon, God's emphasis shifted from His extraordinary works to His ordinary works. Our attention and concern as New Testament Israelites (Christians) follows God's emphasis. God's ordinary means are more important than His extraordinary means, and they always have been because the purpose of the extraordinary has been to establish the ordinary.

PROPHECY

Next on Paul's list is prophecy (*prophēteia*). According to the Greek lexicon *prophēteia* is a discourse emanating from divine inspiration and declaring the purposes of God, whether by reproving and admonishing the wicked, or by comforting the afflicted, or by revealing things hidden, and especially by foretelling future events. The difficulty with the idea of prophecy is that people have a pagan, superstitious, crystal ball understanding of the word and of the process. So, to get at the biblical meaning of the word we need to disabuse ourselves of this common error.

In the Old Testament, prophets were preachers who foretold God's plan and the coming of Christ. Part of that foretelling was a forth-telling, a telling forth, a bringing out into public view, and a clarification of the things of God. With the advent of Christ, New Testament prophets are preachers who clarify that God's Old Testament promises have been fulfilled in Jesus Christ by setting Christ in public view as the fulfillment of Old Testament prophecy, and who foretell of the return of Christ in judgment in the fullness of time.

These New Testament prophets are not always the commonly accepted church leaders, just as the Old Testament prophets were not always the commonly accepted elders, Levites, or priests. The biblical ideal is that church leaders be fluent in the prophecies of God, that church leaders teach and preach God's prophecies correctly, but that doesn't always happen. Leaders are susceptible to sin and error, and so God sometimes brings correction to His people, to His church, by reestablishing prophetic truth outside the ordinary channels of church authority and its leadership. Most of the Old Testament minor prophets provided such correction in the face of a corrupt priesthood. And Paul was dealing with just this kind of situation in Corinth, where church leaders had fallen into sin and were teaching error.

This kind of reestablishment of God's truth from outside of the normal structures of His church is not something to be desired, nor is it to be treated lightly. Rather, it is always a prelude to God's judgment and correction. Yes, the gift of prophecy—full-orbed preaching—produces a time of revival and rebirth for God's people, but it must be noted that birth, while a great blessing and joy, is a painful and bloody process. In the same way, revival is a joy, but it is also traumatic—messy and painful. Think of the guy in a hospital emergency room whose heart has stopped and the trauma inflicted upon him by the emergency room staff to restart it. That's revival.

We have a Romantic understanding of revival, as if it is a sweet and glorious time—like a family reunion or picnic. But real revival, real reformation is traumatic. It divides as well as unites families. It involves struggle and condemnation as well as reunion and affirmation. It always involves stripping people of their treasured illusions, stripping people of false beliefs that they have come to trust. People don't easily change their minds about their most fundamental beliefs and values. But that is exactly what revival and reformation are about.

Suffice it to say that the gift of prophecy that Paul enumerated was nothing more nor anything less than the full-orbed biblical preaching of

Jesus Christ, crucified and risen. It is an explanation of Scripture that brings light to the dark recesses of our hearts and minds.

"And this is the judgment: the light has come into the world, and people loved the darkness rather than the light because their deeds were evil" (John 3:19).

Lord, have mercy.

DISCERNMENT

Next is discernment (*diakrisis*), a kind of distinguishing, judging, and/or disputing. The root meaning of the word (*diakrino*) is to separate, make a distinction, discriminate, to prefer one thing over another. Discernment requires learning by discrimination, judgment, and disputation. It involves the separation of truth from error, and sometimes requires a physical and organizational separation from those who teach or promote sin and error. Such separation can appear to be contentious because it requires a contending for God's truth in the face of sin and denial.

The ESV translates Paul's phrase as the "ability to distinguish between spirits" (v. 10). The distinction is not blood related or genetic. It is not ethnic or national. It is not a matter of intelligence or personal abilities. Rather, the distinction to be made is spiritual. The Greek lexicon defines the word Paul used (*pneuma—Spirits*) as the third person of the triune God, the Holy Spirit. Christians are to discern the presence of the Holy Spirit. Christians are to know the difference between the presence of the Holy Spirit and the absence of the Holy Spirit. And the power to do this is a gift of God—it is the gift of the Spirit because only the Holy Spirit Himself can discern the Holy Spirit in others.

The gift of discernment is a matter of knowing right from wrong, good from evil. It is a matter of knowing what to do and what not to do. It's about perception, aesthetics, and values. It's about morality, duty, and obligation as well as grace, love, and freedom. Discernment is a matter of seeing where God is leading and having the wisdom and courage to actually follow where God leads. Discernment is a gift of leadership.

TONGUES

The gift of tongues is difficult to understand, not because it is shrouded in mystery, but because there is so much historical confusion about it. The first difficulty is to understand what it is, to define it correctly—biblically. We will use the interpretive principle that the plainest,

most ordinary, and simple definition is the most likely to be true. However, this will require that we disabuse ourselves of the contemporary
definition and use of tongues through the widely popular Pentecostal
movement of the last hundred years.

Much of the popular success regarding the understanding and use of
the gift of tongues by the Pentecostal movement must be credited to the
historical Protestant Reformed misunderstanding of the terminology involved. The Reformed doctrinal error is found in a misreading of the
Westminster Confession of Faith. This misreading involves section one of
chapter one, "Of the Holy Scripture." The phrase under consideration
reads, "…those former ways of God's revealing His will unto His people
being now ceased."

The common (and incorrect) understanding of this phrase was that
the practice of glossolalia (understood as inspired speaking and writing)
ceased with the closing of the Canon. However, anyone familiar with the
history of the Christian church and the Pentecostal Movement will know
that glossolalia has *not* ceased, not in the first century or the fourth or the
seventeenth—much less in the twentieth or twenty-first. Glossolalia has
been with us from time immemorial, in Old Testament times, in New
Testament times, and into modern and postmodern times. Indeed, glossolalia is alive and well today, as is evidenced by the phenomenal success of
the Pentecostal Movement over the past hundred years. To say that it has
ceased is nonsense, and to suggest that it *should have ceased* opens the door
to a host of interpretative problems that have not been resolved and are
probably unresolvable.

A better approach is needed. To get at the issue and the problem regarding the gift of tongues we first need to better understand and define
exactly what glossolalia is. It is not a biblical word. The dictionary defines
it as repetitive non-meaningful speech, especially that associated with a
trance state or religious fervor. Pentecostals will take exception with the
idea that it is non-meaningful. Some will argue that it is an ancient language that has been lost. Others will argue that it is a special prayer language that provides for special communication between God and the
believer who uses it. Others will argue that it is a language (or languages)
that only the Holy Spirit can interpret.

The first shortcoming to note is that most Christian examinations of
glossolalia limit their considerations to biblical data, and more specifically
to glossolalia within the Christian tradition. Most of the time these efforts

assume and attempt to justify glossolalia as a legitimate expression of biblical practice. Most Christians, including various Christian scholars in various denominations, understand tongues to be a manifestation of glossolalia because it is part of the history of biblical experience and testimony. The practice of glossolalia understood in this way stretches back into biblical antiquity.

However, if we are going to define tongues biblically, we must distinguish between Paul's use of the word *tongues* and the contemporary definition of *glossolalia*. They are not the same thing. The reality is that glossolalia defined in this way (as being legitimately Christian) has a long and significant tradition that is both unfaithful to God and non-biblical. The roots of this kind of glossolalia belong to Paganism and the ancient traditions of false gods mentioned in Scripture. For instance, glossolalia was exhibited by the renowned ancient Oracle of Delphi, whose origins are associated with the worship of Gaia in the eighth century B.C. At Delphi a priestess of the god Apollo (called a *sibyl*) spoke in unintelligible utterances, supposedly through the spirit of Apollo in the priestess as a kind of prophecy that would then be translated by other priests.[2]

Later in history are found certain Gnostic magical texts from the Roman period that have unintelligible syllables written on them. It is believed that these may be transliterations of the sorts of sounds made during glossolalia and were thought to be prophetic. The Coptic Gospel of the Egyptians also features a hymn of mostly unintelligible syllables which is thought to be an early example of Christian glossolalia.

In the nineteenth century, Spiritism, which investigates the survival of souls after death and communications received from them, i.e., séances, etc., was developed through the work of Allan Kardec (1804-1869). The phenomenon was seen as one of the self-evident manifestations of spirits. While not specifically associated with glossolalia, Kardec's work highlighted and valued ecstatic communication from a scientific perspective. Glossolalia has also been observed in shamanism and the Voodoo religion of Haiti. The point is that these manifestations of glossolalia are clearly not Christian and not faithful to the God of the Bible. I am, then, extrapolating that the roots of glossolalia are intertwined with Paganism and Spiritism (ecstatic communication, which includes communication with the dead, or with spirits).

---

2   Article on *Glossolalia* (2007), http://en.wikipedia.org/wiki/Glossolalia. See also www.indopedia.org/Allan_Kardec.html. Karkec is cited as an example only.

In biblical history, King Saul was involved with glossolalia early in his story. Immediately following Samuel's anointing of Saul as King of Israel (1 Samuel 10:1), Saul himself fell into a swoon of prophecy. We don't know if Saul used glossolalia per se, but nothing of the content of his prophecy is recorded, which suggests that it was meaningless or not significant to God. Scripture provides this story, not to justify Saul's actions, but as a window into the character of Saul. Saul began to prophesy after God gave him "another heart" (1 Samuel 10:1). Note that it was not a *new* heart, and that from that time forward Saul fell increasingly out of favor with God. At the height of Saul's disobedience to God he consulted the witch of Endor and communicated with the dead spirit of Samuel (1 Samuel 28:7). Such communication was forbidden by God. While that communication was not technically glossolalia, it was communication with a dead spirit, which Saul himself had correctly forbidden under the direction of Samuel. God does not want His people communicating with dead or incorporeal spirits.

Again, Saul's experience may not have been glossolalia per se, but it was most certainly not a function of obedience or the understanding of God's truth on his part. Saul's prophesying must be classified as a kind of ecstatic speech, where ecstasy is defined as a state of being beyond reason. The point is that this kind of ecstatic speech—speech that is either nonsensical or unreasonable—is not the kind of communication that the God of Scripture provides for His people. So, while it is not technically or strictly glossolalia, narrowly defined, it was similar enough to be categorized as a kind of glossolalia, broadly defined.

Here's another example: Early in Jesus' ministry He encountered unclean spirit(s) that had inhabited and inflicted people with various maladies. Mark recorded that when Jesus healed a man with an unclean spirit the man convulsed (Mark 1:26). The Greek word (*sparassō*) is the root of the English word *spasmodic*. People reacted spasmodically when the unclean spirits left them, twisting and turning uncontrollably, falling down (Matthew 17:15), probably even barking and growling.[3] The point is that the spirits that manifest these kinds of things in people were expelled from them when they were healed by Jesus, which suggests that they were some sort of evil spirits. These manifestations of spiritual illness and/or possession were not to be celebrated, but were to be overcome and elimi-

---

3   These phenomena have been documented as being part of the "Toronto Blessing," 1994, and the "Brownsville Revival," 1995.

nated from human experience according to the biblical traditions of Jesus' healing work.

The point is that these kinds of ecstatic, trance-induced experiences have always been associated with non-biblical religions—and they still are today. In contrast, the God of the Bible is the God of truth and reason, not of spirit possession and confusion (1 Corinthians 14:33). And God most certainly does not communicate meaninglessness to His people.

The difficulty with understanding tongues and the issues involved with it, however, comes about because people erroneously believe that God had communicated and/or dictated the original writing of Scripture through some kind of ecstatic, glossolalia-like experience. However, there is no evidence that He did. Scripture was written through men, and used the ordinary writing practices of men. The writing of Scripture was not magical or mystical, it was ordinary.

However, Scripture does in fact record that God uses things/experiences like this sort of mystical glossolalia. God does give people over to nonsense and confusion (Exodus 23:27, Deuteronomy 7:23, Isaiah 19:14). God's Word, however, is not a manifestation of nonsense and confusion, but is a manifestation of truth and order.

Granted, we don't know exactly how the Bible was written—and it doesn't really matter. It's like being concerned about the route the UPS driver took to get to your house to deliver a package. You have the package, what difference does it make what route was taken to deliver it? Just open the package and deal with the contents.

So, if Paul's use of tongues does not mean glossolalia in the contemporary or Delphic sense, what does it mean? The Greek word (*glōssa*) simply means *tongue*, the instrument of speech. And by implication and common use at the time it was written, it referred to a foreign language or to foreign languages (in the plural). The Protestant Reformers believed that glossolalia (ecstatic and unintelligible speech) had stopped or ought to stop in the New Testament era, that the manifestation of the Holy Spirit among God's people would put an end to such nonsense. And they were correct because the God of Scripture is not a God of nonsense and/or confusion (1 Corinthians 14:33).

What does *glōssa* mean? It means *foreign languages*. And here's the key issue that will help us understand what Paul was driving at: if some languages are foreign then one particular language is not foreign. Remember that we are talking about God's Word, we might even say "God's language."

God revealed Himself to the ancient Hebrews and established the ancient nation of Israel as a kind of test case study regarding God's law. From Moses to Christ that nation was Israel and its language was Hebrew. That is to say that at that time God's Word was written exclusively in Hebrew. That was God's native tongue, so to speak. The Hebrew Scriptures were not available in any other language. That is important because it meant that all God-language was in Hebrew. If anyone wanted to know what God was talking about, they needed to learn Hebrew.

With the advent of Christ the gospel was opened up to the Gentiles, to the other nations of the world. Those Gentile nations (people) spoke other languages. They didn't speak Hebrew. So, if they were going to understand the gospel, it would need to be spoken (and written) in other languages, languages foreign to the Hebrew tongue. The beginning of this process of speaking genuine biblical gospel God-talk in other languages began at Pentecost when

"divided tongues as of fire appeared to them and rested on each one of
them. And they were all filled with the Holy Spirit and began to speak
in other tongues as the Spirit gave them utterance" (Acts 2:3-4).

"Divided tongues" is comprised of two Greek words, *diamerizō glōssa*. We have determined that *glōssa* means foreign languages, languages other than Hebrew. *Diamerizō* does mean divided, but would be better translated as a division or a distribution.

The phrase "tongues as of fire" is a correct translation, but it isn't very helpful. Note that it does not say "tongues of fire" but "tongues *as* of fire." The word *as* sets up a comparison. Tongues (foreign languages) are compared to fire. The tongues are not made of fire, but are like fire in some way. So, how can foreign languages be like fire? Fire flickers and tongues can be understood to flicker in the mouth when speaking. Thus, the phrase "tongues as of fire" suggests that foreign languages were being spoken with ease. We might say "burning up the airwaves." Tongues were flickering as many people were using foreign languages to speak about the gospel of Jesus Christ and the God of Scripture. Tongues were flickering in a similar way that flames flicker in a fire. That's the comparison.

Acts 2:2 tells us that

"suddenly there came from heaven a sound like a mighty rushing wind, and it filled the entire house where they were sitting."

Think of a school lunchroom or a symphony audience before the show starts. People are all talking at once. Have you ever stopped talking in the middle of that kind of setting and just listened? It sounds like wind rustling forest leaves on a cold Autumn day—except louder. Luke described it as "like a mighty rushing wind" (Acts 2:2).

The Greek word translated *wind* (*pnoē*) can also be translated as *breath*. The word *wind* occurs twenty-six times in the New Testament, but this particular word only occurs twice, here and in Acts 17:25 where it is translated as *breath*. Let me suggest that *breath* may be a better translation. Understood as breath the phrase would mean "like a might rushing breath," or a "mighty gust of conversation." But this rushing breath must not be understood as a temporary or momentary phenomena. The Greek word translated *rushing* (*pherō*) is also unusual. It literally means to bring forth, to bear or carry with endurance. Thus, the phrase suggests a powerful bringing forth of a great and sustaining breath. Let me suggest that this Acts 2:2 tongues as of fire event was the beginning of a great movement of tongue wagging about Jesus Christ in foreign (non-Hebrew) languages that will continue to the end of history.

People were not just talking, they were excited, they were "on fire!" And as more of them began to get excited about the miracle of God's grace in their own lives, they had to speak louder in order to be heard above the crowd. Thousands of people were crowding together, excitedly talking among their friends about their new insights into the gospel of Jesus Christ.

What exactly happened on the day of Pentecost? Suddenly God's Word was being spoken (discussed) in foreign languages (not Hebrew) among the international crowd that had gathered. The Word of God had been given to people who didn't speak Hebrew. For thousands of years all genuine God-talk had been limited to the Hebrew language, and now suddenly, people began to speak about the Hebrew God (or the God of the Hebrews) in their own languages—foreign languages.

The gospel had been given to the Gentiles, but if it was to be received by the Gentiles, it needed to come to them in their own languages —and it did! The point of the Pentecost story was the sudden distribution of genuine God-talk among speakers of foreign (non-Hebrew) languages. If Jesus was to be the savior of the Gentiles, the Gentiles would need to discuss Him in their own languages. And they did, all of a sudden! All at once these gathered Gentiles started talking among themselves about the miracle of Jesus' resurrection and the amazing grace of the gospel. They began talking among their small groups, among their families and friends, groups who didn't speak Hebrew. God's Word had broken out of the Hebrew box that had contained it for thousands of years. The actual understanding of grace and salvation had been given to Gentiles—foreigners, and in their own languages! That was the miracle of Pentecost.

Pentecost was not about mystical unknown languages or special languages known only to God and particular, individual believers. Pentecost was not about gibberish! It was the outpouring of God's grace to the Gentiles in their native tongues.

Later, when the Protestant Reformers said that "tongues" had "ceased" they meant that the Canon of Scripture was closed with the writing of the New Testament—which is true. But in another sense tongues had just begun! The gospel of Jesus Christ is still being translated and spoken in foreign tongues (glōssa) all over the world, and it will continue until the end of time.

Greek was a foreign tongue to the Hebrews. So, part of the tongues experience involved the writing of the Bible (the New Testament) in a foreign language—in Greek, which was the international language of the day. The closing of the Canon was a very important concern. All kinds of stories about Jesus and all sorts of erroneous miraculous events were floating about.[4] And much of it was nonsense. The truth about Jesus Christ needed to be codified. Truth needed to be separated from error. Three hundred years after Jesus, the Roman Emperor Constantine called for the Nicene Council who, among other things, began the process of codifying the books of Scripture as we know them. The authoritative books of the New Testament were established on the basis of common usage. That was a critical issue for the life and viability of the gospel of Jesus Christ, but there were differences of opinion about some relatively popular books.

In the seventeenth century the Protestant Reformers then made a few adjustments to the Canon at the Westminster Assembly when they excluded the Apocrypha from the Canon, which the Roman Catholics have

4   Charlesworth. James H. (ed.) *The Old Testament Pseudepigrapha*, Doubleday, Garden City, N. Y., 1983, 1985, vol. 1.

retained to this day. With that exclusion, Protestants then agreed that the Canon was closed. And to emphasize the closing of the Canon they emphasized in the first chapter of the Westminster Confession the cessation of the gift of tongues, and understood it to mean the end of the writing of the Bible.

But that closing of the Canon did not stop or limit the expansion of God's Word into foreign territories or foreign languages. Rather, the Protestant Reformation began the greatest expansion of Christianity the world had ever seen. Tongues began to flicker for God all over the world, and they still are. Indeed, from this perspective tongues did not cease with the closing of the Canon, but rather they began in earnest as the Bible was translated into every known tongue and exported to every known people. Praise be to God! Praise be to Jesus Christ!

32. The One And The Many

For just as the body is one and has many members, and all the members of the body, though many, are one body, so it is with Christ. For in one Spirit we were all baptized into one body—Jews or Greeks, slaves or free—and all were made to drink of one Spirit. For the body does not consist of one member but of many. If the foot should say, "Because I am not a hand, I do not belong to the body," that would not make it any less a part of the body. And if the ear should say, "Because I am not an eye, I do not belong to the body," that would not make it any less a part of the body. If the whole body were an eye, where would be the sense of hearing? If the whole body were an ear, where would be the sense of smell? But as it is, God arranged the members in the body, each one of them, as he chose. If all were a single member, where would the body be? As it is, there are many parts, yet one body. The eye cannot say to the hand, "I have no need of you," nor again the head to the feet, "I have no need of you." On the contrary, the parts of the body that seem to be weaker are indispensable, and on those parts of the body that we think less honorable we bestow the greater honor, and our unpresentable parts are treated with greater modesty, which our more presentable parts do not require. But God has so composed the body, giving greater honor to the part that lacked it, that there may be no division in the body, but that the members may have the same care for one another.

—1 Corinthians 12:12-25

The body of Christ is one. The body of Christ is many. Which is it? One or many? The answer is Trinitarian. When we look at the construction of chapter twelve we see the following theme: the spiritual unity of the body of Christ through the diversity of gifts. Chapter twelve has so far been a discussion of spiritual gifts. At verse 12 Paul introduced the idea of the body as an example of unity in diversity. The body is one, but is composed of many parts. The body of Christ, like the Spirit of Christ, is composed of diverse elements, and yet it is one in spite of its diversity. The unity of the body requires the cooperation of the parts, and at the same time the diverse parts cannot exist or function apart from their role in the unity of the body.

Note that the unity of the Spirit and the unity of the body are not something that Christians have to achieve. Christian unity is not an individual achievement, not a local church achievement, and not a denominational achievement. Christian unity, unity of the body of Christ, is a given. This unity or oneness already exists. It is a function of Jesus Christ. The unity of the church already exists among Christians and is manifested through the various gifts that God has given to His people, who are "empowered by one and the same Spirit" (v. 11). Paul was teaching about Christian unity here. It is an important lesson, but goes unrecognized for the most part.

Christian unity must be understood as it is manifested—in the diversity of gifts given to God's people. At the heart of Paul's discussion about unity and diversity is the doctrine of the Trinity. The essential question or issue of the Trinity is how something can be one and three, or one and many, at the same time. How can there be unity in the midst of diversity? And how can there be diversity in unity? Again, Paul used the human body as an example of how it works. The human body is made up of various parts—hands, feet, eyes, ears, etc. There is a unity of the body and a diversity of its parts at the same time.

Most people aren't concerned about such issues, but Christians are because Paul is. And Paul raised this issue because it is of ultimate value. It really is important. But why is the doctrine of the Trinity important? What actual difference does it make?

SCIENCE & TECHNOLOGY

The difference that it makes has to do with the development of science and technology, and the role of science and technology regarding human life, among other things. At this point in human history people—the populations of the world—are dependent upon science and technology. Life as we know it could not exist without them. They are the foundation of our contemporary life support systems, i.e., food production, medicine, and shelter.

It is significant that modern science and technology developed in the Christian West. They did not develop in India or China, both of which have very long histories and articulate religions. There was plenty of time for science and technology to develop in either India or China, but they did not. Why not? Why did they develop out of the Christian West? The short answer is that they developed out of the doctrine of the Trinity, and Christianity is the only religion or worldview that incorporates and advances such an explanation of God and of reality. And that is what the doctrine of the Trinity is—an explanation of God and reality that fits the facts.

A full explanation of exactly how the Trinity works is more difficult than simply stating it. For the most part the doctrine of the Trinity has been considered to be a mystery. And it is, but not because it is completely unknown. Rather, it is mysterious because it is both hard to explain and it is not completely understandable. Yet, in spite of this difficulty everyone uses the doctrine of the Trinity every day, and people have always relied upon it, though for the most part our reliance is at a subconscious level. It's sort of like relying on air. We breathe it, but for the most part it goes unseen and unnoticed as we go about our daily lives. The reality of the Trinity is, like air, a common, fundamental condition of ordinary living. People assume it to be true yet rarely acknowledge it, much less consciously think about it. But without the reality of the Trinity, life as we know it would be impossible.

Philosophically, the doctrine of the Trinity answers the fundamental issue posed by Plato known as the one and the many.[1] All human cultures in some way have to account for the myriad of objects and phenomena in the world. We have to make sense of the world in order to live in the world. And the use of science and technology require that we make a particular kind of sense of the world.

We live in a world of objects—things—that are constantly changing. Yet, in this world of objects and change, there seems to be an underlying unity and stability. There is a rational consistency in the way that the world works. For instance, every human being begins as an infant and then grows into an adult and dies. Adults are very different than infants in every regard—in fact, they are in many ways unrecognizable as being the same object. Yet we recognize that they are the same, that something has remained the same, even though the infant has changed into something that is quite different from its original state. And if we trace human life back into the womb or forward into death, we see even more astonishing changes. Yet, in spite of the changes we recognize an enduring consistency, a unique individuality in the midst of drastic change.

Or consider an acorn and an oak tree. They are completely different, yet we recognize that they share an essential identity over time. The one becomes the other such that the consistency between them is absolutely

1   See footnote 3, p. 116.

reliable. Something remains constant between these two very different things. And we see the same rational stability and constancy across the variety of objects that inhabit our world. While the world is full of diverse trees, there is still some constancy and stability to the idea of "treeness" which never seems to change.

This observation of the world of phenomena leads many cultures to believe that the diversity of things and their changes can ultimately be related back to a single thing, a unity or a oneness that remains constant in the midst of the flux of change. It is this constancy, this unity of individual things that gives them their identity. This concern is at the heart of the scientific endeavor and helps us to know how things in the world work.

UNIFYING FACTOR

The problem of finding the oneness—the unity—that lies behind all things—the diversity—in the universe was a primary concern of Plato, the ancient Greek philosopher. Basically stated, the problem of the one and the many begins from the assumption that the universe or the world or anything in the world is one thing, that there is a unifying factor that operates in the background of things, that unity and oneness are real, and that there is a reliable consistency at the center of things. Plato was seeking a philosophical unity or an underlying principle of unity, of identity.

Paul was trying to clarify that assumption, to identify that unifying factor when he wrote of the body as an example of God's Trinitarian character. My body is one thing, yet it is composed of many parts. But because it is one thing, there must be one unifying aspect behind it. There must be something that holds the various parts together so that they make up a single thing—a body—that endures in continuity over time.

Early Greek philosophers thought the unifying factor might be material, such as fire, or water, or air, or earth, or atoms. Others thought it might be an idea, such as number, or mind. Various Greek philosophers are associated with each of these ideas. Paul, continuing to criticize Greek philosophy in his letter to the Corinthians, was working to establish what that one unifying factor was. It was not air, earth, fire, water, or atoms. It was not number or mind. It was—and still is, said Paul, God, manifest in Jesus Christ.

In short, the doctrine of the Trinity tells us that the unifying thing in the universe is God, who exists in three persons, Father, Son, and Holy

Spirit. It is God who holds all things together in unity and in diversity. It is God who has created and given definition to all things. It is God who remains constant through time. God gives identity to things, just as God creates the parts or elements that things are composed of.

Philosophy in the Western world—Greek Philosophy—begins with this concern (the one and the many). The earliest Greek philosophers mainly concerned themselves with this conundrum, but they could not solve the problem. Philosophy has not been able to solve this problem, not the ancient Greeks, not the Indians or Chinese, not the pagans or Muslims, not the Moderns or Postmoderns. As a result, the problem of the one and the many still dominates our understanding of the universe, including modern physics, which has set for itself the goal of finding the theory that will unify the laws of physics. This was the quest that drove Albert Einstein to continue to delve deeper and deeper into the world of physics. It is not a fluke of an idea, but has played a very important role in the world—and it still does. Perhaps you have heard of String Theory, which is an attempt to solve this very problem at the subatomic level.

Follow Christ

But we don't need to go there. We don't need to follow the String Theorists. Rather, we will follow Paul. And Paul says two things that relate to this concern. First, he said that God gives differing gifts to His people and that it is the "same Spirit" (v. 4) that "empowers them all in everyone" (v. 6). God manifests Himself in His people through various spiritual gifts. And, in spite of the differing gifts that people have, the Lord who manifests them is one. God's unity is maintained in spite of the different manifestations of gifts.

Those gifts are manifested in the bodies of different believers, yet they are merely different parts or aspects of one Spirit. The gifts are given through our bodies, and yet our bodies are parts of the body of Christ, the greater body to which we belong, in which we have a greater identity, our true identity in Christ.

Paul said that though there are many bodies that belong to many people, the different gifts that each body contribute to the unity of the body of Christ. In Christ, those differing gifts are parts of Christ's body— His church. Do you see it? Christ is the unifying factor. Christ, the Spirit of Christ, the Holy Spirit is the glue that provides Christian unity, that holds all Christians together in the one body of Christ, though composed of different people with different gifts.

We don't have to work to establish Christian unity. It is not a function of denominational administration. It is simply given. It is given through the differing gifts. It is a function of the Trinity. So, where those gifts are, there is unity. And where those gifts are not, there is no unity. And the one identifying thing about God's gifts is that they all pull in the same direction, toward the same goal and/or purpose. They are all working together toward the same end, with the same Spirit through the manifestation of the same Lord, who is Jesus Christ.

And yet, denominational separation is a reality, but it is not an ultimate reality. It is important, but not ultimately important. It is not as important as the gifts of God, not as important as the manifestation of the Holy Spirit in the lives of believers. Denominations are not as real as the gifts given to God's people. And where denominations do not pull together toward God's purposes, the denominational unity they express is less real, less important, than the unity of gifts that all pull in the service of God's purposes. Paul does not speak of denominations as the elements of Christian unity. He speaks of gifts, which are the manifestation of the Holy Spirit.

DIVISION OF LABOR

At the same time Paul warns us of gift envy, of jealousy and opposition among Christians. We don't all have the same gifts. That's not the way that God has designed things. We are all different. God has provided for specialization, for the division of labor. The division of labor is an essential element of human society, and particularly for the development and use of science and technology. The division of labor provides for maximum social development because it provides for maximum skill specialization. We can't all be eyes or ears, hands or feet. Rather, we each must develop our unique gift, which provides for our unique identities as unique individuals. Our individuality, our uniqueness is tied to the gifts that God has given us.

We are all different and we must celebrate our differences, our diversity. But at the same time we must not allow the focus on our diversity to overwhelm our unity in Christ. The division of labor is essential, and works best when it functions within the same economy (*oikos*), when it contributes to the common good, to a common culture. All of the various gifts (parts) are necessary to the well-being of the whole.

Paul wrote,

"the parts of the body that seem to be weaker are indispensable, and on those parts of the body that we think less honorable we bestow the greater honor, and our unpresentable parts are treated with greater modesty, which our more presentable parts do not require. But God has so composed the body, giving greater honor to the part that lacked it, that there may be no division in the body, but that the members may have the same care for one another." (vs. 22-25).

Was Paul talking about our individual bodies? Or the body of Christ? Both!

You have heard the old adage that a chain is only as strong as its weakest link. That is the idea that Paul is discussing here. The strength of the chain (church) is dependent upon the weakest link (person). The chain is a whole, a unit, though it is composed of many links. Each link of a chain must be in unity, in relationship with the other links. The strength of the chain is dependent upon the relationship between the links. And so it is with the body, as well. The strength of the body requires that the parts of the body have strong relationships with one another. Each part is in relationship with each other part, some relationships are closer than others, but all must be strong—real, personal, hearty, familiar—in order that "that there may be no division in the body, but that the members may have the same care for one another" (v. 25).

This mutual care and concern is a critical issue that Paul will address in the next chapter.

LOVE

The unity of the body, the unity of the universe, is a function of love. God loves the world and His love holds the world together. God's love is the unifying factor in the laws of physics. Similarly, in like fashion, inasmuch as we are created in the image of God, we must love one another because our mutual love—our mutual concern, our mutual attachment, our mutual bond—helps hold the body of Christ together. In an ultimate sense, Christ alone holds it together. But in a practical, relative sense, the glue of God's church is the bond of love and fellowship between the members.

Friends love each other, but when they argue and fight, the friendship is ruined. Friends fight and walk away from each other. In contrast, family members also love each other, but when families argue and fight, the family relationship remains intact. Families find it much more difficult to walk away from each other. And even when they do, the family relationship remains for life. Family relationships cannot be undone.

Christian fellowship is more like family relationships than friendships in this regard, except stronger. The bonds of Christian fellowship are stronger and more durable than friendships, even more durable than family relationships. Relationships in Christ are as strong and durable as Christ Himself. Our relationship with Christ is as strong and as eternal as Christ because we are held in that relationship by the love of Christ for us, and not merely by our own love for Christ. Our love is weak and fickle, Christ's is not. Our love is temporal, worldly. Christ's is eternal, heavenly.

When Paul wrote to the Romans he said that nothing can separate us from the love of Christ. Nothing, not "tribulation, or distress, or persecution, or famine, or nakedness, or danger, or sword" (Romans 8:35). This is the bond that holds Christ's church together in unity.

33. PAUL'S LIST

...that there may be no division in the body, but that the members may have the same care for one another. If one member suffers, all suffer together; if one member is honored, all rejoice together. Now you are the body of Christ and individually members of it. And God has appointed in the church first apostles, second prophets, third teachers, then miracles, then gifts of healing, helping, administrating, and various kinds of tongues. —1 Corinthians 12:25-28

Verse 25 sums up the central concern of 1 Corinthians 12—"that there may be no division in the body." The general theme of the chapter is the unity of the body of Christ, the church. Paul had been writing to the Corinthian church because some of the church leaders had created a division as a result of their apostasy. Paul's mission was to bring healing through the teaching of right doctrine to the church. He was now explaining that the building blocks of that unity are the spiritual gifts that have been given to God's people. The building blocks are a set. If the set is broken, the unity of the church is broken. When all the pieces are working, we have one set. But if a piece is missing or broken, we have less than one set.

As with a human body, the various parts work together to make the body whole. Each part has a unique function, and without that function the entire body suffers and is thrown off balance. No function is more or less important than another. They are only different. If your little toe hurts, your whole body limps.

Paul found that the Corinthian church was limping and that limp was the impetus for Paul's next major concern—the care and maintenance of the body. Paul introduced the idea of care and maintenance in the latter half of verse 25, "that the members may have the same care for one another."

The lack of unity or wholeness in the church results in both additional sin and pain. And just as in the human body, the pain is not the real problem, it is a symptom of the problem, a symptom of sin. Pain provides a warning signal. If the cause of the pain is not resolved, increasingly serious consequences will unfold. The lack of unity produces corporate pain in the churches. Paul dealt with this pain in two ways. First, he addressed the prevention of corporate pain. And second, he addressed its care and treatment.

This an issue because the Corinthian church was limping. Was the whole body broken? Were all of the members in pain? "If one member suffers, all suffer together; if one member is honored, all rejoice together" (v. 26). The Corinthian church had a migraine headache. Some of its leaders were out of whack, and were not seeing straight.

Paul's point was that it wasn't just a problem with the leadership, it was the whole body that was in trouble. Yes, leaders are important. They provide key functions in the body. But without followers, leaders are nothing. Leaders can only lead if followers follow. When followers don't follow, leaders aren't leaders. So, when Christian leaders don't lead in the right direction, Christian followers should not follow. That means that Christian followers must know which leaders to follow and which direction is the right direction to go. Trusting church leadership is good, of course. But Christians must do more than simply trust their leaders. They must be Bereans. They must know God and know Scripture.

The Bereans "were more noble than those in Thessalonica; they received the word with all eagerness, examining the Scriptures daily to see if these things were so" (Acts 17:11). The Bereans not only received the leadership of their leaders (preachers), but they honored them by making sure that what they said and did were in line with Scripture. The Berean followers honored their leaders by testing their leadership against the biblical model.

Some people might think that such testing was not a function of trust and honor, but of doubt. Some people might argue that it was a lack of trust that caused the Bereans to check what they heard from their leaders against Scripture. And that may be partly true because, knowing Scripture, the Bereans knew the reality and extent of sin. But when their leaders were proven to have provided genuine biblical leadership, leadership that was in conformity with Scripture, that leadership was doubly honored because the Bereans had erased all doubt as a result of their own examination. Leaders that passed the muster were worthy of honor, and those who didn't were corrected or abandoned. Thus, the body of Berean followers were not led astray by errant leaders. The followers gave legs to the right leadership and cut the wrong leadership off at the knees.

Blind followership is as bad as blind leadership. Jesus warned, "if the blind lead the blind, both will fall into a pit" (Matthew 15:14). The corollary of Jesus' warning is that if the blind try to lead the sighted, it is the obligation of the sighted to keep them both out of the pit. So, if you can see, if you are not blind, then your obligation is to avoid the pit, and to help others do the same. The Berean followers insured the strength and veracity of the Berean leaders. Contrary to popular opinion, the real strength of the Christian church is not in her leaders, but in her followers. Followers always get the leaders they deserve. So, an increase in the quality of leaders will require a corresponding increase in the quality of followers. There is an application of this to both civil and religious politics that is rather distressing, but you will need to make that application yourself. Lord, have mercy.

If one member suffers, all suffer together. If one leader suffers, all suffer together—members and leaders. So, to avoid suffering, each part must do its job—and the job of Christian followers is to examine the Scriptures daily to see if these things are so, to be like the Bereans. Paul reminded the Corinthians that they were "the body of Christ and individually members of it" (v. 27). Each individual member had a role to play, a function to perform. Each follower must examine the Scriptures, to be "diligent to make your calling and election sure" (2 Peter 1:10). Worthy leaders will not be threatened by that role. Rather, they will be strengthened and honored by it.

There are no Christian spectators. This is why spectator worship is such a crime against the Spirit! Worship that treats the congregation as spectators trains Christians to be blind followers. The congregation must participate in worship, not just watch. Remember that true Christian worship is more than what happens on Sunday mornings. Worship is a way of life. Worship is a matter of bringing all your life to God as a sacrifice of daily living. Worship is the exchange of our personal worthlessness for the worthiness of Christ. The gift of Christ's worthiness is freely bestowed upon the unworthy, and produces a life of worship, not just a life that goes to church.

Paul went on to list various gifts that are essential to the church.

"God has appointed in the church first apostles, second prophets, third teachers, then miracles, then gifts of healing, helping, administrating, and various kinds of tongues" (v. 28).

APOSTLES

An apostle (*apostolos*) is a delegate; specifically an ambassador of the Gospel; officially a commissioner of Christ. The traditional understanding is that apostles were responsible for writing the New Testament. Miracles were associated with their ministry. Miracles provided a method of evaluation or proof of their calling, their ability to speak accurately for God.

The purpose of miracles in the Bible was to establish the authority and authenticity of God's prophets, known here as apostles. The purpose of biblical miracles was not the blessing of the recipients of those miracles, though the recipients were indeed blessed. Miracles were the traditional way of identifying and authenticating God's prophets, in order to give glory to God. The purpose of the prophets—the apostles—was to produce the Bible, to set God's Word straight by producing the New Testament.

So, with the closing of the Canon, it has been traditionally understood that the age of miracles was passed—not because God could not perform any more miracles, but simply because their purpose was complete. In the light of Scripture, miracles are no longer necessary. God's Word has eclipsed them. Miracles are like flashlights in the dark. But in the light of day, flashlights are no longer necessary. Flashlights still work, but in the light of day they don't provide any significant help.

Thus, the role of the apostles ceased with the closing of the Canon. The New Testament had been written. But in the first century Corinthian church (and in other churches) the production of the Canon was in full swing. The apostles were busy writing the New Testament. And the writing of the New Testament was the number one job of the Christian church at that time. So, Paul rightly listed it first in his list of gifts.

PROPHETS

Second in Paul's list were prophets (*prophētēs*). We know those who have this gift as preachers. The prophet's job was to expound Scripture, to multiply the gift of the apostles, the gift of Scripture (the New Testament, but not the New Testament alone—also the Old Testament) by illustrating and applying it to God's people, to the churches. Once the Scripture was complete and available, it was to be proclaimed to the nations, to the Gentiles, to all of the people in the world. With the closing of the Canon and cessation of the role of the apostles, the role of the prophets took first place in the churches. Indeed, preaching God's Word is still the primary job of every church.

TEACHERS

The next gift on Paul's list was teaching. Teachers (*didaskalos*) were to help people incorporate Scripture into their lives. Teachers instruct, train, and disciple others. Teaching is an outgrowth of preaching. Teaching takes preaching to the next level. Where preaching is the proclamation of God's Word, teaching involves the assimilation and application of God's Word. The teacher must master the subject before teaching it, and then help others master it. So, the first job of the teacher is learning.

And every Christian is called to be a teacher. Husbands are to teach their wives. Parents are to teach their children. Older students are to help teach younger students, etc. Teaching is the main staple of Christianity. Every Christian needs to be taught, not just the essentials of the faith, but the fullness and richness of the faith. Christianity is not just about the main points of biblical doctrine, it's about the entire story of the Bible in all of its amazing details. "All Scripture is breathed out by God and profitable for teaching, for reproof, for correction, and for training in righteousness" (2 Timothy 3:16).

MIRACLES

Next on Paul's list are miracles. But didn't I say that miracles had ceased with the closing of the Canon? I did, and what I said is true. However, it is not the whole truth because the closing of the Canon was not the end of Christianity. Rather, it was the beginning of God's Christian mission to the whole world. Paul's inclusion of miracles on the gift list was the result of Jesus' instructions in John 14:12: "Truly, truly, I say to you, whoever believes in me will also do the works that I do; and greater works than these will he do, because I am going to the Father." James taught the same thing: "You see that a person is justified by works and not by faith alone" (James 2:24).

You might say that Paul used the word *miracles* where the verses I have quoted above use *works*. And indeed, they are not the same Greek words. Nonetheless, the meaning and intent of the two verses are the same. Paul used the word *dunamis*, which means power. Paul's use of the word *miracles (dunamis)* here referred to going out in the power of Christ and changing the world. Paul was not talking about carnival tricks or healing aunt Sally's sore elbow. Paul was talking about using the wisdom that God had provided in Scripture to change human culture and society into the likeness of Christ. Paul was talking about the application of biblical principles and truths to the endeavor of being human in a fallen world. Paul was talking about walking in the Spirit, about living in regeneration, about being used by God in the accomplishment of God's purposes for His church, to extend the biblical mission to reach the whole world.

With the light of Jesus Christ and completion of the Bible, miracles that were like flashlights in the dark were no longer necessary in the light of Christ. Again, it is not so much that miracles that worked like flashlights in the dark ceased to work, but that in the light of Christ flashlights were no longer necessary. But note that if the light from the flashlights was miraculous, the light of Christ was a miracle of infinitely greater proportion. The flashlights were simply abandoned in favor of the superior light of Christ.

Miracles are like tongues. Rightly understood, we see that speaking in tongues did not cease, but rather began in earnest with the closing of the Canon as the gospel was translated (spoken and written) into foreign tongues (languages). Similarly, miracles did not cease with the closing of the Canon, either. Rather, the closing of the Canon provided the platform for the launching of new generations of miracles, new kinds of miracles previously unknown, miracles that could only be manifest in the light of the Trinitarian Christ. Indeed, the application of the Trinitarian understanding of God and the Trinitarian understanding of reality brought about the development of science and technology, which have utterly and miraculously changed the world.

What we call science and technology today, Christians of the first century would have called miracles. What we assume as commonplace today, would have been considered to be absolutely miraculous in any other period of human history. I'm talking about modern communications, transportation, media, agriculture, population increase, etc. Think about the transformation of the world from the time of Christ to the twenty-first century and it is nothing short of absolutely miraculous, particularly from a first century perspective. This is the gift of miracles that was on Paul's list.

The rest of the gifts on Paul's list are lumped together as if the order is not significant, "then gifts of healing, helping, administrating, and various kinds of tongues" (v. 21).

The previous gifts on the list are in the order of importance. The most important was the apostolic, the writing of the New Testament. Second was the preaching of the New Testament gospel. And third was the teaching of the New Testament gospel. The direct result of that preaching and teaching would be—and were—miracles. The preaching and teaching of the Trinitarian gospel of Jesus Christ utterly changed the world for the better and forever. The continuing unfolding of God's gifts would then include things like "healing, helping, administrating, and various kinds of tongues" (v. 21), which are not listed in the order of importance, but are lumped together in a group.

HEALING

Healing (*iama*) included everything that would contribute toward increased human health and well-being as a result of the preaching and teaching of the gospel of Jesus Christ and the application of the Trinitarian perspective that produced modern science and technology. Indeed, increased health and healing of people under the influence of Christianity have resulted from faith in Jesus Christ. Modern medicine and the health industry must be included in the fruits of this gift.

HELPING

Helping or helps (*antilēpsis*) is a very interesting word. It means aid or help and is correctly translated. And yet, to translate it as *helping* doesn't really say very much. What does helping mean? Helping what? Helping how? The Greek Lexicon provides this definition: a laying hold of, apprehension, perception, objection of a disputant. It sounds like the gift of helping is a perspective.

The word is composed of two parts: *anti* and *lēpsis*. *Anti* means opposed, and *lēpsis* is a medical term that means seizure. Together they literally mean opposed to seizure. We can see how the word suggests a kind of helping. And it could be taken in one of two senses. It could suggest a kind of medical helping that would serve to prevent or treat seizures. Here it would be a kind of helping to oppose or overcome or treat seizures in the medical sense.

Or it could suggest that it was opposed to the medical (or medicinal) treatment of seizures, where seizures may be associated with demon possession. Demon possession was common in Christ's time, and the Lord treated several cases of it that were related to seizures. The word *seizure* can also mean to take possession of something. In this sense demon possession was a kind of seizure of the person who was being possessed. Consider this story:

> "And he asked them, 'What are you arguing about with them?' And someone from the crowd answered him, 'Teacher, I brought my son to you, for he has a spirit that makes him mute. And whenever it seizes him, it throws him down, and he foams and grinds his teeth and becomes rigid. So I asked your disciples to cast it out, and they were not able.' And he answered them, 'O faithless generation, how long am I to be with you? How long am I to bear with you? Bring him to me.' And they brought the boy to him. And when the spirit saw him, immediately it convulsed the boy, and he fell on the ground and rolled about, foaming at the mouth. And Jesus asked his father, 'How long has this been happening to him?' And he said, 'From childhood. And it has often cast him into fire and into water, to destroy him. But if you can do anything, have compassion on us and help us.' And Jesus said to him, 'If you can! All things are possible for one who believes.' Immediately the father of the child cried out and said, 'I believe; help my unbelief!' And when Jesus saw that a crowd came running together, he rebuked the unclean spirit, saying to it, 'You mute and deaf spirit, I command you, come out of him and never enter him again.' And after crying out and convulsing him terribly, it came out, and the boy was like a corpse, so that most of them said, 'He is dead.' But Jesus took him by the hand and lifted him up, and he arose. And when he had entered the house, his disciples asked him privately, 'Why could we not cast it out?' And he said to them, 'This kind cannot be driven out by anything but prayer'" (Mark 9:16-29).

This may have been the context for Paul's inclusion of helps on his list of gifts. The father of the boy wanted help, but the disciples could not give the help that was needed. With the dispensation of the Holy Spirit upon the whole Christian church in Acts 2, this kind of help may have been provided more widely.

Here the sense might be that the treatment of demon possession would be more spiritual than medical. The opposition (*anti*) would be directed more against the purely medical or physical aspects of seizures and focused more on demon possession. This perspective would then point to Christ's preferred treatment of demon possession, which was to cast them out. With the coming of the Holy Spirit upon the church, this gift— which would have been a gift of prayer according to the context above— may have been given to Christians as part of the dispensation of the Holy

Spirit. And perhaps we don't know much about it because it was so successful in its elimination of demon possession as the Holy Spirit was poured out on Christ's church in Acts 2. Demon possession appears to be rare today, but it was not rare then.

I'm out on a limb here, but there isn't much that is known about this particular gift. Calvin suggested that it may have to do with some church function or office that has been lost in antiquity. Most other commentators suggest that it indicates a generic kind of helping one another. And, of course, helping one another is good, and particularly helping through prayer. We may be content with such a definition because of the value of prayer in the lives of believers. In addition, it may be that prayer itself serves to keep the demons at bay. If so, this is a wonderful gift that we cannot afford to lose. Everyone needs the gift of prayer and the help that prayer affords.

Administrations

The next gift on Paul's list is administrations (*kubernēsis*), which again is not a very helpful translation. The KJV translates it as *governments*. Calvin understood this gift to mean the Presbyterian functions of the church—oversight of the church by the elders. And that is a sufficient understanding, as long as we don't limit it to the modern or contemporary understanding of church government. Paul had more in mind than a kind of board of directors who would meet monthly to discuss church administration.

I suspect that Paul had in mind a system of church courts that would be much like the Old Testament elder system that had been developed by Moses on the model given to him by his father-in-law Jethro.

> "The next day Moses sat to judge the people, and the people stood
> around Moses from morning till evening. When Moses' father-in-law
> saw all that he was doing for the people, he said, 'What is this that you
> are doing for the people? Why do you sit alone, and all the people stand
> around you from morning till evening?' And Moses said to his father-
> in-law, 'Because the people come to me to inquire of God; when they
> have a dispute, they come to me and I decide between one person and
> another, and I make them know the statutes of God and his laws.'
> Moses' father-in-law said to him, 'What you are doing is not good. You
> and the people with you will certainly wear yourselves out, for the
> thing is too heavy for you. You are not able to do it alone. Now obey
> my voice; I will give you advice, and God be with you! You shall repre-

sent the people before God and bring their cases to God, and you shall warn them about the statutes and the laws, and make them know the way in which they must walk and what they must do. Moreover, look for able men from all the people, men who fear God, who are trustworthy and hate a bribe, and place such men over the people as chiefs of thousands, of hundreds, of fifties, and of tens. And let them judge the people at all times. Every great matter they shall bring to you, but any small matter they shall decide themselves. So it will be easier for you, and they will bear the burden with you. If you do this, God will direct you, you will be able to endure, and all this people also will go to their place in peace.' So Moses listened to the voice of his father-in-law and did all that he had said" (Exodus 18:13-24).

Moses set up a system of courts that served to adjudicate conflict among God's people. At the time of Jesus' ministry the Pharisees and Sadducees were teaching wrong doctrine, substituting the teaching of men for the teaching of God (Matthew 15:9). And if that was true, then it could be surmised that the Temple courts were also corrupt. Paul would have been acutely aware of such corruption because of his experience as a Pharisee. In addition, because Paul was dealing with the grand design of Christ's church, he probably had such courts in mind when he put governments on his list of gifts. I suspect that this is the case. Consequently, Paul's gift of governments must include the whole of the biblical teaching regarding government, which includes self-government, family government, civil government, and church government, all of their various jurisdictions and courts.

And indeed, we know that the Early Church set up a system of church courts to adjudicate disputes. Roman courts had become corrupt and inadequate. They could not deal with the flood of local conflicts that came with the expansion of the Roman Empire. And as a result of this backlog and failure of the Roman court system, people turned to church courts, and even brought civil matters to the church courts. Paul no doubt saw the beginnings of this as he journeyed up the Roman government appeal system to Rome[1] and anticipated this need by putting governments on his list of gifts. He was able to anticipate it because of his knowledge that the Mosiac court system had grown corrupt in his own time.

---

1   For more on Paul's journey see Ross, Phillip A. *Acts of Faith—Kingdom Advancement*, Pilgrim Platform, 2007.

VARIOUS KINDS OF TONGUES

"Various kinds of tongues" is a translation of two Greek words: *genos glōssa*. The first word literally means kin, as in kindred—family. And the second means tongue, by implication a language, and specifically the language of one's kin (family). The Greek Lexicon expands the definition to mean the language or dialect used by a particular people distinct from that of other nations. So a literal translation might be *kindred languages*, and again it suggests the language of one's kin or family, the language spoken by one's parents, one's native tongue. It is an untenable stretch of the imagination to think that it means unknown languages of any kind.

In the light of our previous discussion of tongues, we find that this gift of "various kinds of tongues" is about speaking the gospel in the native tongue(s) of believers in order to share it with one's family at home. Remember that the purpose of tongues is to bring the gospel of Jesus Christ to the nations, to the Gentiles, to the people of the world. Through Christ the gospel of the God of the Hebrews was exported to the world in the native tongues of the various nations.

Paul's mention of this gift is a repetition of verse 10, and biblical repetition serves to emphasize importance. Various kinds of tongues would serve the expansion and dissemination of the gospel to the world. Paul was not instructing disciples to speak in languages they didn't know, nor in forgotten languages, nor to speak in languages known only to God. Rather, he was instructing disciples to take their knowledge, experience, and love of the gospel of Jesus Christ and share it with their family and friends at home, in their native countries, in their native tongues, as a means of evangelizing the Gentiles, non-Hebrews.

This gift, rather than being a fanciful flight into realms of so-called higher spirituality, was the most common, ordinary thing imaginable. Because the gift of tongues that was given in Acts 2 was the gift of speaking (and writing) the gospel of Jesus Christ in non-Hebrew languages for the sake of world evangelization, this repetition of that gift simply emphasizes its importance. Paul was acknowledging that foreigners, Gentiles, had indeed received God's grace of salvation and the power of the Holy Spirit, and was directing and empowering those Gentile Christians to take the gospel to their homelands and to do so in their own native languages.

The application for us is the same now as it was then. Christians everywhere are directed and empowered to share their faith in Jesus Christ in any and every language, but particularly to do so in their most common and familiar language. Sharing the gospel in one's native tongue by a true believer will do much to alleviate the difficulties that accrue to those who try to translate it into a language that is not their own native tongue. In short, the biblical gospel of Jesus Christ escaped the confines of the Hebrew language as Gentile Christians carried it home in their native tongues. And this has been a great gift of the Spirit, a continuing gift. In fact, this gift will continue into eternity because sharing the love of Jesus Christ is at the heart of the gospel.

34. The Best Gift

Now there are varieties of gifts, but the same Spirit; and there are varieties of service, but the same Lord; and there are varieties of activities, but it is the same God who empowers them all in everyone. To each is given the manifestation of the Spirit for the common good. —1 Corinthians 12:4-7

Are all apostles? Are all prophets? Are all teachers? Do all work miracles? Do all possess gifts of healing? Do all speak with tongues? Do all interpret? But earnestly desire the higher gifts. And I will show you a still more excellent way. —1 Corinthians 12:29-31

In order to understand Paul's questions we need to put them into context. So, I have intermixed a few verses from chapter twelve to remind us of the context for verse 31—Christian unity or the unity of the body of Christ. There is unity of Spirit in the diversity of gifts. Paul emphasized this Trinitarian relationship between unity and diversity several times because it is so important. The diversity is obvious, we can all see it. And we all experience it.

But the unity is not obvious. The unity is invisible or informal.[1] The unity is a function of the Holy Spirit and is, therefore, seen by faith, which is "the assurance of things hoped for, the conviction of things not seen" (Hebrews 11:1). Those who are not regenerate do not see the unity. They do not know the unity, and they cannot live in the unity. The diversity is easy. It's natural. The unity is harder. It's supernatural.

Paul's questions sound a bit like chastisement because the obvious answer is *no*. Are all apostles? No. Are all prophets? No. Are all teachers? No. Do all work miracles? No. Paul was addressing the jealousy that makes us envy those who have different gifts than we do. He was addressing the tendency to think that the grass is always greener on the other side of the hill, to think that other people have it better or easier than we do. And by impli-

---

1   See Ross, Phillip A. *Informal Christianity—Refining Christ's Church*, Pilgrim Platform, Marietta, Ohio, 2007.

cation, Paul was calling Christians to spend their time and energy developing their own gifts rather than being jealous or envious of other people who have other gifts. Paul was calling Christians to bloom where God has planted them, to use the talents and resources that God has given them, to not neglect the station to which each has been called.

POOR ME

Part of our sin state is the "poor me" complex that captures and keeps people feeling trapped by their circumstances. In contrast, the central message of the gospel is that we are not trapped by our circumstances. We are not trapped by sin, not by our own sin, and not by the greater sins of the world that often—usually—appear to dominate our lives. Yes, the sin is there. Yes, the sin is real. Yes, the sin is powerful and pervasive. But "the law of the Spirit of life has set you free in Christ Jesus from the law of sin and death" (Romans 8:2).

Christ Jesus has set us free from the tyranny of our circumstances and set us free from those circumstances in the joy of the Lord. And the Spirit of that joy is the Spirit of unity in the body of Christ. The joy of the Lord is supernatural. It supersedes or superimposes or superintends the natural state of sin.

It is this joy in the Lord to which Paul now turned. We all want the joy, but we all feel stuck in the sin. We want the freedom to be all we can be in Christ, but we feel like victims captured by our circumstances. We look at other people and think, "if only I could be like him or like her. If only I could do what he does or what she does, then I'd be happy or rich or free or whatever."

"No!" said Paul. That is not the way things are. Are all apostles? No. Are all prophets? No. Are all teachers? No Do all work miracles? No. Does everyone have to be this way or that way? No. Is everyone the same? No. And thank God! Indeed, thank God in Jesus Christ for the diversity of the kingdom that gives rise to the division of labor, which in turn is the engine of human culture that drives the development of modern culture, including science and technology.

Joy is not found by trying to be like someone else. Joy is not a function of imitation, except inasmuch as we can imitate Christ. But our imitation of Christ is not a matter of trying to be like Him. Rather, the imitation of Christ is a matter of being who God made us to be. Inasmuch as we can imitate Christ we imitate His authenticity. In Christ we know and celebrate and develop our own unique gifts. Christians are not to pretend to be like other Christians, not at all! Nor are we to pretend to be like Jesus. Christians are not called to pretend at all. Christians are called to be real, to be unique, to be authentic, to be—as the old King James Version reads—*peculiar*.

> "But ye are a chosen generation, a royal priesthood, a holy nation, a peculiar people; that ye should show forth the praises of him who hath called you out of darkness into his marvelous light: Which in time past were not a people, but are now the people of God: which had not obtained mercy, but now have obtained mercy" (1 Peter 2:9).

Christianity is not a cookie-cutter religion where people try to match or reach some perfect ideal. Quite the contrary! Christianity is a religion rich in diversity. No two Christians are the same—nor should they be! If you are trying to be like someone else, you are barking up the wrong tree. God does not want you to be like someone else. God wants you to be like He made you. God wants you to use the gifts He gave you in the circumstances in which He planted you. Someone else's gifts and talents won't work for you where you are, in your circumstances.

When we try to be like someone else, we are driven by envy and jealousy and will experience frustration and sorrow because, no matter how hard we try, it won't work. I can't be you, you can't be me. We can't be like someone else. Trying to be like someone else is a guaranteed route to failure because we are not them. The feeling of being trapped by our circumstances is the result of trying to be someone that we are not meant to be, or trying to do something we are not meant to do. The feeling of being trapped by our circumstances is always a function of sin. It is the very thing that Christ came to free us from.

We are not victims of our circumstances, though God has certainly bound us to our circumstances. The gift(s) that God has given us are for use in the midst of the circumstances that God has given to us. And as we learn to use our gift(s) we will see that those gifts require our particular circumstances. Our circumstances provide the context in which our gifts make sense. Our circumstances provide the foil that sharpens and strengthens our gift(s), which unleash God's blessings upon our circumstances, and which in turn give glory to God. Indeed, God has a better way!

God's grand plan unfolds through the exercise of the ordinary means of grace—Word and Sacrament—in the midst of His people who make use of their God-ordained gifts, and are intended to bring blessing to us and glory to God through ordinary living. In verse 31 Paul alludes to "higher gifts." Gifts (*charisma*) is in the plural. So there actually are some higher or better gifts. These higher gifts are the simple gifts of love and service. They are the gifts of Christian leadership that Jesus taught to His disciples.

> "You know that those who are considered rulers of the Gentiles lord it over them, and their great ones exercise authority over them. But it shall not be so among you. But whoever would be great among you must be your servant, and whoever would be first among you must be slave of all" (Mark 10:42-44).

The higher gifts are the very mundane gifts of love and service exercised in the midst of ordinary life.

HIGHER GIFTS

Paul had two such gifts in mind. The first higher or better gift is the unique gift(s) that God has given to each of His people, those various skills, abilities, and personality quirks that makes each of us unique. These are the gifts of the diversity of the body of Christ.

The second better or higher gift that Paul has in mind is a gift that is more valuable than all the others he has so far mentioned, more valuable than apostles, more valuable than prophets, more valuable than teachers, more valuable than miracles, more valuable than gifts of healing, more valuable than helping, more valuable than administrating, more valuable than various kinds of tongues, and more valuable than the interpretation of tongues. This gift is the gift of Christian love. God's love is the gift of grace He has given us. Love is both root and fruit, seed and flower. It is a gift given to us by God Himself, and a gift that we are to pass along to others (Genesis 12:2).

This second higher gift of Christian love is more spiritual than the others. It is more a function of the Holy Spirit, more a manifestation of the Spirit, more an expression of the Spirit. And as such it is a gift of the unity of the Spirit. It is different than the other gifts mentioned because its central characteristic is unity rather than diversity. It issues out of unity. It creates unity. And it celebrates unity. As such it is a gift that is shared by all Christians. All of Christ's people have this gift (to varying degrees), and those who don't have it, aren't Christ's people. It is an identifying mark of God's people, the body of Christ, the church. It is what holds the body of Christ together. It is the glue of Christian fellowship.

And it goes hand-in-hand with the first gift, the unique and personal gift(s) that make us all different from one another.

The gift Christians share in common provides the context for the blossoming of the different gifts that make us unique. And conversely, our unique differences provide the context for the common glue that holds us together. The diversity requires the unity in order to function. Our different gifts must work together toward or with a common purpose. Without the unity the diversity is just chaos.

And without the diversity the unity produces death. If all of the parts of the body tried to be eyes or ears or hands or feet, the body would die because the body needs the different parts to function as God created them to function. The unity needs the diversity, and the diversity needs the unity. Paul has been speaking about the diversity in chapter twelve. In chapter thirteen, he turned his attention to the unity, the greatest gift that God has given to His people, the gift that cannot be seen apart from the eyes of faith and cannot be exercised apart from the power and presence of the Holy Spirit.

35. LOVE ENDURES

If I speak in the tongues of men and of angels, but have not love, I am a noisy gong or a clanging cymbal. And if I have prophetic powers, and understand all mysteries and all knowledge, and if I have all faith, so as to remove mountains, but have not love, I am nothing. If I give away all I have, and if I deliver up my body to be burned, but have not love, I gain nothing. Love is patient and kind; love does not envy or boast; it is not arrogant or rude. It does not insist on its own way; it is not irritable or resentful; it does not rejoice at wrongdoing, but rejoices with the truth. Love bears all things, believes all things, hopes all things, endures all things. —1 Corinthians 13:1-7

Note that the very first gift that Paul set love over and against is tongues. In Paul's day as in ours tongues was a special concern. Two kinds of tongues are mentioned here: tongues of men and tongues of angels. This is the only time that the phrase "tongues of angels" occurs in Scripture. The obvious references can only be to human languages and angelic languages. No doubt Paul had encountered glossolalia among some of the Corinthian members. Given what we have seen about the desire of some of the Corinthians to mix Greek ideas into their Christian theology, it should come as no surprise that the highly valued spiritual practices of the Greeks at the highly valued Oracle of Delphi, and no doubt elsewhere, had found their way into Corinthian worship. People seem to have a natural propensity for religious syncretism.

Indeed, the idea of mystical communication and its interpretation by specialized priests has a very long history in the religions of humanity. Even the Roman Catholic Church held on to vestiges of this practice into the twentieth century. Until Vatican II the Roman Catholic Church recommended that church members not read the Bible because of its interpretative difficulties. Rather, Catholics were to rely upon the clergy in this regard. The clergy would read and explain the Scriptures for the people. The point is that such a practice was simply the continuation of God's mystical communication and its interpretation by specialized priests.

Angels

Paul's mention of tongues of angels is, I believe, an allusion to the practice of mystery glossolalia that had become part of the Corinthian church experience. If so—and I believe it was, Paul was placing the gift of love (*agapaos*) above it. He said that Christian love is more important than mysterious communication with God, even more important than translating the gospel into foreign languages. Apart from the primacy of Christian love, any translation of the gospel into a foreign tongue would be inadequate and inaccurate because the person doing the translating would lack the main ingredient of faithfulness—love.

In addition, Christian love is more important than communication with angels because Jesus Christ has been given all authority. Anything divine that needs to be communicated has been or will be communicated through Him and/or through the structures of authority that have been given in Scripture. Angels take a back seat in the light of Christ.

In essence, Paul was saying that Christian love is more important than anything anyone can say, more important than words. As the old adage goes, "Actions speak louder than words." Apart from the actual manifestation of Christian love, words are just noise.

In verse 2 Paul said that love is more important, more valuable than the ability to perform miracles. This is a big one. To be able to miraculously move mountains from one place to another is nothing compared to Christian love. Even perfect and complete understanding of all religious mysteries and all knowledge of the world are nothing compared to Christian love. Paul was saying that not only are words without love nothing more than meaningless noise, but that thinking itself, thought and understanding are nothing without love. Any thought or ideas that anyone may bring to the table in defense of some position—any position about anything—is nothing but noise apart from Christian love. Paul essentially and effectively undermined all opposition to the love of Jesus Christ, which manifests as Christian love among God's people.

"If I give away all I have, and if I deliver up my body to be burned, but have not love, I gain nothing" (v. 3). Here Paul suggested that people can do sacrificial things, good things, noble things, and still lack the essential ingredient of Christian love. But to do so amounts to nothing. Even martyrdom can be nothing but an effort of works-righteousness apart from the actual manifestation of Christian love provided through regeneration by the power and presence of God's Holy Spirit in the lives of believers. This is a very significant statement because it identifies Christianity as an expression of Christian love, not theology, not mystery, not personal sacrifice or commitment to some ideal. Agape is love in action.

Having said this Paul moved on to define Christian love or agape.

"Love is patient and kind; love does not envy or boast; it is not arrogant or rude. It does not insist on its own way; it is not irritable or resentful; it does not rejoice at wrongdoing, but rejoices with the truth. Love bears all things, believes all things, hopes all things, endures all things" (v. 4-7).

This is a call to Christian faithfulness. Here is the very heart of Christianity. Here are the characteristics that necessarily mark all Christians. And conversely, anyone who claims to be a Christian but does not manifest these characteristics is deluded about his or her membership in the body of Christ.

What is patience other than the good-natured tolerance of delay and incompetence? Patience means not flying off the handle when things don't go they way that you think they ought to go. Patience means endurance and perseverance in the face of difficulty, complexity, and confusion. Patience means not chomping at the bit. Patience and worry are opposites.

Kindness and patience go hand-in-hand. Kindness means being warmhearted, considerate, humane, and sympathetic toward others. Patience and kindness are related to manners, social deportment. Manners are the commonly understood and practiced behaviors that communicate kindness and patience. Manners provide various ways to demonstrate kindness and patience. Manners give legs (or wings) to kindness and patience.

Not

Paul then shifted gears and set out some limitations to his definition of love by expressing what it is not. The definition of a thing in the negative, saying what something is not, is a way to provide for maximum freedom of definition. The Ten Commandments employ this method. By saying what a thing isn't, you allow the widest possible interpretation of what a thing is by setting the limit at what it is not.

Love is many things to many people, and we are free to understand love in many different ways. There are as many ways to understand love as there are people, and yet the various understandings of love have much in common. So, rather than trying to provide a detailed list of everything that love is—an impossible task, Paul simply said what it is not. And by implication, then, as long as these negative characteristics are avoided, all other definitions of love are viable.

Love is not envious or boastful, said Paul. Both envy and boasting are functions of pride. So, Paul was saying that love and pride are opposites, and that they don't and cannot mix. Nor is love arrogant or rude. Arrogance issues from feelings of unwarranted importance or overbearing pride. To be rude is to lack civility or good manners. And again, we see that arrogance and rudeness are functions of pride.

In addition, love "does not insist on its own way" (v. 5). Of all of the characteristics Paul enumerated, this may be the most important. It means that love understands itself to be a servant, not a master. To love another is to live in service to him or her. And to keep this service from simply feeding the ego of the person loved, Christian love is first given to Jesus Christ. Christians love Christ first and foremost, and then love their brothers and sisters in Christ as an expression of their love for Christ. This means that our service to those we love is not a matter of simply doing whatever they want us to do for them. But rather it means that our service to those we love in Christ is a matter of doing what Christ wants us to do for them. Christ is the governor of our love and service. By loving Christ first and foremost our love for others in Christ does not serve or feed the selfish desires that abide in the breast of every person. Rather, our love for and service to others is directed, not by them, not by their felt needs, but by Christ.

CYNICAL

Nor is love irritable or resentful. Love is not easily annoyed, nor is it bitter or indignant. We could add that love is not cynical either, in that cynicism is closely related to irritability and resentment. This means that these characteristics are expressions of faithlessness. Faithlessness often expresses itself as irritation and resentment. Faithlessness is often bitter and indignant, and conversely, to be bitter and indignant are expressions of faithlessness. And of course, those who are bitter and indignant often slide into cynicism, which is another expression of faithlessness.

Paul may have had the ancient Greek Cynics in mind when he penned this verse. Cynicism originated in the philosophy of a group of ancient Greeks who rejected all conventions, whether of religion, manners, housing, dress, or decency, and advocated the pursuit of virtue in a simple, unmaterialistic lifestyle. (Sounds like the Hippies of the sixties!) The ancient Cynics almost sound spiritual to our modern ears, but not to Paul's. Paul rejected the cynical rejection of the world. Christian spirituality is not a matter of rejecting the world. Christianity is not found or expressed through a rejection of the world. Of course, Christians reject sin, but not the world. God loves the world. Life as we know it is not possible apart from the world.

When we think of the world we think of John 3:16, and yet to really understand John 3:16 we need to hear it in context.

> "For God so loved the world, that he gave his only Son, that whoever believes in him should not perish but have eternal life. For God did not send his Son into the world to condemn the world, but in order that the world might be saved through him. Whoever believes in him is not condemned, but whoever does not believe is condemned already, because he has not believed in the name of the only Son of God. And this is the judgment: the light has come into the world, and people loved the darkness rather than the light because their deeds were evil. For everyone who does wicked things hates the light and does not come to the light, lest his deeds should be exposed. But whoever does what is true comes to the light, so that it may be clearly seen that his deeds have been carried out in God" (John 3:16-21).

We are not called to hate the world—sin, yes, the world, no. We must remember that God intends to change the world by eradicating sin. So, we must not become cynical, even in the midst of a world where there are very good and sound reasons for cynicism. Cynicism, not the world, must be rejected. Christian love is the antidote to cynicism. Christian love is not irritable or resentful, even in the face of irritability and resentfulness. It is not cynical, even in the face of cynicism. Love turns its back on irritability and resentment, and refuses to engage or express them, regardless of our personal feelings.

COMMITMENT

Love, as Paul has defined it here, is not a function of feelings. Love is simply not subject to human feelings. Rather, love is a commitment, a commitment to Christ first and foremost and then to His people, come what may. Love is commitment to biblical principles regardless of how we feel in the moment. Love understands that its commitment to these things—to Christ, to God's people and to Scripture—is greater than life itself. Love understands that commitment to Christ will survive this temporal life and continue into eternity.

Paul went on to say that love "does not rejoice at wrongdoing, but rejoices with the truth" (v. 6). Other translations translate the Greek (*adikia*) as *unrighteousness* or *iniquity*. Love does not rejoice in unrighteousness. Love does not rejoice in iniquity. The word literally means injustice. Love hates injustice, unfairness, unrighteousness, and iniquity. But love loves truth (*alētheia*)—verity, equity, fairness, justice, and righteousness. It cannot be otherwise because true love loves Jesus Christ, and Jesus Christ is the manifestation of verity, equity, fairness, justice, and righteousness. Because Christians love Christ first and foremost, they love the things of Christ first and foremost, more than other things. Christians rejoice in these things. These things provide joy for those in Christ.

This great Love Chapter provides a call to faithfulness that cuts through the fog of theology and doctrine without denying or belittling theology and doctrine. It makes Christian love real, more than words, more than feelings, more than commitment to an ideal or a cause.

"And this is love, that we walk according to his commandments" (2 John 1:6).

36. Love Abides

Love never ends. As for prophecies, they will pass away; as for tongues, they will cease; as for knowledge, it will pass away. For we know in part and we prophesy in part, but when the perfect comes, the partial will pass away. When I was a child, I spoke like a child, I thought like a child, I reasoned like a child. When I became a man, I gave up childish ways. For now we see in a mirror dimly, but then face to face. Now I know in part; then I shall know fully, even as I have been fully known. So now faith, hope, and love abide, these three; but the greatest of these is love. —1 Corinthians 13:8-13

Love never ends" (v. 8), or as the KJV reads, "Charity never faileth." *Fails* is the better translation of the Greek (*ekpiptō*). To say that love never ends makes it into a statement about time and duration, whereas to say that love never fails makes it into a statement about effectiveness and perseverance. Over against love Paul has put prophecies and knowledge, both of which will fail, and tongues, which will cease.

The reference to tongues ceasing has, no doubt, given credence to the idea of cessationism as it was interpreted by the Reformers—that the mysterious phenomena of Delphic-like glossolalia would end. And if you come to the text with the idea that tongues means mysterious glossolalia (babbling), then the ceasing of babbling would be an acceptable meaning to assign to the phrase. However, it must be understood that babbling should not cease because of the reign of Christ or because of the completion of Scripture, but babbling must cease because it is not and has never been a methodology of God. The God of Scripture doesn't babble. Never has. Nor does God encourage His children to speak without understanding (1 Corinthians 14:33).

And what is more, the idea of the cessation of babbling doesn't fit with the larger context of the passage. Paul set the temporal gifts of prophecies, knowledge, and tongues over against the eternal gift of love. Prophecies, tongues, and knowledge exist on the earth now and are for use with these earthly bodies, but love will carry forward into eternity. There will be no need for prophecy in eternity, nor for knowledge, because in eternity all things will already be known.

The exercise of tongues involved the use of foreign (non-Hebrew) languages to carry the content or orthodox meaning of Scripture to people of every nation. Tongues is a matter of translating the gospel into foreign languages for the sake of those who don't understand the "mother tongue" (Hebrew). In eternity all of God's saints will speak the same language. Whatever it may be, it will be a common language. Thus, the need to translate into other tongues will be unnecessary in eternity. And the practice of tongues—translating the gospel into other languages—will cease.

Or, if we want to press the passage for a stronger meaning, we can understand Paul to say that language itself will one day fail. Language itself as we know it will one day cease, but love will never fail. Love is not a function of language, rather, arsy varsy, language is a function of love.

INVERTED PRIORITIES

Again, Paul's point was to contrast the temporal gifts of the Spirit with the eternal gift of love in order to show the superior character of love. The problem that Paul encountered in Corinth was that too many people had overvalued the temporal gifts, particularly tongues, and undervalued the eternal gift of love. The Corinthian priorities had become inverted, preferring the gifts that are exercised in the flesh over the greater gift of love that is exercised in the Spirit.

Verses 9-10 emphasize the difference between part and whole: "For we know in part and we prophesy in part, but when the perfect comes, the partial will pass away." In this temporal world our knowledge and our ability to use our knowledge in prophecy is only partial. The world has been rent asunder by sin. It is broken, flawed, incomplete, not whole. But when "the perfect" (teleios) comes, things will be fixed, restored, made whole again. What is this "perfect" that will come? Scripture uses the word in several places. For instance:

> "You therefore must be perfect, as your heavenly Father is perfect" (Matthew 5:48).

> "If you would be perfect, go, sell what you possess and give to the poor, and you will have treasure in heaven; and come, follow me" (Matthew 19:21).

"Do not be conformed to this world, but be transformed by the renewal of your mind, that by testing you may discern what is the will of God, what is good and acceptable and perfect" (Romans 12:2)

"And he gave the apostles, the prophets, the evangelists, the pastors and teachers, to equip the saints for the work of ministry, for building up the body of Christ, until we all attain to the unity of the faith and of the knowledge of the Son of God, to mature (perfect) manhood, to the measure of the stature of the fullness of Christ, so that we may no longer be children, tossed to and fro by the waves and carried about by every wind of doctrine, by human cunning, by craftiness in deceitful schemes" (Ephesians 4:11-14).

The idea contained in the use of the word *perfect* in Scripture pertains to the end of time, at which Christ will return and restore all things to their original purpose. Our perfection in Christ suggests the culmination of our sanctification, even our ultimate glorification in Christ in eternity, the endpoint of our growth in grace in eternity, or as it is translated elsewhere, our maturity in Christ.

BROKEN

Paul was saying that now we are broken, our understanding is broken, and our ability to communicate with one another is broken. But one day everything will be fixed. One day things will be restored to their original purpose. On that day we will look back on our brokenness and weep tears of sadness for our foolishness and tears of gladness for God's grace and mercy. On that day the temporal (temporary) gifts of prophecy, tongues, and knowledge will fade in the light of the infinitely superior gift of love that will manifest in full bloom. On that day, we won't need what is broken. We will release it and embrace what is whole. Rather, God's wholeness will embrace us and wrap us into the fold of perfection, completeness, maturity.

Looking back on the process of his own spiritual growth and maturity, Paul reflected, "When I was a child, I spoke like a child, I thought like a child, I reasoned like a child. When I became a man, I gave up childish ways" (v. 11). There is nothing wrong with thinking and speaking like a child, as long as it is understood that such thinking and speaking are temporary phenomena that are outgrown in maturity. Thinking and speaking like a child is fine for a child. But they are inappropriate for an adult. One day we will look back upon what we consider to be our adulthood today and see it as only another stage in our childhood. Every new stage of maturity engaged in the flesh will in eternity be seen as temporary aspects of our childhood. Only in eternity will we find our perfection and our complete maturity in Christ.

And yet, through regeneration by the power and presence of the Holy Spirit that process of perfect maturity in Christ has begun here and now, in the flesh, in these sinful and inadequate bodies. It is not that we must disregard or discount the various stages of our growth and maturity, but that we must not hold on to them when we are beckoned by God to continue to grow in grace through faith. We must continuously honor our past—as sinful as it is, we must acknowledge our history, our fallen condition, and the various stages of our growth in grace, without fearfully clinging to what has past. We must not ignore or dishonor the past, those stages of growth that provide identity and continuity. The past is important, but the future in Christ is determinative. It is not that the past is pushing us into the future, but that Christ is (teleologically) pulling us into greater faithfulness, and eventually into eternity.

DIMWIT

We cannot see clearly as we try to peer into the future. "For now we see in a mirror dimly, but then face to face. Now I know in part; then I shall know fully, even as I have been fully known" (v. 12). It's not just that we see dimly, but that we see *as in a mirror* dimly. Seeing dimly is bad enough, but to see as in a mirror dimly suggests that we not only see poorly, but that we see backwards (arsy varsy). Mirror images are reversed. Right is left and left is right. The allusion to a mirror image suggests that we currently see things from an inverted, backwards, or reversed perspective. In our perfection, in our maturity, this reversal of vision and values that has resulted from the Fall, from sin, will be corrected. The reversal of sin will itself be reversed, restored to its original order. But for now it remains as in a mirror dimly.

Our vision and our values are in need of correction. Of course, Christ has reversed the effects of sin in this present world, but not completely. And yet, Christ's victory is certain because it is the central purpose of God. It is so certain that we proclaim Christ's victory in history now. And we proclaim it as complete because we trust in the power of God to finish what He has begun.

The light of Christ not only brings additional illumination, but it brings about a reversal of vision and values. In Christ, our worldly values are turned upside down and inside out. In Christ everything is different, everything is new.

The allusion to seeing "face to face" (v. 12) has a long biblical history that helps us understand what Paul meant by it. When God revealed Himself to Moses in the dessert, He said, "I am the God of your father, the God of Abraham, the God of Isaac, and the God of Jacob." And what was Moses' response? He "hid his face, for he was afraid to look at God" (Exodus 3:6). Later, Moses wanted to see God and asked,

> "'Please show me your glory.' And he said, 'I will make all my goodness pass before you and will proclaim before you my name "The LORD." And I will be gracious to whom I will be gracious, and will show mercy on whom I will show mercy. 'But,' he said, 'you cannot see my face, for man shall not see me and live.' And the LORD said, 'Behold, there is a place by me where you shall stand on the rock, and while my glory passes by I will put you in a cleft of the rock, and I will cover you with my hand until I have passed by. Then I will take away my hand, and you shall see my back, but my face shall not be seen'" (Exodus 33:18-23).

This is the biblical context for Paul's phrase "when the perfect comes" (v. 10) because it will come to reveal the face of God. Is this a contradiction because Moses wrote that no one could see God's face and live, while Paul wrote that we will see God face to face? Not at all. Christians are baptized in Christ.

> "Do you not know that all of us who have been baptized into Christ Jesus were baptized into his death? We were buried therefore with him by baptism into death, in order that, just as Christ was raised from the dead by the glory of the Father, we too might walk in newness of life" (Romans 6:3-4).

The regeneration—the passing from death into new life—that believers experience this side of glory is but a dark reflection of the resurrection that believers will experience in glory. Through regeneration believers do see God's face, but darkly. Regeneration begins the reversal of vision and values that works to undo the effects of sin, but that reversal takes more than a lifetime to complete to perfection. In the meantime, we still see God's face darkly, dimly, barely, in fits and starts, as in a mirror.

The vision of seeing God face to face, of seeing and being seen by God is awesome. We want to see God to satisfy our curiosity and to answer our questions. But there is another aspect of this face to face meeting that is threatening. We will not only see God, but we will be seen by God. Seeing is one thing, but being seen is another. Most people—sinners —want to see God like Peeping Toms. We want to see without being seen ourselves. We want to look on God, but we don't want God to look on us. But that is not how it works. In order to see, we must also be seen. So, what's the problem with being seen?

BEING SEEN

Shame, guilt, and sin, that's what! We are afraid to be seen with all of our follies and foibles, all of our shame, guilt and sin. We'd be embarrassed. We don't want anyone to see this side of us, so we hide it. We cover it up however we can. We not only try to hide it from God, but we try to hide it from others, and even from ourselves. The problem with knowing fully is that we will also be fully known.

"Now I know in part; then I shall know fully, even as I have been fully known" (v. 12). But as scary as it is to think about being fully known, in the love of Christ we trust God. We trust that God loves us and has our best interests in mind. Being fully known by God, who loves us, is a little like being fully known by our spouse. Husbands and wives love each other and in this world they come as close as possible to being fully known by one another. That's why marriage is difficult. But in spite of the difficulties, that knowledge creates a bond, and the bond strengthens the love over time (at least that's the way it is supposed to work).

Faith, hope, and love are braided into a "threefold cord" (Ecclesiastes 4:12) that is not easily broken. We're are not talking about the marriage bond here, but rather our covenant bond in Christ. This bond cannot be broken, and it will not be broken. Even if we fail on our side, God will not fail on His side. Even if God's love brings us through a time of discipline and chastisement, God will not renege on His covenant promises.

Faith and hope belong to us, to God's people. Our part, our responsibility regarding the covenant bond with God is to be faithful and hopeful. Our response to God's love is faith and hope. In contrast, love belongs to God. God's part is to lead with love. Oh, we love God, without a doubt— because He "first loved us" (1 John 4:19). But it is not *our* love that holds us in covenant with God. Rather, we are held in covenant, in relationship with God, by *His* love. And His love will not fail. His love will not let us go, even if we lose our grip on God, God will not lose His grip on us. Even if our love for God grows pale and dim, God's love for us will not. God's covenant grip of love for His people will not fail. God, who is love itself, will not fail. God "who began a good work in you will bring it to completion at the day of Jesus Christ" (Philippians 1:6). Of this you can be sure. And so Paul concluded, "faith, hope, and love abide, these three; but the greatest of these is love" (v. 13).

37. Huh?

*Pursue love, and earnestly desire the spiritual gifts, especially that you may
prophesy. For one who speaks in a tongue speaks not to men but to God; for no
one understands him, but he utters mysteries in the Spirit. On the other hand,
the one who prophesies speaks to people for their upbuilding and encouragement
and consolation. The one who speaks in a tongue builds up himself, but the one
who prophesies builds up the church. Now I want you all to speak in tongues,
but even more to prophesy. The one who prophesies is greater than the one who
speaks in tongues, unless someone interprets, so that the church may be built up.
Now, brothers, if I come to you speaking in tongues, how will I benefit you unless I bring you some revelation or knowledge or prophecy or teaching? If even
lifeless instruments, such as the flute or the harp, do not give distinct notes, how
will anyone know what is played? And if the bugle gives an indistinct sound,
who will get ready for battle? So with yourselves, if with your tongue you utter
speech that is not intelligible, how will anyone know what is said? For you will
be speaking into the air. There are doubtless many different languages in the
world, and none is without meaning, but if I do not know the meaning of the
language, I will be a foreigner to the speaker and the speaker a foreigner to me.*

—1 Corinthians 14:1-11

Chapter fourteen begins right where chapter thirteen left off. Love
is the object of Christian pursuit. Love is the goal to be achieved.
Love is the "pearl of great value" (Matthew 13:46) for which from
the human side we should be willing to sell all that we own in order to attain, but which from the divine side is a gift of grace. Love is to be pursued,
but not in the sense that we must do everything we can to attain it. But
rather because love has been given as a gift of God's grace we must endeavor to give ourselves completely to it. Love—the love of God—is not
ours to own and possess. Rather, we belong to God's love in Christ, who
alone owns and possesses us.

While verse 1 is Paul's advice to believers, it is more than a request. It is
a command. We are commanded to pursue love. Can love be commanded?

Can the command to love be obeyed and still be love? What if I don't feel like loving?

Paul's next phrase commands believers to "desire the spiritual gifts." Again the word *gifts* has been added to to the English. It's not in the Greek. It's okay to use it because Paul has been talking about gifts. And yet, to add it tends to limit Paul, as if he is speaking only about gifts. It could also be translated as "spiritual things" as Jay Green does in his *Literal Version*, which suggests that what Paul says could pertain to anything and everything spiritual. The latter is closer to the original.

IMPOSITION

There are two issues in this simple phrase that need clarification: the verb and the object. The object is "that which is spiritual," the verb is "desire." The idea is to desire that which is spiritual. The phrase is situated in or as part of an imperative sentence, a command. Paul has not only commanded believers to pursue love, but he has commanded us to *desire* what is spiritual, as well. Again we must ask whether human wants and desires can be commanded. Can people be commanded to want or desire a particular thing? Doesn't desire just well up from within a person? Can human desire be imposed by a command?[1]

It is an interesting question. Most people believe that they are subject to their desires, rather than their desires being subject to them, subject to their willful control. If Scripture is to be believed and trusted, then the answer must be *yes* because Paul here commands believers to control their love and desire. Yet Paul was not content to leave it at that, but he added further clarification.

We are not only to chase after love with fervent passion, but we are to want what is spiritual. We are to desire the gift(s) that God has given us. We are to desire our own gifts and not chase after gifts that are not ours. By implication we are not to want or covet someone else's spiritual gifts. We are to want what God has given us. And most especially, said Paul, we should want to prophesy, by which he means to speak meaningfully about Scripture. Believers should especially want and engage this particular gift. The implication is that God has given this particular gift much more widely than most people think. Paul is calling it a common gift among believers, not a rare gift, an ordinary gift, not an extraordinary

1   For more on the idea of God commanding willing obedience, see Ross, Phillip A. *Informal Christianity—Refining Christ's Church*, Pilgrim Platform, Marietta, Ohio, 2007, p. 68-71.

gift. Sure, some people will do it better than others, but all Christians are called to engage in meaningful explanation about God, Jesus, and the Bible.

We understand that Paul was teaching that New Testament prophets are to be preachers of the gospel of Jesus Christ, to forth-tell or explain the New Testament and how Jesus Christ is the fulfillment of Old Testament prophecy, and to foretell the return of Christ in glory. Does this mean that Paul thinks that all Christians should be preachers?

Well, yes and no. No, Paul doesn't mean that all Christians must be employed as pastors or professional evangelists. But, yes, Paul agrees with Peter that every Christian needs to be "prepared to make a defense to anyone who asks you for a reason for the hope that is in you" (1 Peter 3:15). We all need to speak about Jesus Christ and to be ready to explain Scripture as best we are able to anyone who asks. Is this a realistic expectation? Can ordinary Christians really be expected to explain Scripture?

Peter said that Christians are a

> "chosen race, a royal priesthood, a holy nation, a people for his own possession, that you (they, we—Christians) may proclaim the excellencies of him who called you out of darkness into his marvelous light" (1 Peter 2:9).

All Christians are to proclaim the excellencies of Jesus Christ and to explain how they came from darkness to the light of Christ, and how Christ is the fulfillment of Scripture.

It's a tall order, but it's not my order. It's Paul's and Peter's, and Jesus' as well. The way this works is that prophesying is an overflowing of teaching, and teaching is an overflowing of learning. Learning leads to teaching, and teaching to prophesying (or preaching). Each builds upon the other and takes the accumulation of wisdom and knowledge to new levels. It's a matter of sanctification, of growth and maturity in the Spirit.

Verse 2 should be pretty straight forward, but there are some interpretive difficulties—not with the Scripture, but with our understanding and perspective.

"For one who speaks in a tongue speaks not to men but to God; for no one understands him, but he utters mysteries in the Spirit" (v. 2). Note the punctuation. As we have seen previously, too many interpreters have brought faulty assumptions to the discussion of tongues. Among those assumptions is the belief that the gifts of tongues and prophesying are extraordinary and miraculous—even mystical. I contend that they are none of these things. Rather, when they are properly understood and engaged, they are to be common and ordinary among God's people.

ORDINARY

To get at some of this let's start with the first word of verse 2: *for* (*gar*). It appears twice in this verse. Remember also that there is no punctuation in the Greek. I mention this because I believe that the translator's punctuation is wrong because it breaks the flow of what is actually a single thought. The Lexicon says that *gar* is a conjunction that assigns a reason to something, that it is used in an argument, explanation, or intensification, and is usually translated as *for, and, as,* or *because*. So, *for* is a correct translation, but it needs to be understood as supplying a reason or defense, thus it really means *because*, (i.e., for the purpose of).

Verse 2 could then read, "*Because* one who speaks in a tongue speaks not to men but to God *because* no one understands him, but rather he utters mysteries in the Spirit." Verse 2 is given as a reason for something. Verse 2 is given as an explanation of verse 1, as if to say, "verse 1 because verse 2." The same pattern occurs in the clauses of verse 2.

Verse 1 told us to prefer love to the other gifts, and then (next) to prefer prophecy above the other gifts. Among those other gifts are, of course, tongues. There are other gifts, but tongues appears to be a special case that requires some special treatment. We are to prefer prophecy over tongues, according to verse 1. Why? Paul began verse 2 with *because* and went on to explain that speaking in a foreign language—foreign to those to whom one is speaking—doesn't make sense to anyone, except maybe God. Let's give the benefit of the doubt to the Charismatic understanding here and suggest that Paul may be referring to the practice of mystical glossolalia and not simply to a known foreign language. Regardless of whether it is a foreign language, foreign to those listening or an instance of mystical, angelic glossolalia, Paul's point is the same: no one understands it except maybe God. And therefore, such practices are not helpful to the body of Christ.

We are to prefer prophesying—explaining Scripture, making sense of the Bible—to speaking in such a way that people do not understand what we are saying. Again, paraphrasing verse 2:

> because he who speaks in an unknown tongue does not speak to men but to God because no one hears or understands him, he is, then, speaking mysteries in or to the spirit.

Paul was pointing to the uselessness of such communication. Language is of no use to people who don't understand what is said or what it means. Maybe it is meaningful to the Spirit, but whether it is or not is a mystery to Paul because he doesn't understand it either.

"On the other hand, the one who prophesies speaks to people for their upbuilding and encouragement and consolation" (v. 3). He contrasts the practice of saying something to people that they can't understand to saying something to people that they can understand. Whether someone is practicing mystical glossolalia in some special spirit language or just speaking in a foreign language makes no difference to people who don't understand it. So, said Paul, it is better to prophesy, to explain Scripture in a meaningful way, a way that will provide upbuilding (edification—*oikodomē*), encouragement, and consolation for God's people. Remember that to edify means to make someone understand something or to make something understandable to someone.

Paul had nothing to say about someone speaking in tongues to God, using tongues for a private prayer language. Because he didn't know the meaning of what such a person was saying he couldn't comment on it. But it would seem out of character for God to be concerned with meaningful communication and not contributing to confusion and chaos, and then recommend that people speak to Him in languages that they themselves don't understand. Rather, it makes more sense for God to recommend that people make their prayer time meaningful. God already knows what we need. So, we are not informing Him. Rather, He is informing us, and meaning is critical to that task.

COMMUNICATION

"The one who speaks in a tongue builds up himself, but the one who prophesies builds up the church" (v. 4). If you are saying something that only you understand, you are talking to yourself, building yourself up, edifying yourself. But if you are saying something that others can understand, then you are building them up, edifying them, making them understand. This is so basic that it is hard to get a hold of. The purpose of language (tongues) is communication, common understanding. So, if the language (a particular tongue) is meaningless to those who hear it, it is useless to them. Giving the benefit of the doubt, Paul suggested that it may mean something to the speaker, and so it may be useful to the speaker. But again Paul doesn't really know because he doesn't understand it.

Verse 5 authorizes the practice of speaking in tongues. "Now I want you all to speak in tongues…." Paul did not forbid speaking in tongues. But what does he mean? We've seen that Paul used the word *tongues* with two meanings: 1) foreign languages and 2) babbling (unknown or spirit languages). Actually, both kinds of tongues are foreign languages. One is foreign to other nationalities, and one is foreign to humanity. So, by encouraging speaking in tongues Paul was saying that he wants the gospel translated and spoken in foreign languages. He wants people to speak in languages that they know, languages other than Hebrew.

It seems that Paul didn't mind even if someone was intent upon speaking in some unknown or angelic language. It can't hurt anything because no one knows what is being said. It might be helpful to the person speaking it, who knows? But it is at best a waste of time for the gathered body of Christ.

OUTER LIMITS

Paul understood that the gospel of Jesus Christ stretches the very limits of human language as people struggle to proclaim the magnitude and miracles of Christ to the watching world. Is it any wonder that Christians stutter when they try to speak about the gospel, the virgin birth, Christ's resurrection, or the Holy Trinity?

Paul spoke of groaning when he wrote to the Romans,

"For we know that the whole creation has been groaning together in the pains of childbirth until now. And not only the creation, but we ourselves, who have the firstfruits of the Spirit, groan inwardly as we wait eagerly for adoption as sons, the redemption of our bodies" (Romans 8:22-23).

And again in his second letter to the Corinthians,

"For in this tent we groan, longing to put on our heavenly dwelling, if indeed by putting it on we may not be found naked. For while we are still in this tent, we groan, being burdened—not that we would be unclothed, but that we would be further clothed, so that what is mortal may be swallowed up by life" (2 Corinthians 5:2-4).

Indeed, explaining the gospel of Jesus Christ pushes human language beyond its limits. Is it any wonder that Christians struggle and stutter and groan when speaking of Christ? No, not at all. Paul himself groaned in frustration at the limits of language to express the gospel of Christ. Human language is inadequate to the excellencies of Christ, but we try to understand it and to explain it as best we can, trusting that the presence and power of the Holy Spirit will convey what we cannot.

And that is Paul's next point. As much as Paul wanted people of every language to speak the gospel, he wanted even more for them to speak with understanding, to explain Scripture meaningfully. Listen again to Paul's words:

> "Now I want you all to speak in tongues, but even more to prophesy.
> The one who prophesies is greater than the one who speaks in tongues,
> unless someone interprets, so that the church may be built up" (v. 5).

Do you hear it? The one who speaks meaningfully is greater than the one who speaks without meaning, unless someone interprets the foreign tongue. It doesn't do me any good to hear someone speaking Russian, unless someone interprets it for me. Or we could understand Paul to say, "Speaking a foreign language is good. You all should master a foreign language. But it is even better to speak meaningfully about God's Word."

Unnecessary

Of course! It is so basic, so simple a statement that people are tempted to read some mystical meaning into it to make it "spiritual" in some abstract, Greek, Gnostic way. The point is that the mystical meaning related to charismatic angelic languages is completely unnecessary and foreign to the text. It introduces what Paul *doesn't* say.

We don't have to go so far as to say that mystical glossolalia is demonic. Who knows if something is demonic or not unless they understand the meaning. Paul was just saying that it isn't helpful to the church, to those gathered. So, don't waste our time with it.

> "Now, brothers, if I come to you speaking in tongues, how will I benefit you unless I bring you some revelation or knowledge or prophecy or teaching? If even lifeless instruments, such as the flute or the harp, do not give distinct notes, how will anyone know what is played? And if the bugle gives an indistinct sound, who will get ready for battle? So with yourselves, if with your tongue you utter speech that is not intelligible, how will anyone know what is said? For you will be speaking into the air. There are doubtless many different languages in the world, and none is without meaning, but if I do not know the meaning of the language, I will be a foreigner to the speaker and the speaker a foreigner to me" (vs. 6-11).

Even musical instruments convey meaning. This is so clear. Meaning of some kind—revelation, knowledge, or prophecy—must accompany speech. If it doesn't you may as well be baying at the moon.

Robert McCloskey said, "I know that you believe you understand what you think I said, but I'm not sure you realize that what you heard is not what I meant." For communication to be successful there needs to be a common, agreed upon understanding of the meaning of the words spoken. If communication is relative and people are free to assign their own meanings to words, then communication will be impossible. Maybe that's what happened in the Tower of Babel.

38. Understanding

Even so you, since you are zealots of spiritual things, seek to build up the church, in order that you may abound. So then he speaking in a language, let him pray that he may interpret. For if I pray in a tongue, my spirit prays, but my mind is unfruitful. What is it then? I will pray with the spirit, and I will also pray with the mind; I will sing with the spirit, and I will also sing with the mind. Else, if you bless in the spirit, he occupying the place of the unlearned, how will he say the amen at your giving of thanks, since he does not know what you say? For you truly give thanks well, but the other is not built up. I thank my God that I speak more languages than all of you; yet in a church I desire to speak five words with my mind, so that I might also teach others, than ten thousand words in a tongue.   —1 Corinthians 14:12-19

Paul said that "one who speaks in a tongue builds up himself" (v. 4), and now repeated his insistence that it is preferable to build up the church rather than one's self. He does not say to do both of these things, but contrasts them as if they are in opposition to one another. And rightly so! The contrast is between self-service and service to others, between self-centeredness and Christian service, between the pride of self-concern and the humility of concern for others. In self-service the love and attention flows inward, to one's self. In Christian service the love and attention flows outward, to others.

And again we note that the word *gifts* has been added to the English. It is not in the Greek. And again we see that it is not necessarily wrong to add it, but it tends to limit Paul's admonition. And again, Jay Green gets it pretty right in his Literal Version, "since you are zealots of spiritual things, seek to build up the assembly that you may abound." Other translations use the adjective *zealous* rather than the noun *zealots*, and the adjective is to be preferred. The meaning is: since you are zealous for the spirit or for spiritual things, then work to build up (edify) other Christians so that you may grow in the process.

Paul has identified those who speak in tongues as being zealous for the Spirit of God. They are full of enthusiasm, zeal, and eagerness to be used by God's Holy Spirit, and Paul knew that such desire is a good thing. So, he encouraged it while at the same time redirecting it. He wanted them to use their zeal (enthusiasm) to serve the growth and maturity of the church, and in the process they would themselves grow and mature in faithfulness. Since they wanted to think of themselves as being special because they think that they have a "higher" gift or experience in that they can speak some special fandango language, or can speak a real but unknown language of the Spirit, Paul advised them to actually become special by serving the growth and maturity of other Christians. And if they do that well, they will actually grow in maturity themselves and will then have the real thing—a true tongue that speaks meaningfully about God, Jesus, and Scripture rather than a counterfeit tongue that speaks unknown or meaningless babble.

The desire to be used by God is good, but it should not be self-directed. It should be other-directed. We are not to try to use God for our own edification, but rather we should try to be used by God for the edification of others. To speak in a tongue that others don't understand does nothing for anyone else. It is just a way to draw one's attention inward, as if a higher truth lies within one's own heart and mind. Rather, said Paul, build up the body of believers by prophesying, by speaking meaningfully about God and Jesus and Scripture. Seek to excel in the ability to prophesy, to explain Scripture.

INTERPRETATION

Paul said in verse 13 that the person who speaks in a tongue—in a foreign language (human or angelic)—would do better to pray to be able to interpret, to say something meaningful. Again Paul contrasted speaking meaninglessly with speaking meaningfully. The Greek word translated as *interpret* (*diermēneuō*) literally means to explain thoroughly or expound. The speaking in tongues that Paul encouraged involves the translation and explanation of God's Word in foreign languages, which is important. But Paul knew that the words alone, even completely accurate words, are not enough.

While anything is possible with God, it is God's preferable means of grace that the words of Scripture be accompanied with the right understanding, the right explanation from a regenerate or Spirit-filled (Spirit-led, Spirit-dominated) perspective (Romans 10:14). Anyone can read the

words of Scripture, but only born again, Spirit-filled disciples can understand it—not perfectly, but sufficiently. The Holy Spirit must be in the
words spoken in order to communicate to the Holy Spirit in others. Of
course God can send His Holy Spirit through someone who doesn't
know what he is talking about, but again God's preferred method is to
use people who have some understanding of the gospel.[1]

"For if I pray in a tongue, my spirit prays but my mind is unfruitful"
(v. 14). Verse 14 is a lament. But Paul was not saying that it is a bad thing
for a person's spirit to pray (or to pray in the spirit). In fact, such prayer is
good. People should pray. But there is something about this kind of
prayer that is not quite right. The emotional impetus is good, but without
meaningful, communicable content the prayer is not all that it could be,
not all that it should be.

The Greek word *nous* can be translated as mind or understanding and
points to the rational ability of the mind or the rational content of thinking. Paul did not want one's thinking, praying, or communicating to be
unfruitful, to be without reason or without meaning. Indeed, all Christian
thought, prayer and communication should overflow with rational, communicable meaning.

HEARTMIND

"What are we to conclude from this?" Paul asked in verse 15. He
concluded that the best approach is to join the enthusiasm of the spirit
with the understanding of the mind, whether praying, singing, speaking,
or thinking. For a Christian, heart and mind are one. Christians are not to
be torn between matters of the heart and matters of the head. Rather,
Christians are whole, complete—even perfect in Christ, who joins heart,
mind, soul, and strength (Matthew 12:30) as an element of Christian
unity.

In Christ, not only are believers in unity with other believers, but
each believer is in unity with him- or herself. Each believer is a whole, a
unit. Satan is divided against himself (Luke 11:18), Christians are not
(Matthew 6:22). The first step toward genuine Christian unity is not
unity among denominations, but the unity of heart, mind, soul, and
strength in the presence and power of the Holy Spirit in the lives of indi-

---

1   For more on the uniqueness of biblical understanding from a genuinely spiritual
     perspective see Ross, Phillip A. *The Wisdom of Christ in the Book of Proverbs*, Pilgrim
     Platform, Marietta, Ohio, 2006.

vidual believers. Individual believers must be in personal unity before groups of believers can be in unity.

Paul's mention of singing suggests an application of this regarding Christian music. Good Christian music must be meaningful. Lyrics must be meaningfully biblical. Singing is a very affective way of teaching and reaching—teaching the saints and reaching the lost. Indeed, when biblical lyrics, rich in doctrine and teaching, are supported with godly tunes, tunes that are excellent, appropriate, and passionate, God's Word will better accomplish its purpose. It should also be noted that God's people sing. They are not all great singers, but they do sing greatly by giving themselves enthusiastically to the song. To refuse to sing in worship is to refuse to worship God, to fail to share in the praise of worship. The failure to sing is a failure of faithfulness.

Verse 16 shows an application to evangelism. Paul's emphasis was not just on the edification of believers, but was on evangelism as well. The meaningful content that is to be communicated between and among believers for their edification is also to be shared with "outsiders" (*idiōtēs*). Other versions translate the word as *unlearned* or *uninformed*. A literal translation would be *ignoramuses* or *idiots*.

> "Else, if you bless in the spirit, he occupying the place of the unlearned (ignoramuses or idiots—the unbeliever), how will he say the amen at your giving of thanks, since he does not know what you say?" (v. 16—MKJB).

It's the same concern that Paul has been pressing for several chapters now—that communication must be meaningful, comprehensible, and rational. Meaningful communication about the content of Scripture from a born again perspective will serve to edify believers and evangelize unbelievers. This is so basic, so simple, so much a function of common sense that it is hard to imagine how people can get it wrong. And yet, legions of Christians throughout the ages have gotten it wrong in their quest for a "higher" spirituality or a "mystical" experience. It is well past time to close the door on this kind of nonsense, to call it what it is, to call it what Paul called it in verse 33—*akatastasia* (instability, a state of disorder, disturbance, confusion).

BRASS

And yet Paul was gracious in his assessment. "For you may be giving thanks well enough, but the other person is not being built up" (v. 17).

Again, Paul didn't know what these tongues speakers were saying. They may be praising God, but if no one knows what they are saying then there is no edification, nor any evangelism. The only thing that could be happening in such a situation is that the person speaking is polishing his own brass. That's not necessarily a bad thing, but it isn't ministry.

Verse 18 is used by many people to justify glossolalia, speaking in angelic or otherwise unknown languages (babbling). But to do so it is necessary to rip the verse from its ordinary context and impose extraneous presuppositions upon it. The context suggests that Paul was using the word *tongues* (*glōssa*) to mean foreign languages. So, Paul was saying that he spoke more foreign languages than those to whom he was writing, or that he spoke more often in foreign languages than they did. And because of Paul's travels, either interpretation of this verse is acceptable. There's not much difference between them.

In order to cement the point Paul said, "Nevertheless, in church I would rather speak five words with my mind in order to instruct others, than ten thousand words in a tongue" (v. 19). All other considerations aside, Paul preferred to speak with understanding than without it—in any language. The purpose of speaking is communication, and communication requires the understanding of rational content. While Paul said that this was his preferred behavior in church, it is unthinkable that Paul would do anything different in any other context. Whether in church or on the road, speaking to a brother in Christ or to a heathen, Paul preferred to speak intelligently.

Sure, he groaned occasionally when words fail to contain and convey the excellencies of Christ. Nonetheless, he pushed language to its limits in order to rationally and intelligently express his faithfulness, Christ's righteousness, and God's mercy as best he could, without relying on tricks or gimmicks. Paul was preaching faith alone in Christ alone according to Scripture alone, and that's all he needed. And it is all we need.

Praise be to God in Jesus Christ!

39. Peace & Order

Brothers, do not be children in your minds, but in malice be like infants, and in your minds be mature. In the Law it is written, "By other tongues and other lips I will speak to this people, and even so they will not hear Me, says the Lord." So that tongues are not a sign to those who believe, but to those who do not believe. But prophesying is not to those who do not believe, but to those who believe. Therefore if the whole church has come together, and all speak in languages, and if uninstructed ones or unbelievers come in, will they not say that you rave? But if all prophesy, and some unbeliever or one not instructed comes, he is convicted by all, he is judged by all. And so the secrets of his heart become revealed. And so, falling down on his face, he will worship God and report that God is truly among you. Then how is it, brothers? When you come together, each one of you has a psalm, has a teaching, has a tongue, has a revelation, has an interpretation. Let all things be for building up. —1 Corinthians 14:20-26

Beginning at verse 20 Paul takes another swipe at communicating his essential message regarding tongues. Here he accused the brethren, his brothers in Christ. By calling them *brethren* he established common ground, but in regard to his argument he did not seek to put them at ease. Rather, he set before them his clear opposition to their errant thinking. By calling them *brothers* he established that he was speaking to the whole Corinthian church, and yet his major point stands in opposition to a particular group. He opposed those who have misunderstood and misapplied the speaking in tongues—however defined—as if tongues were more important or more spiritual than the other gifts, as if Delphic glossolalia was a blessing to the church!

Prophesying in tongues, properly defined and understood, actually is a function of genuine Christianity. Once it is properly defined it is clearly seen that the gospel of Jesus Christ has been given to people of every tongue.

Paul's basic message in verse 20 is: *Grow up! Don't be immature in your thinking and understanding of tongues.* The subject of the immediately preceding verses is tongues. He continued with that subject, "Be infants in evil" (v. 20). Other versions translate the word *evil* (*kakia*) as *malice* or *maliciousness*. It literally means badness, depravity, or wickedness. Paul told them not to engage evil, not to be malicious or wicked in their assessment of his opposition to their Delphic understanding of tongues, but to be mature, to be men about it. The Greek word translated as *mature* or *men* is *teleios*. We've seen the word before. It means whole, complete, and is often translated as *perfect*. Paul was calling them to Christian maturity in the same way that he called the Ephesian church to maturity in Christ.

> "And he gave the apostles, the prophets, the evangelists, the pastors and teachers, to equip the saints for the work of ministry, for building up the body of Christ, until we all attain to the unity of the faith and of the knowledge of the Son of God, to mature manhood, to the measure of the stature of the fullness of Christ, so that we may no longer be children, tossed to and fro by the waves and carried about by every wind of doctrine, by human cunning, by craftiness in deceitful schemes. Rather, speaking the truth in love, we are to grow up in every way into him who is the head, into Christ, from whom the whole body, joined and held together by every joint with which it is equipped, when each part is working properly, makes the body grow so that it builds itself up in love" (Ephesians 4:11-16).

Paul quoted Scripture to establish his point. His reference to the law was a reference to the Old Testament, to the established body of truth.

> "For by people of strange lips and with a foreign tongue the Lord will speak to this people, to whom he has said, 'This is rest; give rest to the weary; and this is repose;' yet they would not hear." (Isaiah 28:11-12).

Paul didn't quote the verse exactly, but gets the point across. Paul paraphrased it, "By people of strange tongues and by the lips of foreigners will I speak to this people, and even then they will not listen to me, says the Lord" (v. 21).

NOT UNDERSTOOD

It doesn't matter whether Paul meant foreign languages or angelic languages because his point was that the language being spoken was not understood by the hearers. And it wasn't so much that they would not listen to the Lord, but that they could not hear the Lord because they were not regenerate. They did not have ears to hear (Matthew 11:15). This is a very common problem that has plagued God's people from time im-

memorial. By reaching back into Isaiah, Paul was speaking of the fulfillment of Isaiah's prophecy in the second chapter of Acts and beyond. Paul
was saying that God would speak to His people (Hebrews) through foreigners (non Hebrews), that Gentiles would be given the Word of the
Lord (the gospel), and in spite of the gift of tongues (translation into other
languages, into the native tongues of the Gentiles) God's Word would
not be heard (or listened to) by many, regardless of the language in which
it was spoken.

Moses also made note of this problem.

> "And Moses summoned all Israel and said to them: 'You have seen all
> that the Lord did before your eyes in the land of Egypt, to Pharaoh and
> to all his servants and to all his land, the great trials that your eyes saw,
> the signs, and those great wonders. But to this day the Lord has not
> given you a heart to understand or eyes to see or ears to hear'"
> (Deuteronomy 29:2-4).

Isaiah (Isaiah 28:12, 30:9, 42:20) and Jeremiah (Jeremiah 5:21, 6:10,
11:10, 13:10, 17:23, 19:15, 25:4, 36:31) struggled against it, as did Jesus
and Paul. Paul confronted this particular problem at Corinth here in the
issue of tongues. It wasn't just that people did not understand the foreign
languages that were being spoken, or that they did not understand the so-
called angelic languages. People did not understand Paul who was speaking in their mother tongue! The deeper lack of understanding was not a
function of the language being spoken, but was a function of not having
ears to hear, regardless of the language. The issue of understanding the
gospel is intimately related to the issue of speaking in tongues.

Those who understand the gospel will speak with understanding, regardless of the language they use. And those who do not understand it,
will always speak without understanding. Those who speak without understanding cannot communicate understanding, regardless of the language. The proof of this is that this definition of tongues in conjunction
with the lack of regeneration (not having ears to hear) provides the context for the correct understanding of the next verse.

MISTRANSLATION

The long history of misdefining the word *tongues* as Paul was using it
has led to a minor mistranslation of verse 22. The sentence structure is
awkward to begin with. The KJV translates the word *pisteuō* as "to them
that believe" and *apistos* as "to them that believe not." In a later clause of

the same sentence the Greek words are repeated, but this time they are translated as "*for* them that believe not" and "*for* them which believe." Note that the prepositions are different, *to* verses *for*. Note also that there is no preposition in the Greek at this point. A literal, word for word translation might be "Therefore tongues are for sign not believers but unbelievers but prophesying not unbelievers but believers."

It's awkward because it doesn't flow in English, but uses the Greek order of words. The word *for* is out of place in the English. It should be placed after the word *sign* so that it reads "Therefore tongues are sign for not believers but unbelievers but prophesying (implied *for*) not unbelievers but believers." The word *for* (*eis*) would be better translated as *of* in this case. "Therefore tongues are sign of not believers but unbelievers but prophesying *of* not unbelievers but believers."

Whenever the word *tongue(s)* is used it always refers to a different language, not common to the one currently in use. Because Paul was in the process of chastising the Corinthians for their immaturity, he was at this point using the word *tongues* to mean glossolalia (as in Delphic babbling). That is what he has been opposing in the last couple of chapters, and that is the sense of the word in verse 22. So, Paul's basic message in this verse is that tongues are a sign of unbelief or a lack of understanding (which amounts to the same thing), whereas prophecy (speaking meaningfully about God) is a sign of belief or understanding of the gospel. Here tongues are a sign of unbelief because what is spoken, whether a foreign language or an angelic language, is not understood. And unbelievers do not understand the gospel in any language.

SIGN

He called it a *sign*. A sign always signifies something. In this case, speaking without understanding or communication (speaking in tongues, speaking in a way that people don't know what you are talking about) signifies that the speaker is an unbeliever. And speaking with understanding (prophesying) signifies that the speaker is a believer. If I tell you a bunch of wrong things about the gospel, and you are a believer, you will know I'm not a believer because I've got the gospel wrong. If that's what I believe, then I can't yet believe the true gospel because I don't understand it. It's not that belief follows understanding, but that understanding follows belief.[1] This is both hugely important and mostly misunderstood by the unregenerate.

Whatever unbelievers say about the gospel will always be nonsense. Because they speak ignorantly of what they do not know. And conversely, prophecy defined as making sense of Scripture is a sign of belief because only believers can make sense of the gospel. Believers speak knowledgeably about the gospel because they are instructed by the Holy Spirit through regeneration.

The reasons for this suggestion about the translation of the preposition (*eis*) in verse 22 are somewhat complex, but the result provides a simple translation that eliminates confusion, facilitates understanding, and fits the context—both the context of the surrounding verses and the larger context of the chapter, and of the whole letter. It's the only meaning that is consistent with what Paul has been saying, and simply serves to drive the point home.

Verses 23-25 serve as a kind of case study of how this works. Suppose, said Paul, that an unbeliever comes into a worship service and people are all speaking foreign languages, the poor unbeliever will have no idea about what's going on. He won't understand what is being said, and will think that the people are crazy. At best he won't have any understanding of what they are saying or doing because the tongue is foreign to him.

But, on the other hand, if an unbeliever comes into a worship service where people are all talking intelligently and making sense of the Bible through prophecy, and he is called to say something himself, and in the process the secrets of his heart are exposed in a meaningful way, he will fall on his face in worship of God and will declare God's reality and presence. The differences between these two scenarios are stark, and Paul's meaning is absolutely plain and simple. Making sense makes sense.

However, because the gospel was in the process of being translated into foreign languages as Paul was writing, because the gospel had just broken out of the limitations of the Hebrew language and culture (Acts 2), people from many countries and regions were gathering together, learning, and sharing the gospel of Jesus Christ. In every church and gathering of Christians there were people of foreign heritage (non-Jewish

---

1   Anselm of Canterbury stated well the proper relation between reason and revelation: "I do not seek to understand so that I may believe; but I believe so that I may understand. For I believe this also, that 'unless I believe, I shall not understand'."

people) who probably spoke a smattering of Greek because Greek was the International language of the day, the language of the business world. Greek was a common language for many Christians, but as the gospel spread it was not the mother tongue of many. Several languages were undoubtedly spoken at every gathering as the gospel moved into the Gentile world.

Paul reproved the Corinthians for their pride and selfishness in wanting to show off when they came together for worship. Paul was not here suggesting that everyone should have something to share at worship, whether a "hymn, a lesson, a revelation, a tongue, or an interpretation" (v. 26). Rather, he was chastising them for their disorderliness. Too many of them had been vying for a place in the proverbial sun during worship and babbling nonsense of various kinds, in various languages. Paul was still contrasting their desire for self-service with Christ's call to Christian leadership, "whoever would be great among you must be your servant, and whoever would be first among you must be your slave" (Matthew 20:27).

Paul was calling them to the practice of discipline and order in worship, in their understanding and in their personal lives—in their practice of the faith. It wasn't that Paul didn't want people to participate in worship. He did! But more important than individual participation was the purpose and order of worship. Worship is service to God. It is to be God-directed and God-centered, and when worship is God-centered it will provide edification for God's people. In contrast, the people are *not* the subject of worship. Worship is not to be directed at the people. Worship is not for the people. It is not about the people. Worship is for God. It is about God.

There is a very interesting dynamic at work in worship. When worship is directed at the people, the quality of the worship suffers because it is not what it could be, not what it should be. It falls short of giving God the glory that is His alone because it is intentionally crafted to conform to the understanding of the people. When the people are the subject of worship, when worship is directed to the people, God's Word gets twisted and watered down in order to make it palpable to those who are gathered. When we aim worship at the gathered congregation we tend to aim at the lowest common denominator in an effort to be inclusive and relevant. The result is that the quality of worship is degraded by the effort to be inclusive and relevant to the people who are gathered.

Best Effort

But when we aim worship at God we tend to give our best effort. We are not trying to dumb down the explanation of God's Word for the guy in the fourth row who only has an eighth grade education. Rather, we are making every effort to reflect the actual meaning of God's Word back to God, who is infinitely intelligent and perfect in every way. Rather than trying to make the gospel fit the understanding of the people who are gathered in worship, we need to reflect the actual meaning of God's Word accurately, to speak God's Word as God intended it to be heard, not as we think it can best be heard by some subgroup of Christians (a particular gathering, congregation or denomination, church, youth, women, men—whatever). Paul's call for unity is a call to abandon all appeal to Christian subgroups.

Understanding the gospel is not a function of intelligence, education, experience, or relevance. It is a function of regeneration. Understanding the gospel is a gift. The best thing that we can do to help people understand God's Word is not to try to make it relevant to this or that person (church, denomination, etc.), but to get it right from God's perspective. To understand it correctly ourselves—from God's perspective, from a regenerate perspective—and communicate it accurately so that people can hear what God actually says and not what *we* think about what God says.

But, Paul said, "Let all things be done for building up" (v. 26), for edification of the saints, for building up the church, the people of God. Am I contradicting this? Not at all.

We are to be in service first and foremost to God through Jesus Christ, and that means that we are to be in service to God's people, not to do for them what they themselves want us to do for them, but to do for them what God wants for them. And the best thing that we can do to help God's people better hear and understand the gospel is to better reflect it back to God in worship accurately, to see it as God sees it and to say it as God said it. If people are going to hear the Word of the Lord, then those who proclaim it must stop trying to make it relevant. It is already relevant because it is God's Word. Those who think that this is not enough will only be convinced by their own regeneration. We must get our own perspectives out of the way, stop telling people what we think about it or what our favorite theologians or scholars think about it. We must become transparent in order that people may hear God's Word through us, through our words and through our actions.

The saints are built up—edified (*oikodomē*)—through very specific activities. Paul wrote to the Thessalonians about building up the church. On Paul's edification list were the following: 1) encourage one another, 2) build one another up, 3) respect those who labor among you, Christian leaders who minister in your midst, respect those who are over you, respect those who admonish you, 4) esteem your leaders very highly because of their work, 5) be at peace among yourselves, 6) admonish the idle, 7) encourage the fainthearted, 8) help the weak, 9) be patient with everyone, 10) avoid revenge (don't return evil for evil), 11) seek to do good to everyone, 12) rejoice always, 13) pray without ceasing, 14) give thanks in all circumstances, 15) do not quench the Spirit, 16) do not despise prophecy (the careful explanation of Scripture), 17) hold fast to what is good, and 18) abstain from evil (1 Thessalonians 5:11-22).

This is a very interesting list, and difficult to accomplish. These recommendations all sound good and noble, but when we actually try to engage them we encounter difficulties because of our own sin. It sounds good to encourage one another, but when someone sins against you it becomes more difficult to encourage them. It sounds good to be at peace with other Christians, but when someone attacks your character, it is not so easy to remain at peace with him. It sounds great to be patient with everyone, but have you ever actually tried it? It sounds noble to pray without ceasing, but who can actually do it? And these are the easy ones!

The harder ones involve respecting those who admonish us. We are to be at peace with *them*. And more than that, we are to esteem them very highly, those who are over us and admonish (*noutheteō*) us, those who warn us that our thoughts, speech, and actions are not what they need to be. The hard work of Christian churchmanship is the giving and receiving of biblical admonishment and warning while remaining in peace, even esteeming those who deliver the admonishment, the warning, the exhortation, the instruction.

Notice that the instruction that Paul gave to the Thessalonians, and to all Christians by implication, is not to withhold admonishment and exhortation. But rather, Paul's instruction is not simply about *giving* admonishment to others, but the instruction is to *receive* admonishment from others with peace—not chafing at those who bring it because they dare to criticize you, but holding the admonishment itself in esteem because it is of the Lord. This is the hard work of building up the church, of admonishing the saints, making them understand God's Word, and being made to understand it better ourselves. Christians are called to be mutually accountable, to give and receive.

May all of God's people be blessed with ears to hear and tongues to speak the gospel with such understanding.

40. Are You Able?

If any speak in a tongue, let there be only two or at most three, and each in turn, and let someone interpret. But if there is no one to interpret, let each of them keep silent in church and speak to himself and to God. Let two or three prophets speak, and let the others weigh what is said. If a revelation is made to another sitting there, let the first be silent. For you can all prophesy one by one, so that all may learn and all be encouraged, and the spirits of prophets are subject to prophets. For God is not a God of confusion but of peace. As in all the churches of the saints, the women should keep silent in the churches. For they are not permitted to speak, but should be in submission, as the Law also says. If there is anything they desire to learn, let them ask their husbands at home. For it is shameful for a woman to speak in church. Or was it from you that the word of God came? Or are you the only ones it has reached? If anyone thinks that he is a prophet, or spiritual, he should acknowledge that the things I am writing to you are a command of the Lord. If anyone does not recognize this, he is not recognized. So, my brothers, earnestly desire to prophesy, and do not forbid speaking in tongues. But all things should be done decently and in order.

—1 Corinthians 14:27-40

Those gathered for worship with the Corinthians were a diverse bunch. Corinth was one of the largest and most corrupt cities in the Roman Empire. Five times as large as Athens at the time, Corinth was also a port city full of international travelers. If too many languages were spoken during a worship service, people would loose track of what was going on. So, Paul suggested a limit of two, possibly three different languages—and the translations should be given sequentially, not all at the same time. In addition, each message (prophecy or explanation) should be translated so that all present would be able to understand what was said.

And if someone came with a message in a tongue that was not known to anyone, and there was no one to interpret what he said, he should keep it to himself. There was no point in saying something that couldn't be understood. So, if there was no interpreter present for a particular language, that language should not be used. Greek was the international language and most people spoke enough Greek to get along. Most of the international travelers were probably bilingual. And as is common, when a bilingual person is speaking in his inferior language and comes to a more complex thing to say, he will revert to his native tongue simply because he doesn't know how to say it in the inferior language—hoping that someone in the crowd would be able to interpret. So, said Paul, if there was no one to interpret, such a person should hold his tongue. There was no sense trying to share something that couldn't be shared. He should just think it through to himself and share it with the Lord—save it for a time when he was with others who spoke his language.

Paul not only limited the languages spoken to two, possibly three, but he limited the points that prophets should make in whatever language as well. As we know, the job of prophets was the clarification, explanation, and application of Scripture. Here Paul suggested that too many explanations in any one worship service would leave people confused. The Corinthians leaders were probably overwhelming people by saying too much. Paul sought an optimum communication level. It was an error to speak in a language that people didn't understand. But it was also a mistake to say too much in a language that they could understand. We should understand this problem today because in our contemporary world the Word of God is all but lost in a flood of Godless words that demand and distract our attention.

Again, the point of speaking, especially in worship, is communication. So, not more than two or three points should be made during any particular worship service. And those points could then be considered and weighed by any other prophets/preachers who were there. Two things can be noted.

First, that various people participated in worship leadership. Paul's point was that the leaders should cooperate. Perhaps one person would make a particular point, and another person would further clarify it. And secondly, the worship leaders should be cautious about bringing up too much, about making too many different points in any one worship service. Communication fails when the language spoken is not understood, but it also fails when people are overwhelmed with too much information —even if the information is good.

APPLICATION

Verse 30 is about making biblical applications. Suppose one of the leaders is clarifying and explaining a particular point, and in the midst of that explanation he makes an application of the point that involves someone present. Something is revealed about someone. The fact that something is revealed suggested that whatever it was had been previously hidden, maybe intentionally, maybe not. Usually, biblical application involves some spiritual growth and reveals some sin or failure and the application involves some way to avoid or overcome that sin or failure through better reliance on God. So, said Paul, when such an application is in the process of being made, it should not be interrupted or derailed by someone who wants to say something else. When a biblical point is being made, stay with it. Clarify it. Explain it fully. And if an application is made, particularly if it involves someone who is present, let it take its course. Don't interrupt it by changing the topic. Let it play out because biblical application is one of the central elements of Christian worship.

Verse 31 makes the important point that all Christians, all those whom Paul addressed in this letter, could (even should) prophesy (clarify and explain Scripture), some translations use "may."

"For you can (or may) all prophesy one by one" (v. 31). Both ability and permission are given. The Greek is interesting. The word translated as *could* or *may* (*dunamai*) literally means to be able, to have power whether by virtue of one's own ability and resources, or because of a state of mind, or through favorable circumstances, or by permission of law or custom. It means being able to do something, being capable, being strong and powerful, having the ability. It is related at the root to the word *dunamis*, which is often translated as miracle or power.

ORDINARY GIFT

Paul was saying that all Christians have the power to prophesy, to clarify and explain Scripture, because that power resides in the Holy Spirit who has regenerated them. It is on this basis that prophecy is an ordinary Christian gift, not an extraordinary gift. Indeed, the explanation of Scripture is common among Christians, at least it should be. And the purpose of this gift, said Paul, is learning and encouragement in faithfulness. All should learn, all should be encouraged, and all should encourage others, all should clarify and explain what they know to be true about Scripture. The only thing unusual about this gift is that so few people who call themselves Christians can do it. And even fewer can do it well! This, however, does not mean that the gift of prophecy is rare among Christians. Rather, it suggests that faithful Christians may be more uncommon than people think.

To say that "the prophets are subject to the prophets" (v. 32) suggests that biblical explanation should not contribute to contention or division, as if my explanation is better than yours so it is your obligation to agree with me. But rather, those who explain Scripture should be in submission to others who explain Scripture. In other words, different explanations are not necessarily in conflict, and the prophets/ preachers need to make every effort to reconcile the differences according to Scripture. Faithful adherence to this dictum will go a long way to encourage Christian unity.

This does not mean that the majority rules regarding biblical interpretation, or that the commonly held view is always without error. Rather, it means that those who interpret Scripture, those who preach and teach, must have submissive, teachable spirits themselves. Biblical interpretation must be understood and practiced as a team effort. There would surely be fewer denominations if more people actually practiced this.

"For God is not a God of confusion but of peace" (v. 33). The idea behind *peace* (*eirēnē*) is that peace is a function of both unity and prosperity. The punctuation of this verse is disputed. It seems that the older versions treat verse 33 as one sentence, and the newer versions make the latter half to be the beginning of a new sentence that carries over to verse 34. The issue is whether the phrase "as in all the churches of the saints" goes with the idea of peace without confusion or with the idea that women should not preach or prophesy in worship.

Not Women

The first thing to notice about Paul's admonition against women taking leadership in worship is that it limits or clarifies what Paul just said about all Christians prophesying (clarifying and explaining Scripture). Here he says that women should keep silent at church during worship.[1] In verse 34 Paul links the submission of women to Genesis 3:16, "Your de-

---

1　This may be at odds with 1 Corinthians 11:5, which implies that women may pray or prophesy as long as their heads are covered. The issue may be that they are not to do so at church or during formal worship, but that other venues may be okay. The issue may also be one of permission in that the issue is headship and submission. Whatever the case, it is beyond the scope of our concern here.

sire shall be for your husband, and he shall rule over you." John Gill noted,

> "By this the apostle would signify, that the reason why women are not to speak in the church, or to preach and teach publicly, or be concerned in the ministerial function, is, because this is an act of power, and authority; of rule and government, and so contrary to that subjection which God in his law requires of women unto men. The extraordinary instances of Deborah, Huldah, and Anna, must not be drawn into a rule or example in such cases. ... All speaking is not prohibited; they might speak their experiences to the church, or give an account of the work of God upon their souls; they might speak to one another in psalms, hymns, and spiritual songs; or speak as an evidence in any case at a church meeting; but not in such sort, as carried in it direction, instruction, government, and authority. It was not allowed by God that they should speak in any authoritative manner in the church."[2]

Worship leadership was given to men, not because they were better at it, nor because they enjoyed a superior status. Rather, I suspect that it was a function of need. It is for our sanctification.

We know that the leader always gets more out of the lesson than the student, if only because the leader has spent more time in preparation. And because men are naturally lazy and irresponsible, God chose them to lead worship because they need to spend more time in preparation, because they need the additional burden of leadership responsibility to counteract their natural tendency to be irresponsible, and because they need the additional sanctification that results from additional effort.

Women tend to suffer from a different character flaw. Women, following Eve's lead (Genesis 3), tend to usurp authority. Women, because they are the natural caretakers of children, have a natural tendency to take charge of everything. That tendency, coupled with the character flaw of men toward irresponsibility, is socially and culturally deadly because it encourages the growth of male irresponsibility. Thus, God requires each sex to counteract their natural tendencies. Women are to submit rather than to take charge, and men are to be responsible rather than irresponsible. Each sex is required to grow in sanctification by denying their natural tendency to engage their weakness—submission for women and responsibility for men—in order to grow spiritually. Clearly, team effort, mutual

---

2   Gill, John. *Exposition of the Whole Bible,* 1763.

support and mutual encouragement are required. Men and women are mutually dependent upon each other for their spiritual growth.

FOLLOWERSHIP

As mentioned previously, the real strength of Christianity is not so much in Christian leadership, as in Christian followership. All Christians are followers. Men are to model Christian followership outside the home through submission to church and civil authority, and to model representative leadership in the home by representing the authority of Christ to their families. Women are to model Christian followership inside the home through submission to their husbands (who are to be in submission to Christ), and to model representative leadership by representing the authority of her husband to her children. Representative authority is always a chain of command. And to break any link of the chain is to break the whole chain.

Paul also said that women should look to their husbands for spiritual instruction and leadership as an expression and exercise of biblical social order because every Christian husband serves as a priest to his family. John wrote in Revelation,

> "And they sang a new song, saying, 'Worthy are you to take the scroll and to open its seals, for you were slain, and by your blood you ransomed people for God from every tribe and language and people and nation, and you have made them a kingdom and priests to our God, and they shall reign on the earth'" (Revelation 5:9-10).

Christians are to become a kingdom of priests. Paul had written earlier that "the head of every man is Christ, the head of a wife is her husband" (1 Corinthians 11:3). Thus, the best thing a wife can do for the spiritual growth of her husband is to look to him for spiritual leadership by taking her questions to him, to model submission to him as a way to encourage his growth in responsibility and counteract his tendency toward irresponsibility. The best thing a wife can do for the spiritual growth of her husband is to teach the importance and structure of biblical authority to her children and to the society at large by modeling submission to his representative authority. However, submission is not just for women, men also need to model submission to Christ. Indeed, no issue is more important, more neglected, or more needed than the this issue of living in submission under representative authority.

Consequently, the reason that "it is shameful for a woman to speak in church" (v. 35) is that it undermines the authority of God's intended social structure for human society—God's representatives—and leads to anarchy—not right away, of course, but eventually. Because all authority belongs to God, the undermining or ignoring of any authority leads to the eventual destruction of authority, to anarchy, the denial of authority.

NOT WAGGLING

In verse 36 Paul provides his primary argument against the pagan (Delphic) idea of speaking in tongues. That kind of mystical speaking in tongues tends to make people believe that God Himself is speaking His Word through the tongue waggler. If God has always spoken through His people in this manner—by directly possessing and dictating their every word or syllable, if God wrote the Bible in this way (in some mystical and/or angelic language), then whatever comes out of the mouth of such a person would be, if not equivalent to Scripture itself, then nearly so, because God is perfect and makes no errors. If Scripture is God's Word and God's words come out of someone's mouth, then those words must be taken as divine, or nearly so. This kind of Delphic speaking in tongues far exceeds what Paul understood as prophesying, the clarification and explication of Scripture. Christian prophesying/ preaching is not infallible.

Paul, with his tongue firmly planted in his cheek, asked if they—the speakers in tongues—thought that God's Word was limited to their own mouths, or if they thought themselves to be the only people who were able to hear or speak God's Word. The question drips with sarcasm and suggests that this is precisely what they thought—that they had exclusive possession of God's Word or its interpretation through their mystical babbling and its interpretation by union priests.

Paul was telling them that they were dead wrong. Paul had been arguing for the exact opposite, that prophesying was a common gift among Christians, that speaking and explaining God's Word was the obligation and the gift of every Christian, and that it was a function of making sense, not a function of nonsense. Some can do it better than others, of course, but all are called to do it. Christian prophets are to be subject to Christian prophets. Preachers and teachers need to know the truth before they can preach or teach the truth. So, said Paul throwing down the gauntlet, "If anyone thinks that he is a prophet, or spiritual, he should acknowledge that the things I am writing to you are a command of the Lord" (v. 37).

To contradict Paul is to contradict the Lord. All biblical teaching will be in conformity with Paul's teaching. Paul knew himself to be correct because he knew himself to be in complete submission to Jesus Christ. Paul's martyrdom proved his submission, and the universal acceptance of his teaching among Christians proved his orthodoxy. And to fail to recognize the authenticity, authority, and orthodoxy of Paul's teaching must result in the failure to be recognized yourself as having authenticity, authority, or orthodoxy by God's people. The recognition of biblical truth is the most basic element of Christian experience and fellowship. Those who do not recognize biblical truth in Paul's teaching must not be given any church authority.

Therefore, Paul concluded, "earnestly desire to prophesy, and do not forbid speaking in tongues" (v. 39). The Westminster Confession was wrong in the way that it framed the idea that tongues had ceased, but it was not wrong in the essential argument that mystical babbling has no place in New Testament Christianity.

Prophecy is not described by Paul here as an extraordinary gift, at least it is not intended to be. It should not be unusual or uncommon, but should be ordinary and common among Christians. Every Christian can and should earnestly strive to learn to prophesy—to clarify, explain, and apply Scripture (God's Word) to every situation and in any and every language possible, to anyone who asks—and to many who don't. The clarification, explanation, and understanding of God's Word is the foundation, the means and the purpose of Christian worship. Nothing should inhibit these things, but rather, "all things should be done decently and in order" (v. 40).

41. An apostle

Now I would remind you, brothers, of the gospel I preached to you, which you received, in which you stand, and by which you are being saved, if you hold fast to the word I preached to you—unless you believed in vain. For I delivered to you as of first importance what I also received: that Christ died for our sins in accordance with the Scriptures, that he was buried, that he was raised on the third day in accordance with the Scriptures, and that he appeared to Cephas, then to the twelve. Then he appeared to more than five hundred brothers at one time, most of whom are still alive, though some have fallen asleep. Then he appeared to James, then to all the apostles. Last of all, as to one untimely born, he appeared also to me. For I am the least of the apostles, unworthy to be called an apostle, because I persecuted the church of God. —1 Corinthians 15:1-9

Paul began this chapter by stating in no uncertain terms that the gospel that he had been preaching and teaching to them is the true gospel. He reminded them that he had preached it, that they received it, and had been standing in it (or because of it), that it was the source of their salvation, that there is a condition to it—that they must "hold fast" (v. 2) to it, and that it may be possible for them to believe in vain, to believe falsely, or to believe without substance.

Paul said these things precisely because he was confronting them about differing versions of the gospel of Jesus Christ, one of which was true, and many of which were not. He was differentiating the true version from the counterfeit versions. This is exactly what Paul had been doing from the very beginning of this letter to the Corinthians. From the beginning, Paul had been talking about the differences between the wisdom of Christ and the foolishness of the world. Paul was suggesting that the foolishness of the pagan religious world had infected the church and was the source of the different versions of the gospel.

Note that verse 2 teaches that salvation, while it begins in a moment, is a process that unfolds over time. Those who are saved persevere in faithfulness over time, and because their faith is sustained over time it is not empty, not fruitless, not in vain. It was important to keep the gospel that Paul taught in mind because some of the Corinthians had slid into either a false understanding of the gospel or a vain and empty kind of belief. All of this means that it is possible to believe rightly, at least correct intellectually, but vainly. It is possible to believe the right gospel correctly, but to believe it in such a way that no gospel fruit comes of it, to believe without substance, to believe in vain. This surely is the bane of those who are too often spoken of as the frozen chosen. In other words, having the correct intellectual content of the faith is not a guarantee of salvation. There is more to salvation than understanding the gospel correctly, more than an intellectual understanding, more than words.

UNDERSTANDING FOLLOWS BELIEF

It was Augustine who said that understanding the gospel correctly is a consequence of belief. Augustine said this in opposition to those who thought that understanding the gospel correctly would produce belief. The difference between these two perspectives is huge. One says that belief produces understanding, the other says that understanding produces belief. If belief results from a correct understanding of the gospel or a correct understanding of Scripture, then all we need to do is to teach it correctly and people will believe. In contrast, Augustine's view is that belief is necessary in order to acquire a correct understanding of the gospel or of Scripture.

The difference involves regeneration by the Holy Spirit versus enlightenment through education. Augustine was saying that regeneration is different than a correct understanding. He said that the one leads to the other, but the other doesn't necessarily lead to the one. It's a one way deal. He said this because he knew from personal experience that his own regeneration allowed him to see things that he had previously known in a different light. He still knew the same things, but he knew them differently after his regeneration than he had known them before it. There was more involved than information.

One's belief or faith provides a different perspective on things. It allows faithful Christians to see things from the perspective of the Holy Spirit, not completely, not perfectly, not infallibly, but adequately.

Verse 3 tells us that preachers are to pass on to others what they have received. That is what Paul did and, by example what all Christians who share the gospel with others should do. No aspect of the gospel should be left out, and none added. Paul then laid out the essential elements of the gospel: "that Christ died for our sins in accordance with the Scriptures, that he was buried, that he was raised on the third day in accordance with the Scriptures, and that he appeared" (vs. 3-5) to others after His death.

The two essential elements are Christ's death and resurrection. It should be noted that Christ did not simply die for our sins, but died in accordance with the Scriptures. It is essential to understand that Christ's death is the capstone of the Bible. It is essential to understand how Christ's death relates to the Old Testament, how it fulfills the Old Testament prophecies. And it is essential to understand that Jesus appeared in the flesh after He died and was buried. It is not necessary to understand how this was possible, only that it actually happened. If it was necessary for us to understand how resurrection is possible, Scripture would have told us. But it doesn't. So, we must conclude that such knowledge is not necessary.

Jesus appeared to many people, more than five hundred, and many of them were still alive when Paul wrote these words. He mentioned that Jesus appeared to James, "and then to all the apostles" (v. 7). This is probably a reference to Jesus' ascension at the Mount of Olives. A common understanding is that the Twelve Apostles are defined as apostles because they saw Jesus in His resurrection flesh, as if that is an important difference between the Twelve Apostles and the rest of the saints, as if that is why they are Apostles and we are not.

UNITY

But it is hard for me to believe that Paul had that message in mind. Paul was not drawing differences between himself and other Christians. Paul had been drawing pictures of Christian unity through the gifts of the Spirit, pictures of a Trinitarian union with Christ through the power and presence of the Holy Spirit by regeneration. Paul's teaching about gifts was the unity of the Spirit, not the difference between the Twelve and the rest of us. If anything, Paul understood his use of the word apostles (*apostolos*) to mean all who had been called to be ambassadors for Christ. And who were they? Were they a select group of Christians? No! Paul wrote in his second letter to the Corinthians that all Christians are called to be ambassadors for Christ.

> "Therefore, if anyone is in Christ, he is a new creation. The old has
> passed away; behold, the new has come. All this is from God, who
> through Christ reconciled us to himself and gave us the ministry of rec-

onciliation; that is, in Christ God was reconciling the world to himself, not counting their trespasses against them, and entrusting to us the message of reconciliation. Therefore, we are ambassadors for Christ, God making his appeal through us. We implore you on behalf of Christ, be reconciled to God" (2 Corinthians 5:17-20).

This applies to all Christians, not just the Twelve Apostles. That seems to be what Paul had in mind when he used the word *apostles*. He was saying that Christ's appearance to the apostles, to Christians across the board, was a necessary element of the resurrection aspect of the gospel. He was saying that one could not be an ambassador for Christ apart from personally witnessing Christ's resurrection appearance in bodily form, that being a Christian involved a personal seeing or appearance of the resurrected Christ. Exactly what that means is not as clear as the fact that it is what Paul said.

As you might expect, the Greek is interesting at this point (vs. 5-7). The Greek is translated as *appeared* or *was seen*. I suspect that it was a play on words, that many people would describe as a kind of mysterious vision or insight, a seeing of something mysterious. The KJV translates it as "he was seen." There is a change in the subject of the sentence in some of the more recent translations. Again, the KJV reads, "After that, he was seen of James; then of all the apostles," whereas the ESV reads, "Then he appeared to James, then to all the apostles" (v. 7). In the KJV James does the seeing, and in the ESV the Lord does the appearing.

There is also the difference between "appeared to" and "was seen of." There is no corresponding preposition in the Greek. It is assumed or added because of the context. A preposition, of course, suggests a relationship. The word *of* means belonging to or associated with. The contextual assumption is that the seeing or appearance of Jesus belonged to or was associated with the person who saw Him. The seeing, the belonging, and the association are correctly understood as being all tied up together. Consequently, it appears that there is more to this seeing of the resurrected Jesus than meets the eye, if you see what I mean. I don't intend to be cute or witty, that's not the point. I'm not sure what to make of it. Perhaps we can learn something by looking at other uses of the Greek words (*optanomai optomai*).

"Blessed are the pure in heart, for they shall see God" (Matthew 5:8).

"And behold, there appeared to them Moses and Elijah, talking with him" (Matthew 17:3).

"Then will appear in heaven the sign of the Son of Man, and then all the tribes of the earth will mourn, and they will see the Son of Man coming on the clouds of heaven with power and great glory" (Matthew 24:30).

"So when Pilate saw that he was gaining nothing, but rather that a riot was beginning, he took water and washed his hands before the crowd, saying, 'I am innocent of this man's blood; see to it yourselves'" (Matthew 27:24).

That is sufficient to suggest that this is a very special kind of seeing. I suspect that a kind of Trinitarian vision lies at the heart of this kind of seeing.

A Minor Apostle

James saw Him, then all the apostles saw Him ascend into the clouds. And finally, said Paul, "he appeared also to me," or in the KJV "he was seen of me also" (v. 8). Paul noted in the same verse that he (Paul) was "one untimely born" (ESV) or "one born out of due time" (KJV). The Greek is one word (*ektrōma*) and literally means miscarriage or abortion. John Gill said of this verse that

"several learned interpreters think the apostle refers to a proverbial way of speaking among the common people at Rome, who used to call such supernumerary senators in the times of Augustus Caesar, who got into the senate house by favor or bribery." Gill goes on to suggest that such senators were generally very unworthy of their office, and that Paul "calls himself by this name, as being in his own opinion a supernumerary (minor) apostle, and very unworthy of that office."[1]

Thus, Paul seems to be suggesting his own unworthiness with regard to this special kind of seeing or vision of the bodily resurrection of Christ, suggesting that he was unworthy of his calling to be an ambassador of Christ. In support of this view Paul went on to say, "For I am the least of the apostles, unworthy to be called an apostle, because I persecuted the church of God" (v. 9). It should be noted here that Paul probably did not consider himself to be in the same category as we put the Twelve Apostles.

There was symbolic importance to the number twelve because, with God's apparent abandonment of Judas, the Apostles cast lots or elected a replacement for Judas—Matthias by name (Acts 1:23). Obviously, the Twelve Apostles symbolically corresponded with the Twelve Tribes of the Old Testament. With the loss of Judas there were eleven, and with

---

1   Gill, John. *Exposition of the Whole Bible*, 1763.

the election of Matthias the Twelve was restored in order to maintain the symbolism. So, what was Paul? To consider Paul one of the Twelve would require discounting Matthias. But Paul never mentioned Matthias, neither did anyone else. So, I don't think that Paul had any intention of counting himself among the Twelve Apostles. He was denigrating his role, not lifting himself up.

Rather, Paul understood himself to be a model for ordinary Christians to emulate, a model that people would emulate as a mark of simple faithfulness. Paul was modeling the role of a Christian as a prophet. He was prophesying, explaining what he knew about Scripture, about God, what he knew as a result of his own regeneration. Earlier in this letter Paul had called the Corinthians to "be imitators of me" (1 Corinthians 4:16). Paul's use of the word *apostle* was not intended to set himself up as the thirteenth Apostle. Rather, Paul intended the reference to his being an apostle to be understood in the generic sense of an ambassador for Christ, in the sense that all Christians are called to be ambassadors for Christ (2 Corinthians 5:20) in the midst of whatever circumstances God has given them. Paul understood himself, not as a great man, but as an ordinary man who had been called to faith in Christ.

In Paul's own words he was "unworthy to be called an apostle, because I (he) persecuted the church of God" (v. 9). Yes, Paul had impressive credentials:

> "circumcised on the eighth day, of the people of Israel, of the tribe of Benjamin, a Hebrew of Hebrews; as to the law, a Pharisee; as to zeal, a persecutor of the church; as to righteousness, under the law blameless" (Philippians 3:5-6).

Paul had been a thoroughbred Pharisee—smart, well-educated, well-bred, etc. He had more biblical knowledge and skills than any of the other Apostles. But he did not count any of that stuff to his credit. Rather, he found it to be a liability, to be rubbish in the light of Christ.

> "But whatever gain I had, I counted as loss for the sake of Christ. Indeed, I count everything as loss because of the surpassing worth of knowing Christ Jesus my Lord. For his sake I have suffered the loss of all things and count them as rubbish, in order that I may gain Christ" (Philippians 3:7-8).

Paul's impressive credentials were worse than nothing in his own eyes. They were not to his credit, but to his demerit. He threw them away when he became a Christian. In Christ he saw himself as an ordinary sinner—no, rather an extraordinary sinner (1 Timothy 1:15). Paul strove to be an ordinary[2] Christian, not to be a great saint. And if we are to imitate Paul, we too should strive to be ordinary Christians who live ordinary lives in the midst of ordinary circumstances, to prophesy in the midst of our ordinary circumstances, which means to endeavor to understand, explain, and apply Scripture in our ordinary lives. Therein we will find many of the blessings that issue from salvation in Christ.

---

2   The word *ordinary* needs to be understood in its older sense of suggesting immediate jurisdiction—without an intervening medium, as opposed to jurisdiction by delegation or deputation. The point being that an ordinary Christian is one who is connected directly to Christ through the power and presence of the Holy Spirit through regeneration. This, however does not mean that there is no place for the church or for submission to other authorities, but rather establishes the jurisdiction of personal conscience in the light of Christ, such that ordinary Christians have ordinary access to Christ (John 15:15).

42. I Yam What I Yam!

But by the grace of God I am what I am, and his grace toward me was not in vain. On the contrary, I worked harder than any of them, though it was not I, but the grace of God that is with me. Whether then it was I or they, so we preach and so you believed. Now if Christ is proclaimed as raised from the dead, how can some of you say that there is no resurrection of the dead? But if there is no resurrection of the dead, then not even Christ has been raised. And if Christ has not been raised, then our preaching is in vain and your faith is in vain. We are even found to be misrepresenting God, because we testified about God that he raised Christ, whom he did not raise if it is true that the dead are not raised. For if the dead are not raised, not even Christ has been raised. And if Christ has not been raised, your faith is futile and you are still in your sins. Then those also who have fallen asleep in Christ have perished. If in this life only we have hoped in Christ, we are of all people most to be pitied. But in fact Christ has been raised from the dead, the firstfruits of those who have fallen asleep.　　　　　　　　　　　　　　　　—1 Corinthians 15:10-20

After having confessed his untimely birth and his mistaken persecution of the church, Paul said that by the grace of God he was what he was. Though the timing and circumstances of his birth seemed unfortunate to Paul, he trusted that it was not so to God, that God had brought him into the world at the right time and in the right circumstances. He even trusted that his persecution of the church was a function of God's providence—not that God was responsible for his sin, nor that he had been justified in persecuting Christians. But rather, the fact of his persecution of the church facilitated a great outpouring of God's grace and mercy—even providing a large endowment of personal remorse that Paul would use to fuel his ministry.

Note that Paul did not say that he was what he was because he had persecuted the church. He did not accuse God of being responsible for his sin, or wallow in his guilt. Rather, he thanked God for being responsible for his salvation, and pressed forward in service to Jesus Christ, his Lord and Savior.

Of course Paul was motivated by the power and presence of the Holy Spirit through regeneration, and had received and accepted God's grace and forgiveness. And yet at the same time Paul felt acute remorse. He did not question God's grace or his forgiveness, yet the shadow of his own remorse lingered. His compunction did not depress him, it highlighted God's ongoing grace and mercy in his life. Apart from an ever present awareness of God's grace and mercy, Paul would have likely crumbled from the weight of his guilt. This is not unique with Paul, we are all like that.

Paul knew that God's grace toward him had not been in vain because Paul was also aware of the extent of his own effort, his work, his struggle. To say that a thing is not in vain means that it is useful and productive. Paul had a particularly productive ministry because God had abundantly blessed him with much grace and mercy, and also because Paul worked harder than the other apostles, or so he said (v. 10). Paul worked hard at ministry. He tried to take advantage of every opportunity to preach, teach, and reach. And yet, Paul knew that he could not succeed by his own efforts.

This is a critical point: Paul made a huge personal effort to work at ministry, though it was not him or his work that made the critical difference. Rather, he said that it was the grace of God that was with him that got the credit. God's grace received the glory. God's grace was the real power of effectiveness that drove his own puny efforts. He knew that his effort was necessary, but he also knew that it was not sufficient.

Not Alone

"Whether then it was I or they, so we preach and so you believed" (v. 11). This is a curious verse. Having mentioned the other apostles, he continued with that thought by referring to them here. Paul had not been the only apostle to preach among the Corinthians. Other apostles and preachers had taught what Paul was teaching. Paul was not a Lone Ranger. Rather, he claimed unity with other gospel preachers that they had heard.

A sub-point here is that it doesn't matter who preaches or teaches, as long as the communication of God's truth is facilitated. The power of the Word does not attach itself to the preacher. It is not that the preacher uses the Word, but that the Word uses the preacher. The power and effectiveness of God's Word is in the Word itself, not in the preacher. God's

Word is not attached to the preacher, rather the preacher is attached to God's Word. It's like nailing a sign to a tree. The sign is attached to the tree, the tree is not attached to the sign.

It didn't matter who had preached the true gospel. Paul acknowledged that there had been many people who had preached what he was preaching. But there had also been many people who had preached a false gospel. Paul made a point to differentiate between what was true and what was false, and called upon the Corinthians to acknowledge the difference by remembering back to when they first believed. There is a link, a causal connection between the preaching and the believing indicated by the Greek word *houtō*, which is translated as *so* and literally means "in this way." We preached, said Paul, and in this way or because of this you believed.

Paul then turned to a practical application or a case study of the relationship between preaching and believing. Apparently, some of the Corinthians had been quibbling about the reality of the resurrection. It provides a stumbling block for many people. Note that Paul did not tell us how it could happen, only that it did.

"Now if Christ is proclaimed as raised from the dead, how can some of you say that there is no resurrection of the dead?" (v. 12). The logic of this verse is so simple that it is easy to miss. We might think that one person preaches the resurrection and another denies it. So, who's to know for sure. It's not the kind of thing that can be proven. So, we tend to think that either option is viable. This kind of thinking is quite common in our relativistic culture. But that is not at all the way that Paul reasoned. We may catch Paul's meaning if we emphasize the word *you* in the verse. "Now if Christ is proclaimed as raised from the dead, how can some of *you* say that there is no resurrection of the dead?" (v. 12).

DO YOU OR DON'T YOU?

Let me fill in some of Paul's assumptions. Paul said something like this: now if Christ is proclaimed by those who preach the true gospel (Paul and the apostles), which includes the resurrection, which you have believed and through which you have received regeneration, and there are witnesses to Christ's resurrection among you, how can some of you who have believed the true gospel say that there is no resurrection? Paul was raising the same question that he raised to the Galatians: "O foolish Galatians, who bewitched you not to obey the truth, to whom before your eyes Jesus Christ was written among you crucified?" (Galatians 3:1—MKJB).

The logic in verse 12 is not about the relative merits of resurrection versus no resurrection, but about the power and consistency of belief. Paul was saying, *You used to believe and now some of you don't believe.* So, which is more likely to be true: Jesus' resurrection or the quality of a belief that flip-flops between two mutually exclusive positions. Clearly, the only thing that had changed was the belief of some of the Corinthians. Christ had not changed. History had not changed. The weak link in this line of argumentation was not the resurrection of Jesus, but the vacillating belief of those who changed their minds.

Nonetheless, Paul then entertained the possibility that the doctrine of the resurrection may be in error by noting that it logically follows that "if there is no resurrection of the dead, then not even Christ has been raised" (v. 13). If we assume that there is no resurrection, then Christ cannot have been raised. And the conclusion of the argument is the loss of hope and the installation of pity upon those who make such an assumption.

But that's not the end of it. The no resurrection scenario is worse than just killing hope because "if Christ has not been raised, your faith is futile and you are still in your sins" (v. 17). If Christ has not been resurrected, then there is no cure for sin. And if there is no cure for sin "those also who have fallen asleep (died) in Christ have perished" (v. 18).

Paul said that if there is no resurrection, then it would follow that Christ was not resurrected. He stated it as simply as possible. Next Paul called attention to the fact that everything hangs on the resurrection. Christianity is holistic. It all works together or it doesn't work at all. Christianity is a comprehensive worldview. It affects everything. Note also that Paul did not suggest a kind of intellectual systematic theology as if the various elements of faith and belief are like puzzle pieces that we need to fit together in order to make a whole. Rather, Paul jumped from what may be considered to be an intellectual idea (resurrection) to the passions of hope and pity.

One of the reasons that the doctrine of the resurrection is important is that it is a kind of bridge between three different elements of our personhood. It is intellectual, of the mind. It is physical, of the body. And it is emotional, of the heart. The idea of resurrection is an idea (an abstraction), but it is an idea about the physical body. If it is true, there is a physical element to it. In addition, it produces the emotions of hope or pity.

Paul's argument was that if the doctrine of the resurrection is not true, then those who believe it are the most pitiful people in the world because resurrection is about the ultimate state of our being. And if we are deluded about that, then we are ultimately deluded—and beyond hope.

BLASPHEMY

But worse than being beyond hope, if we are wrong about resurrection we have been "misrepresenting God, because we testified about God that he raised Christ, whom he did not raise if it is true that the dead are not raised" (v. 15). To misrepresent God is both blasphemous and idolatrous, which are the opposite of faithful. If resurrection is not true, but God is real, then we are preaching and teaching false hope and false belief.

But not only are those who preach falsely condemned by Paul, but those who believe falsely—vainly, or without effect, those whose belief does not result in repentance or the works of repentance (Luke 5:22, Romans 2:4, 2 Corinthians 7:10, 2 Peter 3:9)—are also condemned. Does this mean that those who believe and preach false doctrine are without hope? Not at all. Everyone believes wrongly at some point in their growth, "as it is written: 'None is righteous, no, not one'" (Romans 3:10). We are all sinners. We are all damned, but some are saved from damnation by the grace of God.

So the critical issue is not false belief per se, but clinging to false belief in the light of Christ. The critical issue is the rejection of the increasing light of Christ in our own lives in favor of holding fast to old beliefs that may be comfortable, but which impede ongoing sanctification or continuing personal growth in grace. The critical issue is ongoing growth and maturity in Christ. It is a process without end. Growth that stops along the way is growth that leads to damnation.

There is more to faithfulness than belief, more than thinking about the Bible or about God or about Jesus. There is more to faith than the talk. There is also the walk. There are consequences to faithfulness. Believing in vain is equivalent to believing all the various biblical doctrines correctly, having a bulletproof intellectual understanding of Christianity, but failing to live it out, failing to walk the walk, failing to continue growing, failing to continue in perseverance. It is stopping somewhere along the way because you think you have arrived. It is thinking that your understanding or system of belief cannot be improved upon.

I'm not downplaying the importance of getting doctrine right. It is important, even critical! But it is not everything. There is more to living than thinking. There is more to the gospel than thinking about Jesus. There is the living, the daily grind, the relationships, the family, the job, etc. We cannot live in our heads, nor can we think without our minds. We are called to wholeness, which includes "all your heart and … all your soul and … all your mind and … all your strength" (Mark 12:30). In other words, all of your life.

CALLED TO PERFECTION

Christians are called to be perfect, to be whole, to be complete in Christ. We sinners can only do that in Christ, who is perfect. We cannot do that apart from Christ. Nor can we do that unless we continue to grow and mature in all of the various aspects of our personhood—the intellectual, the physical, the emotional, the spiritual. Remember that we are not called to perfection in our own strength, nor will anyone complete this calling in this life. In order to complete this path, this journey, we need to continue growing in Christ beyond this life in glory, in heaven, in eternity. So, if there is no resurrection (contrary to what Paul and the apostles have taught), then we are still in our sins, and we are still damned —and without remedy. "But," wrote Paul, "in fact (*nuni*) Christ has been raised from the dead, the firstfruits of those who have fallen asleep" (v. 20).

The ESV translates *nuni* as *in fact*, whereas the KJV and most other translations translate it as *now*. Paul's point by the use of the word *nuni* is that because the doctrine of resurrection is true, Christ has indeed been raised. The Pharisees had been arguing about resurrection for centuries, but in Christ it was now an historical fact, registered in history. Resurrection is true, and we have not been left in our sins, and Christ is the first of many who will die and be raised in resurrection, and you will be raised in resurrection as well.

We are who we are on the basis of the grace of God. We are what we are on the basis of the grace of God, not on the basis of some misunderstanding about resurrection. We are who we are because we have been snatched out of the fire by the grace of God (Jude 1:23). We are not our own, but have been bought with a price. Our purpose, our job, our task as Christians is to glorify God in all that we think, say, and do here and now, in this life, with these bodies (1 Corinthians 6:19). Praise be to God in Jesus Christ!

43. ALL GOD'S CHILDREN

For as by a man came death, by a man has come also the resurrection of the dead. For as in Adam all die, so also in Christ shall all be made alive. But each in his own order: Christ the firstfruits, then at his coming those who belong to Christ. Then comes the end, when he delivers the kingdom to God the Father after destroying every rule and every authority and power. For he must reign until he has put all his enemies under his feet. The last enemy to be destroyed is death. For "God has put all things in subjection under his feet." But when it says, "all things are put in subjection," it is plain that he is excepted who put all things in subjection under him. When all things are subjected to him, then the Son himself will also be subjected to him who put all things in subjection under him, that God may be all in all. —1 Corinthians 15:21-28

The first few verses of this section (vs. 21-22) provide a clear statement of the representative nature of biblical governance. Death and resurrection are dispensed to the whole of humanity through a covenantal head who serves as a representative, who represents the people to God, and who represents God to the people. The Greek word translated *by* (*dia*) is a primary preposition denoting the channel of an act, and literally means through. So a man, a covenantal head or representative—Adam, then Christ—is the channel through which either death or resurrection has come to … who? Verse 22 tells us that "in Adam all die, so also in Christ shall all be made alive."

All (*pas*) here means all as in everyone and suggests a whole or undivided measure. The question is, all of what? All of who? All of some portion, or all of a whole? Calvinists understand the various issues surrounding the word *all*. And yet we know that God does not stutter or misspeak His mind.

There is no problem with understanding that all have died in Adam, that use of the word *all* means every single person who has been or ever will be born this side of Christ's return in glory (Christ excepted, of course). But we must be careful not to fall into the apostasy of Universalism as we try to understand what is meant by "in Christ shall all be made alive" (v. 22). We must be careful to read Scripture, particularly sections like this one, in the light of the whole of Scripture.

All

We must keep in mind the Westminster Confession 1:7,

"All things in Scripture are not alike plain in themselves, nor alike clear unto all: yet those things which are necessary to be known, believed, and observed for salvation, are so clearly propounded and opened in some place of Scripture or other, that not only the learned, but the un-learned, in a due use of the ordinary means, may attain unto a sufficient understanding of them."

Understanding all the riches of Scripture is not easy because some ideas are balanced and nuanced by others. And yet, all of God's people can attain a sufficient understanding of Scripture to continue in faithfulness and to grow in sanctification.

Many of the issues that are dealt with in this section of First Corinthians are deep and complex, and we need to take care to not close our minds before we consider everything that Scripture says about a particular concern. However, my purpose here is not to be comprehensive, but to be suggestive, to sketch some of the broad outlines of God's concerns and invite you to further consideration under the guidance of the power and presence of the Holy Spirit (1 John 2:27). Let's look to Romans for help.

"Therefore, just as sin came into the world through one man, and death through sin, and so death spread to all men because all sinned—for sin indeed was in the world before the law was given, but sin is not counted where there is no law. Yet death reigned from Adam to Moses, even over those whose sinning was not like the transgression of Adam, who was a type of the one who was to come. But the free gift is not like the trespass. For if many died through one man's trespass, much more have the grace of God and the free gift by the grace of that one man Jesus Christ abounded for many. And the free gift is not like the result of that one man's sin. For the judgment following one trespass brought condemnation, but the free gift following many trespasses brought justification. If, because of one man's trespass, death reigned through that one man, much more will those who receive the abundance of grace and the free gift of righteousness reign in life through the one man Jesus Christ. Therefore, as one trespass led to condemnation for all men, so one act of righteousness leads to justification and life for all men" (Romans 5:12-18).

The same Greek word for *all* is used in both occurrences in Romans 5:18. Paul's meaning is that Adam's sin has condemned *all* of humanity, all who are under Adam as a covenantal head. And in a like manner Christ's propitiation on the cross provides sufficient justification for *all* of humanity, all who are under Christ as a covenantal head. This issue of the meaning and extent of the word *all* and its use in various places in Scripture has a very long and bloody history in the church. And it is not easily resolved. But it is not an error or a misspeaking by the Holy Spirit. Rather, God has given us this issue to wrestle with because through our wrestling with it we must wrestle with the Holy Spirit Himself. The point is that we are changed by the struggle, as we wrestle with God— and that's His purpose.

The result of the struggle, of coming to grips with this issue, is the confirmation of our individual covenantal head, whether it remains Adam unto condemnation or becomes Christ unto salvation. All in Adam will receive condemnation, and all in Christ will receive salvation. The primary question anyone should have concerning the word *all* this is: am I still under Adam or am I now under Christ? God knows your ultimate status. Do you? If you don't, you need to wrestle through it. Be prepared for it to take longer than a night, and be advised that you will come away with a limp.[1]

Our Own Order

"But each in his own order: Christ the firstfruits, then at his coming those who belong to Christ" (v. 23). The sense of our "own order" is that each individual will have a specific place or position in resurrection (in heaven). This lobbies against the idea that those in heaven will all occupy the same place or position. Do all Christians occupy the same position in Christ? No. There is, of course, the watershed issue of justification and the new position the justified person occupies under the headship of

---

1   Jacob the patriarch wrestled with God one night—and won! But Jacob's hip was put out of joint. It's not that Jacob defeated God, but that Jacob won salvation. He emerged a changed man. In honor of that change God renamed him Israel, and from that day forward Israel limped. See Genesis 32. I contend that the only significant answer to this theological conundrum is the answer *you* give about your own inclusion in or exclusion from this "all" of Christ's people. You can answer for no one else, and no one else can answer for you.

Christ. But beyond that initial justification, there is the matter of the identification and development of God's gifts. The idea that Paul was suggesting is that God's order is hierarchical on earth just as it is hierarchical in heaven, and consequently, each resurrected individual will have a specific position in God's order, on earth and in heaven, subject to the Holy Spirit. Each individual will be uniquely positioned in God's hierarchy to follow the Spirit. God is working to make it "on earth as it is in heaven" (Matthew 6:10).

Paul had previously discussed the unity of the body of Christ on earth as being a function of individual giftedness, and that each individual has a specific role as well as a unique position in Christ's body (the church) on earth. Here he suggests that Christ's body is not limited to its earthy manifestation as His church, but that Christ's body spans (or bridges, or includes) heaven and earth.

While gold and silver—worldly riches—do not translate into heaven, our new character in Christ does. There is a continuity of character in Christ through regeneration and resurrection into eternity. Christians are changed upon regeneration, grafted into Christ (Romans 11:17-24), which means that our spiritual gifts, our individual endowments of character, interests, and abilities, will continue to grow and develop and be used in heaven as well as on earth. Heaven will not be a grand retirement center where the saints sit in rocking chairs and reminisce about the good old days. Rather, in heaven the saints will actively engage their gifts in the work of praise (Revelation 19:4-10).

Christ has lead the way in resurrection. Paul describes Christ as the firstfruits (*aparchē*). The reason that firstfruits is plural is that the Greek word means a beginning of sacrifice, and is an allusion to Old Testament worship: "The best of the firstfruits of your ground you shall bring into the house of the Lord your God" (Exodus 23:19). It is also plural because Paul understood that Jesus is Trinitarian, and is always in the Godhead. It is also plural because the saints are grafted into Christ.

"Then comes the end, when he delivers the kingdom to God the Father after destroying every rule and every authority and power" (v. 24). The word *end* in view is the Greek *teleios*, which means end, purpose, or goal. God's purpose is not to destroy the world, but to reboot it. God is not out to destroy the world—He loves it (John 3:16)! And yet God is out to destroy something. Here we see that He is out to destroy "every rule and every authority and power" (v. 24). Yet, neither is God out to establish anarchy. He is not out to destroy authority itself, but rather to establish it rightly, to establish all authority in Christ (Matthew 28:18).

REBOOT HUMANITY

God's purpose is to remake humanity in the likeness of Jesus Christ (Romans 6:5) through regeneration (John 3:3). While the Greek word translated *destroying* (*katargeō*) is not wrong, it does not (and cannot) convey the whole of God's intentions here. The KJV translates the word as *shall have put down*, others translate it as *abolish*. It is important to see that God intends to get rid of one kind of rule, authority, and power, and to establish another. Thus, we can think of the whole of this action as a kind of reconfiguration. God intends to reconfigure the world's operating system, which will require a reboot in order to function correctly (if I may use a more contemporary analogy).

"For he must reign until he has put all his enemies under his feet. The last enemy to be destroyed is death" (vs. 25-26). The principle enemy in mind here is Satan, who inaugurated death in the world at the Fall, when he deceived Adam and Eve into understanding themselves as autonomous individuals who could think and act apart from God. While this did not threaten the character of the Trinity itself, it did damage the Trinitarian image in which humanity had been created. It damaged the bond or relationship between humanity and God. Moses described that damage as death: "in the day that you eat of it you shall surely die" (Genesis 2:17). By destroying death God will reestablish eternal life through the work of Christ. In that Day the "all" of verse 22 will be comprehensive (complete, whole, total, all inclusive), and that aspect of God's promise will be fulfilled exactly as Paul wrote it. All under Adam's covenant headship will perish, and all under Christ's covenant headship will thrive.

> "For 'God has put all things in subjection under his feet.' But when it says, 'all things are put in subjection,' it is plain that he is excepted who put all things in subjection under him. When all things are subjected to him, then the Son himself will also be subjected to him who put all things in subjection under him, that God may be all in all" (vs. 27-28).

Paul was quoting Psalm 8:

> O Lord, our Lord, how majestic is your name in all the earth! You have set your glory above the heavens. Out of the mouth of babes and infants, you have established strength because of your foes, to still the enemy and the avenger. When I look at your heavens, the work of your

fingers, the moon and the stars, which you have set in place, what is
man that you are mindful of him, and the son of man that you care for
him? Yet you have made him a little lower than the heavenly beings
and crowned him with glory and honor. You have given him dominion over the works of your hands; you have put all things under his feet,
all sheep and oxen, and also the beasts of the field, the birds of the heav-
ens, and the fish of the sea, whatever passes along the paths of the seas.
O Lord, our Lord, how majestic is your name in all the earth!

Having mentioned subjection six times in two verses we can trust
that it is the central theme. By subjection Paul meant subordination. He is
talking about hierarchical or representative authority. Elsewhere Paul described this authority: "the head of every man is Christ, the head of a wife
is her husband, and the head of Christ is God" (1 Corinthians 11:3).

Paul was talking about the Trinitarian interrelatedness of all things,
and particularly of all authority on earth and in heaven. He sketched the
major outlines of that authority so that we understand that it is hierarchical. God is at the top and Christ is under God's authority and "all authority in heaven and on earth has been given to" Christ (Matthew 28:18).

TRINITARIAN GLUE

Paul concluded by alluding to the Trinitarian character of God and,
by implication, to the Trinitarian character of God's image, and how, because of that Trinitarian character, God Himself, by the power and presence of the Holy Spirit through regeneration, is the glue that binds all the
various aspects and levels of authority together. Paul was talking about
human authority, but more than that. He had in mind the whole order of
creation. From the stars to the critters, every element in creation has a
unique and specific place of occupation and a unique and specific set of
gifts (interests, talents, abilities, qualities, characteristics, etc.). Our individual placement in Christ is a function of God's sovereignty and dominion in that God "works all things according to the counsel of his will"
(Ephesians 1:11), not some things but all things.

In answer to the earlier concern about the definition or limitations of
the word "all" Paul answers here that God Himself is "all in all" (v. 28).

Scottish Prayer For The Road

God before me
God behind me
I on Thy path, O God

Thou, O God, in my steps.
In the twistings of the road.
In the currents of the river.
Be with me by day.
Be with me by night.
Be with me by day and by night.
    —Anonymous

44. Tsk Tsk

Otherwise, what do people mean by being baptized on behalf of the dead? If the dead are not raised at all, why are people baptized on their behalf? Why am I in danger every hour? I protest, brothers, by my pride in you, which I have in Christ Jesus our Lord, I die every day! What do I gain if, humanly speaking, I fought with beasts at Ephesus? If the dead are not raised, "Let us eat and drink, for tomorrow we die." Do not be deceived: "Bad company ruins good morals." Wake up from your drunken stupor, as is right, and do not go on sinning. For some have no knowledge of God. I say this to your shame.

—1 Corinthians 15:29-34

Verse 29 is a stickler in that it is not easy to determine what Paul was talking about. It helps to keep in mind that the context of the verse is Paul's continuing defense of the reality of resurrection. Much of the problem comes from our sinful desire to turn the Bible and Christianity into something mystical and spiritual, as a way of distancing ourselves from the plain meaning and the personal responsibilities that accrue to a clear understanding of God's Word. And Satan is very willing to help with this effort.

A brief examination of the variety of interpretations and uses of this verse since Paul wrote it provides adequate evidence of Satan's desire to confuse people about God's Word. And one of the more successful ways to sow confusion has been through its mystification. I simply cite the Mormon practice of baptizing the dead as an example of how far people are willing to go with these mystical and spiritual interpretations.

So, if this verse does not mean what the Mormons think it means, what does it mean? Of the many interpretations that have been suggested, I will briefly review two possibilities and suggest what seems to be the most likely to be true.

Some have suggested that the word *baptizō* in this verse does not refer to the ceremony of baptism, but that the word is used in its root meaning of wash. Acts 9:37 and Luke 11:38 are cited in support of this belief.

"Now there was in Joppa a disciple named Tabitha, which, translated, means Dorcas. She was full of good works and acts of charity. In those days she became ill and died, and when they had washed (louō) her, they laid her in an upper room" (Acts 9:36-37).

Note that the word washed (*louō*) in Acts 9:37 is not *baptizō*. So, how can such an argument be made? It is made from the use of the word *baptizō* in Luke 11:38, "The Pharisee was astonished to see that he did not first wash (baptizō) before dinner." Here the word is *baptizō*, and the verse makes no sense if it refers to the ceremony of baptism. It simply means wash.

WASHING CORPSES

The point is that the understanding and use of the word *baptizō* when Paul wrote this letter was not strictly limited to the ceremony of baptism. Therefore, Paul's use of the word in verse 29 could easily have been a reference to the practice of washing corpses before burial. If this was the case, Paul meant something like, "what do people mean by washing the dead? If the dead are not raised at all, why are the dead washed?" The common understanding in the first century, and the common practice among the Jews, was that corpses were washed prior to burial in preparation for resurrection.

Thus, Paul was arguing that this tradition of washing corpses testified to the reality of resurrection. This explanation of the verse is certainly adequate and it conforms to the larger context of this section.

The second and more likely interpretation of this verse comes from Matthew Henry. Henry argues that the definite article *the* (i.e., *the* dead) in Greek is singular, and that the word *dead* (*nekros*) serves as an implied reference to Jesus, who had died. Here the verse is understood to say, "what do people mean by being baptized on behalf of the dead Jesus? If the dead Jesus is not raised at all, why are people baptized for the dead Jesus?

Henry understands Paul to be arguing that if Jesus was not resurrected, then baptism meant nothing. Baptism was (and always should be) a big deal in the lives of believers. Christians in Rome were persecuted because of their baptism. A person could flirt with Christianity and not be in trouble with Caesar. But when they submitted to baptism, Rome released the hounds upon them.

While the great persecutions of Christian history were still yet to come, Paul knew persecution based upon Christian baptism first hand. After Paul was baptized, the Jews began to pursue and to persecute him.[1] Paul was a forerunner of Christian martyrdom, and was arguing here that the reality of the resurrection was the thing that made Christian baptism significant. Again, his argument was to support the reality of resurrection through an appeal to baptism.

IN DANGER

In support of this understanding Paul then asks, "Why am I in danger every hour? I protest, brothers, by my pride in you, which I have in Christ Jesus our Lord, I die every day!" (vs. 30-31). In danger of what? In danger of persecution because of his baptism. The Jews had put out a contract on his life (Acts 9:23). Here Paul attested that he was in danger of death every day because he glorified the church (or the people) of Jesus Christ. He was numbered among his Christian brothers as a disciple of Jesus Christ. And what had made him a member of Christ's body? Of course he had been regenerated on the road to Damascus, but he had been received as a member of Christ's body through baptism (Acts 9:18), as we all are.

These verses are simply an extension of Paul's argument that resurrection was a reality and that everything hung on it, including baptism. This comports well with Paul's next argument for the reality of resurrection. "What do I gain if, humanly speaking, I fought with beasts at Ephesus? If the dead are not raised, 'Let us eat and drink, for tomorrow we die'" (v. 32). Again, he was making another argument for the reality of resurrection. That's the theme that runs through these verses.

According to Strong's (G2351) Paul's reference to fighting with beasts (thēriomacheō) is to be understood as an encounter with furious men. We know this because Paul prefaced this reference by saying, "humanly speaking" (kata), suggesting that he was speaking metaphorically. He was suggesting that, as bad as the false teachers and leaders at Corinth had been, they were nothing compared with those at Ephesus. I suspect that he said this in order to comfort the faithful Christians at Corinth. They could rejoice because their situation wasn't as bad as it had been at Ephesus.

---

1   See Ross, Phillip A. *Acts of the Apostles—Kingdom Advancement*, Pilgrim Platform, 2007.

EPHESIAN BEASTS

Again, his point was that the gospel of Jesus Christ had tamed the beasts at Ephesus. And it had been the gospel based upon the resurrection of Jesus Christ that had done so. Here Paul was saying that if the resurrection was not a reality, he had nothing to gain from struggling to straighten out the poor, misguided Christians at Ephesus. To put it positively, his ministry, his struggle, not only served the glory of God through Jesus Christ, but it would be a feather in his own cap upon his own resurrection. If resurrection is not true, he said, "Let us eat and drink, for tomorrow we die" (v. 32), mocking a common belief of those who denied the reality of resurrection. Paul alluded to the fact that he would be rewarded in heaven because of the reality of resurrection. However you account for the details of the argument, it is simply another argument for the reality of resurrection. But he's not done.

> "Do not be deceived: 'Bad company ruins good morals.' Wake up from your drunken stupor, as is right, and do not go on sinning. For some have no knowledge of God. I say this to your shame" (vs. 33-34).

Here Paul identified the source of their confusion—they had been listening to the wrong people. They had been captured and influenced by sin, as a drunk is captured and influenced by alcohol. They had confused the wisdom of the world with the wisdom of Christ.

Verse 33 is a restatement of a common biblical sentiment. Much of Scripture is about the corruption of God's people. This verse also reflects the sentiments of the fourteenth century Latin proverb "a rotten apple spoils the barrel." A rotten apple spoil the barrel when the spread of mold or other diseases moves from the bad apple to the rest. Mold and other forms of rot spread by proximity and contact. What can the good apples do to counteract the spread of mold and rot? Nothing. Their only recourse is to avoid proximity. Paul's argument here is that sin and the manifestations of sin are contagious and Christians need to avoid sin.

DECEPTION

But more than that, he argued that they had been deceived, that they were in the midst of being deceived, and that deception was at the heart of worldly wisdom. Paul has been arguing for fifteen chapters that the chief enemy of the gospel is worldly wisdom and its many deceits. Here Paul said that trafficking—spending time—with people who have been deceived by worldly wisdom works to corrode the gospel, particularly among new and/or immature Christians. At the very least, traffic with those who have been deceived by worldly wisdom should be kept to a minimum among the saints.

Of course, Christians need to be *in* the world but not *of* it, which means that Christians are not to abandon the world. Rather, we are to serve as God's leaven in the world. We are to shape the world and its culture, we are not to be shaped by it. That is a high calling and a difficult row to hoe.

Paul turned to chastisement, saying in essence, "Wake up from your drunken stupor, stop sinning and realize that some of your cherished leaders of the church do not know God! Those leaders are not regenerate." That's the issue. That's always the issue. In exasperation Paul concluded, "I say this to your shame" (v. 34).

SHAME

Paul used shame as a tool in the service of edification. The fact that Paul used shame as a pedagogical tool speaks volumes about the contemporary churches and their impotent understanding of the gospel of Jesus Christ. The gospel that Paul taught employs shame as a method of edification—not always, but sometimes. Shame is an unavoidable concept because it is unique to humanity. Even the heathen know this. It was Mark Twain who said, "Man is the only animal that blushes. Or needs to." Jeremiah noted that lost people have lost the ability to feel shame.

> "'Were they ashamed when they committed abomination? No, they were not at all ashamed; they did not know how to blush. Therefore they shall fall among those who fall; at the time that I punish them, they shall be overthrown,' says the Lord" (Jeremiah 6:15).

A healthy sense of shame is essential to faithful gospel living.

Consider the following quotation about shame from Marc Miller, Ph.D., a practicing psychotherapist in Berkeley, California. (This is not in support of psychotherapy as a way to deal with shame. Psychotherapy is inadequate for the task. I cite it only because it notes some true things about shame from a person who does not appear to be a Christian.)

> One of the most striking contradictions that I have come across as a therapist is the discrepancy between the centrality of the affect of shame in humans, and the lack of attention shame has received in the study and practice of psychology. In my own training, I was taught to attend to a wide range of feelings: anger, fear, sexuality, excitement, sadness,

but rarely, if ever, the feeling of shame. Shame is also avoided in the "real" world as well. In fact, most of us feel shame about feeling shame. As a result shame is rarely acknowledged to others, or even to oneself. In the last five years I have been paying much more attention to shame in working with my clients, and am amazed at how crucial attending to this feeling is to doing psychotherapy. As with any feeling, when shame is denied it will only resurface to create even more pain and havoc.

Unfortunately, shame is often unbearable. For example humiliation and mortification, which are part of the "shame family of feelings" may be so painful they may lead to violence or suicide. We may equate shame with being worthless, unlovable, unredeemable, or cut-off from humanity. It may evoke other painful feelings, rage at the one we feel shamed by, or terror that we will be abandoned, fragmented and/or overwhelmed with despair. Silvan Tomkins (in Nathanson, 1992) said, "If distress is the affect of suffering, shame is the affect of indignity, transgression and of alienation."

Indeed, shame is at the heart of sin and salvation, of forgiveness and redemption. It is unavoidable. Paul thought that it was downright shameful that some of the Corinthians did not know God, that they could not blush in the face of their own sin, that they were not regenerate.

Paul argued that people who do not believe in resurrection do not believe it because they have not experienced regeneration. And apart from regeneration knowledge of God is merely abstract. It is not personal, not real. So he said that they had "no knowledge of God" (v. 34). There is no negative in the Greek. The Greek is literally translated "have ignorance of God" (YLT). It is not that they are missing knowledge, but that they are holding onto ignorance. This is an important distinction in the light of the first chapter of Romans.

Paul was not ashamed. The gospel had dealt with his shame. Paul wrote to the Romans,

> "For I am not ashamed of the gospel of Christ, for it is the power of God to salvation to everyone believing, both to Jew first, and to Greek; for in it the righteousness of God is revealed from faith to faith; even as it has been written, 'But the just shall live by faith.' For God's wrath is revealed from Heaven on all ungodliness and unrighteousness of men, holding the truth in unrighteousness, because the thing known of God is clearly known within them, for God revealed it to them. For the unseen things of Him from the creation of the world are clearly seen, being understood by the things made, both His eternal power and God-

head, for them to be without excuse. Because knowing God, they did not glorify Him as God, nor were thankful. But they became vain in their reasonings, and their undiscerning heart was darkened. Professing to be wise, they became foolish…" (Romans 1:16-22).

45. REFLECTIVITY

But someone will ask, "How are the dead raised? With what kind of body do they come?" You foolish person! What you sow does not come to life unless it dies. And what you sow is not the body that is to be, but a bare kernel, perhaps of wheat or of some other grain. But God gives it a body as he has chosen, and to each kind of seed its own body. For not all flesh is the same, but there is one kind for humans, another for animals, another for birds, and another for fish. There are heavenly bodies and earthly bodies, but the glory of the heavenly is of one kind, and the glory of the earthly is of another. There is one glory of the sun, and another glory of the moon, and another glory of the stars; for star differs from star in glory. So is it with the resurrection of the dead. What is sown is perishable; what is raised is imperishable. It is sown in dishonor; it is raised in glory. It is sown in weakness; it is raised in power. It is sown a natural body; it is raised a spiritual body. If there is a natural body, there is also a spiritual body. —1 Corinthians 15:35-44

Paul anticipated or repeated a question on the minds of some Corinthians, "How are the dead raised? With what kind of body do they come?" (v. 35). The Greek word translated *body* here is *sōma*, not *sarx*, which suggests that the question is not simply about individual flesh, but concerns a range of meanings related to the word *body*.[1] Paul answered the question in verse 44, "there is a natural body, there is also a spiritual body." He treated the issue of bodily resurrection in the same general way that he treated the issue of the body of Christ in chapters ten and twelve.

---

1   Body: the body both of men or animals, 1. a dead body or corpse, 2. the living body, a. of animals; 2. the bodies of planets and of stars (heavenly bodies); 3. is used of a (large or small) number of men closely united into one society, or family as it were; a social, ethical, mystical body, a. so in the NT of the church; 4. that which casts a shadow as distinguished from the shadow itself—The *New Testament Greek Lexicon*.

"The cup of blessing that we bless, is it not a participation in the blood of Christ? The bread that we break, is it not a participation in the body of Christ?" (1 Corinthians 10:16).

"For just as the body is one and has many members, and all the members of the body, though many, are one body, so it is with Christ" (1 Corinthians 12:12).

"God arranged the members in the body, each one of them, as he chose. If all were a single member, where would the body be? As it is, there are many parts, yet one body" (1 Corinthians 12:18-20).

"Now you are the body of Christ and individually members of it" (1 Corinthians12:27).

We must remember that Paul has been speaking about the unity of the body of Christ and the fact that we are parts of Christ's body. We must not limit our understanding to be narrowly focused on individual human bodies, but must encompass the fullness and wholeness—the unity —of the body that is the subject to which Paul has been speaking. We must understand ourselves to be members or parts of a greater whole, a greater body, the body of Christ. This, I believe, is the gist of Paul's argument here. Let's see how he fleshes it out.

NATURAL & SPIRITUAL

Paul argued for two kinds of bodies—natural and spiritual. However, Paul id not argue from the perspective of dualism. Rather, his argument issued from Trinitarianism. Consequently, it is shrouded in mystery in that we cannot understand it completely, though we can—through the grace of regeneration—understand it adequately.

The question that Paul deals with here pertains to the nature or character of the resurrection body. What kind of body is it? How does resurrection work? Some of the Corinthians thought that they might be better able to believe in resurrection if they understood how it worked, if they understood the nature or character of resurrection existence. People today testify to a similar concern by suggesting that they would believe in Jesus Christ or become a Christian if only Christ would appear to them personally, or if Christ would just perform a *bona fide* miracle in their presence. They say something like, "Show me the truth and reality of Christ's miracles and I'll believe."

But that is not the way that it works. Salvation is not the result of or the culmination of an argument. People are not argued into the kingdom of God. People do not decide to become Christians because they finally understand the truth or because they finally understand reality or God or Jesus Christ from a Christian perspective.

Rather, arsy varsy, people are able to see the truth or to see reality from a Christian perspective only because God has changed their hearts and minds. People begin to see or understand truth and reality from a Christian perspective only after God has given them ears to hear and eyes to see, only after regeneration. Only by actually standing on the promises of God can people see that God's promises are absolutely reliable. Prior to actually stepping out on the promises of God, all personal knowledge of God is mere speculation and hearsay. Such knowledge (speculation and hearsay) is unreliable and issues from faithlessness.

TRINITARIAN RESURRECTION

Paul's argument here regarding the body of resurrection is analogous —similar, even identical—to his argument about the body of Christ dealt with earlier (1 Corinthians 10-12). The argument stands on or is based upon the reality of the Trinity. The most primary character of reality itself is Trinitarian because all understanding of reality comes through human beings who have been created in the image of God, who is Trinitarian. What Paul said in this section is about what it means to say that reality itself is most fully understood as Trinitarian. He was saying that resurrection is a reality because God is Trinitarian.

The first thing that we need to understand is that the Trinity is axiomatic[2] for the regenerate (who assume it) and nonsensical[3] to the unregenerate (who don't). To have faith in Jesus Christ is to assume His reality and truth, which are Trinitarian in that Jesus, God, and the Holy Spirit are in Trinitarian unity. A Trinitarian perspective is essential for the eyes

---

2 *Axiomatic*: adjective; 1. self-evident, taken for granted, evident without proof or argument; "an axiomatic truth;" "we hold these truths to be self-evident." 2. postulational of or relating to or derived from axioms; "axiomatic physics;" "the postulational method was applied to geometry" (S.S. Stevens). 3. aphoristic: containing aphorisms or maxims; "axiomatic wisdom."

3 *Nonsensical*: adjective; 1. having no intelligible meaning; "nonsense syllables;" "a nonsensical jumble of words;" 2. absurd, cockeyed, derisory, idiotic, laughable, ludicrous, nonsensical, preposterous, ridiculous completely devoid of wisdom or good sense; "the absurd excuse that the dog ate his homework;" "that's a cockeyed idea;" "ask a nonsensical question and get a nonsensical answer;" "a contribution so small as to be laughable."

of faith. This is the essential insight and argument that Paul has been making throughout First Corinthians. Paul preached

> "Christ crucified, a stumbling block to Jews and folly to Gentiles, but to
> those who are called, both Jews and Greeks, Christ (is) the power of
> God and the wisdom of God" (1 Corinthians 1:24).

Consequently, Paul does not argue in order to establish the truth and reality of the Trinitarian perspective, rather, arsy varsy, his arguments are based upon the truth and reality of the Trinitarian perspective. He assumes it. But it is more than a mere abstract assumption, for Paul it was a personal testimony. It is the foundation or basis upon which all life and understanding rest. The question that Paul answered here is, What is a resurrection body? What does "resurrection body" mean? How can we understand it? It is intimately related to the question, What is the body of Christ? What does Scripture mean when it refers to the body of Christ?

Paul's first response to this question was to note that the question itself issues from foolishness. "You foolish person!" he said. "What you sow does not come to life unless it dies" (v. 36). It's a foolish question, a futile question that cannot be answered by Paul, or by anyone, except Jesus Christ through regeneration. The question asks, "How?" It's a technical question about the mechanics of resurrection, and is out of bounds because it is beyond our human ability to comprehend. Only God can answer such a question, and the answer will assume a level of comprehension on a par (equal) with God.

SUFFICIENT, NOT COMPREHENSIVE

Paul wrote to the Philippians that even though Jesus "was in the form of God, (He) did not count equality with God a thing to be grasped" (Philippians 2:6). Our human ability to understand is not on a par with God's. Many things are simply beyond us, as individuals and as human beings. We can't explain everything—nor do we need to! God doesn't need to explain everything either. Nonetheless, God gives us what we need. God's explanations are sufficient, but not comprehensive. To insist on a comprehensive explanation is to deny that what God has given is sufficient. To insist on a comprehensive explanation is an act of faithlessness.

Paul tells us that the key to understanding this issue is death. "What you sow does not come to life unless it dies" (v. 36). Paul made an analogous argument from nature. A seed becomes a seed only when it has developed an independent, individual existence apart from the plant. Then, the seed does not germinate until it is planted in the ground, and the resulting germination and maturity of the plant does not in any way resemble the planted seed. In addition, the transformation of the seed appears to be its death and destruction. And lastly, life in seed form is nothing like life in plant form.

He explains that "what you sow is not the body that is to be, but a bare kernel" (v. 37). Our current bodies are resurrection bodies in seed form. These bodies must be planted in death in order to germinate in resurrection life. This life in these bodies that we currently experience is nothing like resurrection life in resurrected bodies. They are as different as seed and plant, egg and chicken, caterpillar and butterfly. Though the seed becomes the plant, the egg becomes the chicken, and the caterpillar becomes the butterfly, they are each so different from one another as to be completely unrelated, except inasmuch as the reality of their continuity is personally experienced. We could never guess that seed and plant are related unless we witness the planting and the growth—the transformation of one form into another. We could never guess that the egg and the chicken are related unless we witness the hatching. We could never guess that the caterpillar and butterfly are related unless we watch the process of chrysalis and transformation.

The continuity can only be observed and witnessed. Thus, the continuity is a testimony, a personal observation, a personal experience. The continuity is not something that can be explained, it is something that we behold in wonder and awe. We call it a fact that seeds become plants, that eggs become chickens, and that caterpillars become butterflies. And scientists provide amazing descriptions and theories about how it all works, about how one phase or stage of the process morphs into another. But the truth is that we have no idea how it works. The truth, explanations about how it works, simply recedes into the infinitesimally small elements of which reality is composed. The more we can see of the process, the more amazing it appears.

TRINITARIAN SCIENCE

"God gives it a body as he has chosen, and to each kind of seed its own body" (v. 38). Why does the seed become the plant? Why does the egg become the chicken? Why does the caterpillar become the butterfly? Because that is the way that God created things. How does this happen? We have no idea other than that God tells us that "each according to its kind" (Genesis 1:11) produces more of its own kind. God does not answer the how question, other than pointing to his own Trinitarian character. The closest we can get to understanding how these things work is to understand the nature and character of the Trinity. The most fundamental and/or essential understanding of the way that the world works (the inquiry of science) requires an understanding of the Trinity. Inasmuch as we know the truth of God, we will know the truth of the world in which we live. And conversely, the more we deny the truth of God the more we block our understanding of the world.

Paul continues with an explanation that God created different kinds of life forms. "For not all flesh is the same, but there is one kind for humans, another for animals, another for birds, and another for fish" (v. 39). We note that Paul associated each kind with a different habitat. Starting with the end of Paul's list we see that the habitat of fish is water, the habitat of birds is air, the habitat of animals is land, and the habitat of human beings is ... what? Isn't that the issue? Isn't Paul talking about the human habitat?

Paul has been arguing for the reality of resurrection. This is another instance of that argument. We know from Genesis that the earth is the human habitat. But earth is only part of the human habitat. Scripture also tells us that there is a heaven, that heaven is also part of the human habitat, even the essential part because it is eternal. Paul set out a fundamental contrast between heaven and earth, celestial and terrestrial, but set the contrast in such a way as to indicate that while they are different, one is a reflection of the other. Which one is the reflection and which the reality? Jesus taught us to pray that God's will would one day be done "on earth as it is in heaven" (Matthew 6:10). For us to hope and pray for that day suggests that heaven is the reality, the model, and earth is the reflection of the glory of heaven—in a "mirror dimly" without a doubt, but one day "face to face" (1 Corinthians 13:12).

What is true in heaven will one day be true on earth. And the one thing that we know for sure about the earth is that we are here in our bodies. We can doubt everything else, but we cannot doubt the existence of our own bodies. We may not know what they are, or how they work, but the reality of our own bodies is an undeniable fact. We eat, we sleep, we go about our business—all of which serves as a testimony to the reality of our bodily existence. If you can hear what I'm saying, or see the words on this page, that hearing or seeing is a testimony of *your* bodily existence.

Therefore, argued Paul, if bodies are an undeniable element of our existence on earth, then, because earth is a reflection of the greater glory, the greater reality of heaven, then heaven will also be populated with bodies. Of what sort he cannot say. But the fact that there are resurrection bodies fitted for heaven is as certain as the bodies that already populate earth.

SEEING THE LIGHT

This is so on the principle of reflectivity. As the moon reflects the light of the sun, but has no light of its own, so, the earth reflects the glory of heaven but has no glory of its own. Paul alluded to this in verse 41, "There is one glory of the sun, and another glory of the moon, and another glory of the stars; for star differs from star in glory."

Paul was struggling to explain how it is that the reality of earthly bodies points to the reality of resurrection or heavenly bodies. He knew that the glory of Christ is reflected in the people of Christ. He had tasted it personally in his own life, in his own body, through his own regeneration, and he saw it in the faces of the saints, as well. He knew it as bedrock reality because it was the reality of his own body.

At verse 42 he applied this principle of reflectivity to resurrection, "So is it with the resurrection of the dead. What is sown is perishable; what is raised is imperishable." Here he contrasted perishable and imperishable, or in some versions corruption and incorruption. The Greek words (*phthora* and *aphtharsia*) literally mean ruin and unruinable, or destruction and not-destroyable. Paul contrasted the deterioration of the earthly body with the inability of the resurrection body to deteriorate or decay. Continuing the analogy Paul wrote, "It is sown in dishonor; it is raised in glory. It is sown in weakness; it is raised in power" (v. 43).

This contrast between the superior and inferior—heaven and earth, the celestial and the terrestrial, the imperishable and perishable—can also be seen in the contrast between dishonor and glory, weakness and power. On earth we experience dishonor, weakness, and perishability, all of which lead to death. And in death the body is sown (planted) as a seed in order that it may sprout in a form that does not resemble the seed, but in which all of the potential of the seed, all of the characteristics of the seed, become manifest in their fullness through the life or fruit of the plant, in the resurrection body. Finally, Paul concluded, "It is sown a natural body;

it is raised a spiritual body. If there is a natural body, there is also a spiritual body" (v. 44).

Again, Paul has been arguing for the reality of resurrection and has used many examples and arguments. Here he has been arguing that the reality of resurrection is an ordinary consequence of the reality of bodily existence on earth that is grounded in the principle of reflectivity. If God's glory is reflected at all on the earth, then that reflection points to the reality of God and His heaven, and to the reality of bodily resurrection. If God's glory is reflected at all on earth, then it is but a shadow of the greater reality of God, of Christ, and of Christ's resurrected people.

46. Imagining Heaven

Thus it is written, "The first man Adam became a living being;" the last Adam became a life-giving spirit. But it is not the spiritual that is first but the natural, and then the spiritual. The first man was from the earth, a man of dust; the second man is from heaven. As was the man of dust, so also are those who are of the dust, and as is the man of heaven, so also are those who are of heaven. Just as we have borne the image of the man of dust, we shall also bear the image of the man of heaven. I tell you this, brothers: flesh and blood cannot inherit the kingdom of God, nor does the perishable inherit the imperishable. Behold! I tell you a mystery. We shall not all sleep, but we shall all be changed, in a moment, in the twinkling of an eye, at the last trumpet. For the trumpet will sound, and the dead will be raised imperishable, and we shall be changed.

—1 Corinthians 15:45-52

Paul continued to contrast the differences and the similarities between the natural body and the spiritual body (v. 44) because this contrast is the main point of this letter to the Corinthians. He has been talking about nothing else from the very beginning of this letter.

"Now we have received not the spirit of the world, but the Spirit who is from God, that we might understand the things freely given us by God. And we impart this in words not taught by human wisdom but taught by the Spirit, interpreting spiritual truths to those who are spiritual. The natural person does not accept the things of the Spirit of God, for they are folly to him, and he is not able to understand them because they are spiritually discerned." (1 Corinthians 2:12-14).

In verse 45 Paul contrasted several elements of the spiritual body with the natural body, all of which are very important. First of all, to suggest that Jesus was like Adam is nothing less than astonishing. Because of the nature of inheritance, Adam is the primary model for all human life. We are what we are because Adam was what he was. He was the original, we are the copies, and the absolute best that a copy can be cannot exceed the quality of the original.

Adam's creation predated the entry of sin into the world. Thus, Adam was created without sin. And the comparison tells us that Christ, who is a type of Adam was also without sin. Scripture goes on to tell us, however, that Adam did sin, and that he sinned prior to the birth of any children, and that Adam's sin changed the relationship between God and Adam that would affect all of his natural children (Genesis 3). As history cannot be erased, so Adam's sin was historical and the reality of that history necessarily continues through time and accrues to Adam's posterity and to us. Adam played a unique role in the history of humanity as the first of a kind.

Adam was unique, so Paul's reference to Jesus Christ as the "last Adam" (v. 45) cannot be overstressed. Paul tells us here that Jesus Christ is the most important person in human history since Adam, since the very beginning. And He goes on to say that Christ's importance far exceeds Adam's. We need to pay close attention to this.

NATURAL/SUPERNATURAL

Paul also tells us that "Adam became a living being" and Christ "became a life-giving spirit" (v. 45). In Genesis 2:7 we learn that "the Lord God formed the man of dust from the ground and breathed into his nostrils the breath of life, and the man became a living creature." The life that God gave Adam has been passed down through the ages through what we call the natural process of generation or reproduction, and Paul referred to the product of natural birth as the "natural man" (1 Corinthians 2:14).

In contrast, Christ was miraculously born from a virgin, suggesting that His biological inheritance was more like Adam's in that both Adam and Christ were more directly related to God than the rest of humanity, whose relationship with God is more distant. Christ's nature was similar to Adam's nature in that both were immediately related to God as Father. While the rest of humanity could claim that God Himself was their great, great, great (ad nauseum) grandfather, both Adam and Christ were immediate or direct sons of God.

And yet Paul also tells us that Jesus Christ "is the image of the invisible God, the firstborn of all creation" (Colossians 1:15). Adam preceded Christ in time, and yet Christ precedes Adam in eminence as the *first born* Son. Paul speaks repeatedly of Christ as the firstborn. Indeed, Adam and Adam's progeny have new life in Christ inasmuch as they are born again in Christ. In fact, the primary story of the Bible is the story of the Fall of humanity into death through Adam and the regeneration or resurrection of humanity into new life through Christ.

Christ is the firstborn of the reborn. The natural person of Jesus is fused with the supernatural Person of the Holy Spirit. When

> "Jesus also had been baptized and was praying, the heavens were opened, and the Holy Spirit descended on him in bodily form, like a dove; and a voice came from heaven, 'You are my beloved Son; with you I am well pleased'" (Luke 3:22).

Thus, Paul's contrast between the first Adam and the last Adam is a contrast between the natural and the supernatural, between generation and regeneration, between the wisdom of the world and the wisdom of God (1 Corinthians 1:20-21). This contrast is the central point of Paul's first letter to the Corinthians.

The KJV contrasts a "living soul" with a "quickening spirit." Within this contrast is the difference between "living" and "life-giving" and between "being" (soul) and "spirit." Rather than getting distracted by the many subtleties of the Greek, let me simply say again that all of these contrasts point to the difference between natural and supernatural, between generation and regeneration, between the wisdom of the world and the wisdom of Christ.

DEGENERATION/REGENERATION

Paul went on in verse 6 to tell us that while Christ was first in eminence, Adam was first in history. It is critically important that Adam was first in history because historical movement from Adam to Christ is a function of regeneration in or through Christ, while historical movement from Christ to Adam would be a function of degeneration. It is significant that history moves toward Christ or into Christ, not away from Him. In Christ is the hope of regeneration, restoration, and wholeness, and that hope is the engine of history. History is powered by hope in Jesus Christ. If history flowed in the other direction, from Christ to Adam, there would be no hope. History would flow from life in Christ to death in Adam. History would be degenerate rather than regenerate, and all humanity could only wallow in hopelessness. But because history flows from Adam to Christ, from death to resurrection, there is hope—and more than hope, proclaimed Paul, resurrection in Christ is a certainty. First "the natural, and then the spiritual" (v. 6).

Continuing this contrast Paul said, "The first man was from the earth, a man of dust; the second man is from heaven" (v. 47). He was paraphrasing Jesus' own words, "You are from below; I am from above. You are of this world; I am not of this world" (John 8:23). Paul call attention to this because those in Adam are like Adam, and those in Christ are like Christ. "As was the man of dust, so also are those who are of the dust, and as is the man of heaven, so also are those who are of heaven" (v. 48). Humanity is divided into two groups: those in Adam and those in Christ, the saved and the lost, the generate and the regenerate, Israel and the Gentiles, the church and the not-church.

The differences between these two groups of people are historic, as well as cultural. These differences run through history and are found in every nation and every people group. And this is why the gospel of Jesus Christ has been sent to every nation. Jesus insisted, "And this gospel of the kingdom will be proclaimed throughout the whole world as a testimony to all nations, and then the end will come" (Matthew 24:14).

Paul knew that "the Scripture, foreseeing that God would justify the Gentiles by faith, preached the gospel beforehand to Abraham, saying, 'In you shall all the nations be blessed'" (Galatians 3:8). Paul drove the point home, "I tell you this, brothers: flesh and blood cannot inherit the kingdom of God, nor does the perishable inherit the imperishable" (v. 50).

Flesh (*sarx*) and blood (*aima*) can also be translated as body and blood. The Greek word Paul used for flesh here is *sarx*, which means that he is presenting the *sarx*/*sōma* contrast here. Again, that contrast is about the definition and use of the word *body*. Which definition of body was Paul using? His use of *sarx* here means that he was talking about more than the definition that pertains to our natural, individual bodies of flesh and blood —*sarx* cannot inherit the kingdom. Flesh and blood bodies are not what Paul has in mind. The point of this verse is to expand our understanding and use of the word *body*. Paul was talking about what will inherit the kingdom, what kind of body will inherit the kingdom of God, not simply in heaven, but on earth—and he was not merely talking about individual bodies of flesh. Of course we cannot live without bodies of flesh. But there is more to our bodies than flesh.

That which is perishable—flesh—cannot inherit the kingdom, but only that which is imperishable. As the KJV reads, "neither doth corruption inherit incorruption" (v. 50). The people of God, those who, from every nation, will inherit the kingdom "on earth as it is in heaven"

(Matthew 6:10) must be above corruption. The Greek Lexicon says the word *corruption* is used in the New Testament in an ethical sense and indicates moral decay. Again, Paul was not talking about *sarx* alone—flesh. He was not talking about growing old, getting sick, and dying. He was not talking about the decay of the flesh, but about the decay of culture and morality. And remember that the definition of morality is concerned with the distinction between good and evil, right and wrong, and focuses on behavior.

ONE WAY STREET

And yet we know that people are not saved by being good, we are saved by grace through faith in Christ (Romans 5:2, Ephesians 2:8). Morality does not lead to heaven or salvation. But salvation does lead to both morality and heaven. Trying to be moral in the flesh (*sarx*) according to the law, even God's law, leads only to death. Paul wrote to the Romans (7:10), "The very commandment that promised life proved to be death to me."

It proved to be death prior to his regeneration because prior to that the only life he knew was *sarx* life, life in the flesh. And life in the flesh cannot escape life in the flesh. Life in the flesh is bound by life in the flesh. Life in the flesh only begets more life in the flesh. Kind produces kind according to its likeness (Genesis 1:25).

But Christ, having been personally begotten by the Father, is of a different order. Christ is another kind altogether. Christ has two natures—natural and supernatural, *sarx* and *sōma*. In Christ our *sarx* is superseded by Christ's *sōma*. "Behold," said Paul, "I tell you a mystery." *Sōma* trumps *sarx*.

"We shall not all sleep, but we shall all be changed" (v. 51). The Greek word translated *sleep* (*koimaō*) usually means sleep, but can sometimes refer to death. The most significant use of this word is found in 1 Corinthians 11:29-30, where Paul wrote,

> "For anyone who eats and drinks without discerning the body eats and drinks judgment on himself. That is why many of you are weak and ill, and some have died."

Most translations read *sleep*. Were they dead or just asleep?

UNRESPONSIVE

I suspect that the word indicates a loss of consciousness, and that is why it sometimes means death and sometimes sleep. Sometimes you don't know if a person is dead or asleep until he wakes up, or doesn't. The thing that the dead and the sleeping have in common is a lack of responsiveness to their actual, immediate surroundings. Substituting "unresponsive" provides some illumination. Speaking of improper management of the body of Christ, Paul said, "That is why many of you are weak and ill, and some are *unresponsive*." And here he said, "We shall not all be *unresponsive*, but we shall all be changed (*allassō*)" (v. 51). *Allassō* means to change, sometimes by exchanging one thing for another, sometimes by transformation. Our *sarx* will be exchanged for Christ's *sōma*, our body for His body, or our bodies into His body.

First His body (*sarx*) was offered as a propitiation on the cross for our sin and in place of our bodies (*sarx*), and some day—suddenly, in the twinkling of an eye—our bodies (*sarx*) will be changed into His body (*sōma*). Our many will become His one. Some day. How long will it take? Only a "moment (*atomos*), in the twinkling of an eye, at the last trumpet" (v. 52).

How long is a moment? The Greek (*atomos*) literally means uncut and, by implication, indivisible. In terms of time it suggests instantaneous. The time between the beginning of a moment and the end of the moment cannot be measured. It is not very small, but is without measure. This kind of moment is immeasurable. It can't be measured because there is nothing to measure. The beginning of a moment and the end of the moment are identical in terms of time.

The "twinkling (*rhipē*) of an eye" is the amount of time it takes to look from one object to another. Our eyes usually dart from one object to another with a jerking motion. A jerk or dart from one object to another is a twinkling.

And when or what is the "last trumpet?" Paul probably had Jesus' Olivet Discourse in mind, where Jesus said that God "will send out his angels with a loud trumpet call, and they will gather his elect from the four winds, from one end of heaven to the other" (Matthew 24:31).

The last trumpet is an allusion to the end or culmination of history, when Christ returns to gather His people and present them to God.

JUST A MOMENT!

Putting it all together, we see that Paul was saying that this change from *sarx* to *sōma* would be completed at the end of history and it would be instantaneous. Is this the moment when Christians get beamed into heaven? Not at all. There is no such moment. Things don't work that way. That is not what Paul has been talking about. I'm not denying the reality of heaven. I'm defending the reality of heaven against the powers and principalities that want to make heaven a function of the imagination.

Is this the moment of rapture? Possibly. But it is not the kind of rapture that has been popularized in contemporary dispensationalism. It is not an escape from reality or an escape from tribulation. Rather, it is the transformation of reality, the transformation of our bodies into Christ's body (Romans 12:5; 1 Corinthians 10:16, 12:12, 12:27) *through* tribulation. Christian's will not escape tribulation, we will overcome it in Christ. Jesus said, "I have spoken these things to you so that you might have peace in Me. In the world you shall have tribulation...."

Did you hear it? We *shall have tribulation*, "but be of good cheer. I have overcome the world" (John 16:33). The apostles taught "that through much tribulation we must enter into the kingdom of God" (Act 14:22). Paul wrote to the Romans, "Who shall separate us from the love of Christ? Shall tribulation, or distress, or persecution, or famine, or nakedness, or peril, or sword?" (Romans 8:35). Tribulation *will* come to God's people, but it will *not* keep us from our divine appointment with Christ.

The point is that tribulation is not the last word. Christ is the last Word, the last Adam. In Christ our tribulation is insignificant. It is not that God will rapture Christians out of the world. Rather, Christ is coming *into* the world, and Christians will be caught up in unity with Christ in the world without regard to the tribulations of the world because the tribulations of the world are part of our regeneration and resurrection in Christ—with Christ, in the world.

47. DEATH

For this perishable body must put on the imperishable, and this mortal body must put on immortality. When the perishable puts on the imperishable, and the mortal puts on immortality, then shall come to pass the saying that is written: "Death is swallowed up in victory. O death, where is your victory? O death, where is your sting?" The sting of death is sin, and the power of sin is the law. But thanks be to God, who gives us the victory through our Lord Jesus Christ. Therefore, my beloved brothers, be steadfast, immovable, always abounding in the work of the Lord, knowing that in the Lord your labor is not in vain.
—1 Corinthians 15:53-58

What is death? Paul was making a case for the reality of resurrection, and death is not simply a related issue but is central regarding resurrection. Resurrection assumes or requires death as a prerequisite—no death, no resurrection. Death is a major concern of the Bible, Old Testament and New. Death was the central consequence for Adam's sin in the Garden. Jesus' death on the cross—the fix for Adam's sin—is the central theme of the Bible, so it is critical that we establish a definition of what Scripture means by death. As important as this is and as simple as it might seem, it is amazing to note how easy it is for us to assume an overly simplified, one-dimensional understanding of death. But that is not what the Bible does.

In response to the Trinitarian character of God, who created man in His own image, we will now examine and define death from a biblical, Trinitarian perspective by suggesting three elements, aspects, or kinds of death: 1) individual death, 2) corporate death, and 3) spiritual death. Each type of death, in this order, suggests an increase in severity. Individual death is bad, corporate death is worse, and spiritual death is the worst or most ultimate. This understanding of death issues from a Trinitarian understanding of human identity in that our identity as human beings is individual, corporate, and spiritual—all at the same time. Thus, each type of death corresponds to each aspect of our human identity. And by contrast, this examination posits three corresponding forms, aspects, or kinds of life: individual life, corporate life, and spiritual life. These different kinds of deaths presuppose actual life in each of these corresponding areas.

Every human being is a unique individual by definition. An individual is not divisible, by definition. The separate parts of our identities are distinctive, but not divisible. Each part has a unique bodily existence, but no part exists alone, independently. There is an individual body, a corporate body, and a spiritual body. Individual human beings live their own lives, have their own bodies, think their own thoughts, eat their own food, etc. We each exist independently from one another to a degree—not entirely, but to a degree.

In reality, human identity is porous. Our individual identities in these areas overlap with one another, and they overlap from person to person, as well. What does this mean? I am who I am because of who my parents were, and because of my relationships with other people—my wife, my children, my parents, my friends, etc. Other people help to shape us as individuals by their love, their responses, their input. Families tend to share family characteristics, churches tend to share certain foundational beliefs, etc. And these things have a real effect upon each of us. They help to shape us into the people we are. My identify is affected by the people I associate with, as is yours.

INTERDEPENDENCE

To the degree that we are not completely independent from one another, we are also corporate beings. We live in families, communities, and societies, each of which have various bodily characteristics. Groups of people are often referred to as bodies, particularly in the modern corporate world where corporations are considered to be legal entities or juristic persons.[1] And we are spiritual beings, as well.

---

1 The *Corporate Personhood Debate* refers to the controversy (primarily in the United States) over the question of what subset of rights afforded under the law to natural persons should also be afforded to corporations as Juristic persons.

Opponents of "corporate personhood" believe that large corporations as juristic persons have enjoyed certain constitutional rights intended for natural humans as the result of a misinterpretation of an 1886 Supreme Court Case, Santa Clara County v. Southern Pacific Railroad. Opponents claim that certain rights of natural persons, such as the right to political and other non-commercial free speech, are now exercised by corporations to the detriment of the American democratic process as provided under the Constitution. Some opponents point to the recent discovery of correspondence between then Supreme Court Chief Justice Morrison R. Waite, and

There is a spiritual dimension or aspect that informs our sense of self. In Genesis 2:16 we find the first reference to death when God said,

"You may surely eat of every tree of the garden, but of the tree of the knowledge of good and evil you shall not eat, for in the day that you eat of it you shall surely die."

The Hebrew word *die* is repeated here and in Genesis 3:4, where "the serpent said to the woman, 'You will not surely die.'" In both cases the word *surely* has been added as an explanation of the repetition of the word *die*. A more literal translation might be something like, God said "you shall die dead," and the serpent said, "you will not die dead." In some sense a double death is suggested.

The repetition is found again when Abraham lied to Abimelech about Sarah, his wife, being his sister. God spoke to Abimelech in a dream saying,

"Now then, return the man's wife, for he is a prophet, so that he will pray for you, and you shall live. But if you do not return her, know that you shall surely die, you, and all who are yours" (Genesis 20:7).

The clarification provided here adds an explanation that the repetition of the Hebrew word means that this particular type of double death includes both individual identity and corporate identity: "you, and all who are yours," you and your family, you and your group. This type of death, a much more serious kind of death, is what I call corporate death. This type of death can be understood as genocide or the death (extinction) of a group, kind, or type.

The repetition of the word is used several times in Exodus and Leviticus and elsewhere, and it appears that its biblical usage does not always suggest corporate genocide. There is another spiritual meaning of

court reporter J.C. Bancroft Davis as proof of a conspiracy among the railroad corporations to intentionally create a misrepresentation of that decision for the benefit of the railroads. ...

Proponents of corporate personhood believe that corporations, as representatives of their shareholders, were intended by the founders and framers to enjoy many, if not all, of the same rights as natural persons, for example, the right against self-incrimination, right to privacy and the right to lobby the government. Some proponents believe that these rights should continue to be extended to corporations regardless of any possible flawed interpretation of the Santa Clara Co. v. So. Pac. Railroad case. – from http://en.wikipedia.org/wiki/Corporate_personhood_debate This issue is cited here to indicate the substantive reality of corporate entities and the real impact they have on us and our world.

"second death" that we will mention later. For now we will take God's meaning to be that the consequence of sin is both individual and corporate death, or the death of a type through the extinction of a typological group of individuals.

TYPOLOGY

The intention here is to invoke biblical typology, in that both Adam and Christ are described as types. The point is that Adam's type would surely die in the sense of Genesis 20:7—"you, and all that is yours"—as a consequence of Adam's sin. Adam and all that were Adam's or all who are in Adam shall surely die. His progeny, his type, would die as a result of his sin. Scripture was speaking about the death or genocide of Adam's race, what I have called corporate death. Adam's sin would be the cause of the genocide of Adam's type. That is the kind of death that resulted from Adam's sin, not his immediate individual death, but the ultimate death of His kind.

Against this backdrop we can now define individual death. In Genesis 2:15 God took Adam and put him into the Garden with orders to dress and keep it. According to Strong's the Hebrew word for Adam can mean either an individual or the species, mankind. In Genesis 2:15-17 it refers to both the individual and the species because it was given when only Adam existed. This was a unique moment in history when Adam was both an individual and the whole of humanity at the same time. As mankind propagated on the earth the difference between individual death and corporate death became more pronounced. As the population increased individuals would die without threatening the existence of humanity as a species or as a particular type or group of people. The more people there are, the less impact an individual death has on corporate death.

Individual death became less serious, less a threat to human existence over time. Individual death has become a natural part of human life in the same way and to the same extent that individual birth has become a natural part of human life. Birth and death are inextricably intertwined, not only as regards individuals but as regards groups, types or corporate existence. The relationship between individual birth and death to corporate humanity is similar to the relationship between, say, the generation and sloughing off of individual cells to the individual body. The death of a cell is not equivalent to the death of the body, nor is the death of an individual human being equivalent to the corporate death of humanity or a type of humanity.[2]

Into this mix God has also poured the Holy Spirit, which provides yet another kind of birth and death. New birth in the Holy Spirit—not the birth of the Holy Spirit in a human being, but the birth of a human being into the Holy Spirit—is called regeneration or being born again (John 3:3, etc.). But before people can be born again, they must die. Paul taught the Romans,

> "Do you not know that all of us who have been baptized into Christ Jesus were baptized into his death? We were buried therefore with him by baptism into death, in order that, just as Christ was raised from the dead by the glory of the Father, we too might walk in newness of life" (Romans 6:3-4).

The death of the "old man" (Romans 6:6) is required for the birth of the new man. Of course, spiritual death began with Adam's sin (Romans 5:12), which has infected all people since, and which means that with each individual born physically, the process of spiritual death begins again in that person. In addition to this, the Book of Revelation also speaks of a spiritual or "second death" that awaits those who reject Christ when the kingdom comes in its full glory. (Revelation 2:11, 20:6, 20:14, 21:8). The point is that spiritual birth and spiritual death are real.

THREE ASPECTS

Human identity (individuality, personality, character) is an amalgamation or coalescence of these three elements: individual existence, corporate existence, and spiritual existence. These are the elements of human life and of human death, and all three must be accounted for in Scripture and in any serious understanding of human existence. We are each and all unique individuals, with unique personalities, unique characters, and unique histories, and yet no one individual can exist by him- or herself for very long. An individual human being is not a viable or sustainable entity. Consequently, human existence is always necessarily corporate (or social). We need others because an individual human being cannot survive very long alone. Not only is the environment too hostile, but we

---

2   This does not denigrate the importance of individuals, nor trivialize individual death. It is simply an attempt to suggest the relationship between individuals and humanity with regard to individual death.

were not designed to exist as individuals. We were designed to exist in community, in families and groups—corporately.

In addition, and in an analogous way, we need the Holy Spirit in order to be whole and complete. The Holy Spirit is a necessary ingredient, perhaps the single most necessary ingredient, of human wholeness. Human unity and human holiness are similarly dependent upon the Holy Spirit. The fullness (or wholeness or unity) of human life requires a robust existence in each and all of these areas, aspects, or domains: individuality, corporality, and spirituality. This is the central composition of our Trinitarian character in the same way that it is the central composition of God's Trinitarian character. God exists in three Persons or three unified but distinct bodies: Father, Son, and Holy Spirit—corporate, individual, and spiritual—as do human beings. I am an individual body, I participate in a corporate body, and I am "caught up" (harpazō—2 Corinthians 12:2-4, 1 Thessalonians 4:17, Revelation 12:5) in a spiritual body through regeneration, as are you and all of God's people.

This is not an argument for one person from three different perspectives or in three different modes. Rather, it is an argument for three different persons, three different and unique bodies whose particular identities and existences overlap one another (somehow). The actual composition of bodily parts is different—unique—for each of these different persons.

And inasmuch as human existence unfolds in each of these areas, so each area is marked by a kind or type of birth and death—a birth and death regarding individuality, a birth and death regarding corporality, and a birth and death regarding spirituality. It is into this complex Trinitarian reality, the reality of human existence, that Paul speaks of death. Listen again to verse 53, "For this corruptible must put on incorruption, and this mortal must put on immortality" (LITV).

The word body is not in the Greek. It is assumed, and rightly so. But which body is meant—individual body, corporate body, or spiritual body. All are real, all are important, all are essential—and all are interrelated (amalgamated or coalesced). They are one in three, and three in one, all at the same time. What is corruptible must put on incorruption. Corruptibility must be clothed in incorruptibility. What is mortal must be clothed in immortality. Mortality must be robed or vested in immortality.

Note that the one exists inside of the other, corruptibility inside of incorruptibility, mortality inside of immortality in such a way that the incorruptibility dominates (or supersedes) the corruptibility, the immortality supersedes (or dominates) the mortality. Paul was speaking of an investiture.[3] Paul was saying here that the office is more important than the man, that the role is more important than the individual. We know this to be true of the nation and of the church. For instance, the office of the President is more important than the particular person who serves in that office. And the office of the pastor is more important than any particular pastor.

Victory

"When the perishable puts on the imperishable, and the mortal puts on immortality, then shall come to pass the saying that is written: 'Death is swallowed up in victory'" (v. 54).

What death? What victory? Paul did not single out any particular type of death, and so we must assume that he means all of the various types of death that have been described. All types of death are swallowed up (consumed and/or destroyed) by victory. He asks, Where is the victory of death? And concludes that there is none. Death is not victory. Death is defeat. There is no successful conclusion or resolution in death. Death has no victory!

If there is no victory in death, then where is death's sting, death's pain? If death is not victorious, and there is a victory over death, then there is no sting or pain in death's defeat. Rather, the defeat of death is a joy, an exultation, and a celebration. Death is robbed of its sting by what victoriously reigns over it. The sting of death is converted into the joy of victory. What victory?

"But thanks be to God, who gives us the victory through our Lord Jesus Christ" (v. 57). Christ supplies the victory. Christ is the victory! That is to say that Christ's resurrection provides the victory, that Christ's resurrection is the victory over death. This is the grand conclusion of Paul's multifaceted argument(s) for the reality and the ultimate victory of Christ's resurrection. Resurrection is real. It is true and can be trusted. Because Christ rose from the dead, death itself is defeated.

There's more! Here also is the resolution of the question about what Paul meant by the "body of Christ." Paul's argument about the reality of resurrection is also his argument about the nature and character of the

---

3   *Investiture*: The ceremonial act of clothing someone in the insignia of an office; the formal promotion of a person to an office or rank.

body of Christ, and the participation of the saints in the body of Christ. The resurrection of the Person of Jesus Christ is also proof of the existence of the body of Christ. And the existence of the body of Christ is proof of the unity of the body of Christ (1 Corinthians 12:12-14) because a body requires a degree of unity and cooperation among its various parts, by definition.

> "For just as the body is one and has many members, and all the members of the body, though many, are one body, so it is with Christ" (1 Corinthians 12:12).

> "The cup of blessing that we bless, is it not a participation in the blood of Christ? The bread that we break, is it not a participation in the body of Christ?" (1 Corinthians 10:16).

> "Now you are the body of Christ and individually members of it" (1 Corinthians 12:27).

In Christ, and only in Christ (or in Christ only) can the fullness of bodily life as a human being be lived in its fullness, its wholeness and holiness. Only in Christ is our unique individuality real, genuine, and complete. Only in Christ is our individuality ultimately meaningful. And conversely, only in Christ is unity real. Only in Christ is corporate unity, the community of humanity in the fullness of its various aspects, real in bodily form. Only in Christ's resurrection and the regeneration of the saints does the reality of the body of Christ take form on earth as it is in heaven. The church exists at the intersection of Christ's resurrection and the regeneration of the saints, and it exists in this world and yet beyond this world, in this life and yet beyond the pale of death.

48. Letting Go

Now concerning the collection for the saints: as I directed the churches of Galatia, so you also are to do. On the first day of every week, each of you is to put something aside and store it up, as he may prosper, so that there will be no collecting when I come. And when I arrive, I will send those whom you accredit by letter to carry your gift to Jerusalem. If it seems advisable that I should go also, they will accompany me. I will visit you after passing through Macedonia, for I intend to pass through Macedonia, and perhaps I will stay with you or even spend the winter, so that you may help me on my journey, wherever I go. For I do not want to see you now just in passing. I hope to spend some time with you, if the Lord permits. But I will stay in Ephesus until Pentecost, for a wide door for effective work has opened to me, and there are many adversaries.

—1 Corinthians 16:1-9

Paul established that the resurrection of Christ is real and that from Christ's resurrection the Holy Spirit provides the regeneration of God's people. Together then, life and Christian service in the Spirit are powered by God Himself and cannot fail. Thus, Paul calls us to be "steadfast, immovable, always abounding in the work of the Lord, knowing that in the Lord your labor is not in vain" (1 Corinthians 15:58). The work of the Lord cannot fail to be fruitful. It does not always appear to be fruitful from a human perspective, but is fruitful in that the Holy Spirit always moves relentlessly forward to accomplish His purposes, sometimes with giant steps, sometimes with baby steps, sometimes with two steps forward and one step back.

Just as Christ's death on the cross did not appear to many people at that time to be a decisive victory over the enemies of God, so humble Christian service does not always look and feel like success—or even progress—in the ways that success or progress are measured by the world. Following Christ's death, the disciples themselves believed that Christ had been defeated because He had died on the cross. They thought that that was it, that it was over, that the movement was dead because of the death of its leader. In defeat, some of the disciples withdrew into the Upper Room, others went home.

A woman engaged in the humble task of preparing the dead body of Christ for burial failed to find the body of Christ in the tomb where He had been laid. At the tomb she had an odd encounter with some body, and ran to the gathered assembly of disciples to tell them about her encounter. It is not insignificant that she, who had been engaged in humble service to the body of Christ, did not find the body of Christ in the grave, but encountered an angel (Matthew 28:2), or a young man (Mark 16:5) or two men (Luke 24:4) or found nothing but folded burial clothes (John 20:5). Each of the gospel writers reported different stories about the encounter with the Risen Christ at the tomb. And because of these differences, we must not succumb to the temptation to think that one or more of these stories is mistaken. Rather, each one is true, though different. Each one has something important to teach us about the body of Christ. And taken together they provide a fuller understanding of the Risen Christ.

FAILURE

Later, two defeated disciples were returning home on the road to Emmaus when the resurrected Lord appeared in bodily form to show them that Christ's death had not been a defeat, but was in fact the very fulcrum of history itself. The Risen Lord walked with them and talked with them and explained how on the fulcrum of Christ's death God Himself had leveraged history to guarantee the success of His Son in the accomplishment of the salvation of the world. What appeared to be the defeat of Christ's cause—His death on the cross—was in reality the springboard of His resurrection and the fountain of salvation for all time. Who'd a thunk it!

Those who had been discouraged and disillusioned by Christ's death had to be further disillusioned of those worldly values and beliefs that blinded them to the greater reality of Christ's resurrection. They could not see the reality of Christ's resurrection until they had been shown by the Lord Himself through the Scriptures how Jesus had fulfilled the prophecies about the propitiation for the sins of His people (Hebrews 2:17). Once the disciples were sufficiently disillusioned of those worldly values and beliefs that kept them from seeing the reality of Christ's resurrection, their discouragement was turned into encouragement as the wisdom of Christ defeated the wisdom of the world, as Christ's resurrection overshadowed His death on the cross.

In chapter sixteen Paul turned to some practical concerns for the ministry and unity of the church as the body of Christ. Paul had been teaching about the unity of the churches for several chapters, and here shows how that unity can be expressed. The Christians in Jerusalem were in need. The persecution of Christians that Paul had been involved in as a Pharisee did not stop with Paul's conversion. Rather, Paul had since become a target of that persecution, and his effectiveness in ministry increased the pressures of persecution. Persecuted people always suffer economic loss as they are increasingly marginalized from society. Food and other shortages increased as the tension between Rome and Jerusalem grew more inflamed. That tension would lead to the destruction of Jerusalem in A.D. 70, but that was still a few years out.

PERSECUTION

For now marginalization and persecution of Christians increased, and the Jerusalem Christians increasingly needed help—food and money. It was an ongoing situation, increasing in severity from year to year, so Paul encouraged Christians everywhere to contribute on a regular basis toward the growing needs of the Jerusalem church. Paul instructed the churches as the body of Christ to help one another as an expression of unity. Paul asked the Corinthians, as he had asked the Galatians and others, to take up a collection on the first day of each week. He did not prescribe any amount to give, nor a percentage, but rather he asked each church and each Christian to give on the basis of their prosperity, to give what they could without putting themselves at risk. Those who prospered much could give much and those who prospered little could give little.

In addition, Paul did not want them to take up a collection while he was with them. He didn't want to give the impression that they were giving the collection to him or that it was for him. Rather, he wanted it to be clear that the collection was for their sister church in Jerusalem. Nor did he want the Jerusalem Christians to think that what they would receive was from him, from Paul. Rather, he wanted the churches to care for one another. Paul insisted that the church at Corinth send its own gifts with its own emissaries. Paul did not want to be in charge, but only to encourage mutual care and support among Christ's churches.

Paul then shared his itinerary and some of the details of his plans in the next few verses. Paul most likely wrote this letter to the Corinthians from Ephesus. Before that he had been in Galatia, and when he left Ephesus he planned to go through Macedonia on the way to Corinth. He hoped to spend an extended time with the Corinthians, maybe even stay the winter. He did not want to cut short his visit with them. But he also wanted to mingle with and preach to the crowds that would be traveling during Pentecost. The fact that there would be crowds of people traveling during Pentecost provided an opportunity for Christian ministry that he did not want to miss. There was so much to do in Jerusalem.

There was much work to do at Corinth, as well. The Corinthian church had gotten off the mark, and much of what he had already written in this letter was given to help straighten them out. Their problems were many and deep seated. He needed to give them more than written instructions, he needed to be there with them. They needed personal help, not just written instructions. So, Paul reassured them that he would visit them as soon as possible and would stay with them as long as possible.

How could Paul be so confident about what he was teaching and doing? What made Paul so sure?

HELP

He knew that he could help them because he knew what he was doing, or rather, he knew what God was doing through Him. The more he wrote and talked to people about the Lord, the more he was convinced himself about the truth of Jesus' resurrection and of the regeneration of the saints. He didn't just talk about Jesus, He embodied the Gospel. He was Christ's chief ambassador. He was aware that the Lord had given him crucial insight about Jesus Christ and about how Christ's churches were to function. In addition, the Lord blessed Paul with a particularly effective ministry. He knew that the Gospel of Jesus Christ was not simply an argument, not mere words. Rather, the Gospel was an embodiment, and enfleshment of the values and virtues of Jesus Christ, an incarnation of Christ's Spirit, the Holy Spirit. The Gospel was not the dead letter he was writing, but the living Word, not a philosophical argument, but an embracing love. It was of the mind and of the heart, of the body and of the Spirit.

He mentioned that "a wide door for effective work ha(d) opened" (v. 9) to him. People everywhere were hungry for the gospel and ready to receive the Word of God. Indeed, there has never been a more effective minister of the gospel of Jesus Christ than Paul.

It is also instructive to note that Paul not only said that "a wide door for effective work has opened" but that "there are many adversaries" (v. 9), as well. Indeed, the more effective a ministry becomes, the more adversaries arise to oppose it. Christian ministry is not easy. The truth is that the Gospel of Jesus Christ is hated by those who love the flesh. Those who prefer the wisdom of the world and the ways of the world will despise the wisdom and ways of Christ. This has been Paul's primary message in this letter to the Corinthians from the beginning. Paul has been hammering on this since chapter one.

He had to hammer on it because it is a hard lesson to receive. We don't want to hear it because hearing it requires our death. As such, this insight is ignored by most of the contemporary Evangelical Christians, who think that unchurched people will simply rush to the head of the line to get all the good things that Jesus has in store for His people.

Most Christians are convinced that Jesus simply wants to make us brighter, better, smarter, stronger, prettier, richer, healthier—whatever, just fill in the blank. It's not that Jesus doesn't want such things for His people—I'm not saying that He doesn't. Such things are fine. But compared to the salvation that Jesus provides those things are secondary. They are not unimportant, but neither are they the main thing. It's not that they are insignificant, but that they are secondary to the main thing. The main thing is new life in Christ—Christ's resurrection and our regeneration. Apart from regeneration in Christ these secondary things are only accouterments on the road to hell. Apart from new life in Christ they are distractions because they tend to keep our attention on ourselves. To focus our attention on these secondary things is to take attention off the main thing—the Gospel of Jesus Christ. And to lose the main thing is to lose Christ and His salvation.

STUMBLE

The characteristics of that new life in Christ are based upon God's values, not ours. The stumbling stone of the Gospel is that the doorway to new life in Christ is personal sacrifice—death. That's the rub. No one wants to give up their hopes and dreams. No one wants to die, whether that means actual bodily death or some kind of personal sacrificial death related to baptism, or the death of one's social (corporate) life as friends are lost because they will not abide with Christ. Life in Christ is not about the fulfillment of our personal hopes and dreams. It's about the fulfillment of God's promises—God's desires, not ours. Life in Christ begins with self-sacrifice, self-surrender. Death in Christ through baptism means the end of self-concern. It means that we no longer put our own concerns first.

God does not want us to be brighter, better, smarter, stronger, prettier, richer, healthier sinners. He wants us to be brighter, better, smarter, stronger, prettier, richer, healthier saints. The Gospel is about the conversion from sinner to saint, about the confession and forgiveness that leads from death to new life. Not that all sin can be eliminated in this life, not that that Scripture teaches a utopian, sin-free life in this world. It doesn't. Sin will dog us all our days. Nonetheless, God intends on reducing sin in this world and eliminating it in the next.

Sinners do not *want* to let go of their sin. In fact, they *can't* let go of it because they identify it as the very essence of their lives. That's the step that sinners don't want to take, that sinner's can't take because to do so is their undoing. It is their death. No sane person will readily embrace his own death. Consequently, the death that leads to new life in Christ is something that sinners cannot—will not—do for themselves. This is where God takes the initiative, the first step, by slaying the sinner through the power and presence of the Holy Spirit, who simultaneously brings the slain sinner to new life in Christ. Just as Christ's resurrection was the result of His death on the cross, so our regeneration is the result of our death through baptism.

People don't want to give up their sins. They like them. They value them. So, Paul encountered adversaries of the Gospel in the churches and out. People didn't like what Paul had to say. They opposed him, not everyone of course. Everywhere that Paul preached and taught, some people received the Gospel and some rejected it. Some who rejected it earlier received it later, and some who received it earlier rejected it later. Some rejected it enthusiastically, some quietly. Others received it enthusiastically, others quietly. But no one was untouched. Indeed, because all authority has been given to Jesus Christ, everyone must either accept or reject the authority of Christ.

The adversaries of the Gospel are not willing to let go of their sins, their lives, not willing to give themselves up to Christ. They oppose the gospel by holding on to their own concerns, their own hopes and dreams for themselves. The desire for self-fulfillment stands in opposition to Jesus Christ. What we want for ourselves is, by definition, selfish and self-centered. Self is the primary actor in the drama of self-fulfillment. In contrast, Christ is the primary actor in a life of service through self-sacrifice.

Living a life of self-sacrificial service to Jesus Christ is what baptism and church membership are all about. In baptism we die with Christ, die to our selves, and we then share in the resurrection of Christ through regeneration. In Christ we die, and through Christ we live. Praise be to Jesus Christ!

49. FOR THE LOVE OF CHRIST

When Timothy comes, see that you put him at ease among you, for he is doing the work of the Lord, as I am. So let no one despise him. Help him on his way in peace, that he may return to me, for I am expecting him with the brothers. Now concerning our brother Apollos, I strongly urged him to visit you with the other brothers, but it was not at all his will to come now. He will come when he has opportunity. Be watchful, stand firm in the faith, act like men, be strong. Let all that you do be done in love.   —1 Corinthians 16:10-14

Paul sent Timothy to Corinth. Think about that for a moment. Timothy was one of Paul's converts. Paul had referred to Timothy earlier in this letter: "That is why I sent you Timothy, my beloved and faithful child in the Lord, to remind you of my ways in Christ, as I teach them everywhere in every church" (1 Corinthians 4:17).

Timothy was a young man whom Paul had been training for ministry. Some of the time that Timothy spent in Corinth he was with Paul, and some of the time Paul was not there. In verse 10 Paul alluded to a time when Timothy would be in Corinth without Paul.

Think about the horrendous condition of the Corinthian church that Paul has been addressing, and then think about Timothy, a young convert in training for ministry. Think about the fact that Paul sent Timothy to Corinth in spite of the fact that Timothy was a minister in training. The point is that Paul did not give Timothy an easy assignment, but threw him into the heat of battle, in a church fraught with conflict and difficulty.

How could Paul do that to Timothy? Wouldn't sending a trainee into a conflicted situation jeopardize both the church and the student? We might think so, but Paul didn't. Paul trusted Timothy to teach the same gospel that Paul taught. Paul knew that the power of God is in the gospel of Jesus Christ, and that the power of God would protect both Timothy and the church. Timothy had the gospel right, and that meant that the power of God would accompany Timothy's teaching and preaching to bring about the consequences that God intended for both Timothy and for the Corinthian Church.

But note also that Paul instructed the church, those who would receive his letter, to put Timothy "at ease among you" (v. 10), or to be "without fear" (KJV—*aphobōs*) regarding the work for the Lord that he was doing in their midst. This instruction was not given to Timothy, but to the church. How could this conflicted, bickering, and unfaithful church put Timothy at ease or take away his fear? If Timothy was to go into *that* church and preach what Paul had been preaching, how could that result in a situation of "ease" for Timothy? How could Timothy get these conflicting parties into a condition of unity which must be the basis of peace? Was Paul asking the Corinthian church to make Timothy's internship easy? And if so, how could they do that?

FEARLESS PREACHING

No. These questions are barking up the wrong tree. This was not what Paul was saying. Rather, it seems more likely that Paul was asking the Corinthians to help Timothy teach and preach the gospel fearlessly. He was asking them not to add to Timothy's hesitation to teach and preach the gospel that brings people face to face with their own fears, the gospel that insists that people face their own fear of death by trusting Jesus in the face of that fear.

The gospel does not alleviate fear, but intensifies it by bringing sinners face to face with the very thing they fear the most—God Himself. Of course the only alleviation of that fear is the grace and mercy of Jesus Christ who alone has propitiated God's wrath by His death on the cross, and who has brokered the exchange of His death in our stead for His life in our stead. He gave up the body of Jesus in order to inhabit the body of Christ—the church.

And how could the Corinthians face that fear? By trusting that Timothy's message was genuinely from God, by trusting that Timothy's teaching and preaching were true to the gospel. So, Paul assured them that Timothy was "doing the work of the Lord, as" (v. 10) Paul was. Paul's message to them was not to doubt Timothy, but to trust him.

There are a couple of very good lessons about ministry here. First, like Paul, we need to trust those who are young in the ministry with significant assignments. We are not to send them into the battlefront without training or testing, but when they have been trained and tested, we should send them out with confidence. Again, our confidence is not in them, but in Christ. Inasmuch as they or we trust the biblical message of the gospel, though it offend us and those who hear it, inasmuch as we deliver Christ's message accurately, He will use that message to identify and sanctify His people.

God's Word will accomplish God's purposes. So, said Paul, give Timothy the freedom to preach the truth in love without fear. "Let no one despise him" (v.11). It is commonly understood that people would be tempted to despise Timothy because of his youth, but that is only part of the story. People don't despise young people because they are young, but because of what they say and do, because they too often have an uppity attitude. People despise those who make them feel inferior, those who criticize and/or belittle them. People would tend to despise Timothy because he was young in the flesh but mature in the Spirit. They would confuse Timothy's maturity and clarity in the Spirit as personal criticism and belittlement. Timothy's spiritual maturity would make others feel inferior, not because of anything he did, but because his maturity would reveal their immaturity, because his spiritual clarity would reveal their spiritual confusion by contrast.

Timothy's message would be mature and clear, direct and to the point, like Paul's. That was the model for Timothy's training, so it is safe to assume that Timothy would bear a likeness to the model. Paul was reminding them that the offense of the gospel should not be attributed to Timothy. If they were offended by Timothy's preaching, then it was because Paul had done a good job training him. Not that preachers should try to be offensive, they should not! But by the same token, the gospel well preached will offend the flesh. It's supposed to!

"Help him on his way in peace" (v. 11). That is, receive his message in peace. Don't fight with him, don't struggle against him. Rather, show him how the gospel can be received in peace, in humble submission and repentance. They were not to get mad at him and chase him away, but honor him with the same respect that you would honor Paul, and then send him on his way because, while his is ministering among you in Corinth, that is not his only place of service. He has other duties to attend to, so don't tie him up with your factious squabbling. Receive him, hear him, honor him, and send him on his way with the assurance that you have heard him and will heed him.

Apollos was another of Christ's assets who was in motion. Paul had spoken of Apollos earlier, and had given Apollos the stamp of his approval. Apollos had been to Corinth before and had baptized some of the Corinthians. So, they knew Apollos. Paul mentioned that he had asked Apollos to go to Corinth, but that for one reason or another Apollos wasn't able to visit with them anytime soon, but he would visit them when he had opportunity. These are various details regarding different personal relationships that are commonly included in letters. Details like this have some historical importance, but they don't usually have much teaching benefit, other than to corroborate the authenticity of the letter.

Grow Up!

Verses 13-14 provide a short summary of the main points of Paul's letter: "Be watchful, stand firm in the faith, act like men, be strong. Let all that you do be done in love." The admonition to be watchful begs the question, be watchful for what? Was Paul calling them to simply be more attentive in life in a general way, as if to arouse themselves from sleepiness? Or did Paul have some particular thing in mind that required additional vigilance? If we take the admonition to be a summary caution, then we can surmise that Paul wanted them to be more attentive to the main issues he addressed in this letter, namely the differences between the wisdom of God and the foolishness of the world. Indeed, Paul thought that the Corinthians had been blindsided by the foolishness of the world that had clothed itself in the various respectabilities of popularity, intellectuality, and practicality.

They needed to understand that the gospel of Jesus Christ was not open and available for syncretism with Greek philosophy or with the ever-changing attitudes of any particular historical moment. Like Yahweh of the Old Testament, Jesus Christ is a jealous God who requires exclusive devotion and loyalty. Jesus Christ shares His authority in a representative way with the various authorities of family, church, and state. But He does not share His authority with other gods, traditions, or worldviews. Just as He has called us to be a one-God people, He has committed Himself to being a one-people God—always keeping in mind that the one-God of Scripture is Trinitarian, three-in-one.

Thus, Paul's admonition to be watchful can be understood as if Paul had said to be faithful. And to affirm that faithfulness is a necessary element of watchfulness, Paul added by way of repetition that the Corinthians should also "stand firm in the faith" (v. 13). Here the call for stability is added to the admonition to be watchful, which adds the quality of endurance. The call to stand at all is the call to acknowledge Jesus Christ as

Lord and Savior. And the call to stand firm is the call to always remain in that acknowledgment in the midst of life's flux. Nothing should ever intermix with or dilute the Lordship of Jesus Christ.

SYNCRETISM

And, of course, syncretism is the temptation of our sinful intellect, our bent toward worldly wisdom and the misguided passion that makes our drive for social acceptance more important than our desire to please God. The passion for religious syncretism is an expression of human intelligence and creativity. It does, in fact, take great intelligence and creativity to devise so many different ways to try to harmonize utterly disparate facts. This is the bane of liberalism which blossoms in a thousand different ways in its perennial and futile effort to reconcile the wisdom of the world with the wisdom of God.

In the face of this passionate and worldly desire Paul calls us to stand firm in the faith—not simply in our personal expression of faith, nor in our particular understanding of the faith, but in our loyalty and allegiance to Jesus Christ as Lord and Savior of the world. We are not saved by our own faithfulness, which waxes and wanes in fickle commitment in the face of the vicissitudes of life. Rather, we are saved by Jesus Christ who stands firm in the face of death—and beyond. In Christ, and in Christ alone, is the truth of God and the truth of the world in which we live, a world created by the only Triune God as a reflection of His glory. We are called to stand fast and firm in the Triunity of God in Jesus Christ, despite the complexities and mysteries enfolded into the covenantal relationships within the Godhead and which are reflected into His creation. In spite of all of this, Paul's admonition to stand firm in the faith is a simple call to fidelity to Jesus Christ as found in Scripture.

Paul was tired of their childish immaturity, and called the Corinthians to "act like men" (v. 13), or in the KJV, "quit ye like men." This phrase is the translation of one word in the Greek (andrizomai). It is the conjugation in the middle voice of the root word (aner) which simply indicates an adult male. In the contemporary vernacular we might translate it, "Man up!" or "Grow up!"

VIRTUE

There is nothing more out of style in the contemporary world than virtue. The concept of virtue is so neglected that not one in a thousand people even knows what it means. At its root virtue is doing what is right and avoiding what is wrong. It is action and activity that are based upon a particular set of values. It requires knowing the difference between right and wrong.

The Latin root of the word *virtue* is *vir* and means man. This root word is also associated with the word *virile*, which means manly and often implies reproduction, and the biblical values related to reproduction, values associated with truth, honor, marriage, family, etc. To be virtuous is to exhibit strength, courage, excellence, and good judgment—judgment that knows what is good, what is right, and what is not. It requires knowing the difference between right and wrong.

Virtue is the lost art of human maturity. Contemporary culture has gone out of its way to blur the difference between good and evil, right and wrong, particularly contemporary media (TV, movies, radio, print, Internet). What is popular today would be considered to be trashy, in poor taste, and essentially evil during any previous era of history. But people don't see it because they are blinded by the cultural bigotry that believes contemporary culture is superior to all others.

American social values have been turned inside out and upside down during the last 300 years, with significant acceleration during the last 50. The loss and recovery of virtue (human maturity) is decidedly a religious matter in spite of the fact that the enemies of virtue unanimously agree that it is not.

The central issue pertaining to virtue is knowing right from wrong. Christianity teaches that right and wrong cannot be understood apart from the Christ of Scripture. The determination of right and wrong apart from faith in Christ and adherence to Scripture can only be done by subjecting God's wisdom to human wisdom, worldly wisdom. Either God informs human beings about right and wrong or human beings judge God's wisdom to be faulty, and put themselves in the place of God regarding this determination. There is no middle ground, no neutral position.

Morality is either godly (biblical) or it is not. Yet, biblical morality is always a matter of growth and development and never a matter of perfect conformity. The essential character of biblical morality is improvement, not excellence. Biblical morality, then, is not a matter of moral excellence (which is beyond human ability), but of moral improvement—regular, ongoing, incremental, concrete, and actual improvement, of increasing conformity to God's biblical standards of morality.

Virtue, then, is moral growth, moral development, moral improvement, moral maturity. It is the reclamation of truth, honesty, and integrity as the values of genuine success, and the repudiation of what mitigates against virtue, and encourages moral immaturity—potty talk and the values of the gutter, dishonesty, deceit, greed, pride, and arrogance—regardless of their packaging or popularity.

Virtue is the blossom of hope for a world of goodness, beauty, truth, justice, and righteousness that is beyond our human ability to bring about —or even to fully envision or understand. It is the work of trusting in the One who has provided the vision (outline or plan) for such a virtuous world, and the only means of its accomplishment—Jesus Christ. This is what Paul was referring to by his use of the word *andrizomai*.

Paul also admonished the Corinthians to "be strong" (v. 13). The Greek word means vigor, strength. Again, it sounds simple, but what does it really mean? Is it like the British dictum to keep a stiff upper lip? Is it a call for perseverance? If so, why didn't Paul use the word *perseverance* (*proskarterēsis*)? He could have. He used it before. But he didn't. So, we must conclude that he had something else in mind.

The problem with the idea of perseverance is that it tends to communicate a passive resolve regarding a situation, where Paul probably wanted to communicate more of an active and aggressive forthrightness. One perseveres a situation when there is nothing left to avert it, to prevent it from happening. But one is forthright in a situation when stirred to make a serious effort to change or affect it. The admonition to be strong is a call to gather together the resources and begin the training required to change a situation. This was Paul's admonition to the Corinthian church. Paul was calling them to change the world. And they did.

LOVE

But there is a caution to all this manly talk about virtue, courage, and action. Recollecting 1 Corinthians 13, Paul cautioned, "Let all that you do be done in love" (v. 14). It is very easy for men to get all pumped up with the adrenalin of nobility in the name of God and go off half-cocked in a destructive rampage of one kind or another and end up doing more harm than good. Yes, the men needed to grow up. Yes, they needed to rekindle the social virtues of manliness. Yes, they needed to be forthright in these efforts. But the effort to reform the Corinthian church, which is what Paul was shooting for, needed to be tempered and bathed in Christian love.

As important as these theological and social reforms were—and they were very important in Paul's eyes, so important that Paul was willing to risk his own death to accomplish them—they were nothing without love. Mere sounding brass, a clanging symbol, nothing but noise apart from love. Love is the attitude and the spirit, the goal and the objective, the content and the meaning. Love is the starting point, the means of advancement, and the goal to be achieved—all at the same time.

And yet it is not our love for one another that will sustain us. As much as we can love one another and as important as it is to actually love one another, our love will fade and die. Our love is fickle and undependable because we are weak in the face of difficulties. Love easily overwhelms us, disarms us, and takes advantage of us. Love is our weakness, the weakness of our flesh.

But neither is it our love for Jesus Christ that will sustain us to the end. Again, as important as our love for Jesus Christ is—and there is nothing in this world that is more important, our love for the Lord is still susceptible to all of the weaknesses and temptations of the flesh. And if, perchance, we master the temptations of the flesh, our love for Jesus Christ is still vulnerable to the pride of life. Indeed, to master the temptations of the flesh is to be delivered into the temptations of the pride of life.

No, it is not *our* love that holds us faithfully to the bosom of the Lord. Rather, it is *His* love, God's love, the love of Jesus Christ for His people that provides the anchor of salvation. It is the love of Jesus Christ that saves. Praise be the Lord!

50. Sum & Substance

Now I urge you, brothers—you know that the household of Stephanas were the first converts in Achaia, and that they have devoted themselves to the service of the saints—be subject to such as these, and to every fellow worker and laborer. I rejoice at the coming of Stephanas and Fortunatus and Achaicus, because they have made up for your absence, for they refreshed my spirit as well as yours. Give recognition to such men. The churches of Asia send you greetings. Aquila and Prisca, together with the church in their house, send you hearty greetings in the Lord. All the brothers send you greetings. Greet one another with a holy kiss. I, Paul, write this greeting with my own hand. If anyone has no love for the Lord, let him be accursed. Our Lord, come! The grace of the Lord Jesus be with you. My love be with you all in Christ Jesus. Amen.

—1 Corinthians 16:15-24

Stephanas was another of Paul's converts in Acacia, along the southern shore of the Corinthian gulf. In all likelihood Stephanas, Fortunatus and Achaicus brought a letter from the Corinthians to Paul, apparently requesting his counsel and guidance. Our present 1 Corinthians is the reply to the letter they brought to Paul. These three men were probably not day laborers, but had some measure of financial independence. They owned property, a home, which they dedicated for the use of ministry.

These Corinthian leaders "devoted themselves to the service of the saints" (v. 15). The KJV translates it as, "they have addicted themselves to the ministry of the saints." The Greek word (*tassō*) actually means to put in order, appoint, even ordain. *Young's Literal Version* translates it, "they appointed themselves to ministry to the saints." The KJV translators probably had difficulty with the idea of the self-appointment of Christians to tasks or offices of ministry (*diakonia*). John Gill said that there was nothing "irregular" about their appointment, but that the verse means that they volunteered for ministry and then funded it from their own pockets. He suggested that there was no indication that they did this on their own authority, but after volunteering, they subjected themselves to the normal authority structures of the church. So, it just means that they were eager volunteers.

Continuing the idea that all things should be done decently and in order under the authority of the church, Paul suggested that the Corinthians

"be subject to such as these, and to every fellow worker and laborer" (v. 16).

Paul understood them to deserve proper respect and submission to their leadership authority. The verse does not teach that people can just appoint and ordain themselves to whatever kind of ministry they desire, but needs to be read in the sense of encouraging people to volunteer their time and resources to the ministries of the church, and that submission to church leaders is not only appropriate but obligatory.

Verse 17 is an expression of Paul's gratitude for these three men, for their willingness, for their service, for their delivery of the now lost letter from the Corinthian church to Paul, and for their fellowship. Paul was refreshed by their visit, no doubt by their zeal for Christ and their commitment to Christ in spite of the difficulties of the Corinthian church. So, Paul commended them back to the Corinthians and recommended that they be acknowledged and appreciated for their leadership and ministry.

GREETINGS

Paul also brought greetings from the churches in Asia. All of the translators agree that the word *ekklēsia* here should be plural, but the word is more often translated in the singular. It can be either singular or plural. It is an important point because it impacts the doctrine of the unity of the church. Is the church in Asia, or are the churches in Asia, or anywhere else, to be considered as singular or plural?

My answer to that question is *both*. If they were in unity, in agreement, of one mind or of the mind of Christ (1 Peter 3:8), then they should be referred to in the singular, as a unit. But if they were not in unity, if they were in disagreement with one another, not of one mind, not of the mind of Christ, then they should be referred to in the plural. Some were of one mind, and some weren't.

The fact that one church brought greetings from another church (v. 19) suggests that the churches recognized each other. That is, that they recognized the validity of the ministry and authority of the other churches. Such mutual recognition is an important element regarding the unity and cooperation of churches. Conversely, the failure to grant such recognition would suggest the kind of adversarial relationship that exists when churches anathematize one another, as too often occurs. The model is mutual care, concern and recognition among Christ's churches, and yet there is a time and a place for anathematization, as well. In fact, the church at Corinth was flirting with the kind of apostasy that could lead to anathematization.

Aquila and Prisca apparently had a church in their house (*oikos*), but the verse could also be understood to mean that they had a household church, a church that was composed of their family and extended family, which is the literal meaning of *oikos*. Driven from Rome during persecution, Aquila, a Jew and likely a slave or servant of a Roman senator, sought refuge in Corinth, where Paul, on his second missionary journey, met him when they were engaged in the same trade. They were fellow tent makers. Paul probably converted—or seriously deepened the faith of —Aquila by sharing the gospel with him as they labored together. Not only did Aquila and Priscilla become Christian leaders, but they also became fast and devoted friends of Paul. Aquila became a teacher of some renown, and his wife, Priscilla, the diminutive form of Prisca, provided such close help and support that they are always mentioned together. And we note that the greetings they brought provided a testimony to their unity in Christ.

The "brethren" who also greeted the Corinthians in verse 20 represented other Christians and churches that were in unity with Paul. Given the character of Paul's New Testament letters we might wonder who it was who enjoyed such Christian unity, since Paul seems to have spent so much time and ink correcting wayward churches. In fact, Paul's New Testament letters were sent to only a small group of churches in existence during that time. And yet, the fact that Paul's letters were valued, passed around and preserved testifies to the fact that many—probably most—of the churches had problems. How could it have been otherwise because the Gospel is so foreign to the flesh? The history of Christianity is the story of troubled churches struggling with the gospel in one way or another.

We can surmise, then, that in almost every church there were not only those who had gone wrong, but there were also those who had it right. There were "brethren" in every church, and it was to those brethren that Paul referred. As the *Westminster Confession of Faith* 25:5 says, "The purest Churches under heaven are subject both to mixture and error." Thus, those brethren who were in unity with Paul sent their greetings, and more. They sent them with a "holy kiss," that is, with special love and regard. Those in unity with Christ sent greetings to those in unity with Christ. Christians recognize one another in Christ.

In verse 21 we find Paul's personal testimony that he himself had penned this letter. The letter we know as First Corinthians was not an impostor, nor did it lack anything in translation. Rather, here we see that Paul himself had personally written it. This does not mean that Paul had physically penned the entire letter himself. He did have people who helped him. But this final salutation would have been part of his signature. People who knew Paul or had other letters from him could compare the handwriting of this sentence with other letters and see that it was genuine. This was a common practice of the time, similar to our use of signatures as evidence of authenticity.

ATTENTION

Verse 22 requires particular attention because of its intensity: "If anyone has no love for the Lord, let him be accursed. Our Lord, come!" The Greek word translated love here is *phileō* not *agape*. Unlike *agape* it is not unconditional. Rather, it means to be a friend, to be fond of someone or something. That is, to have affection, passion and personal attachment—feelings. *Phileō* is a matter of sentiment or feeling and an expression or deliberate assent of the will as a matter of principle, duty, and propriety.

Note that this love (*phileō*) was not to be directed toward one another, but toward Jesus Christ as Lord and Savior. Also note that Paul phrased it in the negative. Paul was not talking about those who had this kind of love and passionate regard for the Lord. Rather, he was talking about those who did not have it. Here was a message, not simply to the faithful saints at Corinth, but a message to the faithless and dispassionate, to all who had no regard or concern for Jesus Christ. Here we see that Paul was not writing merely to the faithful Christians in an errant Church. Rather, Paul was writing to "anyone" who had "no love for the Lord." Anyone! Anyone in Corinth, yes. But also to anyone anywhere anytime. Here we find a message from the apostle Paul to those who don't care about Christianity, not just to those who hate Christ and are actively working against Him—atheists, but to all those who don't care—agnostics.

And what was Paul's message to these people, to those who were not Christians? They are "accursed" (*anathema*)! They were not okay. Jesus did not love them just the way they were. They were at the receiving end of Paul's—and more importantly, God's—curse. But we need to understand that Paul was not so much calling down God's curse upon them, as if Paul was asking God to do a new thing. No. Rather, Paul was simply acknowledging the state or condition of sin into which they had been born. Paul was not so much saying that because they rejected Jesus that God would, therefore, curse them. But rather that they stood in the midst of God's curse given to and through Adam in Genesis 3 to all humanity, and that by rejecting or failing to love Jesus Christ, they had rejected Christ's grace, forgiveness, and mercy, and simply reaffirmed their position in sin and accepted the preexisting curse associated with that sin.

Paul concluded this sentence, and this entire letter, with "Our Lord, Come!" (*Maranatha*). A curious thing happens in the translation of this word, which according to the Greek Lexicon is of Aramaic origin. The Aramaic word means "our Lord *has* come." The Lexicon then goes on to say that the Greek word means "our Lord cometh or *will* come." *Cometh* is an archaic word in the third-person singular present tense. The present tense may be used to express: action at the present, a state of being, a habitual action, an occurrence in the near future, or an action that occurred in the past and continues up to the present. There are a lot of possible meanings here, but the key to this verse is the last meaning—an action that occurred in the past and continues up to the present.

Paul's exclamation of *maranatha* was not merely a call for Jesus to come soon, but was an exclamation that Jesus had in fact already come, that Jesus was also in the process of coming, and that Jesus would come again in the near future. Paul was not simply pining for a Jesus who had left and had promised to come back soon. It was the proclamation of the Christ who had decisively come already and had resolutely defeated Satan and death itself, and who was now actively engaged in the world through His people to bring every aspect of the world to acknowledgment of and submission to Jesus Christ as Lord and Savior, and who will revisit this salvation project upon its completion to provide final judgment and separation of "those who have done good to the resurrection of life, and those who have practiced evil to the resurrection of condemnation" (John 5:29).

Paul's *maranatha* was past, present, and future all at once. It was for a church that had begun, was growing yet struggling in the present, and would one day be fully grown.

JUDGMENT

Thus, it was a cry of both sorrow and celebration that the final judgment of God in Christ at the end of history will bring both unity and division. The saints will be unified together in one group, as will those who reject God and His Son in another group. The two groups will ultimately be separated, divided from one another for eternity to the glory of God.

"If anyone does not love the Lord Jesus Christ, let him be accursed. The Lord comes" (v. 22). Paul acknowledged that God Himself has cursed all who do not love Jesus Christ, and God's curse is not a trifle, but an eternal consignment to damnation. This is serious stuff!

In this verse Paul provided a summary statement of God's earthly reclamation project, the project headed up by His Son, Jesus Christ. But it was not a complete summary statement because it does not include the main thrust of Christ's earthly assignment to provide the grace of salvation. So, Paul added, "The grace of the Lord Jesus Christ be with you" (v. 23).

Paul was not asking the Lord to send or provide grace for His people. Paul does not suggest that God's grace is dependent upon some expression of human passion or human freedom. No! Christ had already been decisively dispatched by God, and had already engaged the enemy and won the decisive victory. Christ is the victor and upon that victory on Golgotha the grace of Christ pours forth into the world. That grace is not weak, but strong. The forces of death and evil melt before it. The grace of Jesus Christ shall have dominion over the whole world. This is the grace that regenerates God's people. This is the grace that Paul here acknowledged to have taken root in Christ's church.

Though the translators suggest that Paul was asking God to provide this grace for His people, that this grace *might or might not* be with His people, that is *not* what Paul said here. The word *be* has been added for clarity, but again the addition fails to clarify. Perhaps it is a subtlety of English or a peculiarity of my own, but when I use the word *be* in a context like this, I instinctively add to it the word *may*—as in *may be*, which then suggests that a thing may or may not be. It communicates a sense of conditionality.

But Paul was not making a conditional statement here. He was stating a fact. *Young's Literal Translation* adds the word *is* rather than *be*, "The grace of the Lord Jesus Christ *is* with you." Isn't that a stronger statement? It is not that Paul was requesting that the Lord dispatch the grace of Jesus

Christ upon the Corinthians. Rather, Paul was simply stating the fact that God had already done so. It was a done deal. The grace of the Lord Jesus Christ was with them. They were not to hope for its arrival, they were to celebrate its presence and reality.

LOVE

The same thing applies to verse 24. The word *be* has been added there too. Paul said, "My love with you all," as well. Paul was not giving his love to particular individuals, not to some select group, but to them all —y'all. Paul was giving his love to their allness, to their togetherness, to their unity, to the unity of all who were/are in Christ. In spite of the fact that there were serious divisions in the Corinthian church, divisions that Paul labored to correct and eliminate, Paul's love was with them in their unity, not simply in their individuality. Inasmuch as they enjoyed unity, they would enjoy Paul's love. Paul loved their corporate unity.

Paul did not love them simply for who they were as individuals. That's not what he said. If he had said that it would have contributed to their pride. They would have understood themselves to be individually better than or more deserving of Paul's love than some other individuals. But Paul was not giving them reason to be proud, not even proud of their faithfulness. Even if Paul suggested that he loved the Corinthians as an individual church, he would have set off rivalries between churches in that the faithful Corinthians could claim that Paul loved them more than he loved some other church. No! Paul's love was not focused on them as individuals or upon them as an individual church, but upon them in their unity, in their corporality. Not simply upon the sum total of their own unity, but rather Paul's love was upon their unity in Christ. Paul did not regard them in the flesh (2 Corinthians 5:16), rather he regarded them spiritually, as being in Christ.

Listen again to *Young's Literal Version*, "my love is with you all in Christ Jesus" (v. 24). Paul's love was in Christ, and through Christ are included all who are in Christ. Paul's love was first and foremost for Jesus Christ, not for the particular individuals who happened to attend the Corinthian church at that particular time. Of course, Paul did love those particular people, but there is more to it than that. Paul's message was for them, of course! But it is also for us today, and for Christians in Christ in all times and places. Paul's confession of love is for "all in Christ," then and now and always.

While Paul's love, like our own weak and fleshly love, was time bound, God's is not. God loves across time, through time, without regard to time. So, all who are in Christ stand with one foot in eternity with God, straddling the limitations of time and the restrictions of our own individual identity and existence. In Christ we are greater (or more) than we would be were we not in Christ. People are more unique, more individual, more peculiar, more whole, more everything in Christ than those who are not in Christ. In Christ the edges and contours of our personal identity, our personal being, our humanity, our very personhood become identified with, yet distinguishable from Jesus Christ, the very Son of God.

Paul's love for the Corinthians was caught up (*harpazō*) in the love of Christ. Paul's love for the Corinthians was subsumed in Christ's love for His people, and in that subsumption it was greatly magnified beyond his own ability to love. Indeed, our love for one another is similarly strengthened and magnified in Christ, when, like Paul, we love the unity of the fellowship of the saints in Christ more than we love anything else. And yet the strength of such love is not in our own ability to love, but in Christ's ability to love. For our love for Him is a mere reflection, a shadow in a mirror dimly reflected of His great and perfect love for us. "We love because he first loved us" (1 John 4:19).

Amen!

SCRIPTURE INDEX

ALPHABETICAL INDEX